Christophe Tournu (ed.)

Milton in France

PETER LANG
Bern · Berlin · Bruxelles · Frankfurt am Main · New York · Oxford · Wien

Bibliographic information published by Die Deutsche Bibliothek
Die Deutsche Bibliothek lists this publication in the Deutsche Nationalbibliografie; detailed bibliographic data is available on the Internet at ‹http://dnb.ddb.de›.

British Library Cataloguing-in-Publication Data: A catalogue record for this book is available from *The British Library*, Great Britain

Library of Congress Cataloging-in-Publication Data

International Milton Symposium (8th : 2005 : Grenoble, France)
Milton in France / [compiled by] Christophe Tournu.
p. cm.
Papers originally presented at the 8th International Milton Symposium held June 7-11, 2005, in Grenoble, France.
English and French.
Includes bibliographical references.
ISBN 978-3-03911-604-1 (alk. paper)
1. Milton, John, 1608-1674–Criticism and interpretation–Congresses. I. Tournu, Christophe. II. Title.
PR3588.I58 2005
821'.4–dc22

2008002553

This publication has been made possible through the support of the following institutions: the *Société d'Etudes Miltoniennes,* the French Ministry of Foreign Affairs, the Regional Council Rhône-Alpes, and the *Agence Universitaire pour la Francophonie.*

ISBN 978-3-03911-604-1

Printed in Germany

A Catherine

Table of Contents

Part III
The Great Poems

1. *Paradise Lost*

Foreword and Acknowledgements

The Eighth International Symposium was a great success,[1] and all the Miltonists gathered in Grenoble – some two hundred people from 21 countries and all continents – enjoyed the majestic setting of the Alps, the pleasant weather, and the intellectual and cultural fare.

I would like to express my deepest gratitude to the University of Grenoble 2 for their support in the organization of IMS 8, and especially to our host, Olivier Ihl, the director of the Institut d'Etudes Politiques (School of Politics). The conference site was exceptional, and the Staff of the School were happy to cooperate. Our two hostesses, Anne and Aurélie, were very professional, and our three law and language students, Anne, Olivia and Hugo, were most helpful.

I am also very grateful to the *Société d'Etudes Miltoniennes.* Our Society, which was officially founded in 2004 in the wake of a Milton conference held the previous year at the Protestant School of Theology in Paris, was in charge of the social programme – most notably the reception in the Salon Bonaparte at the Castle of the French Revolution in Vizille and the concert of the Wilanów String Quartet, two conference breaks which were greatly appreciated.[2]

This publication has been made possible through the support of the following institutions: the *Société d'Etudes Miltonienne*s, the French Ministry of Foreign Affairs, the Regional Council Rhône-Alpes, and the *Agence Universitaire pour la Francophonie.*[3]

We thank you all, speakers, attendees, and sponsors for making IMS 8 a huge success.

1 See report in the *MQ*. Roy Flannagan, "IMS 8: The Eighth International Milton Symposium Grenoble, France, June 7–11, 2005." *Milton Quarterly* 39 (3), 169–179.

2 Many thanks to our friends, Anne and Alain Picard, for they helped me organize the concert. I would also like to thank Alain Chevallier for the reception at Vizille.

3 The following institutions contributed to the organization of IMS 8: the General Council of Isère, La Métro, the Mayor of Grenoble, the University of Grenoble 3, the University of Savoie, the *Centre for Studies and Research on the Reformation and Counter-Reformation* (University of Clermont 2) and the *Institute for Research on the Renaissance, the Neoclassical Age and the Enlightenment* (University of Montpellier 3).

Special thanks to Roy Flannagan for taking his camera with him. The organizer of IMS 7 made a beautiful slide show of the conference highlights, from the opening session to our closing Banquet at the Castle of Sassenage. It can be viewed on our website at http://www.john-milton.org.

Finally, and I have saved the best for last, I would like to thank my wife, Catherine, and my children, Thomas and Sarah, for their enduring patience and love.

Christophe Tournu
27 November 2007

Introduction*

A la majesté du peuple,
A la liberté universelle [...]
Aux pères de notre constitution, à ceux qui en ont posé les bases dans leurs ouvrages immortels: à Locke, à Milton, à Rousseau, à Sidney, à Nedham, à Mably, à Price.

Jacques-Pierre Brissot[1]

The selected papers assembled in the present volume come from the Eighth International Milton Symposium, which was held in Grenoble, France, 7–11 June 2005.

This volume is not a sequel to "Milton, Rights and Liberties," a book I coedited with Neil Forsyth and which was published at Peter Lang at the end of 2006. It is made up of miscellaneous essays, most of which are not relevant to our main Conference theme but which deserved publication for their quality, their specificity, the originality of their approach or their promising character – I think especially of the papers given by PhD candidates.

To begin with, let me say a few words about the Symposium itself.

Everything started eight years ago when I attended IMS 6 at the University of York. I met "the big guns" there, as Neil Forsyth calls them, namely Thomas N. Corns and Gordon Campbell. They told me they wondered why the symposium had never been held in France. Three years later, when I was given the opportunity to deliver a paper at IMS 7 at the University of South Carolina at Beaufort, with the support of my research supervisor,

* I am extremely grateful to John Hale (University of Otago, New Zealand) for reading this introduction.

1 On July 14th, 1790, at the Fête de la Fédération, Jacques-Pierre Brissot, Earl of Warville (1754–93), future leader of the party favouring war against Europe, honoured Milton with the name of "founding father of the French republic."
For a contrasting view, see Auguste Geffroy, *Etude sur les pamphlets politiques et religieux de Milton*. Paris, Dezobry, E. Magdeleine et Cie, 1848, p. 222: «Il balbutie plutôt qu'il ne proclame les nouveaux droits de l'homme, et, il faut le dire, il n'aperçoit pas tous ses devoirs.»

Prof. Bernard Cottret, I declared I intended to make a bid for Grenoble, and incredibly enough, our bid was successful. The idea was to redress what all England and Wales saw as an injustice and, incidentally, to contribute to the promotion of the studies of Early Modern English literature in France: there is a major crisis in French Universities as the so-called democratization of the *études supérieures* leads to a disdain of everything prior to the twentieth century. We have to teach "useful," professional English, and studies of the seventeenth century attract only a few people.

IMS 8 was a challenge and a dream. It was my first Conference ever. I had coorganized a seminar on the political and spiritual heritage of the European identity the year before, and the proceedings were published in 2006. The research vice-president agreed to make a bid for Grenoble only on 21 November 2002, i.e. the day before the deadline for submission expired, and I remember I found myself walking over soaking ground in the industrial area to deliver the parcel at UPS when night was falling. That Prof. Corns got the bid on his desk the morning after was something of a miracle. Then we learnt our bid was successful. Not for long: Marie Zanardi, the secretary I worked with and whom I would like to thank for her help in the very beginning of the project, was transferred, at her request, to another department, the company we took for hotel reservation went bankrupt, the main organizer, *The Historical and Judicial Centre for Human Rights*, lost interest in the project (if they had had any), its director preferred to resign rather than assume the risk of organizing such a big Conference, and six months before the event was held, the Dean of the School of Law and the President of the University wanted to cancel the Symposium altogether. I persevered – to the end, so to speak. The Conference was held, everything went smoothly, so marvellously well.

The organization of IMS8 was an unforgettable, in fact wonderful experience (I am not masochistic): I had to do everything by myself and I enjoyed my independence. I wrote and answered a mass of mails, drafted documents to seek funds from our institutional partners, arranged the social programme (including the concert of the Wilanow String Quartet, who replaced a great show, Handel's *Samson*, we initially intended to organize with Patrick Souillot),[2] I ran the website, I processed your registration or-

2 I would like to apologize to Patrick Souillot and Jean-Paul Stahl, for we worked a lot and should have signed a contract with "L'Orchestre de Grenoble" for the *Samson*. In his never-ending effort to popularize classical music and his taste for high-flying per-

ders – there is not a thing I did not do. Of course, and fortunately, Neil helped me draw up the programme, and *Points Cardinaux* and the three students were very helpful on the days of the Conference. It shows, if need be, that taking initiatives requires much determination – a Miltonic spirit, if I may say so.

Some two-hundred people from twenty-one countries and the five continents gathered in the capital of the Alps, home to the 1968 Olympic Games, to discuss "Milton, Rights and Liberties." There were fifty-two workshops and six semi-plenary sessions. The *De Doctrina Christiana* Team were honoured at the outset of the Symposium, and Annabel Patterson was the speaker at the closing plenary session.[3]

It is now an established tradition to have triennial International Milton symposia – and we can pay tribute to Albert C. Labriola, Duquesne University, and Ronald Shafer, Indiana University of Pennsylvania, for initiating the tradition a quarter of a century ago. And we must also pay tribute to their followers.

That Milton has enjoyed some reputation in France cannot be doubted, and we made much of Milton's relationship to the French Revolution in our programme.

If John Milton is well-known in France for his poetry, most notably for his epic *Paradise Lost* which Chateaubriand immortalized in French in 1855, yet he is much less known for his political writings. While the literary dimension of Milton must be acknowledged, we should reassess him as a political thinker in the numerous pamphlets he has left us. This 8th International Milton Symposium, "Milton, Rights and Liberties" pays tribute to Milton the literary figure and the political writer.

Indeed Grenoble is the cradle of the French Revolution. At Grenoble on June 7, 1788, as regional Parliaments were closed down by Louis XVI, the people rose up and threw tiles at the garrison sent to subdue them (it was called the "Day of Tiles"). The Estates general of Dauphiné were held in Vizille on July 21st, 1788, and they are reputed to have ignited the French Revolution.

English republicans found their way into the discourse of the French Revolution. Milton, Nedham and James Harrington were translated or

---

formances, Patrick has since staged and conducted *La flûte enchantée*, which was a great success.

3 See our website for more details: http://www.john-milton.org

adapted by French revolutionaries to fit their own purposes. Mirabeau, the first President of the National Assembly, adapted and translated Milton's *Areopagitica* as *Sur la liberté de la presse, d'après Milton* and his *Pro populo anglicano defensio* as *Théorie de la royauté, d'après la doctrine de Milton* (London, 1789). This was republished as *Défense du Peuple anglais, sur le jugement et la condamnation de Charles premier, roi d'Angleterre. Par Milton. Ouvrage propre à éclairer sur la circonstance actuelle où se trouve la France* (Defence of the English People, on the Trial and Condemnation of Charles I, King of England. By Milton. A book which is fitting to shed light on the present situation in France. Reissued at the charge of the administrators of the department of Drôme; Valence: P. Aurel, 1792; In-8, 100 p.).

In the preface to *Théorie de la royauté*, Mirabeau explained on what occasion he encountered Milton:

> As everyone knows, Milton is one of the greatest geniuses Great-Britain has ever produced, and yet he is little known among us but as a poet. [...] The questions he dealt with [in his prose] are of so much consequence that they cannot be regarded as mere almanacs of a given period. [...] [Milton] wrote on divorce, on the freedom of the press, and on the respective rights of peoples and kings. These are not things whose interest is limited. The debates they produce are suitable for all times and all countries. [...] It is always essential to know the opinion of a great man on things which day after day draw still more our attention, and finally deserve our full consideration. Hence I have thought I would be helpful if I set myself the painful task of searching into Milton's polemical dissertations so as to dig up the political principles entangled in the circumstantial details and verbose scholarship of his age.[4]

Obviously, the French Revolution wanted to recuperate Milton.

The 8th International Milton Symposium was intended to be transdisciplinary: specialists of English literature as well as specialists from other disciplines (that is, history, philosophy, art, law, politics, and theology) were invited to bring their own contribution to the advancement of Milton studies.

The perspective we suggested was the progress from an age when the main objective of government was to establish rules for the life and well-

4 Mirabeau's comments (pp. i-xiv, lv-lxxviii) are interspersed with his translation of *Areopagitica*, and followed by "Doctrine de Milton, sur la royauté" (1789; BNF MFICHE 8–LEA–63). This is my own translation from the French. See my "John Milton, the English Revolution (1640–60) and the Dynamics of the French Revolution (1789)," in *Prose Studies*, Vol. 24, No. 3 December 2001, pp. 18–38. This essay comes from the paper I read at Beaufort, SC, in 2002.

being of the body politic to an era when people became increasingly aware of deep changes in the structures of society. Up to the eighteenth century nobody paid much attention to the rights of man. We owe the emergence of a new idea of rights to the struggle against the arbitrary power of absolute monarchy between the Magna Carta (1215) and the Petition of Right (1628). The defence of rights and liberties arose much earlier and was more intense in England than anywhere else. Rights and liberties were defended most prominently by John Locke at the end of the seventeenth century and this defence was extended to America in the War of Independence (1776–83). It reached a climax in the Declaration of Human and Citizen Rights during the French Revolution in 1789.

Hence the questions of IMS 8: what status does Milton assign to rights in his works? What is his conception of law and justice? What is his idea of liberty? On what documents and principles does he base the rights and liberties he defends? What kind of liberties does he claim? What heritage has he left us?

This main theme of the symposium was not intended to exclude other topics. The organisers welcomed suggestions for sessions on other themes. Indeed, papers on any aspect of Milton studies were welcomed, and grouped with similar papers to generate themed sessions.

But we ran some risk of being charged with anachronism when we spoke of human rights in the age of Milton.

The first occurrence of the word "rights" in a book title printed in England was only five years after Milton's birth (1608). Sir Henry Spelman's *De non temerandis ecclesijs A tract of the rights and respect due vnto churches* (1613) dealt with tithes or the right of maintenance of the Church. So did William Clarke's *Decimarum et oblationum tabula* (1629). John Harrison described *The Bohemian* [political] *lawes or rights* in 1620, and an official document of the State of Holland gave commercial "privileges and rights" – i.e. liberties – to the West India Company in 1621. In 1632, women's rights [sic] were considered by an obscure lawyer, Thomas Edgar, in *The lavves resolutions of womens rights.* Finally, publications on constitutional "rights and privileges" flourished from 1642 onwards, starting with *A conference… concerning the rights and privileges of the subjects discoursed by Sir Dudley Digges, Sir Edward Littleton, […], Master Selden, Sir Edward Cooke; with the objections by Sir Robert Heath, […], and the answers* and *A declaration of the loyall resolution of the Kingdome of*

Scotland [...] for the preservation of his Maiesties Sacred Person, and for the maintenance of his undoub[t]ed rights and priviledges to his severall kingdomes.

As for civil liberties, the expression appeared for the first time as late as 1659 in a royalist publication entitled *A declaration of the Christian-free-born subjects of the once flourishing kingdom of England. Making out the principles relating both to their spiritual and civil liberties, which they conceive they are bound both in conscience and honour, to vindicate and maintain with sobriety and courage, each one in his proper place and sphere: against all usurpation* (London: [s.n.], 1659). The next occurrence was only in 1689, when the Bill of Rights secured basic civil liberties: Sir George McKenzie of Rosehaugh published *A Letter from the nobility, barons, & commons of Scotland in the year 1320, [...] directed to Pope Iohn [XXII] wherein they declare their firm resolutions to adhere to their King Robert the Bruce as the restorer of the safety and liberties of the people, and as having the true right of succession: but withall, they notwithstanding declare, That if the king should offer to subvert their civil liberties, they will disown him as an enemy and choose another to be king for their own defence* (Edinburgh: [s.n.], 1689).

Yet, "the liberties of the subject," "the liberties of the kingdom," or the king's alleged attempt "to subvert our religion, laws, and liberties" had appeared in 1642. An author bracketed rights and liberties in a booklet called *Equitable and necessary considerations and resolvtions for association of arms throughout the counties of the kingdom of England, and principality of Wales: Against the [...] professed combination of papists, and other enemies of the Protestant religion, and English rights and liberties* (26 December 1642).

As Hugh Wilson rightly says in the opening chapter of "Milton, Rights and Liberties," Milton belongs to a human rights tradition which, from Aeschylus to the United Nations Declaration of 1948, favoured the advancement of liberty in all spheres of life.

Milton symposia are most valuable as they have formally internationalised Milton studies, and are a means of erasing "sectarianism" if I may say so, or parochialism, cliques, for everyone is welcome from any country, any institution, any school of thought.

IMS 8 was a thrilling opportunity to hear and see people I knew by name as I had read their books or had (many of) them on my shelves. Yea, the greatest Milton scholars were there. It was also an occasion to hear people we are less accustomed to hear in Milton gatherings, for they came from different fields. It was finally an opportunity to see new faces, and a new generation of Miltonists met their renowned elders.

This volume

We will start from the impact of the French Revolution on British literary Romanticism with Hugh Wilson's essay on the link between Wordsworth's "Lines composed a few miles above Tintern Abbey, on revisiting the banks of the Wye during a tour" (1798), a poem on the growth of a poet's mind, and Milton's *L'Allegro* and *Il Penseroso*, companion poems on the moods of the poet.[5]

Jean Pironon explores Milton's juvenilia, more particularly the sensory or perceptual experience itself in his minor poetry. Sensation is used to create the fundamental dynamics of Milton's poetic universe. It will be no different, I may say, with his great poems, most notably *Paradise Lost*, which would not be a monument had not the English Revolution happened. Milton's poetry cannot be read as a work of art *per se*. It embodies Milton's responses to his immediate environment, that is, the natural environment (but not only) in his minor poems, and the political environment (and disillusionment) in his great poetry. Whereas Wordsworth found a reassuring divine presence in nature, something which urged him to poetic creativity, Milton described "The tyranny of heaven" in *PL* and he would make the reader sympathise with the devil.

Then Trevor Jockims examines the violent disruption which the event of death has caused to the pastoral landscape in *Lycidas* and which the poem itself attempts to remedy. The shepherd-elegist is left with the role of a healer as he must attempt to reconstitute a disrupted pastoral landscape. David Urban closes the section devoted to Milton's minor poems by exploring, in Milton's Sonnet 19 ("WHEN I consider how my light is spent," 1655? – published 1673) a creative tension in the poet when Milton's tendency to identify himself with the unprofitable servant of the parable of the talents (Matt. 25.14–30) is mitigated by the autobiographical speaker's comparable sense of self-identification with the last-chosen laborers of the parable of the laborers in the vineyard (Matt. 20.1–16).

The second section deals with Milton's prose and opens with a Marxist reading of Milton – *à contre-courant* of revisionist history. Thus Milton's Anti-

5 See David Bromwich, "The French Revolution and 'Tintern Abbey'" *Raritan* 10:3 (1991 Winter): 1–23.

Prelatical pamphlets, Matthew Jordan argues, evince an enthusiasm for a conception of liberation informed by a class-based perspective on social issues. Where the Smectymnuuans look forward to a form of church-government which will enhance the status and power of their clerical caste, Milton enthuses about what he senses is the emergence of a new, more popular, less generally repressive social order, a commitment encapsulated in his coinage of the term "self-esteem." This concern of Milton for the lower social classes can also be seen in *Areopagitica*, where he envisages "the laborers of truth" as ordinary people at work in the "reforming of reformation itself." This apparent democratic stance in the building of the Church as opposed to the *bourgeois* parochial minister's heretical monopoly of what he regards as the truth is utterly rejected in Milton's political scheme in 1654. As a matter of fact, Milton sees with detestation the election to Parliament of "innkeepers and hucksters of the state from city taverns or from country districts ploughboys and veritable herdsmen" (*CPW* 4: 1.682) and limits his definition of the people to "the better or more able part" of the citizens, an elite, the gentry.

In another post-revisionist paper, James Rovira opposes both Stanley Fish's "Driving from the Letter: Truth and Indeterminacy in *Areopagitica*" and Lana Cable's *Carnal Rhetoric* to support a historically grounded reading of Milton's treatise on free speech. *Areopagitica* recovers its status as a foundational document on freedom of the press, the author says, while acknowledging and accommodating the contradictions and complexities of Milton's argument. I have just completed a textbook on the issue for graduate students and my forthcoming book surveys the arguments on both sides.[6]

Antti Tahvanainen investigates Milton's rhetoric in his political pamphlets. As his answer to Salmasius well indicates, Milton was aware of the dangers of rhetoric, which is the language of demagogues and flatterers, and the Huguenot scholar, whom Milton scoffingly calls pedagogue, also pretends to drop rhetoric when addressing the issue of regicide:

> Je traiterai tellement ce grand sujet, que je n'y emploierai rien de l'art oratoire qui me semble en cette occasion & inutile & suspect. Il ne faut pas qu'une si bonne cause, &

6 Christophe Tournu, *Un penseur républicain à l'époque de la première révolution anglaise: John Milton,* Areopagitica: A Speech for the Liberty of Unlicensed Printing to the Parliament of England (1644), The Tenure of Kings and Magistrates (1649). Paris: CNED / Armand Colin, 9 January 2008.

> si juste, se pare des ornements de la rhétorique qui déguisent ordinairement ou qui affaiblissent la vérité (28).

And of course, his book is full of bombastic and theatrical representations of "the truth." As Tahvanainen writes, Milton was well aware of the dangers attributed to rhetoric (see, for example, his letter *Of Education*), but, for him, abuses such as demagogy and flattery could be countered. The truly eloquent, republican orator had to be both virtuous and learned. It is a matter of education: a preventive policy should be implemented to create soothing orators instead of inflammatory demagogues, wise counsellors instead of vicious courtiers. If he ever put a republican educational reform on his agenda, Milton would open himself to jokes at his expense, for the great rhetorician in *Paradise Lost* is Satan and, of course, he appears to us as a republican defying God's absolute monarchy, but his rhetorics is only a false language, he is no better than a liar, a hypocrite and a dissembler, and he is "the Arch-Enemy" (*PL* 1:81).

Kemmer Anderson, a poet and teacher/preacher at a boys' preparatory school in Tennessee, still focuses on the language in *The Tenure of Kings and Magistrates* and makes a rapprochement with Thomas Jefferson's Declaration of Independence (1776). Where a prominent US constitutionalist, Prof. Vincent Blasi, found Milton's principles in *Areopagitica* enshrined in the First Amendment to the American Constitution,[7] Anderson finds a common language between Milton's *TKM* and the "Declaration of Independence":

> We hold these truths to be self-evident, that all men are created equal, that they are endowed by their Creator with certain unalienable Rights, that among these are Life, Liberty and the pursuit of Happiness. – That to secure these rights, Governments are instituted among Men, deriving their just powers from the consent of the governed, – That whenever any Form of Government becomes destructive of these ends, it is the Right of the People to alter or to abolish it, and to institute new Government, laying its foundation on such principles and organizing its powers in such form, as to them shall seem most likely to effect their Safety and Happiness.[8]

This is much very reminiscent of what Milton writes in *TKM*. Anderson's paper focuses on tyranny, arguing that Milton provided a vocabulary and

7 Vincent Blasi, "Milton's Areopagitica and the Modern First Amendment" (March 1, 1995). Yale Law School. *Yale Law School Occasional Papers*. Paper 6. http://lsr.nellco.org/yale/ylsop/papers/6.

8 http://www.law.indiana.edu/uslawdocs/declaration.html.

structure for part of the Declaration. Thomas Jefferson had read and was influenced by *Paradise Lost*: the word "tyrant" became a part of his education and writing. Milton's epic poem offers a narrative definition of a tyrant. Milton and his tract provide vision for the American document of liberation from kings and tyrants.

Danièle Frison (Emerita, U. of Paris 10) considers *TKM* on its own and sees Milton's political treatise as a possible response to Hobbes' *De Cive* in a paper written in French. Then Yuko Noro continues the discussion on Milton's legacy with the concept of *Communitas Libera*, which can be found elsewhere: in the Glorious Revolution, through Locke's writings, in the French revolution, through Mirabeau, in the speech of Abraham Lincoln at Gettysburg (1863) in the American Civil War, in the Preface of the Constitution of Japan (1945) and in the Inaugural Speech by John F. Kennedy.

The last paper of this section envisages what Milton himself may have inherited for his theological beliefs. According to Georgi Vasilev, Milton probably came to know directly some Bogomil manuscript, in their Cathar and Lollard variants, because his violent denunciation of the cross, of icons and of the liturgy resembles what we find there. Milton eulogizes "the divine and admirable spirit of Wiclef" in *Areopagitica*. In *Eikonoklastes*, in a chapter uncovering "the Mysterie and combination between Tyranny and fals religion,"[9] Milton praises the Waldensian churches for making no difference between a bishop and a presbyter. In his defence of the freedom of the press, Milton advances a Manichean dualist conception of knowledge, and his idea of "good men" in his political pamphlets also belongs to the Bogomil tradition.[10]

Turning to the great poems, the third section starts with a fresh reading of *Paradise* Lost by four junior faculty. Thus Matt Dolloff (U. of Texas) considers Milton's Muse, Urania, as the opponent of tyranny in PL VII. In fact, she most significantly stands in contrast to the licentiousness of kings and courtiers even as she remains a vehicle for relating heavenly truths and

9 *CPW* 3: 509.

10 A senior research fellow and chief expert at the State Agency for Bulgarians Abroad, Georgi Vasilev has recently been promoted to full-professorship in European and Medieval Studies at the *State University of Library Studies and Information Technologies* in Sofia. He has just published *Heresy and the English Reformation: Bogomil-Cathar Influence on Wycliffe, Langland, Tyndale and Milton*. Jefferson, NC, McFarland & Co., Inc., Publishers, 2007.

divinely inspired poetry. T. Ross Leasure (U. of Salisbury, Maryland) examines the resemblances between Milton's Belial and Spenser's allegorical figure of Despayre, which appear especially in their rhetorical strategies to supplant the volition of their auditors with their own will-to-inaction, thereby de-moralizing the gullible through pointed argumentation. Martin Dawes (McGill, Canada)'s essay shows Adam learning to manoeuvre God's irony in the conversation about mates (bk. 8), which provides a model, first, for a more equal power relationship in the poem, and second, a model for republican politics, because God reveals himself as a Lord Protector challenging his subjects to become citizens or co-creators. Virginie Ortega-Tillier (U. de Bourgogne, France), a post-doctorate art historian, re-examines in depth the representations of Eden in several editions of *PL* (London, 1795 and 1827, and Paris, 1863). They all show, she claims, the high aesthetic quality of Milton's evocation of Eden and its original character when compared to numerous other illustrations. This brilliant essay, written in French, does not include any images, but we invite our readers to follow the links indicated in the footnotes or go to our website to view them. Finally, Luis Fernando Ferreira Sá (UFMG, Brazil) challenges Martin Evans's reading of *PL* as mimesis of colonial discourse to propose a post-colonial reading of Milton's imperious epic in its ambivalence and various negotiations.

There are also papers by confirmed Miltonists. Charlotte Clutterbuck (Sydney), in "The Sinner's View of God in the Invocations and Book III of *Paradise Lost*", suggests a new reading of the Father's relationship with the persona, whom many readers find repellent in bk. 3. Yet Milton deliberately writes in a false language, and his (unironic) repellent Father appears to be the projection of a sinful, vainglorious poet. Margaret J. Dean (U. of Eastern Kentucky) wonders what purpose the Abdiel narrative, prominent within Raphael's account of the War in Heaven (PL IX), serves in Milton's epic. Antonella Piazza's (U. of Salerno, Italy) considers "An Endless War" in an essay about astronomy in Milton with special reference to Galileo – with the idea of Nature as a book written by God.

Another Italian colleague, Daniele Borgogni, contributes the only essay on *Paradise Regained*: he takes on the problem of the relation between words and things, i.e. what language is supposed to represent, a burning issue in the seventeenth-century.[11] In *PR*, Satan is concerned with deep theological issues when he approaches Christ

> That I might learn
> In what degree or meaning thou art called
> The Son of God, which bears no single sense;
> The Son of God I also am, or was,
> And if I was, I am; relation stands;
> All men are sons of God [...] (*PR* 4: 515–20).

If Satan is also "The Son of God", Christ's reign is deemed ambiguous and non-representative.

Coming to the last great poem, *Samson Agonistes*, which was given a prominent place in *Milton, Rights and Liberties*, we are left with two essays. The first, by Suvi Mäkelä (U. of Tampere, Finland), focuses on the effects of Samson's understanding of beauty, which plays a decisive role in the loss of his freedom. The second, by Sherry Zivley and Chase Hamblin (U. of Houston, Texas), is sustained engagement with the somewhat neglected field of prosody in the two versions of *SA*.

The fourth section of our volume is on "French perspectives." We start with a psychoanalytical reading of Milton with Nicole Berry's essay on "John Milton; or, the Wounded Eagle" (in French).[12] Then we are given two Derridean readings of Milton's work: Miriam Mansur (UFMG, Brazil) examines the visual metaphors of *PL* and attempts to place Milton's epic together with Jacques Derrida's *Memoirs of the Blind* on the post-structuralist's stance towards vision. The approach of Marie-Dominique Garnier (U. of Paris 8, France) is Derridean in the sense that she offers a nano-reading of *SA* by exploring particle poetics (see Jacques Derrida's *The*

11 Think about what Salmasius wrote in *Apologie royale* (1650): the Huguenot accuses the Independents of vampirising words, of emptying them of their substance and of travestying them so that they acquire a new meaning which does not correspond to Truth, e.g. their redefinition of the King as the people's servant is nonsense because what precisely makes a king is his supremacy over and independence from anyone or any human institution. Moreover the hypocritical "Independents" are discovered to have usurped their name; and to restore the relation between the word and the thing, Salmasius redefines them as "ignorant animals" (823)!

12 The argument is developed in her forthcoming book: *Trois Textes: Le Récit, le Paysage, les Sonorités. Essais sur P. B. Shelley, Henry James, Joseph Conrad, John Milton.* Bern: Peter Lang, 2008.

Postcard): *SA* is, quite literally, a "cellular" poem, a text about incarceration, captive thoughts, blind confinement, deprivation, yet about the need to resist and read "on," into the *cellular* possibilities of a new language. Using Deleuze and Guattari's literary theory as exposed in *A Thousand Plateaus* (though arriving as a print artefact, the text was designed as a matrix of independent but cross-referential discourses which the reader is invited to enter more or less at random), the author goes on to explain "Why Milton Matters."

The last section, Part V, is devoted to Milton's Influence in Non-Anglophone Cultures. Luis Fernando Ferreira Sá comes back with an essay on a so far unknown play, Francisco da Costa Braga's *Milton: A Comedy in One Act*, which was staged on April 29, 1866 at the Theatro das Variedades Dramaticas in Lisbon, with much "applause." And through the play, he considers the reception of Milton in the Portuguese world of the nineteenth century. In a very interesting paper, Chia-Yin Huang (National Taiwan University) examines the Chinese appropriation of Milton between the two World Wars. In the wake of the May Fourth Movement, an anti-imperialist, cultural, and political movement, intellectuals fashioned Milton as an ideal poet-statesman committing his pen to the pursuit of liberty and political revolution.

More Food for Thought

When we speak about human "rights" and civil "liberties" as something Milton promotes in his works, perhaps we should seek a link between them. I would like to suggest they originate from a reflection on marriage.

The matter of divorce was brought before the French Senate on 27 January 1999 in the debate over the PACS (Pacte Civil de Solidarité), namely a civil union of two partners whatever their sex, which was subsequently passed into law.[13] The representatives of the main religious faiths in

13 The PACS is different from Civil Partnerships in the UK (available from 21 December 2005), which concerns two same-sex partners, and the US makes a distinction between same-sex marriages and civil unions. The former are banned in the constitutions of twenty States.

France (i.e. Catholics, Protestants, Jews, and Muslims) were asked what their religion taught about marriage. Mr. Olivier Abel, theologian and president of the Ethical Commission of the Protestant Federation of France, answered:

> In the Protestant construction of conjugality, the puritan ethics places man and woman on an equal footing, and considers marriage as an agreement which might be broken. That is why Calvin granted divorce. John Milton, the Puritan poet, the poet of Cromwell's revolution, praises divorce because divorce is freedom – the possibility of freedom.[14]

Then Olivier Abel made a connection between marriage and the French République, since Louis XVI passed the Edict of tolerance on 7 November 1787: "That marriage is a civil act which allows the different communities to weave links between themselves is for us [Protestants] fundamental in our conception of the republican bond."[15]

Once they had established a Republic, the French revolutionaries had established marriage as a civil contract on 7 September 1791 and granted divorce by mutual consent and for *incompatibilité d'humeur* on 20 September 1792. Why did they push for such reforms? They had freed man from the tyranny of the king, and so the next stage in the Revolution, they thought, should be to release women from the shackles of marriage, from the private tyranny of their husbands and parents. In fact, they went from politics to the family. An anonymous broadside called on the National Assembly to establish the liberty to divorce and remarry:

> France is free in her opinions; the slavery of feudalism has been abolished; there are no more monasteries, no more Bastille; let us shake into pieces the bonds of separated

14 Cf. the minutes of the debate at http://www.senat.fr/rap/l98-258/l98-2585.html: «Dans l'éthique protestante de la conjugalité, l'éthique puritaine met à égalité l'homme et la femme et pense le mariage comme un accord dont on sait qu'il peut être trahi. C'est pourquoi Calvin autorise le divorce. John Milton, le poète puritain, le poète de la révolution de Cromwell, fait un éloge du divorce parce que le divorce c'est la liberté, c'est la possibilité de la liberté.»

15 «Pour nous, le fait que le mariage soit un acte laïc permettant de tisser aussi les communautés entre elles est quelque chose de tout à fait fondamental dans notre conception du lien républicain.» (Id.)

> spouses so that they could build new relationships, & the Empire of the French will be the happiest abode in the world.[16]

There was a real debate on divorce, from the anonymous author of *Un mot sur le divorce* (1791) and Albert-Joseph-Ulpien Hennet's *Sur le divorce* supporting (1789) the projected reform, to Suzanne Necker's *Réflexions sur le divorce* (1794) and Jean-Henry Bancal des Issarts against the new legislation in 1797, which he said, "ruins the basis of society," and "attacks the very foundation of liberty."[17]

Milton was quoted on two occasions in the divorce debates during the French Revolution. The first appearance is in Albert-Joseph-Ulpien Hennet, "the most influential pro-divorce pamphleteer of the period,"[18] in a petition to the National Assembly supposedly addressed by Montaigne, Charron, Montesquieu and Voltaire (1791): Hennet draws a list of moralist authors and publicists known for writing in favour of divorce, and Milton is the only foreign writer appearing alongside with French writers:

> Milton. La doctrine & la discipline du divorce rétablie pour le bien des deux sexes & ramenée au vrai sens de l'écriture. Mémoire présenté au parlement d'Angleterre en 1645.[19]

The second appearance is in Félix-Marie Faulcon's *Opinion sur le divorce* (1797) – its author (1758–1841) was a member of a commission on divorce and became provisional President of the Chambre des Députés after Napoleon's destitution in 1814:

16 *Il est temps de donner aux époux qui ne peuvent vivre ensemble, la liberté de former de nouveaux liens.* (BNF): «La France est libre dans ses opinions; l'esclavage de la féodalité est aboli; plus de monastères, plus de Bastille; que l'on brise entièrement les liens des époux séparés, pour qu'ils puissent en former de nouveaux, & l'empire des Français sera le plus beau séjour du monde.»

17 *Opinion sur le divorce*, p. A2.

18 *H-France Reviews*. Vol. 2 (August 2002), No. 74. Carol Blum, *Strength in Numbers: Population, Reproduction, and Power in Eighteenth-Century* France. Baltimore and London: The Johns Hopkins UP, 2002. Review by David Klinck, University of Windsor.

19 *Pétition à l'Assemblée Nationale, par Montaigne, Charron, Montesquieu et Voltaire* (Paris: Chez Desenne, 1791) 25.

OPINION SUR LE DIVORCE.
As a whole people is in proportion to an ill marriage, so is
one man to an ill marriage.
Milton – Discipline of Divorce – Dedication

Today, other French philosophers and sociologists are making a connection for our time between marriage, Milton, and the republican ethos. *They* ordered a translation of Milton's *Doctrine and Discipline of Divorce*,[20] and are rediscovering Milton through the present debates of society.

Their study of Stanley Cavell's comedy of remarriage led them to Milton. They were called as experts by the French government to advise them on so urgent a matter as family life. They have started building their own philosophical systems on Milton.

In the light of IMS 8 and the essays that follow, I suggest we listen to what Sandra and Olivier have to say.[21]

14 January 2008

20 John Milton, *Doctrine et Discipline du Divorce*. Bilingual edition (Paris: Belin, "Littérature & politique," 2005).

21 The French philosophers referred to are Sandra Laugier and Olivier Abel. See Olivier Abel, *Le mariage a-t-il encore un avenir?* (Paris: Bayard, 2005); 165 p. See Sandra Laugier, *Une autre pensée politique américaine: La démocratie radicale d'Emerson à Stanley Cavell* (Paris: Michel Houdiard, 2004); 165 p. They will speak on "Milton's Politics of Divorce" at IMS9 to be held in London, 7–11 July 2008.

Part I

The Minor Poetry

Hugh WILSON

Milton and Wordsworth: Reflections on "L'Allegro," "Il Penseroso," and "Tintern Abbey"

When the sword glitters o'er the judge's head,
And fear has coward churchmen silenced,
Then is the poet's time, 'tis then he draws,
And single fights forsaken virtue's cause.
He, when the wheel of empire whirleth back,
And though the world's disjointed axle crack,
Sings still of ancient rights and better times,
Seeks wretched good, arraigns successful crimes.
-- Andrew Marvell in "Tom May's Death."

Milton's influence on Wordsworth is widely acknowledged. Christopher Wordsworth indicates the poet's early interest in Milton; Raymond Havens observes that Wordsworth's poetry often recalls, "the lofty severity, the intensity of moral purpose, and the organ tone of the most exalted of English poets."[1] Havens observes that "Milton's poetry was more familiar" to Wordsworth "than anything else in English literature (except possibly Shakespeare's plays)" and he calls Wordsworth "the most Miltonic poet since Milton."[2] In *Milton and Wordsworth*, Herbert Grierson discusses the biographical parallels between the two poets; in *Milton and the Romantics*, Joseph Wittreich assembles much of the documentary evidence of Milton's influence; and in *Wordsworth: the Critical Heritage*, Robert Woof excerpts ear-

1 Raymond Dexter Havens, *The Influence of Milton on English Poetry* (Cambridge: Harvard UP, 1922; reprinted, New York: Russell and Russell, 1961), 177. The bulk of this essay was conceived naively in an instant, largely without the benefit of previous scholarship, and composed for the International Milton Symposium in Grenoble, France in June of 2005. In anticipation of its publication as part of the proceedings, I have tried to incorporate a review of previous scholarship. A revised introduction and fuller annotations amend the earlier draft; but the core of the essay is substantially unchanged. Chimegsaikhan Banzar helped me correct a number of errors. Havens quotes one of Wordsworth's friends, "Spenser, Shakespeare, and Milton are his favourites among the English poets, especially the latter, whom he almost idolizes." Havens, 182. He cites J. J. Tayler, *Letters* [1872], 1.72.

2 Havens 190, 197 and 200.

lier critics.[3] Kenneth R. Johnston remarks "Miltonic depth-charges"; he suggests that Wordsworth's meditative poem recalls "Shakespeare's, Milton's and the Bible's heroes in their time of crisis, as they contemplate what Wordsworth himself was contemplating: the need, and the cost, *of public action in the world*."[4] Although the special relationship between Milton and Wordsworth is a given, the full ramifications of that relationship are not always apparent, and there are neglected affinities between "L'Allegro," and "Il Penseroso," the concluding poem of *Lyrical Ballads*, Wordsworth's "Tintern Abbey."

By comparison with the heated polemics over "Tintern Abbey," Milton's wonderful companion poems are only mildly controversial, but Wordsworth's "Tintern Abbey" has been a site where pitched battles have been fought between warring critics for at least three-quarters of a century.[5]

3 Christopher Wordsworth, *The Early Wordsworthian Milieu: A Note of Christopher Wordsworth, and a Few Entries by William Wordsworth*, ed. Zera Silver Fink (Oxford: Clarendon, 1958); Herbert Grierson, *Milton and Wordsworth: Poets and Prophets: A Study of Their Reactions to Political Events* (London: Macmillan, 1937); Joseph Anthony Wittreich, *The Romantics on Milton: Formal Essays and Critical Asides* (Cleveland: Case Western Reserve University, 1970). *Wordsworth: The Critical Heritage*, ed. Robert Woof (New York: Routledge, 2001).

4 The italics appear in the original text. In *The Hidden Wordsworth* [1998] (New York: Norton, 2000), Kenneth R. Johnston offers some fascinating theories I hesitate to assess; he picks up echoes of *Hamlet*, *Samson Agonistes*, the Psalmist, and even Milton's divorce tracts (290; 432–33).

5 Ever since William Empson attacked "Tintern Abbey" in *Seven Kinds of Ambiguity*, the purport and value of the poem has been contested. Helen Vendler contributed to the debate in "'Tintern Abbey': Two Assaults," 173–90, in *Wordsworth in Context*, ed. Pauline Fletcher and John Murphy (Lewisburg: Bucknell UP, 1992). Although Marjorie Levinson has raised a number of interesting and hotly contested issues, in her recent essay, she offers an olive branch and a consensus formulation that many partisans might accept: "'Tintern Abbey' is a more honest, humane, complex, and moving poem than the received readings – the most celebratory readings – had imagined" (125). See Levinson's "Revisionist Reading: An Account of the Practice," *Studies in the Literary Imagination* 30:1 (Spring 1997): 119–40. In 1998, Kenneth Johnston remarked that the poem has become "the focus of an extraordinary controversy, that turns very much on where Wordsworth walked, and what he saw on this trip" *The Hidden Wordsworth* (New York: Norton, 1998, 2000), 428. In "'We Are Two': The Address to Dorothy in 'Tintern Abbey'," *Studies in Romanticism* 40:4 (Winter 2001): 531–46, Heidi Thomson quotes Alan Grob's description of the poem as "that dark and bloody ground over which so many of the battles of Romantic New Historicist historiography have been fought" (531). In "Wordsworth Studies and the Ethics of Criticism: The

The poem enthralls most common readers, but from the beginning of the twentieth century, conservative critics and radicals both attacked it. Norman Foerster called it "a superb expression of unwisdom," and William Empson called it a "muddle."[6] During the nineteen-eighties, several progressive scholars criticized "Tintern Abbey" as an evasive poem that elides serious moral, social and political issues. In marked contrast, other scholars celebrate the poem as a heartfelt, tender, pensive meditation.[7] Some progressives read Wordsworth as a lapsed radical, even an incipient Burkean conservative; some see him as a disillusioned, but unrepentant, reformist; other scholars see him, in 1798, as a chastened, but still committed, radical.[8] Wordsworth never entirely abandoned the moral example Milton set: in his

---

'Tintern Abbey' Debate Revisited," *Concentric* 30:2 (July 2004): 129–54, Eric K. W. Yu reviews the "bitter 'Tintern Abbey' debate" (147).

6 Irving Babbitt, *Rousseau and Romanticism* [1919] (Cleveland: Meridian, 1947, 1966). Norman Foerster, "The Esthetic Judgment and the Ethical Judgment," in *The Intent of the Critic*, ed. Donald A. Stauffer (Princeton: PUP, 1941), 76, cited by James Benzinger, "Tintern Abbey Revisited," *PMLA* 65:2 (March 1950): 154–62; and William Empson, *Seven Types of Ambiguity* [1930] (New York: New Directions, 1947), 151–54.

7 Marjorie Levinson, *Wordsworth's Great Period Poems: Four Essays* (Cambridge: CUP, 1986). Jerome McGann, *The Romantic Ideology: A Critical Investigation* (Chicago: University of Chicago Press, 1983). John Barrell, *Poetry, Language and Politics* (Manchester: Manchester UP, 1989). James Chandler, *Wordsworth's Second Nature: A Study of the Poetry and Politics* (Chicago: University of Chicago Press, 1984), cited by Fred Randel in1993.

8 J. R. Watson, "A Note on the Date in the Title of 'Tintern Abbey'," *Wordsworth Circle* 10 (1979): 379–80. In "The Politics of 'Tintern Abbey'," *Wordsworth Circle* 14:1 (Winter 1983): 6–14, Kenneth Johnston remarks that "beneath the calm surface of its 'still, sad music,' [the author had] turned its clock back twenty-four hours, to avoid setting off the powerful buried charges that would be exploded if this loco-descriptive meditative landscape poem concluding his new volume of poems, were to have been entitled, 'Lines / Written a Few Miles above Tintern Abbey, On Revisiting the Banks of the Wye During a Tour. July 14, 1798'" (13). In "The French Revolution and 'Tintern Abbey'," *Raritan* 10:3 (Winter 1991): 1–23, David Bromwich remarks that the "poem, having done all that it can, in geographical situation and picturesque placement, to put the subject of France out of mind, by this choice of a date brings it back once again" (13, 14n). Bromwich also notes the assumption that Wordsworth's political associates, the Girondins were "moderates" and Jacobins "radicals," oversimplifies the facts: "The Girondins, all along, were the party of war, while Robespierre for a long time resisted their clamor on prudential grounds" (15). Fred V. Randel, "The Betrayals of 'Tintern Abbey'," *Studies in Romanticism* 32:3 (Fall 1993): 379–97. See page 388 for discussion of multiple facets of the poem's date. Randel observes that the "poet who had lived through the recent efforts of both France and Britain to crush dissent, the political and social dimension of this statement would be inescapable" (396).

sonnet, "London, 1802," published a few years after "Tintern Abbey," Wordsworth wished that Milton himself could confront the moral crisis of the era.

Although scholars have recognized the influence of Milton through Wordsworth's allusions to his works, they differ over whether Wordsworth writes in opposition to, or in solidarity with, his predecessor.[9] As best I can tell, none seem to have remarked the way "Tintern Abbey" parallels with both of Milton's companion poems; in my view, most critics have not given sufficient weight to the burden of contemporary repression that forced a measure of justified self-censorship, and encouraged a certain allusive indirection. The following pages discuss some of the ways that Wordsworth's quiet, but not quietist, political meditation alludes to Milton's life and works: Wordsworth drew parallels between Milton's aspirations and his own.[10]

Milton's companion poems can be read as his attempt to find his vocation, to choose between the rival conceptions of the poet available. Al-

9 Harold Bloom, *Poetry and Repression: Revisionism from Blake to Stevens* (New Haven: Yale UP, 1976), 70. (The preceding cited by Damian Walford Davies, 1996.) John Hodgson, "Wordsworth's Dialectical Transcendentalism, 1798: 'Tintern Abbey'," *Criticism* 18 (1976): 367–80. See page 373–74, 379n. Robert A. Brinkley, "'Vagrant and Hermit: Milton and the Politics of 'Tintern Abbey'," *Wordsworth Circle* 16:3 (Summer 1985): 126–33. Lyle Smith, "Reading 'Something' in 'Tintern Abbey'," *Christianity and Literature* 45:3–4 (Spring–Summer 1996): 303–17. See page 314. Fred V. Randel, "The Betrayals of 'Tintern Abbey'," *Studies in Romanticism* 32:3 (Fall 1993): 379–97. Charles J. Rzepka, "Pictures of the Mind: Iron and Charcoal, 'Ouzy' Tides and 'Vagrant Dwellers' at Tintern, 1798," *Studies in Romanticism* 42:2 (Summer 2003): 155–85.

10 For a contrary opinion on Wordsworth's relationship with Milton, and on his alleged quietism, see James Benzinger, "Tintern Abbey Revisited," *PMLA* 65:2 (March 1950): 154–62. See pages 156–57. Still, Nicholas Roe's political reading of "Tintern Abbey" seems more credible. See his "Epilogue: Daring to Hope," in *Wordsworth and Coleridge: The Radical Years* (Oxford: OUP, 1988), 263–75. Mary Wedd suggests that Wordsworth deployed Miltonic allusions to draw a parallel between his position after the French Revolution and Milton's situation after the Restoration (163ff). See "'Tintern Abbey' Restored," *Charles Lamb Bulletin* 88 (October 1994): 150–65. William Richey persuasively argues that Wordsworth "'deliberately engages' social and political issues in 'Tintern Abbey.'" Wordsworth had been harassed by spies, and that he was very much aware of the "increasing repressiveness" of the government. In his view, Wordsworth was composing a "public poem replete with political implications" "during a time of strict government censorship"; he reads the last paragraph as "rededication to humanitarian concerns" (198; 212). See "The Politicized Landscape of 'Tintern Abbey,'" *Studies in Philology* 95:2 (Spring 1998): 197–219.

though Milton's companion poems were probably conceived at leisure and revised in hindsight, he wrote his two companion poems as if he were at or near the fulcrum – the pivot point – of his choice or vocation, contemplating the actual decision. Both poets offer us self-portraits: to use Wordsworth's phrases from "Tintern Abbey," Milton painted a "picture of the mind" near a moment of choice, a time of "sad perplexity," before the poet, in the words of D. C. Allen, found his way.[11]

Milton dramatizes his own personal version of the perennial choice of Hercules that, in some form or fashion, confronts us all. Given his upbringing, there were two plausible choices. As a young man in his twenties, Milton could at least imagine being carefree and cavalier in the spirit of a more austere version of the Caroline *Books of Sports*; he could also imagine becoming a serious student of serious poetry.[12] He could choose Horatian wine or the cold water of asceticism: on one hand, Master Milton could become a refined poetic hedonist, an elegantly tasteful Horatian aesthete, a serious Epicurean seeking the *pleasures* of the mind, the gentry virtuoso, the lover of antique poetry, Italian music, drama, and folklore. In his flattering masque, *Pleasure Reconciled with Virtue*, Ben Jonson, followed by Carew and the other sons of the Ben, pointed the way.

On the other hand, Milton could abandon the tangles of Neaera's hair, burn the midnight oil, commit himself to the studies that would make a higher calling possible, and try to assume the mantle of Elijah: he could try to become a Christian poet, a visionary, "vatic" or prophetic poet. Catholicism had its great poet in Dante, but there was little precedent for an epic poet of the Reformation, a thing "unattempted yet." Given his family's wealth, the first role guaranteed relative security; the second role promised a more hazardous life.

11 "Tintern Abbey," approximately lines 63–64. D. C. Allen, "The Search for the Prophetic Strain: "L'Allegro" and "Il Penseroso" [1954], 106–122, in *John Milton: L'Allegro and Il Penseroso*, ed. Elaine B. Safer and Thomas L. Erskine (Columbus, Ohio: Charles E. Merrill Publishing, 1970). D. C. Allen, *The Harmonious Vision: Studies in Milton's Poetry* (Baltimore: Johns Hopkins University Press, 1954).

12 King James I, *The Kings Majesties Declaration, Concerning the Lawfull Sports to bee Used* [1618] (London: Printed by Robert Barker and by the assigns of John Bill, 1633). Published by James I, and again by Charles I, the so-called "Book of Sports" encouraged recreational activities on Sunday, and provoked widespread Puritan indignation. C. W. Brodribb has suggested that the royal order of October 10, 1633 requiring the 'Declaration of Sports' be read in every parish may have prompted the companion poems. See "Milton's 'L'Allegro' and 'Il Penseroso,'" *NQ* 163 (September 17, 1932): 201.

In his companion poems, John Milton dramatizes the choice of his vocation; in "Tintern Abbey," William Wordsworth meditates on the significance of a choice already made. Both poets were facing dangers requiring prudence, and in Johann Gottlieb Fichte's words, both men were contemplating their own vocations and "the vocation of man."[13]

Both poets wrote in the shadow of wars abroad and repression at home. Milton probably composed his lyrics during the dark years of the Thirty Years War and during the initial years of the "Personal Rule" of Charles I when the king tried to implement the absolutist ideals of his father, James I.[14] During this period, the English monarchy essentially abandoned Protestants on the continent, assumed extraordinary powers at home, and made it an offense – punishable by mutilation – to criticize the royal family; it even became an offense to speak of the convening of a Parliament.

Similarly, Wordsworth wrote in the shadow of the Napoleonic wars, under the threat of Gagging Acts, imprisonment, and treason trials: abroad, Metternich's unsavory "Holy" alliance of Russia, Prussia, Austro-Hungary, and Britain tried to crush the revolution in France and stifle stirrings for democracy throughout Europe; at home, an unreformed Parliament dominated by corrupt, cowardly or mercenary politicians, pocket boroughs, and stock-jobbers used the pretext of Terror to mobilize support for horrific imperialist wars that would enrich cronies, thwart domestic reform, and rationalize repression at home and abroad.[15] The administration drastically

13 Johann Gottlieb Fichte, *The Vocation of Man* (LaSalle: Open Court, 1940).

14 The "Personal Rule" of Charles I begins with dissolution of the Parliament of 1628 and ends with the assembly of the "Short" Parliament of 1640.

15 David V. Erdman, cited by David Bromwich, suggests that "At the time Wordsworth made his tour [1798], both he and Coleridge were on the run – as we would call it today, draft-dodging." See "Wordsworth at Heartsworth: or, Was Regicide the Prophetic Ground of Those Moral Questions?" 12–41, in *The Evidence of the Imagination: Studies of Interactions between Life and Art in English Romantic Literature*, ed. Donald Reiman et alia (New York: New York UP, 1978). David Bromwich, "The French Revolution and 'Tintern Abbey'," *Raritan* 10:3 (Winter 1991): 1–23. Brutality terrorizes and terror begets terror. Bromwich notes that "the actuality of foreign war was used to justify the regime of terror in France" (16). In Wordsworth's view, customary ethical ideals were being betrayed. Fred V. Randel [1993] notes that the "English church joined the state in betrayal by offering prayers for English victories, and Wordsworth recoiled in rage" ([*Prelude* [1805]] 10:263–74). In pursuing their war policy and stifling dissent, the leaders of the English state and church were 'shepherds' perversely bent on 'murder'" (386). In his insightful *Charles Lamb Bulletin* essay of 1997, Damian Walford Davies ar-

abridged the rights of freedom of assembly, speech and press; privacy diminished as spies abounded; the "corresponding societies" sympathetic to the Revolution in France were sabotaged or effectively banned; habeas corpus was suspended, the media was gagged, dissenters were intimidated, and public discussion stifled.[16] Scholars, reformers or journalists like Gilbert Wakefield, Thomas Holcroft, Horne Tooke, John Thelwall, William Hone, and William Cobbett were cashiered or tried on trumped up charges of "sedition."[17] Democratic satirists were censored or silenced; writers and books criticizing the incumbent establishment or defending universal human rights were smeared by the reactionary establishment or suppressed outright: Mary Wollstonecraft's *Vindication of the Rights of Man,* and her *Vindication of the Rights of Woman* [1792] were both derided; Thomas Paine was declared an outlaw, charged with sedition, tried and convicted in absentia; *The Rights of Man* [1789] was banned.

Acknowledged tyrannies were rehabilitated for the sake of allegedly anti-terrorist alliances; pious clergy blessed the knout and the lash, – "A servant will not be corrected by words: for though he understand he will not answer" (Proverbs 29:19) – abolitionists were momentarily paralyzed; the defenders of serfdom and slavery sought shelter from demands for reform under the cover of patriotism and behind the all-purpose alibi of alleged "national security."[18]

---

gues that Wordsworth despised "the unjust aggression of the great European powers," not excluding that of his own country (29).

16 One suspects that Damian Davies' description of the predicament of David Williams in 1793 might have applied to both Wordsworth in the seventeen-nineties and Milton after the restoration, "His reputation was tarnished, his company shunned, his movements monitored and his servants and neighbours questioned." Davies, "Hermits, Heroes and History: Lamb's 'Many Friends'," *Charles Lamb Bulletin* 97 (January 1997): 9–29. See page 19.

17 Kenneth R. Johnston notes "[t]he hysterical political climate in London after the declarations of war (mass meetings, extremist plots, Treason Trials, paid government informers)" (11). Johnston, "The Politics of 'Tintern Abbey'," *Wordsworth Circle* 14:1 (Winter 1983): 6–14.

18 In his *Commonplace Book*, Milton criticized "Amor in Patriam": he remarked, "[t]his virtue should be sought by philosophers warily. For a blind and carnal love of country should not sweep us to deeds of rapine and slaughter and hatred of neighboring nations in order that we may aggrandize our country by power, wealth, or glory; for so did the heathen act. Christians, however, ought to cultivate mutual peace and not covet other men's goods" (Columbia Edition, 17:164–65). Also, see Ruth Mohl, *John Milton and His Commonplace Book* (New York: Frederick Ungar, 1969), 262–63.

Both Milton and Wordsworth were writing under the threat of repression; both men were not so much declaring their political views as much as they were indicating their commitment to be morally engaged.[19] Even that was a potential offense: they knew that repressive regimes sponsor unprincipled and malleable pragmatists; they prefer frivolous persiflage because serious literature encourages attitudes that are inconveniently ethical and inevitably political.

Written in blank verse paragraphs sometimes called "Miltonicks," Wordsworth's poem "Lines Written a Few Miles Above Tintern Abbey, On Revisiting the Banks of the Wye During a Tour, July 13, 1798," recalls Bastille Day,[20] and, at the same time, commemorates Milton's poetry in ways small and large, in turns of phrase, recurrent themes, and verse structures.[21] Milton was the paradigmatic poet of the sublime, and Wordsworth imitates

19 In *Lyrical Ballads*, both Wordsworth and Coleridge wrote under the sign of Milton. There isn't enough time to discuss the full nature and extent of the influence of Milton or his companion poems on *Lyrical Ballads*, but Milton's influence on Coleridge is apparent in "The Nightingale: a Conversation Poem, Written in April 1798," in "Fears of Solitude," in "France, An Ode," "Frost at Midnight," as well as "Tintern Abbey." Coleridge rings changes on several passages from Milton, and Wordsworth was conscious of both poets.

20 The storming of the Bastille on July 14, 1789 – when common criminals and political prisoners were liberated from the prison – is celebrated as the beginning of the French revolution. The proximity of Bastille Day to the date of Wordsworth poem is noted by Henry Weinfield in "'These Beauteous Forms': "Tintern Abbey" and the Post-Enlightenment Religious Crisis," *Religion in the Arts* 6:3 (2002): 257–90. Weinfeld observes that Wordsworth's poem is dated on the fifth anniversary of the assassination of Jean-Paul Marat: July 13, 1793; this assassination, commemorated and nearly sainted in the famous painting by Jacques-Louis David, triggered a wave of recriminations and vindictive executions that discredited the ideals of the revolution.

21 Harold Bloom, *A Map of Misreading* (1975), cited by Brinkley 1985. David Bromwich notes the "Miltonic *or*," and notes that 'Tintern Abbey' is a "blank verse anomaly among the *Lyrical Ballads*" (12). In "Vagrant and Hermit: Milton and the Politics of 'Tintern Abbey'," *Wordsworth Circle* 16:3 (Summer 1985): 126–33, Robert Brinkley rehearses a series of credible Miltonic allusions. Richard Matlak, in "Classical Argument and Romantic Persuasion in 'Tintern Abbey'," *Studies in Romanticism* 25:1 (Spring 1986): 97–129, argues that the poem follows the rubrics of Ciceronian rhetoric. See page 99. In her reading, Deborah Kennedy recalls "the twilight groves of John Milton's 'Il Penseroso'" (81). See "Wordsworth, Turner, and the Power of Tintern Abbey," *Wordsworth Circle* 33:2 (Spring 2002): 79–84.

him in phrasing with inversions like "a sense sublime" and in manner with eloquent blank verse paragraphs.[22]

The allusions to the controversial "blind man," the ascending smoke, the walking tour, and the imaginary hermit echo Miltonic tropes, but the context and the structure of the poems are more important than the surface allusions. Milton published his companion poems during the unfolding of the English Revolution; Wordsworth published "Tintern Abbey" during the unfolding of the French Revolution. Milton probably composed his poems during the Personal Rule, but he first registered them for publication in 1645 after the high hopes revealed in *Areopagitica*, after the battle of Marston Moor and just months before Naseby; they were available during the time of uneasy negotiations that would issue in the second civil war. Wordsworth's *Lyrical Ballads* were issued in the wake of political disasters that shattered naive utopian hopes, and in response, the poet wrote to salvage something from the wreckage: to quietly intimate perennial ideals in a time of domestic repression.[23] In the words that Shelley wrote a generation later, Wordsworth dared "to hope till Hope creates / From its own wreck the thing it contemplates."[24]

The phases of Wordsworth's experience parallel the development of Milton's companion poems and the conception of moral development through aesthetic experience that Schiller explains in his *Letters on the Aesthetic Education of Man* [1794].[25] "L'Allegro" corresponds to the time Wordsworth,

22 My observation may have been prompted by R. A. Foakes, "Beyond the Visible World: Wordsworth and Coleridge in *Lyrical Ballads*," *Romanticism* 5:1 (1999): 58–69. See page 64.

23 Several of Wordsworth's later poems of 1802: the sonnet to Milton, the sonnet on the arrest and incarceration of Toussaint L'Ouverture, – and the betrayal of the ideals of the Revolution – with his invocation of "exultations, agonies,/ And love and man's unconquerable mind," indicate his persistent idealism in the face of transient defeat.

24 Percy Bysshe Shelley, *Prometheus Unbound*, Act IV, ll. 570–578. In his own way, Wordsworth was 'defying power.'

25 Friedrich Schiller, *On the Aesthetic Education of Man* [1794–1795], trans. Reginald Snell (New York: Ungar, 1965). According to Max Hertzberg, Schiller, "the most popular of all German authors in England, as he was also in Germany," "undoubtedly influenced Wordsworth" (313; 342). See "William Wordsworth and German Literature," *PMLA* 40:2 (June 1925): 302–45. If the resemblance is more than just a matter of ideas being "in the air," Coleridge might have been an intermediary between Schiller and Wordsworth. In his study of Schiller's influence on Coleridge, John Michael Kooy has suggested that Schiller's influence on Coleridge is earlier and more profound than it might

having gone beyond the "coarser pleasures of his boyish days," was fascinated by the appreciation of the beauty of nature; Nature, to him, was "all in all." He explains that the spectacle of "sounding cataract," mountains or gloomy woods, haunted him "like a passion," like "an appetite, a feeling and a love," without a deeper thought.[26] "Il Penseroso" corresponds to the subsequent phase in which Wordsworth is chastened and subdued; he has a revelation of a spirit "far more deeply interfused," and begins to hear the "sad, still music" or the "small still voice" of humanity."[27] Like the speaker in the proem of "L'Allegro" who condemns garish, nightmarish Melancholy to some uncouth cell, Wordsworth felt like a man "Flying from something that he dreads" rather than "one who sought the thing he loved."[28]

In contrast to "L'Allegro" and Wordsworth's earlier mood, "Il Penseroso" conveys more of the spirit of the Man of Sorrows, of "sweetest melancholy" that issues in ecstasy and an intimation of the sublime. Both poets move from self-absorption to a sense of a responsibility to something larger than themselves.

As in Schiller's theory explaining the moral potential of the perception of the beautiful in nature or art, man goes through three phases in the progression: from "animal sensations" to the appreciation of beauty to "the moral sentiments." Initially, humankind are absorbed in their appetites and urges, sensations and experiences, without much regard for others. The experience of beauty, of the aesthetic moment, has the power to take us out of ourselves, to make us forget ourselves and our own desires, to liberate us

---

appear to be at first sight. See *Coleridge, Schiller, and Aesthetic Education* (Basingstoke and New York: Palgrave Macmillan, 2002).

26 "Tintern Abbey," ll. 76–85.

27 "Tintern Abbey," ll. 91–105.

28 "L'Allegro," ll. 1–10. "Tintern Abbey," ll. 73–75. Richard Gravil suggests that Wordsworth, in 1793, may have visited Tintern Abbey in order to avoid press gangs and the draft for the Napoleonic wars. Gravil, "'Tintern Abbey' and The System of Nature," *Romanticism* 6:1 (2000): 35–54. See page 50. Richard Gravil's article demonstrates surprising affinities between Wordsworth's attitudes toward nature and those expressed by John Thelwall in *The Rights of Nature* and by Baron d'Holbach in *The System of Nature; or, the Laws of the Moral and Physical World.* (In some respects, Richard Gravil seems to amplify and enrich Alan Grob's suggestion that "*Tintern Abbey* is implicitly a gesture of protest directed toward the existing social order." See Grob's *The Philosophic Mind: A Study of Wordsworth's Poetry and Thought 1797–1803* (Columbus: Ohio State University Press, 1973), 31.) Gravil's encyclopedic eighteenth footnote is especially illuminating.

from our selfishness, and leaves us in a relatively disinterested state of mind. The experience of beauty opens the way for memory, imagination, and empathy, for a recognition of the needs of others; in turn, the exercise of empathy, of compassion, opens the way to a deeper sense of ethics. The recurrence of the experience of beauty evokes compassion: one acquires a sense of something grander and larger than oneself, a recognition and concern for the miseries of others, an ability to hear the "sad music of humanity." Mindless pleasures, irrational melancholy, fear, anxiety, and false joys are put into perspective. Sight yields to insight; wide-eyed credulity in the spectacle of the apparent yields to a deeper understanding and faith in the paradoxical "evidence" of things not seen. Mankind rises from sensation, to feeling, to passive comprehension, and then to a higher intuitive reason. Acute awareness of physical beauty ushers in a sense of the sublime.

In this view, with time, the consciousness of the beauty of nature awakens the conscience and compassion; it arouses a growing awareness of the needs of man; with time, the acquisition of the habit of ethical resolve leads toward a new state of feeling, and the revelation of something divine. The soul opens to the influx of insight, to a new understanding of one's place in the world. One acquires a sense of tragedy, an intimation of death, and an assurance that others, aside from one's mortality, will carry on the continuity of life: the appreciation of the aesthetic, and the consequent development of the moral education of mankind. This unfolding natural order fosters a slow, steady human progress that intimates some kind of cosmic order, whether Platonic, Stoic, Christian, Spinozan or Hegelian, that resonates with the pursuit of truth, the recognition of beauty, and the commitment to love one another.

The appreciation of the beauty of nature rescues man from self-absorption, disillusionment, and despair; it restores a chastened confidence in the spiritual potential of humankind emblematized by the beautiful ruins of Tintern Abbey, and the lovely countryside around the river Wye. The humanitarian idealism that built the monasteries or urged on the generous impulses of the English, American, and French Revolutions suffers from inevitable mistakes, setbacks, betrayals and corruptions, but the aspiration for probity, equity, humanity and justice inscribed on the unfinished monument for Marat's tomb never dies. The people suffer abuse, injustice, poverty and disaster, but there will be other popular repudiations of injustice that seek to implement the universal brother and sisterhood of mankind.

Even as he wrote, Wordsworth knew that innocent sympathizers with the French were being pursued, arrested, and indicted on both sides of the English Channel.[29] For Wordsworth and the partisans of the early phases of the French Revolution as different as Mirabeau and Marat, Milton could serve as an example of principled struggle against injustice. For Wordsworth, composing "Tintern Abbey" in the dark days of 1798, Milton provided an example of a poet who suffered the experience of defeat without abandoning his convictions; he did what he could to denounce oppression and encourage toleration, sympathy, justice and mercy.

In "L'Allegro," after imagining a visit to a sleepy upland hamlet where everyone turns in early, the narrator notes that "Towred Cities please us then / And the busie humm of men [...]" (117–18). In contrast, in "Il Penseroso," the narrator imagines being alone

> Where glowing Embers through the room
> Teach light to counterfeit a gloom [...].[30]

In the spirit of "Il Penseroso," Wordsworth combines the ideas, writing of being "in lonely rooms, and 'mid the din / Of towns and cities."[31]

In "L'Allegro," Milton notices a "Cottage chimney smokes [...] betwixt two aged Oaks"; Wordsworth notices "wreaths of smoke / Sent up, in silence, from among the trees!"[32] In "Il Penseroso," the narrator imagines a "peacefull hermitage, / The Hairy Gown and Mossy Cell" where the poet might learn the secrets of heaven and earth. Similarly, Wordsworth fantasizes that the smoke wreaths that betoken "some Hermit's cave, where by his fire / The Hermits sits alone."[33]

29 J. G. Alger, "The British Colony in Paris, 1792–93," *English Historical Review* 13:52 (October 1898): 672–74.

30 "Il Penseroso," lines 79–80.

31 "Tintern Abbey," lines 27–28.

32 "L'Allegro," lines 81–82. "Tintern Abbey," lines 18–19.

33 "Tintern Abbey," ll. 21–22. Eric K. W. Yu notes John Hunt's observation that the "hermit is a conventional symbol of rural retreat" (134). Tintern's hermit has attracted some especially fascinating commentary: see Robert Brinkley's "Vagrant and Hermit: Milton and the Politics of Tintern Abbey," *Wordsworth Circle* 16:3 (Summer 1985): 126–33; Damian Walford Davies, "'Some Uncertain Notice': The Hermit of 'Tintern Abbey'," *Notes and Queries* 43(241):4 (December 1996): 422–24 and his "Hermits, Heroes and History: Lamb's 'Many Friends'," *Charles Lamb Bulletin* 97 (January 1997): 9–29. Mark English, "'Recognitions Dim and Faint': The Hermit of 'Tintern Abbey' Again," *Notes and Queries* 44(242):3 (September 1997): 324–25. Mark English notes that

In another passage, Wordsworth simultaneously recalls Milton's loss of sight when nature became as "a landscape to a blind man's eye," his 19th Sonnet ("When I consider how my light is spent..."), the invocation to light in Book III of *Paradise Lost,* and the darkness at noon in *Samson Agonistes.*[34] Wordsworth also echoes Milton's description of his predicament after the Restoration in the invocation before Book VII of *Paradise Lost.*[35] "Smit with the love of sacred song," Milton had sung

> with mortal voice,
> Unchang'd though fall'n on evil dayes
> On evil dayes though fall'n, and evil tongues,
> In darkness, and with dangers compast round
> And solitude; yet not alone, while thou
> Visit'st my slumbers Nightly [...].[36]

Wordsworth echoes Milton's wording, his resolve to resist, his sense of something "mysterious meant," and his feeling of being blessed

> With lofty thoughts, that neither evil tongues,
> Rash judgments, nor the sneers of selfish man,
> Nor greetings where no kindness is, nor all
> The dreary intercourse of daily life,
> Shall e'er prevail against us, or disturb
> Our cheerful faith, that all which we behold
> Is full of blessings [...] (128–134).

Like Milton in his meditation on Orpheus – "nor could the Muse defend / Her Son"[37] – Wordsworth contemplates the possibility or the eventuality of

---

Wordsworth might have seen reference to Tintern's hermit-king in contemporary sources noted above and/or in Milton's *History of Britain.* See Richard Gravil's wide-ranging discussion of "hermitude" in "'Tintern Abbey' and the System of Nature," *Romanticism* 6:1 (2000): 35–54.

34 "Tintern Abbey," lines 23–26. *Paradise Lost* 3:1–155.

35 As Robert Brinkley remarks, "the reference to a blind man which immediately follows the hermit in 'Tintern Abbey' serves to reinforce the Miltonic reference" (129). In many respects, Brinkley's meditation on the relationship between Milton and Wordsworth anticipates my own.

36 *Paradise Lost,* 7:24–29. *Samson Agonistes,* lines 67–114. Mark Foster, "'Tintern Abbey' and Wordsworth's Scene of Writing," *Studies in Romanticism* 25:1 (Spring 1986): 75–95. See page 93.

37 *Paradise Lost,* 7:37–38.

his own death. Dorothy may outlive him, but his poem will survive as his testament to her, as a reminder of what they once shared.

"L'Allegro," "Il Penseroso," and "Tintern Abbey" narrate phases in the maturation of their authors as both poets came of age, transcending their early immaturity, abandoning "thoughtless youth" with its "aching joys and dizzying raptures." For both poets, the "wild ecstasies" of youth vitality have matured into "sober pleasure." Something was lost, but for both Milton and Wordsworth, spiritual growth brought an "abundant recompense": "the joy / Of elevated thoughts; a sense sublime / Of something far more deeply interfused [...]."[38] Although Milton lamented his loss of vision, he had heard and honored a higher calling; he would go on to envision "darkness visible," and "things invisible to mortal sight."

In contrast to his hero Milton, Wordsworth could enjoy the beauty of the natural world: the beauty of the earth as "a landscape to a blind man's eye," but he did not over-rate his advantage. He saw the ruins of beauty around him like painterly landscape by Constable or Piranesi, but he dwelt in another, higher realm. Milton heard the call to assume the mantle of the prophet of charity and Christian liberty; Wordsworth heard the appeal of the "still, sad music humanity," and he would try to be its voice for his generation.[39] In glimpses of vision or moments of inspiration, Wordsworth felt he could sometimes see "into the life of things": that he could intuit a mysterious "presence" he could neither see nor hear, something that "im-

38 "Tintern Abbey," line 88, lines 94–96. Milton haunts the poem. In "Metamorphosis and 'Tintern Abbey': Two Notes," *Modern Philology* 81:1 (August 1983): 24–37, Max Byrd suggests that Wordsworth's "abundant recompense" is "surely an echo of Milton's 'large recompence'" in "Lycidas" (36). In *Wordsworth's Counterrevolutionary Turn: Community, Virtue and Vision in the 1790s* (Newark: University of Delaware Press, 1997), John Reider senses a "muted allusion" to *Lycidas* the opening lines of "Tintern Abbey" (186; 202–03). In "Beyond the Visible World: Wordsworth and Coleridge in *Lyrical Ballads*," *Romanticism* 5:1 (1999): 58–69, R. A. Foakes also suggests an echo of *Paradise Lost*, 7:89 in the word "interfused." See page 61.

39 In "The Politics of 'Tintern Abbey'," *Wordsworth Circle* 14:1 (Winter 1983): 6–14, Kenneth Johnston asks, "what kind of music is 'still, sad music'? It sounds more like the andante of a Brahms symphony than the allegro of a Romantic one by Beethoven" (6). In "The French Revolution and 'Tintern Abbey'," *Raritan* 10:3 (Winter 1991): 1–23, David Bromwich remarks, "The still, sad music I believe is the cry of human suffering and human need: the same cry that Rousseau, in his *Discourse on Inequality*, had heard as the original motive for an ideal society founded on nature" (20).

pels all thinking things, all objects of all thought, / And rolls through all things."[40]

"Tintern Abbey," Wordsworth's "sublime" transcendentalist meditation, is a defiantly "Miltonic" poem written in response to "the sneers of selfish men"; it was an implicit repudiation of the power elites of his era. As his sonnet to Milton shows, Wordsworth utterly opposed the mendacity and cold-blooded, one-eyed "pragmatism" of the cynical, self-seeking, proto-Malthusian elitists of his own day. Art was tongue-tied by authority, but we can sense something of what the thoughtful artist saw.

From the vantage of one who has seen the heights of *Paradise Lost* and *Paradise Regained*, Wordsworth's "Tintern Abbey" can be seen a reprise or a recapitulation of some of the issues that Milton had confronted in "L'Allegro" and "Il Penseroso." Wordsworth's poem is a meditation on Milton's life and his own; using Milton as an exemplar, he contemplates the role of poetry and the vocation of the poet. In the hills of Wales around the ivied ruins of the old abbey, Wordsworth fled from the miasma of repression hovering over London; he saw the beauty of nature that preserves and renovates the spirit of man even as it destroys and re-absorbs man's ruins. Although the works and art of man ultimately perish as unhandselled nature returns, nature sometimes incorporates traces of exertion that evince the better potential of the human spirit.

On the grounds of Tintern Abbey, one can see where the nave of the church lay, and hear the wind soughing through the window frames; one can imagine seeing "storied Windows richly dight," and hearing Milton's "Service high, and Anthems clear."[41] In the "frozen music"[42] of the architecture, one can see vestiges of human aspiration that time has not wholly expunged. Wordsworth's poem, like Milton's, commemorates a persistent principle of renewal larger, more memorable and more abiding than its particular manifestations.

40 "Tintern Abbey," lines 94; 51; 103–105.

41 "Il Penseroso," lines 159 and 164.

42 This phrase, applied to architecture, is variously attributed to Goethe or Schelling.

Jean PIRONON

The Five Senses as Origin of Milton's Poetic Idiom in the University Exercises and the Minor Poems (1626–1637)[1]

What motivation do we have to engage in an analysis of the relationships between Milton's poetic art and the bodily senses? Let me begin with an observation: in the past twenty to thirty years, the reading of poetry in general has become increasingly dependent on abstract models provided by sciences distinct from literature – post-modern linguistics in particular – which although claiming to start from text as literal structure, have often imposed on the reader rather abstract considerations and in some measure precluded direct understanding and enjoyment of it. The criticism of Milton's poetry has come out relatively immune from the more lethal manifestations of this tendency. Nevertheless, one might do some service to it in suggesting we read Milton again from less sophisticated perspectives.

One may actually be tempted to resort to a kind of reading in which effect recovers absolute priority, an attitude belonging more or less to empiricist aestheticism,[2] and also at present probably related to a renewed interest in Milton's empiricist attitude.[3] However, it is one thing to uncover the empiricist in Milton and quite another to develop a critical idiom based only on sense impressions, as for instance by Michel Serres in *Les Cinq Sens*.[4] If

1 All quotes from John Leonard, *John Milton: The Complete Poems*. London, Penguin Classics, 1998. Prose works, from *CPW*. Yale.

2 The empiricist criticism of poetry, from Hume (see Renée Bouveresse, ed. *David Hume. Les Essais esthétiques: Seconde partie: Art et psychologie*, Paris, Vrin, 1974), to its resurgence in sensualist or phenomenologist philosophy (Merleau-Ponty: *Phénoménologie de la perception*, 1954, claims – not without some reason – to be able to raise itself to the universal and permanent: see Jean Miquel, *L'Empirisme*. Paris, Armand Colin, 1965; and more recently, Jacques Bouveresse, *Langage, perception et réalité. T. 1: la perception et le jugement,* Nîmes, Chambon, 1995.

3 See Daniel Fried's thoroughly researched article, "Milton and Empiricist Semiotics," *Milton Quarterly*, XXXVI, 3, October 2003, 117–138.

4 Paris, Grasset, 1985.

one would rely entirely on the empirical discourse of poetry, one would soon fall into the fallacies of subjectivism. A certain amount of theorisation is needed, if only not to plunge the reader into perplexity or confusion.

My reading of the early poems will be an attempt to analyse sense-impressions – "percepts" in the course of turning into "affects," in the perspective of Milton's empiricist or newly re-discovered "materialist." I shall begin with what we may know about young Milton's sensory experience of the outside world in his education years. I shall then move on to the view of the passions of the mind he had formed through his reading of the Classics and of the Fathers – this, from his school-days at Saint Paul's, and approximately up to the publication of *Poems of Mr. John Milton* (1645). However, I shall devote my more sustained attention to the sensory or perceptual experience itself in the ten or so listed poems, and particularly how sensation is used to create the fundamental dynamics of Milton's poetic universe. My conclusion will return to some considerations about Milton's "empiricist" view of reality.

Let us start from what may be known, or only conjectured about young Milton's experience of the world outside the classroom. According to a number of sources,[5] this experience was apparently that of a disciplined, studious but somewhat self-centered and perhaps, as the word goes, inhibited youth. Given the constraining yet addictive aspects of the studious routine, vacation periods must have meant a wished-for and somewhat ecstatic release, as we learn from a very early school exercise – a "rhetorical theme", when he was still at Saint Paul's (1623?):

> Up, up, you sluggard [...] You know not the number of Dawn's delights. Would you feast your eyes? Behold the purple hue of the rising sun, the clear brisk sky, the green growth of the fields, the diversity of all the flowers. Would you give pleasure to your ears? Listen to the melodious harmony of the birds and soft humming of the bees. Would you satisfy your sense of smell? You will never tire of the sweet odours flowing from the flowers.[6]

Reactualised as personal experience – a normal process in reading poetry – this may be taken as an example of sense-impressions turning into affect. As an exercise in writing the senses, Spring beyond the walls of the classroom will also be elatedly described in *Elegia Prima* and *Elegia Quinta*, re-

5 Parker's *Milton: A Biography* (Oxford, Oxford UP, 1968) remains the most convenient summary of the question.

6 "Betimes in the Morning Leave thy Bed", *CPW* 1: 1037.

counting, also from a background of conventional mythological terms, the "High nervous excitement" (Parker) of Milton at the age of seventeen, strolling outside in country lanes, and undergoing some sort of a behavioural test – that of walking past groups of attractive persons of the opposite sex.

As the subject of these experiences, young Milton was certainly aware of some mental unrest – a trouble in which the memory of these attractive sights coalesced with the images of sensory or sensuous experiences to be found in the Latin or Greek poets he was reading.[7] He was well-prepared to produce the kind of discourse which might be called "prophylactic," in the sense that it was a discourse of order which would initiate a soul-healing process, and this, by reducing the ethically unfamiliar to the stylistically familiar – a movement of his sensitiveness which has long been identified by all the students of Milton: Wagenknecht was one of its earliest modern exponents.[8]

Milton's experience of the outer world would soon give rise to an examination of Christian ethics conducted throughout his education years – an impressive and unique effort to come to terms with the ambiguity of experience by forcing it, so to speak, into a pre-existing ethical framework.

The amplitude and depth of young Milton's reflexion is revealed by the reading programme to which he submitted himself. Only a small part of this immense, self-inflicted *pensum,* was committed to his *Commonplace Book,* in several stages from 1630 up to 1644, which, as one may observe covers, albeit in part, the time during which the poems we are concerned with were written.[9] I will limit myself to a few observations that are of enduring application in our subject – those concerning Milton's reading of Tertullian and Lactantius. Tertullian is mentioned for two treatises, *De Spectaculis (On Public Shows)* and *De Jejuniis (On Abstinence).* Essentially, these are admonitions against the excesses of two of the senses, sight and taste.[10] Lactantius' *Di-*

7 Some philosophers say that perception of language, and therefore *in* language, is prior to any other perceptual experience (J.-L. Austin, *The Language of Perception.* Trans. P. Gochet, Paris, Colin, 1971).

8 Edward Wagenknecht, *The Personality of Milton.* Norman, OK, U. of Oklahoma P., 1961.

9 Many entries in the *Commonplace Book* were made from 1640 to 1644, that is, some time before the publication of *Poems by Mr. John Milton.*

10 These treatises were well-known of the Church Fathers (Paul); Christian moralists had already lengthily commented upon them (Isidore of Seville). British or Continental historians had also dealt with the same topics (Holinshed, Stow, De Thou).

vine Institutes (Libri Septem Divinarum Institutionum Adversus Gentes), particularly Book VI, 20–2 is also relevant to the case: it deals with sight and touch in relation to lust, also a topic in Milton's *Commonplace Book*.[11] However, let us note that the Fathers or theologians Milton had been reading were mainly conceptual in their method and didactic in their purpose, so that the senses are fused into what might be called an "ethical discourse of the *passions*" – not a "discourse of the *senses*," properly speaking. Their effects are only scantily described in perceptual terms.

So it seems that Milton was mainly concerned at first with the prescriptive aspect of these treatises. Following the Fathers, his interest was in the ethical and ontological status of the passions. As for the senses, contrary to some more idealistic theologians who would consider them as the beneficial flowing of the Divinity into the creation, he believed that man's mind could be changed by them into the gross matter of desire and sin. And it was only after having made his way through the ethical problem of the passions that Milton could write a "discourse of the senses."

Concerning the status of the senses, it is also necessary to consider briefly Milton's relationship with music.[12] As art, music should also be viewed from the double perspective of its aesthetic capacities, and of the ethics of reason versus unreason.[13] Music belongs to the auditory. Richard Hooker,[14] or later Richard Baxter, to mention these only, had considered the auditory as the first among the senses. For them, however, music was of the order of the material, of what Descartes, after the schoolmen, would soon distinguish as *"res extensa,"* in opposition to *"res cogitans"* – the order of the mind. In the cultural consciousness of the period, this resulted in the ambivalent status of music. Musical effects could lift the soul to an experience of the divine; these could also be the opening, the breach, through which the Devil would assault the soul. However, Reformed churchmen, particularly Calvin in his *Commentary* on the Psalms, were not averse to accepting a certain amount of controlled sensuality in the church ritual, especially in the form of music, and from Cardinal Bembo to our French Du Bellay, every hymnologist, musician or poet would theoretically be faced

11 *CPW*, p. 369.

12 Vocal or instrumental. See Parker, 3–181 passim.

13 For recent studies, see John Stevens, *The Well Enchanted Skill: Music, Poetry and Drama in the Renaissance*. Oxford, Clarendon Press, 1990; Robin H. Wells, *Elizabethan Mythologies*. Cambridge, CUP, 1994.

14 *Laws of Ecclesiastical Politie*, 1593.

with the problem of making sense with the senses. Every work of literature, but most of all of poetry, was bound to have as a principle of communication, "audibility," but this fundamental aspect of the poetic art (stanza and rime pattern, and phonation – prosodic devices, essentially), should be controlled by music as regulating process.[15] Practically, the auditory element would compel the words of the poet into an order similar, or figurative, of that of the universe.

In verse in general, the senses appear according to two modes – an observation which, concerning Milton, was first made by Wayne Shumaker.[16] This American critic begins with a notion he calls "auditory awareness" – the consciousness of the effect immediately produced by actual or remembered auditory perception. "Auditory awareness" is of two kinds: related, in part or in totality, to poetic theme; or related to "acoustic data and the sound of the poetry itself" (134). Now, if one changes the word "auditory" into "sensory," this theory can then be expanded to a wider scope, which I propose to reformulate in the following, and of course rather simplified way: in verse, the five senses appear either as thematic, or – which is much more interesting – as genuine "perceptual" elements.

The discourse of the senses is omnipresent in many forms in the Latin Elegies either as themes or as percepts. As theme, these appear in explicit concepts or in diffuse thematisations; images, mythological allusions, or simply through the general rhetoric. As percepts, the sense-impressions may be synaesthesic (when they relate to bodily feeling through a combination of sense perceptions) or kinaesthetic (linked with the perception of movement). When related to the space occupied by the body, they are called "proprioceptive" (Dokic). This complex form of discourse is practically always to be found in poetry; the senses are always active in the text in the form of composite perceptual representation, sometimes needing concepts, be it only to guide the reader's response.[17]

The preceding observations also apply to the early poems in English. Listening to them being recited is enough to realise how skilfully all the five senses are being used in the production of feeling.

15 "Musica reservata" or "musique mesurée" (as advocated by the «Pléiade» poets).

16 *Unpremeditated Verse: Feeling and Perception in* Paradise Lost. Princeton, Princeton UP, 1967.

17 See the theorisation in and round Thomas Campion's four *Books of Airs* – a poet and musician not so distant in time from Milton (1617); also, Shumaker 113–114; and Archie Burnett, *Milton's Style*. London and NewYork, 1981.

The auditory. Is used in the form of composition in time, in the same way as in a piece of music,[18] and of the production of sound patterns and effects – the only aspect we shall now consider. Alliteration may be descriptive only (beginning of *On the Morning of Christ's Nativity*: **t, st,** or **ts** alliterations as creative of the plucking of the strings of an instrument). However, most alliterations are directly creative of feeling, if not of idea: see 132–135 in *Lycidas.* The soft, spring-time breeze, together with the sound of a brook dashing by – a sight associated with the story of Alpheus and Aretusa – is sensorialized in the sound effects uniting **s, z, l, fl**, **lf** and **sh, st** alliterations, which goes with a feeling of renewal:

> Return A**lph**eus, the dread voi**ce is** pa**st**
> That **shr**unk thy **str**eam**s**
> [...]
> An call the va**les** and bid them hither ca**st**
> The bell**s,** and **flow**'ret**s** of a thousand hue**s** (132–135).

However, the transfer of sense impressions to the audio-visual level of the text does not go without some serious problems. First, can anyone believe in a well-defined, univocal correspondence between individual sounds and feelings? Archie Burnett thinks that sense-impressions are governed by conceptual significance.[19] And except for the most obvious effects (**s, fl** alliterations for swift, silent motion), it is often impossible to be sure about correspondences. In *The Passion,* for instance, the **w** alliteration, which goes well with windlike effects, results here in something different: the production of a sobbing, waterish effect, which might as well be created through other sounds (the **l** sound for instance):

> The leaves should all be black **wher**eon I **w**rite,
> And letters **wh**ere my tears have washed, a **w**annish **w**hite (34–35).

So far as **Vision** is concerned, *On the Morning of Christ's Nativity* is the earliest example (1629), of the complete changing of sound into visual effect. Although some of the lines are obviously meant to be auditory (Stanza V, v. 64–68: "the winds with wonder whist / *Smoothly* the waters *kissed*"), it is impossible to ignore the visual effect (the italicised word). We also find

18 See Ivanka Stoianova. *Manuel d'analyse musicale. Les formes classiques simples et complexes.* Musique ouverte, Minerve, 1996. Introduction, pp. 7–10 and 21–31.

19 *Milton's Style*, 1981.

examples in which the visual seems to beg for the auditive, as when the pin-point glitter of the stars is mentioned: ll. 69–70: "the **st**ars with deep amaze / **St**and **fixed** in **st**eadfast ga**z**e." The other side of the dialectic, for instance the smoky dimness of the conjuring scene in Stanza XXIV is materialised by **s** an **z** alliterations of the Osiris lines.[20] All these visual impressions are quite active in the discourse, but it is sometimes difficult to say how and why, although they immediately organize into significant metaphoric patterns in relation with the inner structure of feeling: fixity and motion; eternity and change, and above all, revelation of divine truth as against the doubt, despair and error of the fallen world.

Tactile impressions are to be found early in Milton's shorter poems. *On the Death of a Fair Infant* (1628) offers an exposition of its theme based almost entirely on tactile elements:

O fairest flower no sooner *blown* than blasted,
Soft silken Primrose fading timelessly,
Summer's chief honor if thou hadst outlasted
Bleak winter's force [...]
But kill'd alas, and then bewail'd his fatal bliss (1–7 – my emphasis).

Which, with the same and other consonants, is also the case in *Lycidas*, ll. 1–8.

In the two instances I have just mentioned, contrary to Archie Burnett's view, I find the arrangement of vowels and consonants more suggestive than their individual qualities or their lexical meaning: the above lines play to the full, and contrast with one another, soft and harsh sounds, moving in both poems (twice in the *Lycidas* lines) from the ones to the others, which goes to prove that, even more than the production of abstract structures of ideas which the reader often takes some time to understand, in some cases at least, the meaning seems to rely first of all on the production of sensory effect.

Now remain the last two senses – **the olfactive** and **the gustative.** These, especially the latter, seem to require much more skill to be successfully introduced into verse. In the poems in English, smell and taste appear somewhat later than the other senses. As usual, these are intimately mixed with other sense impressions. The evocation of flowers in *L'Allegro* (47–48)

20 "Naught but profoundest Hell can be his shroud: / In vain with timberelled anthems dark / The sable-stoled Sorcerers bear his worshipped ark" (218–220).

and the flower-catalogue in *Lycidas* (132–151) are opportunities not only for introducing colour, but also sweet smells, through epithets following closely those of Classical poetry. Depending directly on a wide range of sense-data, the effect produced is delicately imitative of actual experience; *L'Allegro*:

> The frolic wind that breathes the spring
> Zephir with Aurora playing,
> [...]
> There on beds of violets blue,
> And fresh-blown roses washed in dew (18–22).

Forms are then defined through touch; colours are mixed with odours or wafted on the wind, in an "ordered disorder" figurative of the approach of an emblematic spring.

Such a view as that advanced half a century ago by Isabel MacCaffrey in *Paradise Lost as Myth,*[21] and according to which, "Milton's image is a matter of perception rather than invention" may prove even now to have stood the test of years. I shall now try to show how the text moves from sensation, or perception to feeling, on the occasion of three fundamental experiences, central to meaning – that of space, of time and of the illusion of the senses. Space and time will be dealt with together.

Space of course is first constructed by visual impressions. In *On the Morning of Christ's Nativity,* space-percepts are related to objects, now fixed now in motion.[22] Fixity may be exemplified by the stars presiding over the birth of Christ: ll. 69–71. Movement, by the use of the **s, sl** alliterations, associated with the silent coming down on the earth of the allegorical figure Heavenly Peace: "She, crowned with olive green, came softly sliding, / Down through the turning sphere" (ll. 47–48). Space is also constructed by audio-visual perception, giving both an impression of distance and of temporal development. In the form of music or song, it is used to substantialise the coming and waning of the time of day, dawn or twilight: *On the Morning of Christ's Nativity; The Hymn,* in its totality, and more especially stanzas IX to XIII.

In these examples, the words seem to stand and act for the things themselves, as if they had appropriated some materialistic dynamism. This we

21 Harvard U. Press, 1959.

22 Several kinds of kinaesthesia have been analysed by Elizabeth E. Fuller in *Milton's Kinesthesic vision in Paradise Lost.* Lewisburgh, Bucknell U. Press, 1983.

may observe in the presence of tactile or gustative impressions. *A Maske* is a case in point. In it, the tactile, the olfactive and the gustative are often bunched together, in long descriptions *("prosopographia")* as in its spectacular and musical ending, a celebration of the characters' feelings towards the rural world – their experience of reintegration with Christianized nature, while the philosophising is left for the Attendant Spirit to do, who suggests that the soul may feed on substances more refined than those of the bounteous Welsh or English countryside. However, even this ethical *pons asinorum* will take the form of human sensation – the rush of air on one's skin, then a gulping of air, as if to regain breath:

> To the Ocean now *I fly,*
> And those happy climes that lie
> Where day never shuts his eye,
> *Up in the broad fields of the sky.*
> There *I suck the liquid air*
> All amidst the gardens fair
> Of Hesperus, and his daughters three,
> That sing about the golden tree […] (976–983 – italics ours).

The sensory approach to illusion is particularly interesting. At first, it uses concepts, for instance that of deceit, as may be observed in the Elegies. In the early poems in English, it is definitely used in the form of percept. Nowhere is it built into words with greater efficiency and scope than in *A Maske.* The central theme of Christian revelation (truth) versus experience (often illusory), is sustained by impressions belonging to a compound of three or four senses: sight, hearing, touch and perhaps taste, immediately leading to the production of synaesthesic impressions. The representation of illusion by auditory impressions makes up both the bulk and structure of Comus's and the Lady's first speeches (respectively, 93–169 and 170–229), in which the successive elements of perception are organised as a passage from auditory deceit to visual certitude. The Lady's speech begins with auditory uncertainty, "This way the noise was […] methought it was the noise / Of riot and ill-managed merriment, […] / This is the place, as well as I may guess, […]" (171–201). Eventually, however, a series of visual impressions due to the moon peeping from the clouds will restore certainty:

> Was I deceived or did a sable cloud
> Turn forth her silver lining on the night? (221–222)

When we turn to Comus – the character emblematic of the other side of the dilemma – he too, when he tries to identify the Lady's song, is a prey to illusion, deceived by the sounds that reach his ears:

> Can any mortal mixture of Earth's mould
> Breathe such divine enchanting ravishment?
> (these raptures)
> How sweetly did they float[23] upon the wings
> Of silence through the empty-vaulted night [...] (244–250).

Visual and kinaesthetic perception in Comus's Fertility speech (706–736), has too often been commented upon for me to do it again. Our attention will be better employed in concentrating on the Spirit's speeches at the denouement: the perceptualisation of the passage from illusion to certainty (814–857), the musical duet between the Spirit and Sabrina (859–975), and the Epilogue proper. A feeling that the natural world can be trusted again – a recovery of the landmarks of legend and of Christian ethics – comes to us through the visual and tactile images. The recitation of the Sabrina myth by the Spirit relies on palpable images of fluidity: the **gl, fl, l** and **s** alliterations of dashing, standing or baptismal waters (807 ff. 831–32, 838–840), to signify the dissolution of the charm which fetters the lady, and the reintegration of the human with the natural world,[24] with here and there as a counterpoint, lingering touches of the former disquieting sensualness: the celebrated "gums of glutinous heat" (*A Maske*, 917).

There remains to be shown how Milton's probable or "implicit" empiricism[25] can be related to his poetic practise. The question of Milton's Empiricism is part of a larger theoretical debate about Milton's ontology, and especially whether he would conceive of matter and spirit as being separate, as did Plato and most of the Fathers, or as belonging to the same "substance."[26] This old debate[27] has been revived with the recent difference

23 A further but very common substantialisation of sound.

24 See Armand Himy, "Poisons, plantes et aromates dans *Comus*," In: *John Milton: Comus or A Maske at Ludlow Castle*," ed. A. Himy, Paris, Editions européennes ERASME, 1990.

25 Daniel Fried, "Milton and Empiricist Semiotics," 124.

26 Also the position of Comenius.

27 See William B. Hunter, "Milton's Materialistic Life-Principle," *JEGP*, XLI, 1946, 68–76; "Milton's Power of Matter." *JHL*, XII, 1962, and Roger Lejosne, *La Raison dans l'œuvre de John Milton*. Thèse de Doctorat d'état, 1979, Chapter XIV.

between two critics – Fallon and Donnelly.[28] With regard to our subject, one should like to know whether young Milton – a philosopher as well as a poet – would consider spirit as being co-substantial with matter. In so far as Milton's attitude to writing will answer a possible theoretical position, he may have thought that the imperfection and dispersion of meaning through man's perceptual experience[29] enabled spirit and matter to fuse together again, or create the feeling that they do.

The art of a Christian poet does not merely consist in producing a pleasing imitation of inner or outer reality. It has for its better aim to tap into the potentiality of words to try and lift the spirit to a contemplation of its divine origin. This view of Christian poetics has long been used by Milton critics to define the working principle of his poetry, an elevation of the soul, which according to many, takes root in a "tension" between the poet's ethics and his actual, sensory experience of the world. Like Paul, Lactantius, and several other Fathers,[30] Milton would not believe that this tension could be solved in the univocal detachment of religious meditation. This had to be lived, or re-lived, through experience itself. Everyone has in mind the famous lines in *Areopagitica* in which Milton eloquently defends the idea that if Christian writing is to have any meaning, or convincing power, it must be rooted in actual experience.[31]

It is easy to see that this "tension" is first caused by the conflict between two aspects of experience, that we may call corporeality and spirituality; the body and the spirit. But this does not necessarily entail that Milton's view of reality depends on a transcendental structure of meaning, in which physical analogy points to an ideal reality situated above and separate from it.[32] On the level of poetic practise, Milton's philosophy of writing does not appear constantly and persistently that clearly, even in the early poems. Even if we grant that meaning is answerable to a transcendent structure as

28 Steven Fallon, *Milton among the Philosophers: Poetry and Materialism in Seventeenth-Century England.* Cornell U. Press, Ithaca and London, 1991; Philip J. Donnelly. "Matter versus Body: the Character of Milton's Monism." *MQ*, 33, 3, Oct. 1999.

29 In *Milton's Kinesthesic vision in Paradise Lost*, Elizabeth E. Fuller argues that the reader is lead through a "sequence of motion," "disjunctions," and "contradictions," so that perception is fragmented or uncertain.

30 Lactantius. *Institutes* III, 29; V, 7 etc.

31 *Areopagitica:* "That which purifies us is trial, and trial is by what is contrary" (*CPW* 2: 515).

32 See Foucault, *Les mots et les choses. Les quatre similidudes,* pp. 32–44 – whose analyses, however, I take with some reservations.

in Patristic philosophy, at the same time, language is also for Milton a contingent construct to be experienced through the corporeality of language. Sensory language often produces feelings and thoughts, apparently unpremeditated by the poet, as we can see in the recurrently favourable interpretations of Comus, Satan or whatever non-Christian feature is to be found in the poetry. This brings to light the frequently semiotic and not merely symbolic nature of Milton's poetic idiom. And it is just what has tempted me to read Milton's early poems in terms of a passage from perception to feeling, which results in the construction of a whole universe, seemingly real, that we can share with the poet through memory of similar experiences. One should envisage Milton's poetics as a very active dialectic or ambivalent instrument aiming at creating the "sensuous" and the "passionate,"[33] or rather at reifying the passionate, that is feeling at its highest, directly in the spontaneity and simplicity of the sensuous, thus giving as word-experience the very dynamism of the spirit.

Works Cited

Burnett, Archie. *Milton's Style: The Shorter Poems.* New York and London, Longman, 1981.

Dokic, Jerôme. *Qu'est-ce que la perception?* Vrin, «Chemins philosophiques», Paris, Vrin, 2004.

Donnelly, Philip J. "Matter versus Body: the Character of Milton's Monism." *Milton Quarterly*, XXXIII, 3, Oct. 1999.

Fallon, Stephen. *Milton Among the Philosophers: Poetry and Materialism in Seventeenth Century England.* Cornell U. Press, Ithaca and London, 1991.

MacCaffrey, Isabel G. *Paradise Lost as Myth.* Harvard U. Press, 1959.

Richard, Jean-Pierre. *Littérature et sensation.* Paris, Seuil, 1954.

Shumaker, Wayne. *Unpremeditated Verse: Feeling and Perception in* Paradise Lost. Princeton, Princeton U. Press, 1967.

33 *Of Education, CPW* 2: 403.

Trevor Laurence JOCKIMS

Pastoral Lost and Regained in "Lycidas"

This paper seeks to centralize the role of generic convention as it functions within John Milton's pastoral elegy, "Lycidas".[1] I do not mean to trace out that poem's generic markers and echoes, as this has been done extensively elsewhere.[2] Rather, I would like to focus on the speaker of the poem, the shepherd-elegist, as a figure who is inscribed by the worldview of a pastoral landscape so that I may, in turn, address the violent disruption to this landscape which the event of death has provoked and which the elegy itself attempts to remedy. The role of the shepherd-elegist as a figure of the pastoral who is attempting to reconstitute a disrupted pastoral landscape has been given very little attention within the voluminous criticism which "Lycidas" has received. Beginning, in fact, with Samuel Johnson's well known commentary on the poem, one may note a paradigmatic trend that has occluded the importance of the shepherd-elegist's generic center:[3]

> In this poem ["Lycidas"] there is no nature, for there is no truth; there is no art, for there is nothing new. Its form is that of a pastoral, easy, vulgar, and therefore disgusting; whatever images it can supply are long ago exhausted, and its inherent improbabil-

1 The sense of "conventional" as a "coming together" (from the Latin *convenire*) is doubly apt with regards to the pastoral. As Paul Alpers notes in *What is Pastoral?*, "pastoral poems make explicit the dependence of their conventions on the idea of [shepherds] coming together … for songs and colloquies" (81). A central trope of "Lycidas" is *the frustration of* such dialogic convening.

2 For an exhaustive cataloging of "Lycidas"'s echoes and allusions see *A Variorum Commentary on the Poems of John Milton Volume II*, pp. 544–734.

3 This paradigm has long held a central position in discussions of "Lycidas." Richard P. Adam's pronouncement in 1949 that "it has been made increasingly evident by critics in recent years that the drowning of Edward King was the occasion, rather than the subject, of 'Lycidas'" (111) suggests that readings centered upon the occasionality of the poem were vital long after Johnson's commentary. Such readings, as I argue below, have tended to blur the epistemological force of the pastoral world inscribed at the center of the poem's shepherd-elegist by shifting focus away from genre and toward occasionality.

ity always forces dissatisfaction on the mind [...]. We know that they [Milton and King] never drove a field, and that they had no flocks to batten (60–1).

Johnson's comments polarize convention and sincerity, suggesting that the shepherd figure is both hackneyed and improbable, since neither Milton nor King were in fact shepherds. In his essay "Literature as context: Milton's *Lycidas*," Northrop Frye seeks to qualify this fission by expanding the notions of sincerity into two concepts: "personal sincerity" and "literary sincerity."[4] "If we start with the fact that "Lycidas" is highly conventional and that Milton knew King only slightly," Frye argues, then "we may see in "Lycidas" an 'artificial' poem" which lacks "personal sincerity" (210). However, Frye continues, "*Lycidas* is a passionately sincere poem" (210) in terms of "literary sincerity" (210) precisely because of "Milton's [deep interest] in the structure and symbolism of funeral elegies" (210).

My present interest is in highlighting the shepherd-elegist's literary sincerity – his full generic weight – as an interpretive crux that is inscribed at the center of the poem. Granting the seemingly transparent assumption that the speaker of "Lycidas" is a shepherd from a harmonious pastoral setting confronted by the event of death, certain more provocative questions arise: How prepared is this figure to mourn? What capacities can a shepherd, a wandering emanation from the pastoral, have for elegy? How, indeed, is this figure's pastoral center inflected by the death-event which brings the poem into being? And how, in turn, is the mourning of this death inflected by the elegist's pastoral center? These questions are essentially questions of place, and it is my aim to show that the shepherd-elegist, as a survivor of a disrupted pastoral place, speaks an elegy that strives not only to place the deceased within an otherworldly, protective enclosure but, perhaps more urgently, to reconstitute the unstable boundaries of the pastoral itself. Death has caused intense disruption within the pastoral landscape, cutting the dialogic pair in two. At the center of this cut is the pastoral elegist who has lost companion, dialogue and – most traumatically –

4 Frye is certainly addressing Johnson, but as an exemplum of the "fallacy [which confuses] personal sincerity and literary sincerity" (210). The concepts are readily apprehended in terms of their everyday meaning – "personal sincerity" being a direct, subjective expression of feeling and "literary sincerity" being an expression mediated through conventional, recognizable tropes. Conventionality, in Frye's view, as it pertains to his notion of literary sincerity, is a vehicle which makes articulation possible: "one may," Frye writes, "burst into tears at the news of a friend's death, but one can never spontaneously burst into song, however doleful a lay" (210).

place. Cast as a figure of placelessness, an *unheimlich*[5] wanderer, the shepherd-elegist works through the elegy to restore his own sense of place within the altered pastoral landscape. He must, after all, go on living there. It is his place.

Mourning the death of Hans-Georg Gadamer, Jacques Derrida remarks upon the ontological position of the surviving friend in terms which are pertinent to our current discussion.[6] Evoking Freud and Heidegger, Derrida speaks of the surviving friend as *unheimlich*: the survivor, Derrida suggests, becomes homeless, or placeless, following the death of his companion. "Survival carries within itself the trace of an ineffaceable incision," writes Derrida. This incision, or cut, begins with the event of death itself, the "blind Fury with … abhorred shears / [Who] *slits* the thin-spun life" as Milton describes it in "Lycidas" (ln. 8; emphasis added). Following the event of death, the incision "multiplies itself" (Derrida 7) and the cut which had begun as an external event becomes internalized by the survivor. "One interruption affects another" (7), asserts Derrida. Death begins by cutting one person off from another, and then it proceeds to cut the survivor off from himself. The dialogic world which the friendship, the coming together, had constituted is violently severed and although, as Derrida writes, "the dialogue … will forever be wounded by [death's] ultimate interruption" (6) the survivor persists, cut in two, speaking singly in a once dialogic landscape. "Death," Derrida contends, "is nothing less than an end *of the world* … every time" (8), not only for the deceased but for the survivor who is left "in the world, outside the world, deprived of the world" (8) which that dialogue had once constituted.

Derrida's speaking of death as a lost dialogue directly suggests pastoral elegy itself, where the fundamentally dialogic world of pastoral becomes the

5 *Unheimlich*, as Derrida notes, is "untranslatable" (3); however, its lineage as a concept may be usefully traced. As Svetlana Boym has noted in her chapter "On Diasporic Intimacy" in *The Future of Nostalgia*, "Freud examined multiple meanings for the word *homey (heimlich)* from 'familiar,' 'friendly' and 'intimate' to 'secretive' and 'allegorical.' The word develops greater ambivalence until *homey (heimlich)* finally coincides with its opposite, the *uncanny (unheimlich)*" (251). See Sigmund Freud, "The Uncanny," in *Studies in Parapsychology* (New York: Collier Books, 1963.) Derrida's use of the word certainly includes these nuances but emphasizes, as I do, *unheimlich* as a condition of homelessness or placelessness analogous to Heidegger's notion of homesickness or restlessness as communicated in *Being and Time* (cf. 188–91).

6 "Béliers: le dialogue ininterrompu: entre deux infinis, le poème," Paris: Galilée, 2003.

monologic voice of elegy.[7] Pastoral elegy's lost dialogue, further, suggests a loss of home, a loss of the world which the now-absent dialogue had constituted. This, I would argue, is the status of the shepherd-elegist as "Lycidas" begins: a placeless, *unheimlich* figure mourning a lost companion and, moreover, mourning the loss of pastoral's prototypically dialogic construction. Where there were two, now there is one, and that one must now make his way through an altered landscape. Even on the surface of taxonomy, the ontological disruption of place with which the surviving shepherd is confronted is clear: the genealogy indicated by the rubric pastoral elegy (the mode's status as the offspring of two independent modes, pastoral, and elegy)[8] is about as fundamentally incongruous a meeting as one can imagine. What, after all, has the pastoral to do with elegy? "Pastoral feeling," (6) in Paul Alper's phrase, is characterized not by mortality but by "the warmth of the sun, fresh air, and … free perambulation with purpose temporarily suspended" (*What is Pastoral?* 6), characteristics which all suggest a harmonious view of time. As a representative anecdote, harmonious, cyclic time presents itself as perhaps the central fact of the pleasant landscape which pastoral affords its inhabitants by running on natural, not historical, time. As Orlando observes in *As You Like It*, "there's no clock in the forrest" (III.ii.291–2). Contrary to the harmonious temporality of pastoral, elegy's temporality is, as Peter Sacks writes in *The English Elegy*, a setting of "extreme discontinuity" (23), a linear urgency which is decidedly "unpastoral" (Alpers 6). The coming together of *pastoral* and *elegy* in *pastoral elegy* repre-

7 Pastoral expression, as Alpers notes, is most often cast dialogically: two shepherds, that is, singing to one another (Alpers 21–5). The way in which the act of dialogue itself represents – gives form to – other concerns of the pastoral may be noted in the various dichotomies which it plays out – country/courtly; nature/art and, as exemplified by William Empson's well known dictum, the complex/simple dialectic by which pastoral puts the "complex in the simple" (*Some Versions of Pastoral* 14). Significantly, when we enter the realm of pastoral elegy we see Milton's elegist singing monologically. "Lycidas" in fact emphasizes this in the prefatory note added to the 1645 edition, declaring itself a Monody.

8 This statement is problematic, but necessary, even though a proper explanation would be far beyond the scope of the current paper. As Ellen Lambert notes in *Placing Sorrow*, it is not known "what would be most useful to know" (xxii); namely, "the extent to which the origins of the pastoral elegy are involved or distinct from those of the pastoral genre as a whole" (xxii). However, there is an important distinction to be made here regarding the types of temporality which both modes suggest – the former a cyclic, harmonious view of time presented within the *locus amoenus*, the latter an urgent, linear view of time dealing with "mortal loss and consolation" (Sacks 3).

sents, I would suggest, a coming together of antithetical temporalities, and it is the shepherd-elegist (as my hyphenated nomenclature indicates) who embodies this antithesis.[9]

The notion that death moves violently counter to the pastoral is centralized in the opening lines of "Lycidas":

> Yet once more, O ye Laurels, and once more
> Ye Myrtles brown, with Ivy never sere,
> I come to pluck your Berries harsh and crude,
> And with forc'd fingers rude,
> Shatter your leaves before the mellowing year.
> Bitter constraint, and sad occasion dear,
> Compels me to disturb your season due:
> For Lycidas is dead, dead ere his prime (ln. 1–8).

In part conventional, self-protecting modesty – "denial vain and coy excuse" – the poem's opening also establishes early the troping of death as a violence done to the pastoral landscape. "Bitter constraint and sad occasion dear / Compels me to disturb your season due." The survivor's elegy, figured as an unripe, unskilled picking of foliage before fruition ignores pastoral's harmonious, cyclic flow – its *season due* – and damages the pastoral landscape, "shatter[ing]" its "leaves before the mellowing year." Thus the shepherd, a steward of the pastoral becomes – in his initial reaction to death – an instrument that damages the pastoral landscape. This oddly inverted relationship speaks of the cut, the fission, which the event of death has triggered between the surviving shepherd and his pastoral landscape. In another Miltonic pastoral elegy, "Epitaphium Damonis," we also witness a surviving shepherd whom death has violently cut off from his landscape. In that poem, in fact, the speaker's sense of dislocation serves as an organizing principle for the entire elegy, given in the refrain *"Ite domum impasti, domino iam non vacat, agni."* [Go home unfed, my lambs, for your master has no time for you."] Both pastoral elegies present responses to nature which display

9 This is not to say that the pastoral world is without threats. As Lambert writes, "neither suffering nor death has ever been excluded from this paradise. And one can make at least a plausible case for the view that the pastoral dirge is the original pastoral song" [Lambert is here refererring to Theocritus's lament for Daphnis in his 'First *Idyll*'] (xv). Although this may seem to problematize my view of pastoral's harmonious temporality, I do not think that it substantively does. Yes, the pastoral is a threatened landscape but its horizon, in the here vs. there construction which I express, is composed precisely of the pastoral's ability to stay these threats.

not only the shepherd-elegist's severance from a harmonious relationship with his surroundings but, moreover, scenes which mimic each elegist's respective concern over prematurity and belatedness: Lycidas has died too young, and the shepherd-elegist is, thus, a (self-styled) premature talent who shatters leaves before fruition; Damon, for whom the speaker of "Epitaphium Damonis" mourns, has been dead two years, thus casting his mourner as not premature but decidedly belated. As "Lycidas"'s elegist's concern with prematurity is troped as a premature plucking of fruit, the belatedness of Damon's elegist is analogously reflected in his response to his surroundings: rather than breaking the fruit before its time, the elegist of "Epitaphium Damonis" lets his surroundings overgrow (cf. lines 63–7). In both instances place – the pastoral place – is damaged by the event of death, by the shepherd-elegist's encounter with death, either through neglect or direct violence.

The theory of place extended in this essay is deliberately (and necessarily) selective: primarily, I take Aristotle's pronouncements in the *Physics* as my organizing hypothesis (cf. *Physics* 212a14–21). It is in the *Physics* that Aristotle provides the metaphor of place as being something very much like a vessel.[10] This metaphor is instructive, as it emphasizes place as a collocation whose purpose it is to gather, hold together, and protect. The pastoral landscape of the eponymous genre is itself a bounded, protective enclosure. Place, within the pastoral, in every sense, *holds*. This holding operation of place is predicated as much by what is inside the pastoral place as by what is outside of it: in the *Januarye* woodcut of *The Shepheardes Calender*, as Colin turns toward the city, one recognizes that he must, simultaneously, turn his back to the pastoral.[11] As Edward Casey writes of the holding operation of place, "what holds the collocation there is the landscape's horizon within which [one is] situated by means of a distinguishable *here vs. there* that forms the epicenter of the place where [one is] at" (Casey 248–9).[12] This Aristotelian "here vs. there" notion of bounded place is pertinent to our current discussion of the surviving shepherd, the *unheimlich* figure, of "Lycidas"

10 Aristotle writes: "just as the vessel is transportable place, so place is a non-portable vessel" (212a13–15).

11 Reproduced, among other places, in *The Yale Edition of the Shorter Poems of Edmund Spenser.*

12 See Edward S. Casey's "Keeping the Past in Mind," collected in *American Continental Philosophy*. In terms of the Aristotelian notion of place, Casey draws directly from *Physics* (cf. 208b10–25).

who is attempting to reconstitute and regain the boundaries of his own pastoral place, for this restoration of place can only be achieved by reconstructing the *horizon* of the pastoral. The "here vs. there" boundaries of the pastoral, that is, must be rebuilt. The transgressing element – death and the deceased himself – must be, in a physical, spiritual, and ontological sense *moved.* It is only through the creation of a "there" – a new landscape, a new place – for the deceased that the shepherd-elegist's "here," the pastoral, may be reconstituted.

The first step toward the recovery of place for the elegist is the bringing to presence of the deceased. As Lloyd Kermode notes in "To the Shores of Life: Textual Recovery in *Lycidas*," until the deceased can be possessed in some measure, it is impossible to fully mourn the loss and, paradoxically, to release it. "[The] double-bind of the community's need to settle the lost one in a context of absence and safety (e.g., the woods, heaven) yet also to possess some token or reminder, some presence relating to the lost one" (13) is central to the work of mourning. But it is precisely this impulse which cannot be satisfied within "Lycidas". The deceased's body is no where to be found. The poem immediately draws us into the surviving shepherd's perplexity over the physical absence of the other, as the speaker invokes the deceased's name in an effort to bring him to presence:

> For *Lycidas* is dead, dead ere his prime,
> Young *Lycidas*, and hath not left his peer:
> Who would not sing for *Lycidas*? [...] (ln. 8–10)

The effort here is to orientate oneself, using the repetition of the deceased's name as a form of recovery and a bringing to presence.[13] The name "Lycidas" is spoken three times in as many lines in the poem's opening stanza; it is spoken only twice in the poem's subsequent 145 lines, and then three times again in quick succession in the song's final strophe. "The survivor leans upon the name," (26) Sacks writes, discussing elegiac convention. "The name, by dint of repetition, takes on a kind of substantiality" (26). "The griever must be convinced of the actual fact of loss" (Sacks 24); but in

13 It would be difficult to overstate the importance of the play between presence and absence within (pastoral) elegy. In Peter Sack's view, the mode presents "a perspective from which to reexamine the connection between language and the pathos of human consciousness" (xii) by animating an extreme instance (i.e. death) of one of the absences "which the use of language may seek to redress or appease" (xi).

"Lycidas" there is no body to sing over, no hearse to cover with conventional flowers, even though the desire to do so abides:

> Throw hither all your quaint enamell'd eyes,
> That on the green turf suck the honied showers,
> And purple all the ground with vernal flowers.
> Bring the rathe Primrose that forsaken dies,
> The tufted Crow-toe, and pale Jessamine,
> The white Pink, the Pansy freakt with jet,
> [...]
> To strew the Laureate Hearse where *Lycid* lies (ln. 139–44; 151).

The shepherd-elegist's frustrated desire to invoke convention and cover the hearse of the deceased with flowers represents a double longing for the presence both of the body and the ontological solidity which pastoral elegy's self-reflexive and self-repeating structure entails.[14] As Barbara Johnson notes, the strewing of the hearse with flowers is a "conventional mode [ ] of consolation [...] of pastoral elegy" (69); critics tend to emphasize the poem's inability to enact this convention as a testing of the pastoral. However, since the breakdown of the flower convention is a corollary of a deeper absence – the absence of the corpse of Lycidas – it is this which must be addressed.[15]

As I have suggested, the shepherd-elegist must *place* the deceased's body outside of pastoral's "here" so that he may reconstruct his landscape's horizon. The inability to possess the body of Lycidas, the inability to bring it to presence, I would argue, tropes the shepherd-elegist's desire to locate and move the deceased to an identifiable "there." This desire is made visible when one notices just how frenetically cast is the body's present, undesirable status in the *no-place* of the sea. The description of the body of Lycidas is given vivid motion – and, one might add, intensely ironic and disturbing motion, given that it is a corpse – as it travels through the poem, ungraspable: Lycidas, in the poem's opening, "float[s]," and "welter[s]" in a "parching wind" until the "remorseless deep/close[s] o'er [his] head," and "s[i]nk[s] so low [his] sacred head," which the sea then "wash[es] far away" as Lycidas is "hurled [by the] sounding seas," "under the whelming tide"

14 As Sacks has noted, pastoral elegies (perhaps none more so than "Lycidas") are often "repetitions in themselves"of the entire genre to which they belong (23).

15 Barbara Johnson describes the generic *un*conventionality of the elegist's search for the body in "Lycidas"as "unprecedented in the history of pastoral elegy" (69).

and, finally, cast to "the bottom of the monstrous world." The descent of Lycidas's body begins at line twelve and does not reach the 'bottom of the monstrous world' until line 158.[16] The body's "downward trajectory" (Johnson 22) reaches its nadir at line 167 ("sunk though he be beneath the watery floor"). This *end* is a place, as Barbara Johnson notes, at which the narrative of Lycidas's body "has finally reached a resting point" (22). If we recall the Aristotelian notion of place as constructed by a here vs. there relationship, we see just how suggestive the descent of Lycidas is: he ends up, as Johnson correctly notes, "as far outside the pastoral world as it is possible to go" (23). (Until, of course, his ascent, which is able to begin only after this lowest point has been reached.) To begin to repair the rift of pastoral place which the event of death has occasioned, the elegist precisely needs to get "Lycidas" "as far outside the pastoral as it is possible to go." He also needs to make sure that he stays "there" by combating motion with the spatial fixity of place. The elegist's, and indeed the elegy's, first success is in sinking the body in an identifiable "there" far outside the pastoral and stopping its motion.

The most important "failure" of the elegy is enacted by another effort to bring the deceased to presence, this time not physically but within the mind – the memory – of the shepherd-elegist. The project of utilizing memory as a surrogate mode of recovery is presented in lines 23–36:

> For we were nurst upon the self-same hill,
> Fed the same flock, by fountain, shade, and rill.
> Together both, ere the high Lawns appear'd
> Under the opening eyelids of the morn,
> We drove afield, and both together heard
> What time the Gray-fly winds her sultry horn,
> Batt'ning our flocks with the fresh dews of night,
> Oft till the Star that rose, at Ev'ning, bright
> Toward Heav'n's descent had slop'd his westering wheel.
> Meanwhile the Rural ditties were not mute,

16 An important subtext involved in the distancing motion of the body is the critique of Platonic dualism which runs through the poem. "The image of the dead Lycidas," Barbara Johnson writes, "is continually evoked as the swain attempts to picture where he is and what has happened to his body as well as his soul" (70). The body retreats, corporeality retreats but, Johnson argues, the poem ultimately suggests Milton's monistic view of the relationship between the body and the soul in its apotheosis: "the image of Lycidas in heaven is not that of a shade or a disembodied soul; his corporeal nature is emphasized in heaven, just as it had been in the poem" (72).

Temper'd to th'Oaten Flute;
Rough *Satyrs* danc'd, and *Fauns* with clov'n heel
From the glad sound would not be absent long,
And old *Damaetas* lov'd to hear our song.

What is being remembered is not merely a specific person, but a specific *place*, a pastoral place; in fact, one might remark that what is being remembered is the landscape of the pastoral mode itself. The memory contains all the markers of pastoral: nature "nurse[s]" the pair "upon the self-same hill," as they, in reciprocity, feed "the same flock," in a landscape of "fountain, shade, and rill." What is remembered is a mode of existence, an activity of reciprocity between nature and man running the full, pastoral daily cycle. The elegist remembers not only the deceased but himself as well. As such, memory becomes another means by which the surviving shepherd attempts to recover not only the deceased but the pastoral, through a nostalgic turn toward the reassuring power of the memory of a place which predates the event of death. As Casey writes of the restorative power of placial memory: "place is eminently suited for the keeping operation which we found earlier to lie at the core of remembering … the past itself can be kept in place, right in place, especially when place is taken in its full landscape being" (284).

Since place and memory are conjoined one sees, in stanza three's recollection, a unification of place, deceased, and elegist: "*we* were nursed upon the *self-same hill* /Fed the *same* clock," "*together* both," "*together* heard," "*our* song." But the precise problem with memory lies within its very effectiveness: that is, just as the dialogic construction of the memory – *we, together, our* – comforts, it also destabilizes the memory. The other is, after all, gone, and it is clear that what the elegist misses most intently is the image of himself *with* his lost companion. He remembers, and longs for, *them* – the hills, *otium*, the dialogism of pastoral. Even as the elegist recalls his own pastoral past he reveals his sense of severance from that pastoral inheritance, proclaiming:

But O the heavy change, now thou art gon,
Now thou art gone, and never must return!
Thee Shepherd, thee the Woods, and desert Caves,
With wild Thyme and the gadding Vine o'ergrown,
And all their echoes mourn (ln. 37–41).

Following the Derridean paradigm of mourning, one observes that death has penetrated deep into the surviving shepherd, down even into his memory. Just as the surviving shepherd had once inhabited, and was inhabited by, the pastoral landscape he recollects as a *self-same hill*, so now he is inhabited by, and inhabits, a landscape inscribed by the heavy change of death:[17] "As killing as the canker to the rose … Such, Lycidas, thy loss to shepherd's ear."[18] The failure of the memory to provide consolation is an important failure because it tells us that the rift, the cut, of death has passed through the shepherd-elegist's surroundings, into him, all the way into his own past.

I would like to conclude by focusing on the perplexing emergence of the new voice at the close of "Lycidas," suggesting that the coda is a necessary framing device that recovers the landscape of lines 23–36 and by which the poem speaks of the shepherd-elegist's ultimately successful recovery of, and replacement in, the pastoral landscape. As we reach the coda, Lycidas has already been placed into the secure "there" of heaven, a placement which ends his floating and weltering and, as a corollary, makes it possible that the shepherd-elegist may too find an end to his ontological drift. "So *Lycidas*, sunk low, but mounted high, /…/In the blest kingdoms meek of joy and love" (ln. 172; 177). The work of the elegy has been successful in mourning, celebrating, and placing the deceased, but what now is to become of the surviving shepherd? This seems to be the question which the coda is interested in addressing, and it is the emergence of the coda's new voice which equips the poem to frame a response.

From the perspective of the framing coda, the reader looks back – looks, one might say, into – the pastoral landscape which the shepherd now, again, inhabits, the coda:

> Thus sang the uncouth Swain to th'Oaks and rills,
> While the still morn went out with Sandals gray;
> He touch't the tender stops of various Quills,

17 Inhabitation, that is, is bi-directional: as Heidegger writes in *Being and Time*, "what keeps us in our essential nature holds us only so long, however, as we for our part keep holding on to what holds us" (246).

18 The phrase "as killing as the canker to the rose … Such, Lycidas, thy loss to shepherd's ear" is not pathetic fallacy but an analogy which centralizes and unifies the shepherd-elegist's knowledge of death (given in the synedochal "ear," itself a locus of knowing) *and* connects this knowing to a corruption of his natural surroundings. Death, as in the poem's opening stanza, works against the pastoral setting.

With eager thought warbling his *Doric* lay:
And now the Sun had stretch't out all the hills,
And now was dropped into the Western bay;
At last he rose, and twitch't his Mantle blue:
Tomorrow to fresh Woods, and Pastures new (ln. 186–93).

Returning to lines 23–36, we may note the ways in which the coda recalls and recovers the pastoral memory sequence of stanza three. To facilitate a clearer discussion of the echoes present between the two sections, I provide them here, side-by-side:[19]

ll. 23–36	*Coda*
For we were nurst upon the self-same **hill**,	Thus *sang* the uncouth Swain to th'Oaks and **rills**,
Fed the same flock, by fountain, *shade*, and **rill**.	While the still **morn** went out with Sandals **gray**;
Together both, ere the high Lawns appear'd	He touch't the tender stops of *various Quills*,
Under the *opening eyelids* of the **morn**,	With eager thought *warbling* his *Doric lay*:
We drove *afield*, and both together heard	And now the **Sun** had stretch't out all the **hills**,
What time the **Gray**-fly winds her sultry horn,	And now was *dropt* into the **Western** bay;
Batt'ning our flocks with the fresh dews of night,	At last he **rose**, and twitch't his Mantle blue:
Oft till the Star that **rose**, at Ev'ning, bright,	To-morrow to fresh *Woods*, and *Pastures* new.
Toward Heaven's *descent* had slop'd	
]his **westering** wheel.	
Meanwhile the *Rural ditties* were not mute,	
Temper'd to th'*Oaten Flute*;	
Rough *Satyrs* danc'd, and *Fauns* with clov'n heel	
From the *glad sound* would not be absent long,	
And old *Damaetas* lov'd to hear our *song*.	

The echoes between the coda and the earlier passage are numerous. The direct repetitions of single words between the two sections include: "hill," and "hills"; "rill," and "rills"; "morn," and "morn"; "gray," and "gray"; "western," and "westering"; "rose," and "rose." In addition, various topical echoes may be identified: "song" is answered by the coda's "sang"; the "glad sound" and "oaten flute" of stanza three become the coda's "warbling" and "Doric lay"; "descent" is echoed in "dropped"; "pastures" in "afield." These surface repetitions constitute a larger, essential pattern which the two passages share – a movement from morning to evening, across the whole pastoral daily round, with an emphasis on song. Missing, however,

19 Words in **bold** denote direct repetitions among the coda and lines 23–36; *underlined* words and phrases mark not specific repetitions but echoes in subject, theme, or idea.

from the coda are the dancing satyrs and the dialogic singing patterns, but we have already had our song – the monody itself – which has functioned as a surrogate for the pair's singing. Despite the reading of the coda as a harbinger of Milton's desired movement toward epic, the coda clearly emphasizes the pastoral: the shepherd-elegist is going to pastures, however 'new' they may be. The final, framing voice creates a new landscape to be sure (since it now includes a direct apprehension of death), but it is a decidedly pastoral one.

With the echoing coda one can see the poem offering up the ontological solidity which the shepherd-elegist has been lacking all along: the elegist's memory of the pastoral, recalled and spoken by a new, detached voice, loses its nostalgic longing and becomes, as it echoes through the coda, a bracing known whose presence the reader feels at the core of the coda. The elegy is suddenly framed, by the coda, as a singing that has unfolded across a full pastoral day decidedly similar to the prototypical pastoral day recalled in the third stanza. (Lycidas's ascent, too, in being associated with the "day-star," enacts this return to cyclicality.) It is by once more recalling the memory sequence of the earlier passage that the coda makes the shepherd-elegist's return to the pastoral clear. After placing Lycidas in the secure "there" of heaven, the shepherd-elegist leaves off the work of mourning: he stops speaking the poem. Instead, the poem speaks him. The new framing voice allows the reader to view the pastoral-elegist not as an actively mourning figure within a disrupted pastoral landscape but, rather, as a figure within a conventional setting. In a remarkable pulling back, the coda presents a placing of the shepherd-elegist by which the framing voice provides another point – a "there" – which solidifies the boundary into which the "uncouth swain" is placed, locating him within a reconstituted, regained, pastoral place.

Works Cited

Adams, Richard P. "The Archetypal Pattern of Death and Rebirth in *Lycidas*." *Milton's Lycidas: The Tradition and the Poem.* Ed. C. A. Patrides. Columbia, Missouri: University of Missouri Press, 1983. 111–16.

Alpers, Paul. *What is Pastoral?* Chicago: University of Chicago Press, 1996.

Aristotle. *Physics I–II.* Oxford: Oxford University Press, 1970.
Boym, Svetlana. *The Future of Nostalgia.* New York: Basic Books, 2001.
Bush, Douglas. Ed. *A Variorum Commentary on The Poems of John Milton* Volumes One and Two. New York: Columbia University Press, 1970.
Casey, Edward S. "Keeping the Past in Mind." *American Continental Philosophy.* Ed. Walter Brogan. Indianapolis: Indiana University Press, 2000. 241–61.
Cullen, Patrick. *Spenser, Marvell, and Renaissance Pastoral.* Cambridge: Harvard University Press, 1970.
Derrida, Jacques. *Béliers: le dialogue ininterrompu: entre deux infinis, le poème.* Paris: Galilée, 2003.
Empson, William. *Some Versions Of Pastoral.* Norfolk, Connecticut: New Directions, 1935.
Freud, Sigmund. "The Uncanny." *Studies in Parapsychology.* New York: Collier Books, 1963.
Frye, Northrop. "Literature as Context: Milton's Lycidas." *Milton's Lycidas: The Tradition and the Poem.* Ed. C. A. Patrides. Columbia, Missouri: University of Missouri Press, 1983. 204–16.
Heidegger, Martin. *Being and Time.* Trans Joan Stambaugh. New York: State University of New York Press, 1996.
Johnson, Barbara. "Fiction and Grief: The Pastoral Idiom of Milton's Lycidas." *Milton Quarterly.* 18 (1984): 69–77.
Johnson, Samuel. "from The Life of Milton." *Milton's Lycidas: The Tradition and the Poem.* Ed. C. A. Patrides. Columbia, Missouri: University of Missouri Press, 1983. 60–2.
Kermode, Lloyd Edward. "To the Shores of Life: Textual Recovery in *Lycidas.*" *Milton Quarterly.* 31(1997): 11–26.
Lambert, Ellen Zetzel. *Placing Sorrow: A Study of Pastoral Elegy Convention from Theocritus to Milton.* Chapel Hill: The University of North Carolina Press, 1976.
Milton, John. *Complete Poems and Major Prose.* Ed. Merritt Y. Hughes. Indianapolis: The Odyssey Press, 1957.
Sacks, Peter. *The English Elegy: Studies in Genre From Spenser to Yeats.* Baltimore: The Johns Hopkins University Press, 1985.
Shakespeare, William. *As You Like It.* Oxford: Clarendon Press 1993.
Spenser, Edmund. *The Yale Edition of the Shorter Poems of Edmund Spenser.* New Haven: Yale University Press, 1989.

David V. URBAN

Talents and Laborers: Parabolic Tension in Milton's Sonnet 19*

When I consider how my light is spent,
E're half my days, in this dark world and wide,
And that one Talent which is death to hide,
Lodg'd with me useless, though my Soul more bent

To serve therewith my Maker, and present
My true account, least he returning chide,
Doth God exact day labour, light deny'd,
I fondly ask; But patience to prevent

That murmur, soon replies, God doth not need
Either man's work or his own gifts, who best
Bear his milde yoak, they serve him best, his State

Is Kingly. Thousands at his bidding speed
And post o're Land and Ocean without rest:
They also serve who only stand and waite.

In *Milton's Burden of Interpretation*, Dayton Haskin notes that while a fair amount of Milton criticism has discussed the poet's fascination with the parable of the talents (Matt. 25.14–30; cf. Luke 19.11–27), surprisingly little has addressed his proclivity "to think of himself as a version" of the "unprofitable servant" of Matthew's parable (33). We recall that, having been entrusted by his master with a talent of money, this servant fearfully buries his talent, unlike his two fellow servants, who busily put their talents to work and double their money. When the master returns, he chastises the servant for his lack of industry, pronounces him "wicked and slothful," and has him "cast [...] into outer darkness." Haskin does much to explain Milton's "uneasy" relationship to the parable and his tendency to identify

* I would like to thank Calvin College, whose Calvin Summer Research Fellowship helped me complete this essay. Special thanks also to Michael Lieb for his consistent help throughout my work on Milton and the parables and Robin S. Grey, who greatly helped me refine an earlier version of this essay.

himself with the unprofitable servant. As valuable as Haskin's study is, he does relatively little to analyze Milton's connection to the unprofitable servant in light of his comparable self-identification with the last-chosen laborers of the parable of the laborers in the vineyard (Matt. 20.1–16; hereafter referred to as the parable of the laborers).[1] These parabolic figures, unlike the unprofitable servant, receive God's grace and reward in spite of their limited work in their master's vineyard. Very significantly, Milton makes use of this parable in a number of the same works in which his identification with the parable of the talents appears so prominently, including the early Sonnet 7 ("How soon hath Time the suttle theef of youth") and its companion letter "To a Friend," as well as Sonnet 19. In these works, Milton employs the parable of the laborers as a mitigating factor that offers him the hope of God's favor amidst his failures. Although we cannot assert finally that Milton's autobiographical speakers – or Milton himself – ever escape completely the horrible fear of being judged "unprofitable" by God, we do see the parable of the laborers serve, even if only temporarily, to assuage such spiritual anguish. This essay will focus on such parabolic tension in Sonnet 19 ("When I consider how my light is spent").

As I have noted elsewhere, although in Sonnet 7 and the letter "To a Friend" Milton employs the parable of the Laborers to mitigate the parable of the talents' harsh judgment upon the unprofitable servant, he offers no such mitigation in his 1642 depiction of the latter parable in *The Reason of Church Government* (Urban, "The Talented" 11).[2] Roughly a decade later,[3] however, when Milton in Sonnet 19 again identifies with the unprofitable servant in his most famous reference to the parable of the talents, he re-introduces the parable of the laborers. This re-introduction is used at first

1 Haskin does address the relationship between these two parables briefly with reference to *Samson Agonistes* (see 169–70). He does so in response to John Guillory's discussion of the two parables (see 158–59). For a more extended discussion of the tension – and eventual resolution – between the two parables in *Samson*, see Urban, "The Parabolic Milton," 60–84.

2 The present essay is largely drawn from my *Milton Studies* article listed below, which also addresses in detail the tension between the two parables in Sonnet 7 and the letter "To a Friend" and discusses the parable of the talents in *Ad Patrem*. Used with permission.

3 Although some have argued for 1642 or 1644, most commentators contend that Sonnet 19 was written between 1651 and 1655. In an intriguing variation, Annabel Patterson "suggest[s] that Milton wrote the sonnet in the early 1640s; but then resituated it, sometime in the late 1650s, in a sequence formed by hindsight" (35).

to expose a weakened, discouraged Milton whose desire to serve God as a prophet/poet ironically manifests itself in bitterness towards God himself; by the end of the poem, however, the parable of the laborers is a vehicle of grace to teach the self-important, self-condemning Milton that his service to God is under the authority of a sovereign Lord who will accomplish his perfect plan with or without Milton's heroics.

The sonnet's octave is characterized by Milton's autobiographical speaker's discouragement and bitterness, a condition that his combined use of both parables works to accomplish.[4] When the parable of the talents is referred to explicitly in line three, we see its connection with all that precedes and follows in the poem. There has been plentiful speculation concerning exactly what the "one Talent which is death to hide, / Lodged with me useless" (3–4) really is. Traditional scholarly consensus holds that the "Talent" in question is Milton's poetic gift, and that his "light" that has been "spent" is his eyesight.[5] These designations, while not wrong, are too limited. As Haskin points out, Milton's notion of "talent" in the sonnet includes his poetic gift but encompasses a broader gifting (96). It is better to recognize his poetic gift in conjunction with the prophetic office with which he has been entrusted, even as it is more appropriate to view Milton's vocation as a poet in conjunction with his calling as a prophet.

In the same way, the "light" of Sonnet 19 on one level is certainly Milton's eyesight. However, as with "Talent," Milton moves beyond a limited interpretation of such a potent word. In the context of the poem, "light" encompasses the spiritual enlightenment and direction given to believers, as well as the responsibility of the believer to shine forth God's glory and goodness before the world. These aspects of "light" are especially pertinent to Milton's prophetic "office." We may understand his anxiety in relation to his perceived failures as a prophet of God, one whose prophetic energies, for the past decade or more, have been dedicated inordinately to political

4 Although my present essay places some stress on the autobiographical dimensions of Sonnet 19, I also agree with John T. Shawcross's following observation: "We can recognize Milton within the sonnet, but we also should translate its substance – the 'I,' the contemporary problems for humankind, and the resolution of action and inaction – to our own individual world. We read the poem and are thereby read ourselves" (67).

5 William Riley Parker demonstrates the consensus position when he writes: "'That one talent' must have seemed to him his long-felt, God-given capacity for composing a truly great poem – a capacity which, in the analogy of the parable, might have been taken from him as his failure to use it" (1:470).

pamphleteering. Milton's self-doubt here includes his dissatisfaction with his poetic output, but only as his role as a poet is viewed within the larger context of his prophetic office. Indeed, in retrospect we may see the occasion of Sonnet 19 as a turning point of sorts in Milton's prophetic career, one in which he seems to eschew the parochialism of his prophetic role within the Puritan political cause in favor of a more universal prophetic office that is conducted more properly through the vehicle of poetry. This vehicle finds its apex in *Paradise Lost*, but it is displayed with immense power in this very sonnet, a sonnet that has impacted countless readers in a way that Milton's political prose – the vehicle through which so much of his "light" had already been "spent" – has never done.

Early in the poem, then, we see a discouraged, disconsolate prophet, one whose blindness exacerbates his situation with a stinging and seemingly perpetual irony. We also may note the speaker's sincere desire to labor for God in spite of his crippled condition. Although his "Talent" is "Lodg'd with me useless," he announces that "my Soul [is] more bent / To serve therewith my Maker, and present / My true account" (4–6). His desire to serve, however, is not based on genuine New Covenant faith, but rather is a response to his own fear of the unfair, even malicious God he perceives. The sonnet continues: "lest he returning chide; / Doth God exact day-labor, light denied, / I fondly ask" (6–8). That Milton's speaker is thinking wrongly about God here is evidenced by the resolution of the sestet, and Michael Lieb correctly notes the absence of Christian sentiment in the octave (49). Indeed, the speaker here demonstrates a misunderstanding of the parable, even as he misunderstands God himself. In his resolution "[t]o serve," the speaker is not demonstrating "a right will" (contra Roger Slakey), nor, for that matter, right reason. He is falling into the same error as the unprofitable servant, whose misperception of his lord as "an hard man" (Matt. 25.24) inspired him to hide his single talent in the ground.[6] In the case of the speaker, his misperception of the parable and God drive

6 Calvin states that the unprofitable servant's perception of his lord ought not to be seen as the parable's endorsement of such a view of Christ, whom the lord represents: "This hardness [see Matt. 25.24] is not part of the essence of the parable, and they are philosophizing irreverently who here dispute how God acts towards his people. [...] Christ only means that there is no excuse for the slackness of those who both suppress God's gift and consume their age in idleness. From this we also gather that no form of life is more praiseworthy before God than that which yields usefulness to human society." (2:289)

him to try to earn God's favor apart from recognizing his grace,[7] and the result of such self-justifying efforts is further frustration and bitterness.

This bitterness is particularly evident when Milton's speaker rejects his once-beloved parable of the laborers, the parable that had offered him in Sonnet 7 and the letter "To A Friend" such relief from the judgment of the parable of the talents (see Urban, "The Talented" 4–8). We see that the question "Doth God exact day-labor, light denied" contains a scornful allusion to the parable.[8] It is ironic that this parable, the very text that acted as Milton's "rescuer" from his struggles with the parable of the talents in the 1630s, should now reappear in the "fond murmur" of line seven. Clearly the grace that was received appreciatively by a late-blooming priest in training is less than satisfactory for a middle-aged prophet/poet mired in depression. Indeed, his spurning of the parable here demonstrates a frightening degree of *hubris* that transcends even the self-importance of *The Reason of Church-Government* (1642). In that work, Milton, identifying strongly with the unprofitable servant of the parable of the talents even as he presents himself as a divinely inspired prophetic spokesman for the Puritan cause, notes "that God even to a strictnesse requires the improvement of these his entrusted gifts" (*CPW* 1: 816) and claims that were he to neglect his prophetic gifts and fail to defend the Church, he would certainly be judged "timorous and ungratefull" and "slothfull" (804). But Milton's *hubris* in Sonnet 19 exceeds that of *Reason*, for the sonnet's speaker has, in essence, transferred his own self-loathing to God himself; that is, because the speaker experiences such disgust towards himself, he portrays God, through the vehicle of the parable of the talents, as effectively rejecting him. What is more, the speaker has turned that perceived divine rejection into an accusation against the character of God. We see here that Milton is, in fact, "playing God" on two levels, for he simultaneously pronounces God's judgment on himself even as he pronounces judgment on God.

The speaker's rejection of the parable of the laborers manifests itself through his distortion of its message of grace. In the parable, the lord of the vineyard exemplifies God's grace by granting a full day's wage to those laborers whom he hired only for the final hour of the workday. The speaker's "fond murmur" – which echoes the complaint of the discontent

7 Here I concur with Dixon Fiske, who writes, "the sonnet does not criticize the implications of the parable of the talents, but rather the speaker who sees the wrong implications" (45).

8 Fiske notes, but does not elaborate on, this allusion (46).

workers in the parable of the laborers, who "murmured against" the lord of the vineyard (Matt. 20.11) – turns this idea on its head. Milton's speaker insinuates that, unlike the generous lord of the parable, God would expect a full day's work from one who lacks the ability to work in the first place. Given the occasion for Milton's poem, we rightly may see in this line the image of a blind man groping helplessly to perform a task that requires sight, or perhaps that of laborers struggling to harvest their crop in the dark of a starless night. At the same time, we can imagine our prophet/poet striving to serve the very God who has withheld blessing from him. In all this, the speaker displays a marked self-righteousness, and to the reader familiar with Milton's earlier affection for the parable of the laborers, this self-righteous striving is particularly noteworthy. Indeed, we can see that here Milton has lapsed even further away from a focus on God's mercy than he did in *The Reason of Church-Government.* There, Milton's public spiritual anxiety strikes us as odd, but it reflects the feelings of a man who, having completed his extensive preparation, earnestly desires to prove himself useful. In Sonnet 19, however, Milton's speaker actually belittles the parable he formerly cherished, rejecting its message of grace. And although Milton's blindness and the obvious sadness expressed in the octave give us genuine sympathy for the speaker, we still may recognize on his part a certain spiritual betrayal even as he accuses God himself of betraying him.

The speaker's words end at this point. Sonnet 19's remarkable turn takes place in the middle of line 8, introducing the character "Patience," whose rebuttal of the speaker's murmur makes up the sestet. The speaker's silence is highly revealing, for what had been the active complaint of an achievement-consumed individual is replaced by his passive reception of Patience's words. We do not get the impression that Milton's speaker willingly steps aside from his posture of active complaint; rather, we see that he has been moved by a higher power – a messenger of the very God he has been accusing. And we sense that there is something at the same time irresistibly strong and disarmingly gentle about this displacement. To be sure, on one level there is great force behind Patience's words; for the speaker to attempt a rebuttal would be not only foolish but also impossible. And yet, as he hears Patience speak, he recognizes that the God he has distrusted has, indisputably, the best interests of his cantankerous servant in mind.[9]

9 The similarity between Sonnet 19 and Herbert's "The Collar" comes to mind here. We recognize that for Herbert's speaker, the simple call "My child" is enough to quiet his

Even as Patience's words demonstrate God's compassion towards Milton's speaker, they also reveal a justification of God's character and a clear articulation of the speaker's relationship to him. God's absolute sovereignty is seen throughout Patience's speech, and the need for the speaker to accept this humbly is reinforced by the biblical allusions in the sestet. The words "God doth not need / Either man's work or his own gifts" call to mind Psalm 50, in which God rebukes the Israelites for thinking that he somehow is dependent on their sacrifices. God declares,

> I will take no bullock out of thy house, nor he-goats out of thy folds. For every beast of the forest is mine, and the cattle upon a thousand hills. [...] If I were hungry, I would not tell thee; for the world is mine, and all the fullness thereof (50.9–10, 12).

In both Sonnet 19 and Psalm 50, those who receive God's rebuke are chastised for thinking that they can act in a way that somehow will enhance God's position. In Psalm 50, those individuals are commanded, "call upon me in the day of trouble; I will deliver thee, and thou shalt glorify me" (15). God does offer them a chance to glorify him, but only through their utter dependence upon him. Having been rebuffed in their attempts to add to his glory, they are told in no uncertain terms that they are the needy ones and that their most acceptable service to God is a humble display of such need.

A second, and oft-mentioned allusion appears in Patience's statement, "who best / Bear his mild yoke, they serve him best" (10–11). As many have noted, the words "mild yoke" echo Jesus' words in Matthew 11.29–30, where Jesus tells his listeners to take his "easy" yoke upon them. For purposes of our discussion of Sonnet 19, however, we do well to quote that passage in its larger context:

> At that time Jesus answered and said, I thank thee, O Father, Lord of heaven and earth, because thou hast hidden these things from the wise and prudent, and hast revealed them unto babes. [...] Come unto me, all ye that labor and are heavy laden, and I will give you rest. Take my yoke upon you, and learn from me; for I am meek and lowly in heart, and ye shall find rest unto your souls. For my yoke is easy, and my burden is light (Matthew 11.25, 28–30).

---

discontented ranting and bring him to a state of humble worship. Milton's speaker requires a polemic of sorts to bring him to silent submission, and this contrast may testify to the degree to which he has convinced himself of God's cosmic injustice.

Jesus' opening statement declares that God's wisdom and blessings are not given to those commonly considered wise, but to the humble. This statement is followed by an invitation to the hurting to place themselves in a relationship of total reliance upon Jesus himself. Again, this biblical passage parallels the message of Sonnet 19. Especially if we expand our understanding of "light" to include the spiritual inspiration offered to our author, we see that, because of his own pride, he finds himself in a state of spiritual deprivation. We see in Jesus' words that the invitation to take up his yoke is also an invitation to learn from him. This dual invitation, however, is predicated upon a faith in him that exhibits complete dependence on him, imitating the humility of the one who describes himself as "meek and lowly in heart" (11.29). For our exhausted prophet/poet, the admonishment to "Bear his mild yoke" is, ultimately, the gateway to restored spiritual light, a light that is superior to that previously expended, for it is purified by the humble obedience of one who better serves a humble master.

These two biblical allusions set the stage for the allusion to the parable of the laborers seen in the concluding line: "They also serve who only stand and wait." These words, Patience's final utterance, reinforce the emphasis on humble dependence on God and the true service rendered by such an attitude. This line recalls the situation of the laborers who have been "standing idle in the marketplace" (Matt. 20.3) for the first eleven hours of the workday, waiting to be hired. Having been hired by the lord of the vineyard at the eleventh hour, they work a single hour and are given a full day's wages equal to those workers who were hired early in the morning. Noting the connection between this parable and the sonnet's final line, E. A. J. Honigmann points out that Milton uses "wait" to mean "stay in expectation" (176); the "idle" workers, by virtue of their willingness to wait to be chosen, demonstrate their total dependence on the call of the vineyard's lord to be made useful. When they finally are called, they are rewarded as much for their patient waiting as for their actual work in the vineyard.

Clearly this kind of "service" is hardly the sort that Milton the prophet/poet, the busy, experienced veteran of the pamphlet wars, would value for himself or anyone else. Indeed, the early-hired laborers, who scornfully "murmured against" the lord of the vineyard for granting the others an equal wage (20.11), have essentially the same attitude as that of the speaker earlier in the poem: an attitude that disdains the grace of God in favor of calling attention to their own strenuous efforts. As with Milton's speaker, these murmuring laborers are silenced. Reminding them of their agreement to work for "a penny" for the day, the lord instructs them, "Take what is thine, and go thy way; I will give unto this last, even as unto thee" (20.14). In a word, these laborers have no right to complain, for they have not been cheated. Ultimately, what they are angry about is the lord's generosity – and the preposterous notion that eleven hours of useless waiting combined with one hour of work should be of equal value in his sight as their twelve hours of hard labor. Yet it is this very same absurd notion that the speaker is forced to accept by the final line of Sonnet 19: God's economy, quite simply, is not that of humankind, not even that of a prophet/poet who has considered all his previous labor as service unto God. As with the early-hired laborers, such an idea is offensive to the speaker. It is in the end, however, the very thing that can rescue him, both from his self-hatred and from anger towards God.

At this point I wish to briefly interact with the intriguing argument of Carol Barton, who takes issue with what she calls traditional Milton scholarship's assertion that the sonnet's final line is "an anthem to passive resignation" that exhibits a "namby-pamby 'pity poor me'" attitude (109, 110). Barton instead asserts that Sonnet 19 is "the first major milestone in [Milton's] progress toward reformation of the heroic ethos of classical antiquity," noting that the sonnet represents "the first in a series of penetrating inquiries that lead from the personal ('What can I do now') to the universal ('What can any Christian man do now?')" (115). Although it seems clear that Barton is indulging in a kind of rhetorically overstated dismissal of earlier criticism, and although such rhetoric obfuscates and minimizes the genuine spiritual weariness of the sonnet's speaker and his utter need to depend completely on God's grace, her observation that the final line anticipates the speaker's re-entry into vigorous action is valuable indeed, and we ought to remember that obedient resignation before God precedes such action in a number of Milton's later works. As Barton also notes, in *Samson Agonistes*, "'patience' [...] is the corollary – not the antithesis – of the 'invincible might' of the heroic Deliverers who 'with winged expedition / Swift as the lightening glance' (*SA* 1283–84) execute God's errands" (115), and we remember that Samson's own final victory is preceded by his complete submission to the Law of God (1386–87). We may also observe that, in *Paradise Lost*, Adam's entrance into his new life of active service before God in a fallen world is preceded by his meek resolution to obey and depend on God for all things (12.561–71). Similarly, in *Paradise Regained*, the Son's active resistance against Satan's temptations is preceded by his own obedient following of his Father's mysterious leading into the wilderness, a leading that offers no specific information concerning the purpose of the Son's journey (1.290–93); he reaffirms his dependence upon his Father in his very first words to the disguised Satan (1.335–36). So too may we recognize that, for Milton's speaker in Sonnet 19, submission to God's will does in fact offer hope for the kind of active service that he longs for.

Such hope, however, in no way diminishes the utter weariness of the sonnet's speaker and his need for complete dependence on God. Any active service must wait for God's bidding in God's time. In light of the struggles of the octave, and in light of the struggles of Milton's life, we may surmise that the resolution of the sonnet's final line is hardly an easy one for Milton's speaker – or Milton himself – to accept. While he finally must be thankful for this resolution, we sense that he accepts it not because it is palatable to him, but because it is a divine decree that he has not the strength to fight; furthermore, we recognize that the demons that torment the speaker in the octave of Sonnet 19 have not been vanquished permanently; they shall return often enough to plague him. Nonetheless, we see that here again the parable of the laborers has acted to relieve Milton from himself and his burdensome relationship to the parable of the talents. Clearly, as the years have elapsed and as his battles, his accomplishments, and his disappointments have accumulated, it becomes increasingly difficult for him to accept the grace of God exemplified by the parable of the laborers. At the same time, here in his blindness, his exhaustion, his despair, he recognizes that he ultimately has no other recourse than to receive the very grace that so much of him wishes he didn't need. This acceptance of grace also demonstrates a maturing in Milton's relationship to the parable of the laborers. Whereas in the letter "To a Friend" and Sonnet 7 that parable serves to stave off his self-condemning tendencies while he prepares for his visible entry into labor in God's vineyard, in Sonnet 19, with Milton having more of life to look back on than to look forward to, the parable does much more than enable him to bide his time. It offers a divine perspective that transcends the self-focused concerns of his autobiographical speaker. By turning Milton's attention away from his own situation and onto God's transcendent power, the parable is a vehicle of grace that offers relief from past failures and divine hope for an uncertain future.

Works Cited

Barton, Carol. "'They Also Perform the Duties of a Servant Who Only Remain Erect on Their Feet in a Specified Place in Readiness to Receive Orders': The Dynamics of Stasis in Sonnet XIX ('When I Consider How My Light Is Spent')." *Milton Quarterly* 32 (1998): 109–22.

Calvin, John. *A Harmony of the Gospels: Matthew, Mark, and Luke.* 3 vols. Trans. T. H. L. Parker. 1972. Grand Rapids, MI: Eerdmans, 1979.

Fiske, Dixon. "Milton in the Middle of Life: Sonnet XIX." *ELH* 41 (1974): 37–49.

Guillory, John. "The Father's House: *Samson Agonistes* in Its Historical Moment." *Remembering Milton: Essays on the Texts and Traditions.* Ed. Mary Nyquist and Margaret W. Furgeson. New York: Methuen, 1987. 148–76.

Haskin, Dayton. *Milton's Burden of Interpretation.* Philadelphia: U of Pennsylvania P, 1994.

Honigmann, E. A. J., ed. *Milton's Sonnets.* London: Macmillan, 1966.

Lieb, Michael. "Talents." *A Milton Encyclopedia.* Gen. ed., William B. Hunter. Vol. 8. Lewisburg, PA: Bucknell UP, 1980. 48–51.

Parker, William Riley. *Milton: A Biography.* 1968. 2nd ed. Ed. Gordon Campbell. 2 vols. Oxford: Clarendon P, 1996.

Patterson, Annabel. "That Old Man Eloquent." *Literary Milton: Text, Pretext, Context.* Ed. Diana Trevino Benet and Michael Lieb. Pittsburgh: Duquesne UP, 1994. 22–44.

Slakey, Roger L. "Milton's Sonnet 'On His Blindness.'" *ELH* 27 (1960): 122–30.

Shawcross, John T. *Rethinking Milton Studies: Time Present and Time Past.* Newark: U of Delaware P, 2005.

Urban, David Vincent. "The Parabolic Milton: The Self and the Bible in John Milton's Writings." Ph.D. diss., University of Illinois at Chicago, 2001.

–. "The Talented Mr. Milton: A Parabolic Laborer and His Identity." *Milton Studies* 43 (2004): 1–18.

Part II

The Prose

Matthew JORDAN

The Bourgeois Utopianism of Milton's Anti-Prelatical Tracts

What is sometimes called historical "revisionism" has been concerned to downplay the significance, as a causal factor in the political turmoil of the 1640s, both of a commitment to liberties of various kinds, and of class conflict. John Morrill agrees that the century to 1640 witnessed major social and economic changes, "Yet by 1640 the pressures were easing."[1] It is simply not true, despite what both sides asserted, that Parliament's support came chiefly from "the middling sort" (Morrill, 217). According to Conrad Russell, it is impossible to divide the parties to the conflict into "two clearly differentiated social groups or classes," while the actions of the Long Parliament do not suggest that it was "mainly concerned with social issues."[2] Nor, in contradiction of a story which is old but not dead, was there any "great militancy about the constitutional demands of the parliamentary activists in 1642" (Morrill, 10). Indeed, initially the struggle could be said to have

> [...] concerned issues not of parliamentary sovereignty, still less of popular liberties; it was concerned with the restoration of the ancient peerage to its dominant role around the Crown. At one level, the civil war began as an aristocratic coup (Morrill, 11, 300).

The circumstances which had fostered such a possibility were above all a consequence of widespread hostility to Charles's repressive religious policy, but the result was by no means a desire for liberty, at least among those leading the campaign: the

> [...] "puritan" drive was not common to all parliamentarians, but it was characteristic of most parliamentary activists. It was also largely a preoccupation with removing one

1 John Morrill, *The Nature of the English Revolution* (London: Longman, 1993), 4. Throughout, when multiple references to a text are made, subsequent citations will be given in the text, with an abbreviated title where convenient.

2 Conrad Russell, *The Causes of the English Civil War* (Oxford: Clarendon, 1990), 2–3.

> coercive, unitary national church and replacing it by another. Freedom of individual conscience, the key issue ten years later, was not a major issue in 1642 (Morrill, 14).

Anyone looking for evidence in support of this view would find ample in the writings of Smectymnuus, the pseudonym of a group of godly divines in support of whom Milton's anti-Prelatical tracts are generally held to have been written. The Smectymnuuans write in response to Bishop Joseph Hall's defence of episcopacy. Hall's position is that the "spirituall power" the bishops possess is the same as that which "was by Apostolique Authority delegated unto" the successors to the apostles, and thus divinely established; and that in "the genuine and undeniable writings of those holy men, which lived both in the times of the Apostles and some yeers after them, and conversed with them, as their blessed fellow-labourers" there is evidence of "a cleare and received distinction, both of the names and offices of the Bishops, Presbyters, and Deacons, as three distinct subordinate Callings, in Gods Church."[3] As he clarifies in his next tract, to the bishops alone is given the task of "Ruling": there "is a just distinction to be made, betwixt the government of soules, in severall Congregations, and the government of the Church, consisting of many Congregations; that task is yours, this is the Bishops."[4] Although the Greek term *"presbuterion"* (51; I have transcribed from the Greek alphabet), meaning council of elders, "was at first promiscuously used … the Office of Bishops, and Presbyters differed" (344 / 53). Presbyters are subordinate to bishops in a "sacred Hierarchy" (*Defence*, 51, 53, 111).

For the Smectymnuuans, by contrast, this common use of the term is the basis for their affirmation that "in the Apostles times there were no Bishops distinct from Presbyters."[5] The "Church was not governed by Bishops, but by Presbyters." They contend that "all such as watch over the soules of Gods people, are entitled *to rule* over them" (*Answer*, 19, 25). This stress on their right to rule in the Church is recurrent.[6] What they object to

3 Joseph Hall, *An Humble Remonstrance to the High Court of Parliament* (London, 1640), 23–4 (the latter mispaginated 14). I have used modern "s" throughout.

4 Joseph Hall, *A Defence of the Humble Remonstrance…* (London, 1641), 53.

5 Smectymnuus, *An Answer to a Book Entituled, An Humble Remonstrance…* (London, 1641), 16.

6 Compare e.g. *Answer* 88; *A Vindication of the Answer to the Humble Remonstrance…* (London, 1641), 71, 211.

is the bishops' claim to superiority over the presbyters of individual congregations:

> we finde in Scripture [...] that Bishops and Presbyters were *Originally* the same, though afterwards they came to be distinguished: and in process of time, Episcopacy did swallow up all the *honor* and *power* of the *Presbytery*; as *Pharaohs* lean Kine did the fat (*Answer*, 21).

Thus

> [...] the Apostles Bishops and ours are two: there was no other then a Parochiall Pastor, a Preaching Presbyter without inequality, without any Rule over his brethren. Ours claim an eminent Superiority, and a power of Ordination and Iurisdiction unknowne to the primitive times (*Answer*, 32).

If "the name Bishop" is to be retained, they ask, should it not "bee made common to all Presbyters"? (*Answer*, 91).

As may already be apparent, the Smectymnuuans are not against superiority *per se*: rather, they object to having been deprived of it themselves. Despite their affirmation of the importance of *"the lay presbytery"* (*Answer*, 72; cf. e.g. *Vindication*, 192), and that "The people specially have power either of chusing worthy Priests, or rejecting the unworthy ... from *Divine Authority*" (*Answer*, 33), it is difficult not to gain a strong impression of a bid for self-empowerment – that in relation to the other elders, the minister would be first among equals. The likes of Hall were not slow to pick up on this, of course, asking rhetorically "whether themselves, if they did not hope to carry some sway in the Presbytery, would be so eager in crying up that government" (*Defence*, 156). But to feel that Hall has a point is surely not simply to repeat the terms of the debate. The Smectymnuuan argument is not against superiority in the Church, but

> [...] that a superiority and inferiority betweene Officers of different kindes, will not prove that there should be a superiority and inferiority between Officers of the same kinde. [...] no man will deny but that there may be superiority and inferiority, as there is amongst us between Presbyters and Deacons (*Answer*, 63).

They refer to "Gods Ministers and *their* people" (*Answer*, 12; emphasis mine). They are open to the idea of "a superiority of the Ministers over the people" (*Vindication*, 155), and see in the Church "a plaine distinction betweene the *Governours*, and the *governed*" (*Vindication*, 140). Thus, as part of an argument with Hall about how Laud has denied ministers the right to extemporary prayer in services, they object that "the Minister is to exhort the people to pray … in what words he shall think fit" (*Vindication*, 41). Nowhere is their tenor clearer than when, in response to Hall's asseveration that the English Church is, as it should be, *"Aristocraticall,"* they object

> […] if it were *Aristocraticall*, then ought every Minister to be a member of that Aristocracy; for certainely no man will account the Minister *de plebe*; in the judgement not onely of the ancient Fathers, but of reason it selfe, none can be accounted *plebs* but the Laicks (*Vindication*, 82).

Although Milton is prepared at one point to describe the ministry as having been elected to a "holy and equall *Aristocracy*" by *"Gods people"* (*CPW* 1: 600), his outlook is very different and fits much less well into Morrill's scheme.[7] It could not be argued that at this stage he is a clear advocate of liberty of conscience, but in *Of Reformation*, his first contribution to the debate, in May 1641, there is certainly an enthusiasm about the spiritual potential of the general populace which evinces a sense of liberation entirely lacking in the Smectymnuuans:

> If we will but purge with sovrain eyesalve that intellectual ray which *God* hath planted in us, then we would beleeve the Scriptures protesting their own plainnes, and perspicuity, calling to them to be instructed, not only the *wise*, and *learned*, but the *simple*, the *poor*, the *babes*, foretelling an extraordinary effusion of *Gods* Spirit upon every age, and sexe, attributing to all men, and requiring from them the ability of searching, trying, examining all things (*CPW* 1: 566).

Admittedly there is a late swerve from all humanity being called to learn from Scripture, to the duty, incumbent on all *men*, of the independent use of critical reason, inspired of course by the Spirit. Nonetheless, it is worth noting, despite the desirability of instruction, the elision of any human agent but the reader from this process; and while it may be that the force of Milton's refusal to reserve such activity as the prerogative of the wise and learned has waned a little by the end of the sentence, Milton is certainly not careful to avoid such a conjunction of ideas. Indeed, he goes on to contrast unfavourably the innumerable and useless volumes of the Fathers with taking "a sound Truth at the hand of a plain upright man that all his dayes

7 John Milton, *Of Reformation* (London, 1641), in Don M. Wolfe et al., eds, *The Complete Prose Works of John Milton* (New Haven, Yale UP, 1953–83), Vol 1, 600. Subsequent references will take the form *CPW* 1: 600.

hath bin diligently reading the holy Scriptures, and thereto imploring *Gods* grace" (*CPW* 1: 568).

Paul Christianson has described such an emphasis on the spirit as a typically sectarian trait.[8] Simply to label Milton thus would be unwarranted; but nonetheless his position on the sects seems to be on the positive side of ambiguous. The Smectymnuuans remark that "some few *Prelats* by their over-rigorous pressing of the *Service-book* and *Ceremonies* have made more Separatists, than all the preachers disaffected to the Ceremonies in England" (*Vindication*, 38). This, however, is less a justification of separation than an aspersion against the Laudians. Those who had declined, despite their disaffection, to separate from the Church generally frowned on those who had so chosen as having deserted their post; and when Stephen Marshall sought accommodation with those on an "Independent trajectory," it foundered upon his insistence that they distance themselves from what he regarded as sects.[9] Milton, on the other hand, avers that they are no "rabble of sects … but a unanimous multitude of good Protestants" who, with the passing of the bishops, "will then joyne to the Church, which now because of you stand separated" (*CPW* 1: 787–8). Indeed, although *Reason of Church-government* contains a paean to "discipline" as the "axle" upon which "all the moments and turnings of humane occasions are mov'd to and fro" (751), his later description of the proper practice of excommunication could even be construed as a bid to address the fears of the sects regarding coerciveness, so concerned is he to stress that it is a last resort, coming after much persuasion for the sake of the individual's "dearest health" (846), and the action of "the whole Church" rather than an autocratic individual (847). (For Smectymnuus, it is the responsibility specifically of the elders (*Answer*, 38).) Certainly, it seems of a piece with a more general espousal of the empowerment and rights of ordinary believers. In his account of the qualities which will be fostered by reform of the Church, and which must be exhibited by those entrusted with responsibility within it, Milton evokes the "honourable duty of estimation and respect towards his own soul and body" which makes up a proper "self-pious regard" in "he that holds him-

8 Paul Christianson, *Reformers and Babylon: English apocalyptic visions from the reformation to the eve of the civil war* (Toronto: U of Toronto P, 1978), 169.

9 Tom Webster, *Godly Clergy in Early Stuart England: The Caroline Puritan Movement c. 1620–1643* (Cambridge: Cambridge UP, 1997), chap. 14; Murray Tolmie, *The Triumph of the Saints: The Separate Churches of London, 1616–1649* (Cambridge: Cambridge PP, 1977), 126.

self in reverence and due esteem" (*CPW* 1: 842). This Christian virtue can be promoted by letting each believer know that "by the high calling of God" he is "ordain'd [...] to such offices of discipline in the Church to which his owne spirituall gifts [...] have autoriz'd him." (842–3) Milton rejects "the scornfull terme of Laick," so important to the self-image of the Smectymnuuans, seeing it as a mark of "the exclusion of Christs people from the offices of holy discipline through the pride of a usurping Clergy" which "causes the rest to have an unworthy and abject opinion of themselves" (843). Rather, "every good Christian" should

> [...] be restor'd to his right in the Church, and not excluded from such place of spirituall government as his Christian abilities and his approved good life in the eye and testimony of the Church shall preferre him to, this and nothing sooner will open his eyes to a wise and true valuation of himselfe, which is so requisite and high a point of Christianity (844).

This "will stirre him up to walk worthy the honourable and grave imployment wherewith God and the Church hath dignifi'd him," fearing only that "something unholy from within his own heart should dishonour and profane in himselfe that Priestly unction and Clergy-right whereto Christ hath entitl'd him" (Id.). Such sentiments make it not incidental that, while the Smectymnuuans refer to "blessed Constantine" (*Answer*, 9), Milton associates him with clerical ambition and "Tyranny" (*CPW* 1: 551). Even more to the point, he remarks of those churchmen who see in Constantine's reign a desirable example of the state supporting the Church in securing religious unity, "They extol *Constantine* because he extol'd them" (554) As Paul Christianson remarks, "No writer in 1641 more ferociously deflated the image of Constantine and, thereby, the concept of the godly prince" (Christianson, 193).

The differences between Milton and the Smectymnuuans have often been thought of as "distinctions of emphasis," although Christopher Hill instanced his remarks on Constantine as an example of "the wide discrepancies between himself and them" of which "he must already have been aware."[10] But if, as Thomas Corns argues, Milton is aiming at "the devastation of the middle ground emerging in 1641–1642," and coalescing around

10 Arthur Barker, *Milton and the Puritan Dilemma, 1641–1660* (Toronto: U of Toronto P, 1942), 27; Christopher Hill, in *Milton and the English Revolution* (London: Faber and Faber, 1979), 84. Space precludes a thorough summary of positions on this matter here.

various schemes for limited or reduced episcopacy, Milton is close to an outright opponent of the Smectymnuuans.[11] As Webster has observed, "the Smectymnuuan works are masterpieces of ambiguity and opaqueness" (Webster, 320), but they do remain open to the possibility of a satisfactory Episcopal settlement, as when they assert that

> [...] we acknowledge no *Antiprelaticall Church*. But there are a company of men in *the Kingdome, of no meane ranke or quality*, for *Piety, Nobility, Learning*, that stand up to beare witnesse against the *Hierarchie* (as it now stands)" (*Answer*, 81).

As Webster summarizes the main thrust of their position, they reject

> [...] a separate order of bishops that reserves to itself the sole right of ordination and discipline. Ordination was not solely an Episcopal power but involved the "presbyters or chorepiscopi who actually had the joint power to ordain without him. This is not to demand the extirpation of episcopacy, for they immediately proclaim that the bishop is bound "in all his Ordinations to consult with his Clergy." The assumption is that a properly constituted church will include bishops but that they will be of the same order as their Presbyters or *Chorepiscopi,* and that they will join with them in administration (Webster, 321).

Here and there, there is "the vaguest hint of an alternative order" (Webster, 321, 325), but in the main they are seeking to draw on the powerful appeal of the notion of "the godly, primitive bishop" to the majority in the House of Commons, and among the godly.[12] Their aim is to capitalize on the desire of those members "yearning for a middle way."[13] Overall, Webster suspects, this espousal of primitive, "reduced" episcopacy "might have been seen as a way to encourage the moderate godly to take the first step away from diocesan episcopacy" (Webster, 326). Although, if Hugh Trevor-Roper is correct, it is a settlement that would have appealed to Pym, and Pym and Marshall are generally held to have been of one mind on such matters.[14]

11 See "Milton's antiprelatical tracts and the marginality of doctrine," in Stephen B. Dobranski and John P. Rumrich, eds, *Milton and Heresy* (Cambridge: Cambridge UP, 1998), 40.

12 William M. Abbott, "The Issue of Episcopacy in the Long Parliament." Diss. University of Oxford, 1981, 46, 113.

13 Anthony Fletcher, *The Outbreak of the English Civil War* (London: Edward Arnold, 1981), 123.

14 Hugh Trevor-Roper, *Religion, the Reformation and Social Change* (London, 1967), 297, 311.

Milton proffers his own model of reduced episcopacy: "he that will mould a modern bishop into a primitive, must yeeld him to be elected by the popular voice, unrevenu'd, unlorded" (*CPW* 1: 548–9). Of course, the substantive position conveyed by this reduction is exactly what those seeking compromise were avoiding. This division between Milton and the Smectymnuuans may explain Milton's declaration in *Reason of Church-government* that "Neither shal I stand to trifle with one that will tell me of quiddities and formalities, whether Prelaty or Prelateity in abstract notion be this or that" (*CPW* 1: 824). Haug's note remarks "None of the writers in *CBT* [*Certain Brief Treatises*, the collection Milton is addressing] had discussed this point." Clerical politicians like the Smectymnuuans – three of whom had, until May 1641 (between the publication of their two tracts) sat with bishops on the subcommittee of divines to the Lords committee for religion, and had compromised or reached agreement on a number of issues, in an atmosphere in which "'all passages of discourse were very friendly between part and part,' despite the presence of Bishop Hall" – might well have found useful just such a distinction between the form and substance of a bishop (Abbott, 135–8; Webster, 323).

Milton's opposition is not outright, or else there are passages in the tract the title of which is sometimes abbreviated to *An Apology for Smectymnuus* that would be explicable only as acts of outright dishonesty. It seems that in the final analysis he still believed in the category of "the godly," and in the overriding desirability of a degree of unity amongst them. But it should be borne in mind that, although his contribution to the campaign for reform of the Church may have begun with the anonymous "Postscript" to *An Answer to a Book*,[15] the title of this final offering is his first explicit reference to the Smectymnuuans; and that it occurs after a (short-lived) truce has had to be negotiated, at the Smectymnuuan Calamy's house in November 1641, between those on "Independent" and "Presbyterian" trajectories, in order that their mutual differences should not detract from the desired end of reform (Tolmie 48, Webster, 328–30). It may be that the understanding of Milton as writing *in support* of the Smectymnuuans, rather than advancing his own particular views, is in part a consequence of reading backwards from this final title. Even this – *An Apology against a Pamphlet Call'd a Modest Confutation of the Animadversions upon the Remonstrant against Smectymnuus, etc.* –

15 Cf. e.g. Barbara Lewalski, *The Life of John Milton: A Critical Biography* (Oxford: Blackwell, 2000), 128.

is principally a defence of his own intervention, although he suggests that in so doing he is combating an aspersion against them (*CPW* 1: 875). While he describes the Smectymnuuans as "my respected friends" (872), they are first introduced as "those reverent men whose friend I may be thought in writing the Animadversions" – certainly a slightly oblique formulation – and his relation to them is presented as consisting not quite in a common cause but in "having the same common adversary" (871). It may be that his description of their "unnecessary patience" in failing to respond to Hall's "coy flurting stile" refers not only to a humble excess of this virtue, but to their strategy and tactics (872–3).

As part of the ecclesiological cease-fire, the "Independents" had agreed to persuade religious radicals to lie low:

> [...] since "the preaching of some laymen, tradesmen and mechanics in the public congregations was a great stone of offence in the building of the Temple," presumably by bringing discredit upon the whole anti-episcopal movement, the Independent clergy (or at least those "judged to be most gracious and powerful with them") undertook to dissuade the lay preachers from appearing in public pulpits "especially at that time" (Tolmie, 48–9).

It is surely significant that in the wake of this Milton, in *The Reason of Church-government*, engages in a partial defence of the sects, and then in *An Apology* inveighs against the "injurious and alienat condition of Laity," since "the title of Clergy S. *Peter* gave to all Gods people," and affirms that "the privilege of teaching was anciently permitted to many worthy Laymen" (*CPW* 1: 838–9).

Another indication of Milton's dissociation from the mainstream of the religious opposition is his coinage, in *An Apology,* of the term "self-esteem" which, although it is used in reference to himself, is clearly a linguistic refinement of the earlier "pious self-regard" (890). Those with a vested interest in the existent order suspected that the social ambitions of those who should know their place were finding expression in the campaign against the bishops, and expressed disgust at their presumption, and anxiety about the social order.[16] This view could only have been confirmed by Milton, while more orthodox churchmen commended a "base esteem" of oneself or, as did Marshall, proclaimed that "the generality of the people of *England*

16 Cf. e.g. Fletcher, 110–12; Dagmar Freist, *Governed by Opinion: Politics, Religion and the Dynamics of Communication in Stuart London, 1637–1645* (London: I. B. Tauris, 1997), 2, 77, 175, 198.

is extreamly wicked."[17] Milton condemns those who are "so queasie of the rude multitude" when really there is a plentiful supply of "divers plaine and solid men" (935). (The first two references – both of later date than Milton's employment of the term – the OED cites for "self-esteem," from the Benedictine monk Augustin Baker, and the broadly Presbyterian Richard Baxter, are unequivocally negative.)

Indeed, there can be discerned in these texts the lineaments of Milton's vision of an emergent social order. Its outlines are nicely thrown into relief by a comparison of different treatments by the various participants in this particular controversy of a specific image, that of a picture. In *An Answer to a Book,* the Smectymnuuans expound Beza's distinctions between the "Divine Bishop ... as he is taken in Scripture, which is one and the same with a Presbyter"; the "humane Bishop ... chosen by the Presbyters to be President over them"; and the puffed-up "Diabolicall Bishop." This latter they illustrate by means of a story about a painter who painted two identical pictures, kept one secret, and altered the other according to "every man's fancy." After seeing this picture "swell into a monster," he brought out the other and proclaimed "This the deformed one the People made: This lovely one I made" (*Answer*, 86–7). Hall, in response, turns the Smectymnuuans into the populists, asking whether

> [...] the Painter that dressed up his Picture after the fancy of every passenger, do not more fitly resemble those, that frame their discipline according to the humour of their people, varying their projects every day, then those which hold them constantly to the only ancient and Apostolical form (*Defence*, 153).

(This is probably a specific reference to the politicking of the Smectymnuuans.) Lastly, Milton picks up the analogy and applies it to the workings of the Church so as actively to promote the right of the people to a voice in the Church in a way which is foreign to the Smectymnuuans, and includes them in ordination:

> [...] the care [...] and judgement to be us'd in the winning of soules, which is thought to be sufficient in every worthy Minister, is an ability above that which is requir'd in

17 Stephen Denison, cited in Peter Lake, *The Boxmaker's Revenge: "Orthodoxy," "heterodoxy" and the politics of the parish in early Stuart London* (Manchester, Manchester UP, 2001), 26; Stephen Marshall, "Reformation and Desolation" in Robin Jeffs, ed., *The English Revolution I: Fast Sermons to Parliament Vol. 2, Dec 1641–April 1642* (London: Cornmarket, 1970), 129.

> ordination: For many may be able to judge who is fit to be made a minister, that would not be found fit to be made Ministers themselves, as it will not be deny'd that he may be the competent Judge of a neat picture, or elegant poem, that cannot limne the like (*CPW* 1: 715).

Milton's Modest Confuter objects that such judgements are "the office of a Critick. Who but you thinks an inspired Cobler may judge of *Apelles* his workmanshop?" It is an irresponsible act of social elevation that amounts to an attempt at rabble-rousing:

> Who but you, against the command of God himself, dare bring not the Congregation onely, but the very beasts of the people, within the borders of the Mount? Sober and wise Christians, I doubt not but they know where to stay; neither will they follow such Ringleaders as you, to their own destruction.[18]

(The prognostication was to prove optimistic.)

Nonetheless, although Milton is quite capable of emphasizing the abilities of the plain and unlearned, especially in order to contrast them favourably with the bishops – remarking, for instance, "that if any Carpenter, Smith, or Weaver, were such a bungler in his trade, as the greater number of them are in their profession, he would starve for any custome" (*CPW* 1: 934) – it may well be here that we find something of the essence of a social vision which is more formally than substantively egalitarian. Milton clearly believes that the Church should be a meritocracy. However, he also believes that the ministry should not be granted prelatical riches because "a middle estate is most proper to the office of teaching" (951). This can be described as a commitment to competition and choice which, while it may, arguably, benefit all, will reward disproportionately those from what Milton perceives to be his class background, if they educate themselves suitably (it is the minister's "own painfull study and diligence that manures and improves his ministeriall gifts" (*CPW* 1: 715)). By contrast "many of the Gentry, studious men, as I heare" (Milton appears not even to know such people), have allowed themselves to be so miseducated as to have "crackt their voices for ever with metaphysical gargarisms" (*CPW* 1: 854). Milton will later say much the same in respect of civil government: it is "the middle class, which produces the greatest number of men of good sense and knowledge of affairs" (*CPW* 4: 1.472).

18 Anonymous, *A Modest Confutation…*, in William Riley Parker, *Milton's Contemporary Reputation* (Columbus: Ohio State UP), 23.

Morrill believes that the revolution "was not, in any simple or obvious sense, the completion of a process begun in 1642. It was more the product of the traumas of civil war" (Morrill, 17). It is wrong to assume, as does Brian Manning in his consideration of the Levellers' "plan for the total reconstruction of political institutions [...] a continuity with 1640–3, whereas the more obvious source of these ideas lies in the experience of war" (Morrill, 220). But could it not be that the nature of Milton's intervention in this religious controversy is a result of his enthusiasm for a more general social process he feels to be underway, an enthusiasm sufficient for him to believe in an almost magical resolution of the tensions and contradictions which were already beginning to shatter "the godly" into bitterly rivalrous factions? His response to apprehensiveness about disorder among "moderate Puritans" is not to downplay the potential for popular empowerment, but to argue for its benefits; to the fears of coercion of the sects, he addresses a vision of discipline as rational, caring, and non-authoritarian. Of course the desired outcome is a religious hope, but is it not also something like a *bourgeois* utopianism? And might this not in part explain why we find in Milton's early texts, if not in the concerns of the parliamentary and clerical leadership, more continuity than discontinuity with 1649?[19]

Works Cited

Abbott, William M. "The Issue of Episcopacy in the Long Parliament." Diss. University of Oxford, 1981.

Anonymous. *A Modest Confutation.* William Riley Parker, ed., *Milton's Contemporary Reputation.* Columbus: Ohio State UP.

Barker, Arthur. *Milton and the Puritan Dilemma, 1641–1660.* Toronto: U of Toronto P, 1942.

19 For instance, although Conrad Russell, in *Unrevolutionary England* (London: Hambledon Press, 1990), 296, remarks that "it is dangerous to underestimate the constitionalism of any Englishman in 1641," Milton in *Of Reformation* appears to have a republican understanding of the constitution. See Janel Mueller, "Contextualizing Milton's Nascent Republicanism," in Paul G. Stanwood, ed., *Of Poetry and Politics: New Essays on Milton and His World* (Binghampton, NY: MRTS, 1995), and *CPW* 1: 600–1. Milton's concern with questions of esteem, rights and liberties feeds directly into his assertion, in *The Tenure of Kings and Magistrates*, that men as conceived in Royalist theory "can in due esteem be thought no better than slaves and vassals born" (*CPW* 3: 237).

Christianson, Paul. *Reformers and Babylon: English Apocalyptic Visions from the Reformation to the Eve of the Civil War.* Toronto: U of Toronto P, 1978.

Corns, Thomas N. "Milton's antiprelatical tracts and the marginality of doctrine." Stephen B. Dobranski and John P. Rumrich, eds, *Milton and Heresy.* Cambridge: Cambridge UP, 1998.

Fletcher, Anthony. *The Outbreak of the English Civil War.* London: Edward Arnold, 1981.

Freist, Dagmar. *Governed by Opinion: Politics, Religion and the Dynamics of Communication in Stuart London, 1637–1645.* London: I. B. Tauris, 1997.

Hall, Joseph. *An Humble Remonstrance to the High Court of Parliament.* London, 1640.

–. *A Defence of the Humble Remonstrance.* London, 1641.

Hill, Christopher. *Milton and the English Revolution.* London: Faber and Faber, 1979.

Lake, Peter. *The Boxmaker's Revenge: "Orthodoxy," "Heterodoxy" and the Politics of the Parish in Early Stuart London.* Manchester, Manchester UP, 2001.

Lewalski, Barbara. *The Life of John Milton: A Critical Biography.* Oxford: Blackwell, 2000.

Marshall, Stephen. "Reformation and Desolation." Robin Jeffs, ed., *The English Revolution I: Fast Sermons to Parliament Vol. 2, Dec 1641–April 1642.* London: Cornmarket, 1970.

Milton, John. Don M. Wolfe et al., eds, *The Complete Prose Works of John Milton.* New Haven, Yale UP, 1953–83.

Morrill, John. *The Nature of the English Revolution.* London: Longman, 1993.

Mueller, Janel. "Contextualizing Milton's Nascent Republicanism." Paul G. Stanwood, ed., *Of Poetry and Politics: New Essays on Milton and His World.* Binghampton, NY: MRTS, 1995.

Russell, Conrad. *The Causes of the English Civil War.* Oxford: Clarendon, 1990.

–. *Unrevolutionary England.* London: Hambledon Press, 1990.

Smectymnuus. *An Answer to a Book Entituled, An Humble Remonstrance.* London, 1641.

–. *A Vindication of the Answer to the Humble Remonstrance.* London, 1641.

Tolmie, Murray. *The Triumph of the Saints: The Separate Churches of London, 1616–1649.* Cambridge: Cambridge UP, 1977.

Trevor-Roper, Hugh. *Religion, the Reformation and Social Change.* London, 1967.

Webster, Tom. *Godly Clergy in Early Stuart England: The Caroline Puritan Movement c. 1620–1643.* Cambridge: Cambridge UP, 1997.

James ROVIRA

Milton's Ontology of Books and *Areopagitica*

Milton begins his argument in *Areopagitica* with a series of definitions. He defines his audience as, ostensibly, the English Parliament; he defines himself as one qualified to address his audience (even though qualifications are irrelevant to those who employ reason to seek the truth); then he defines his subject: Parliament's 1643 reinstatement of state licensing after its repeal in 1641. Milton conveniently ends his introduction with a four point outline before moving directly into the bulk of his argument, which opens with a controlling comparison that serves as the basis of his discussion of books throughout – a comparison between books and people, which is essentially another type of definition: the definition of a book itself as a reasoning agent much like a person. The specific ontological claims about the nature of books central to the argument of the *Areopagitica* will be explored below, claims which place books, and the *Areopagitica*, in a privileged position in the Miltonic canon and which require special consideration be given to both in this light. The ontological claim asserting books are reasoning agents also deflect some recent criticism arguing that Milton didn't care for freedom of speech at all in the *Areopagitica*.

In the *Areopagitica* Milton associates reason with immortality, the human intellect, the image of God, and the content of books, claiming that books "preserve as in a violl the purest efficacie and extraction of that living intellect that bred them" (Patrides 200), and "are the breath of reason itselfe [...] an immortalitie rather than a life," and that the one who destroys a good book kills "reason it selfe, kills the Image of God" (Patrides 201). Positioning himself solidly upon assumptions underpinning the humanism of his age, Milton echoes Epictetus: reason is what humanity has in common with the gods. Underlying Milton's comments are the assumptions that virtue, goodness, and the most godlike qualities a human being can possess are all mediated through reason.

This view of human reason is long and deeply embedded in Western history. Gregory the Great, from the mid-sixth century, is one good representative of medieval thought, saying that "man has existence in common with stones, life with trees, and understanding with angels" (Lewis 153). He describes the well-known three-fold division of the soul, named the vegetable, sensitive, and rational souls, the lower forms both transcended by and included in the higher. Chaucer, Trevisa, and Donne also expressed some form of this belief (Lewis 155).

Milton himself asserts this belief in *Paradise Lost*:

> Therefore what he gives
> (Whose praise be ever sung) to man in part
> Spiritual, may of purest Spirits be found
> No ingrateful food: and food alike those pure
> Intelligential substances require
> As doth your Rational; and both contain
> Within them every lower facultie
> Of sense, whereby they hear, see, smell, touch, taste,
> Tasting concoct, digest, assimilate,
> And corporeal to incorporeal turn (5.404–414).

Activities sustaining the human body sustain the human mind, the seat of reason, thus turning "corporeal" food into "incorporeal" thought, the physical sustaining the spiritual, the rational. Milton doesn't understand the corporeal and incorporeal facets of human existence as completely separate but as part of a larger, organic whole, a whole arranged in a specific hierarchy – rational, then animal, then vegetable. It is very important to notice Milton's organicism at this point. He didn't divide up rational agents into separate physical and spiritual compartments, but saw the physical and spiritual as different parts of an indivisible whole.

Milton's claims about books in the *Areopagitica*, that books are a slice of the divine capacity, an expression of the author's rational soul, should be understood as firmly rooted within this philosophy of human nature. Milton believed that books, just like people, have corporeal and incorporeal natures, and that the two together make up an organic whole. Milton seems to want his audience to take his identification of books with reason as literally as his language will allow. Books are indeed "the breath of reason itself." On the other hand, Milton employed metaphors to describe the *physical nature* of books, the characteristics of books as objects. Metaphorically books "preserve as in a violl" what is to be literally understood as an "extraction of the living intellect that bred them." Milton does assert a dichotomy between books as objects and books as reasoning agents, but this is a dichotomy between interdependent halves, like a human body and a human soul, not an insurmountable juxtaposition between objects irreconcilable by nature.

So the assumptions underlying Milton's ontology of books could be restated in this way: human beings are reasoning agents and language, for Milton, is the arena in which reason parades itself. Therefore books are, naturally, repositories of reason because they are made up of language. The scene in *Paradise Lost* where Adam names the animals illustrates this last point:

> As thus he spake, each Bird and Beast behold,
> Approaching two by two, these cowring low
> With blandishment, each Bird stoop'd on his wing.
> I nam'd them, as they pass'd, and understood
> Thir nature, with such knowledge God endu'd
> My sudden apprehension (8.349–354).

Representatives of the vegetable and animal are "cowring" low as God *calls* them to Adam, the animals presumably bowing before a king who *names* them. Adam's naming of the animals represents the subordination of nature to reason, language here standing in as the vehicle of Adam's dominion over nature, a sign of his "sudden apprehension" or rational grasp of the nature of the animal before him and the sign of his rule. This subordination of nature to language and reason subverts the idea of a hostile juxtaposition between books *as objects* and books *as reasoning agents* in the *Areopagitica.* Books as reasoning agents are literally a slice of the image of God because they employ reason through the use of language, language which must always be embodied in some sort of object.

In fact, books as reasoning agents are so important to Milton that in some instances, at least, they are more valuable to him than a bad person. To lose a bad person is not necessarily a great loss, "Many a man lives a burden to the earth [...] no age can restore a life, whereof perhaps there is no great losse" (Patrides 201). It seems odd to at least some modern sensibilities that Milton could consider any book more important than any person, but this is Milton's belief. He does need to be clearly understood at this point, however. When we lose a book, we lose an expression not only of the highest human faculty (a divine faculty within this context), but an expression of "a master spirit [...] the living labours of publick men" (Patrides 201). Milton elevates writers and their product to almost divine status in order to persuade Parliament to exercise less control over printed material. An attack on a book is a direct attack on the most valuable expression of a person and, more importantly, the most valuable expression of the *best* people. Again, "hee who destroyes a good Booke, kills reason it selfe, kills the Image of God" (Patrides 201). This is not to say that there is no such thing as a bad book, of course. It is not the suppression of bad books that Milton is concerned with, but the suppression of good ones, which Milton argues will not only inevitably be suppressed along with the bad through licensing, but are actually more likely to be suppressed than false books: "if it comes to prohibiting, there is not ought more likely to be prohibited than truth it self; whose first appearance to our eyes blear'd and dimm'd with prejudice and custom, is more unsightly and unplausible then many errors" (Patrides 244).

So when Stanley Fish insists in his essay "Driving from the Letter: Truth and Indeterminacy in Milton's *Areopagitica*" that this tract is un-Miltonic because it "locates value and truth in a physical object" (Fish, *How Milton Works* 190), this insistence seems surprising, almost blasphemous, within the context of an ontology of books which sees books, like people, as reason *incarnate.* It is apparent that Fish can only ignore Milton's mixture of metaphor with literal language in the *Areopagitica* – a mixture which reflects his organic understanding of the body and soul, the rational and the physical – by ignoring Milton's ontology of books. Rather than beginning from any of the several relevant contexts of the *Areopagitica*, Fish simply asserts that Milton "could not have *really* meant" to elevate books to such a high status because he would not have placed such a high premium on a physical object.

Fish accurately paraphrases Milton's argument by saying, "even if one went to the impossible lengths of removing all objects, the flourishing of lust and other sins would continue unabated" (Fish, 238) because lust is a property of persons, not objects. On the surface, it does seem self-contradictory to assert both that "books are extractions from the author's rational soul," and "books are capable of promoting evil." But these statements do not contradict when contextualized within Milton's argument, part of which consists of a description of the nature of books and their relationship to reason. Fish argues that once Milton admits virtue and vice reside in the human heart, what difference can a book make? So what difference can licensing make? At this point, Fish seems to be ignoring that Milton argued persons denied the company of books are denied an important opportunity to exercise their reason. Books add nothing to the human capacity for lust because, theoretically, *anything* can be an object of lust. But even "bad books" can work against vice by providing opportunity to reason, and this is Milton's argument against licensing in a nutshell, an argument that finally asserts that books should not be suppressed prior to publication because they can work against evil without significantly contributing to it.

Lana Cable in *Carnal Rhetoric: Milton's Iconoclasm and the Rhetoric of Desire* begins her discussion of the *Areopagitica* by critiquing Fish along these lines as she wrestles with Milton's use of contradictory images. Once again an emphasis upon books as *objects* leads to the seemingly absurd image of "items of printed matter languishing behind bars" (Cable 120). But is this image so absurd? A book behind bars is as inaccessible as a book burnt, meaning the real prisoners in this case are those excluded from the prison, from the place where reason and free thinking have been contained. While of course the book itself is not languishing, the life of the mind is. Cable does progress beyond Fish's position to the recognition that "it is not the mere corporality but the vitality of men that books can be said to resemble" (Cable 120). Though conceding the weakness of Fish's argument, she still has a great deal of affinity with it. Her iconoclasm proceeds along lines parallel to Fish's deconstruction, setting image against image so that Milton's rhetoric deconstructs. In this way she sees Milton upholding "the sanctity of the idea" (Cable 122) at the expense of visual images, at the expense of metaphor, and *necessarily* at the expense of visual images, metaphor, and the corporeality of books, the latter being most affected by licensing.

Cable's thesis is exciting at times and worthy of reflection, but as she applies it to the *Areopagitica* her discussion of books as *objects* becomes disturbing as well as absurd when we consider how it might extend to all objects. In her chapter about the *Areopagitica* Cable follows Milton's argument through a description of the acts of past licensors, concluding that what the licensors feared "was never to be found *there* (neither in bodies nor in books) in the first place" (Cable 127, her emphasis). But if ideas do not exist within books or people, where do they exist? How is it that a licensor can restrain ideas without restraining either the persons or the books in which they are found? We seem to be seeing another example of Cable's "ontological longing," where the destruction of the physical image takes place to liberate the pure idea. By liberating ideas from books and people we leave nowhere else to look but an incorporeal realm, perhaps something like Plato's world of ideal forms, a world that, for political purposes, threatens nothing so long as it is not spoken of through any physical medium.

This move is problematic because Cable's iconoclasm does violence not only to the physicality of metaphors, but to the legitimacy of the physical itself, the very source of metaphor's power. Cable, like Fish, commits her own form of violence to the distinction between books as physical objects and books as reasoning agents, for the juxtaposition between "objects" and "ideas" entails a dichotomy inapplicable to Milton as it is being used in her argument. Ideas do not exist and are not accessible apart from objects any more than human beings exist as disembodied souls. Consequently, ideas do exist in both the writer's flesh and in books, and nowhere else for a licensor's immediate purposes. Once again we are forced to return to our ontology of books as a corrective. Two independent agents – books and reason – are not being set against one another, nor are they identified with one another. Ideas are not objects and objects are not ideas. However, ideas are inaccessible apart from objects because they are only held within objects, objects such as books or the human mind. As with the human body, so with a human book: ideas and objects are indivisible parts of a single whole. Milton's ontology of books requires that we recognize that for him licensing therefore matters, as does censorship, and how books as objects are treated.

Of the two great problems of Milton's *Areopagitica*, Milton's restriction of freedom of expression for Catholics, and the fact that Milton himself served as a licensor for a time five years after the publication of the *Areopagitica*,[1] at least the first may be tentatively addressed by our understanding of his ontology of books. Books, like people, should be allowed the freedom to live and act in the world until they transgress, and only after they transgress should they be restrained or punished. The rhetorical benefit of Milton's association in the *Areopagitica* of the practice of licensing with the Catholic Church needs no elaboration; the Westminster Assembly, a uniformly Presbyterian body, would take great umbrage at the thought that the very course of action they pursued found its origin in the Catholic Church.

1 I would like to suggest that Milton's description of an ideal licensor in the *Areopagitica* is essentially a description of himself, so that when asked to serve as a licensor he could reasonably justify it by claiming his own qualifications for the position, perhaps even considering himself a martyr of sorts since the job of licensor is described as a burden to those qualified to do it. The latter observation may serve, in part, as wry commentary on the motives of those who appointed him.

But I would also like to suggest that Milton's attacks on Catholicism are consistent with his ontology of books as well. The Catholic Church, acting freely in the world, had repeatedly shown itself to be a transgressor against religious and civil liberty in Milton's opinion and should legitimately be suppressed. Therefore a recognition of Milton's ontology of books smoothes out some of the apparent contradictions of the *Areopagitica*, though not all, and addresses some facets of the text problematic to modern readers, possibly even serving as a bridge from Milton's reasoning to our own, as we also acknowledge individual freedom until the moment of transgression for both people and for books, the former exemplified by the very nature of our legal systems and the latter exemplified, to cite one example, by relatively recent legislation against hate speech in the United States.

Works Cited

Cable, Lana. *Carnal Rhetoric: Milton's Iconoclasm and the Poetics of Desire.* Durham, NC: Duke University Press, 1995.

Fish, Stanley. "'Driving from the letter': Truth and Indeterminacy in Milton's *Areopagitica*," reprinted in *Re-membering Milton*, ed. Mary Nyquist and Margaret W. Ferguson. New York: Methuen Inc., 1987.[2]

–. *How Milton Works.* Cambridge, MA: The Belknap Press of Harvard University Press, 2001.

Lewis, C. S. *The Discarded Image, Canto Edition.* Cambridge: Cambridge University Press, 1994.

Patrides, C. A. ed., *John Milton: Selected Prose.* Columbia, MO: University of Missouri Press, 1985. All citations from Milton's prose works are taken from this edition.

2 Stanley Fish substantially revised "Driving from the Letter" between its 1987 republication in *Re-membering Milton* and again for its 2001 republication in *How Milton Works*, the largest revision being an excision of a comparison of the *Areopagitica* with Milton's theological works. "Driving from the Letter" seems oddly out of place in *How Milton Works*, not really fitting Fish's engaging and credible argument in the book's first chapter, "The Miltonic Paradigm." The fact that two strong theses, Fish's in *How Milton Works* and Cable's in *Carnal Rhetoric*, don't seem to fit Milton's *Areopagitica* serves as further evidence that the *Areopagitica* requires special interpretive principles and that Milton did indeed consider books alone among physical objects to be enough like human beings to be treated like us.

Shawcross, John. *The Complete Poetry of John Milton.* New York: Anchor/Doubleday Books, 1971. All quotations from Milton's poetry are taken from this edition.

Antti TAHVANAINEN

The Role of Rhetoric in the Political Thought of John Milton

Rhetoric has historically been a controversial art in political thought. It has often been viewed as conducive to democratic values and ideals, yet it has also been condemned as the art of sedition and treachery, undermining political order and rational decision-making.[1] My argument in this paper is that Milton was well aware of the dangers attributed to rhetoric, but he consistently argued that abuses such as demagogy and flattery could be countered. His answer was even more rhetoric, and of the kind that would follow the rhetorical ideals of morality, learning and eloquence.

These three ideals were also the essentials in Milton's views on republican education. The truly eloquent, republican orator had to be both virtuous and learned. In Milton's political thinking this was a question of preventive policy: how to create soothing orators instead of inflammatory demagogues, wise counsellors instead of vicious courtiers.

1 Literature on the subject is abundant, for a recent contribution, see Fontana. Examples of the classical precedents in the republican tradition can be found in Miller.

Demagogy[2]

That Milton was aware of the dangers traditionally associated with seditious rhetoric is evident from the "Second Defence of the English People," where Milton admitted how "times may often come when a majority of the citizens are wanton, preferring to follow Catiline or Antony" (*CPW* 4: 1.648). Catiline, *satis eloquentiae, sapientiae parum*, was the classical archetype of a demagogue, but reference to him need not be interpreted as showing only the danger of rhetoric. After all, it was Cicero's use of rhetoric which saved the republic. The image of Milton as Cicero, reliving the ethos of the golden age of republican liberty and oratory, was thus reinforced (Smith 190).

Milton, like his fellow republicans Marchamont Nedham and James Harrington, often saw Presbyterian ministers as prime examples of seditious demagogues. In *The Tenure of Kings and Magistrates* these "Ministers of sedition," or "Mercenary noisemakers" were portrayed acting "as if sedition were thir onely aime" (*CPW* 3: 236). Yet Milton was careful to lay

2 I use the term demagogy instead of rabble-rousing, fomenting discord, etc., since it was a term deliberately appropriated by republican writers to distinguish those orators without real care for the public – a use of the term remaining to this day. Although Milton attacked "the affrightment of this Goblin word [Damagogue, sic]" in "Eikonoklastes" (*CPW* 3: 392–3), the term had been in use since 1629, when Thomas Hobbes wrote against "the Demagogues" ("Of the life and history of Thucydides" a1–2). Hobbes, of course, regarded both republican form of government and rhetoric as inherently harmful, but as I will argue, Milton made a distinction between different uses of rhetoric. This applies also to other republican authors, such as Marchamont Nedham, who wrote of "the ancient Demagogues of Athens, or popular Orators in Rome," associating them with the "sad examples" of "Pulpit-Politicians" like Savonarola, who could "chain the hearts of the people to their own tongues, and lead them by nose which way they please" (Nedham 11). That was an abuse of rhetoric clearly different from the beneficial "cure of mutinous and dis-affected Spirits" which was achieved "by the still small voice, the smooth oyle of gentle language, persuasive Admonitions and Declarations" (Nedham 4). Later on James Harrington, using Hobbes's translation of Thucydides extensively, used demagogy consistently in the pejorative sense: as Athens "was cast headlong by the rashness of her demagogues or grandees into ruin," similarly Civil War England had "been tossed with every wind of doctrine, lost by the glib tongues of your demagogues" (Harrington 262, 265). And similarly to Nedham, there also existed the kind of oratory that was "of great benefit unto [...] the whole nation" (Harrington 286).

the blame only on the demagogues, not on the whole "party calld Presbyterian, of whom I believe very many to be good and faithfull Christians, though misledd by som of turbulent spirit" (238). As in ancient times, the demagogues were to be opposed by learned oratory, a task Milton took in writing so "that men may yet more fully know the difference between Protestant Divines, and these Pulpit-firebrands" (Id.).

Thus demagogy could be opposed by eloquence, but in this respect *Eikon Basilike* presented a problem, despite being "the artificialest peece of fineness to perswade men into slavery that the wit of Court could have invented" (*CPW* 3: 392). Its author used paradiastole to make the virtuous conduct of Parliament appear self-seeking and corrupt (Skinner, "Visions of Politics" 281, quoting *CPW* 3: 501), and similarly, "by smooth and supple words" aimed "to make som beneficial use or other ev'n of [king's] worst miscarriages" (*CPW* 3: 377). Milton admitted how "Wee have heer, I must confess, a neat and well-couch'd invective against Tumults; expressing a true feare of them in the Author, but yet so handsomly compos'd, and withall so feelingly" (382). Faced with such talent, Milton had to attack the content behind the words instead. As "the matter heer considerable, is not whether the King, or his Houshold *Rhetorician* have made a pithy declamation against Tumults" (383), Milton chose to write page after page of arguments to show that there were not any tumults, and those near to the term were in fact the king's own fault.[3]

Besides *Eikonoklastes*, Milton could make easier attacks on the eloquence, learning and character of his opponents. When Salmasius attempted to be more persuasive by claiming not to use rhetoric, Milton turned the argument around in the *Defence of the People of England.* There was "no need for what you cannot accomplish": from such "dull, stupid, ranting, wrangling advocate" there was to be nothing "requiring toil, clarity or taste," and the best Salmasius could manage would be "flowery rhetoric" (*CPW* 4: 1.324). The "empty windbag" could not "avoid the use of such

3 One argument why Milton did not write "a rhetorical tour de force" was that he wanted to persuade his readers "not with lavish rhetoric but with the simple truth" (McKnight 150). It could also be that the quality of the opponent caused Milton to choose a different rhetorical approach, but it should also be noted how, to a certain extent, Milton did not completely refrain from taking advantage of rhetorical redis-criptions: the people designated in "Eikon Basilike" as "Demagogues" were to Milton "good Patriots" (*CPW* 3: 393). Of course, this is also another presentation of the view that virtuous men cannot possibly be demagogues.

rhetorical coloring as [he] can manage," being closer to "some brazen hawker at a country fair," and should therefore have abstained from any claim to "ability at rhetorical narration" in the sense of a true orator (325–6).

Similarly, in the *Defence of Himself*, Milton argued how "nothing is farther removed from the very nature of decorum," than that someone like his opponent "should employ language which is elegant, or reproach that which is foul" (*CPW* 4: 2.744). Besides eloquence, morals and utility needed to be taken into account when distinguishing seditious demagogy from virtuous oratory:

> No orator known for the baseness of his life, not even if he were the most eloquent of the Athenians, should have the right to speak on public matters to the people [since] more harm proceeds from the example of a base character than good from the most chaste and holy oration (Id., 761).

In a way, Milton's view on the relationship between demagogy and rhetoric can be compared to that between demagogy and books. In *Areopagitica*, Milton wrote how books could be "as lively, and as vigorously productive, as those fabulous Dragons teeth; and being sown up and down, may chance to spring up armed men" (*CPW* 2: 492). But the fault lay not so much in books, as in their user, since even the "best books to a naughty mind are not unappliable to occasions of evill" (512). Likewise, the art of rhetoric was not to be blamed for its abuse.[4]

Flattery

In *Areopagitica*, Milton acknowledged the danger of epideictic rhetoric degenerating to a point where "all praising is but Courtship and flattery" (487). To an extent, avoiding this danger required an audience that was

4 This was the approach of Aristotle: "If it is argued that one who makes an unfair use of such faculty of speech may do a great deal of harm, this objection applies equally to all good things except virtue, and above all to those things which are most useful" (1.1.1). Interestingly, Thomas Hobbes left this part out from his translation of Aristotle.

"better pleas'd with publick advice" rather than being delighted "with publicke flattery" (488). It meant being ready to hear unpleasant things from those orators brave enough "in publick to admonish the State" (489). But unlike with demagogy, Milton saw flattery as an abuse of rhetoric, more closely associated with monarchy than with republic. As he attested in *The Readie & Easie Way to Establish a Free Commonwealth*, in a republic its leaders "may be spoken to freely, familiarly, friendly, without adoration" (*CPW* 7: 356), "whereas a king must be ador'd like a Demigod" (420).

In this vein, Milton traced in the *Eikonoklastes* the troubles of the English Civil War to court fawners and flatterers, as "those neerest to this King and most his Favorites, were Courtiers and Prelates; men whose chief study was to finde out which way the King inclin'd, and to imitate him exactly" (*CPW* 3: 350). This was repeated more strenuously as "None were his [Kings] friends but Courtiers, and Clergimen, the worst at that time, and most corrupted sort of men" (370).

The classical basis for such an interpretation lay in the Tacitean distinction between republican eloquence and imperial flattery. But in early modern Europe the new ideals of courtesy theory and civil conversation were an added obstacle to the civic humanist ideals of oratory. It was in the "language of a Courtier," that words such as "honour and civilitie" meant mainly "complement, Ceremony, Court fauning and dissembling" rather than "as they did of old, discretion, honesty, prudence, and plaine truth" (539).

Flattery in political sphere was not the only aspect where ideals of courtesy and civil conversation were opposed to Milton's ideals. Rhetorical, ornamented speech did not accord with some of the ideals of conversation – supposed spontaneity, inclusiveness and equality (Burke 92). In his *Prolusions*, Milton recognised the problem that "it is often asserted that the learned are as a rule hard to please, lacking in courtesy, odd in manner, and seldom gifted with the gracious address that wins men's hearts" (*CPW* 1: 295). But for Milton, there was no reason to embrace modern civil conversation. Classical examples would show that there was nothing "more delightful and happy than those conversations of learned and wise men" (Id.). Inclusiveness was required only among the learned – as for the rest, they could enjoy such conversations "in spell-bound silence" (Id.).

Milton kept up his opposition to courtesy and civil conversation in *De Doctrina Christiana*, as he argued against "crafty and hypocritical playing down of one's merit, when one is really fishing for compliments" (*CPW* 6:

734). Significantly, unlike elsewhere Milton omits scriptural quotations. It could be that Milton could find no quotations for this aspect of the courtesy theory, but nevertheless deemed it important enough to inveigh against it. At other points, Milton continued to argue for humanistic ideals against flattering abuses. Comity was a virtue, but not when it was "counterfeit or affected." Urbanity was a virtue when it entailed elegance and wit in conversation, but only "of a decent kind." And especially frankness, "what makes us speak the truth fearlessly" (769–70), is praised as a virtue, unlike in courtesy theories.[5]

Education

In the *Prolusions*, Milton presented his views on the qualities an ideal orator should profess. The orator must possess skills of the highest calibre, "nothing common or mediocre can be tolerated" as well as a "thorough knowledge of all the arts and sciences" (*CPW* 1: 288–9).[6] As Milton was aware that even "men eminent for learning" could be "of bad character" and slaves to "evil passions," it was imperative that the orator should have "integrity of life and uprightness of character" (292). This view was summed up in *An Apology against a Pamphlet* as "how he should be truly eloquent who is not withall a good man, I see not" (*CPW* 1: 874).

In *Of Education*, Milton presented humanist ideals and learning as the cure to avoiding the dangers due to abused rhetoric. If those who "betake them to State affairs," do it "with souls so unprincipl'd in vertue, and true generous breeding," then "flattery, and Court shifts and tyrannous

5 This last point could also used against the often made attack on rhetoric as untruthful. On this matter, *De Doctrina Christiana* includes an important argument. In Milton's "better definition of falsehood," "parables, hyperboles, fables and the various uses of irony are not falsehoods since they are calculated not to deceive but to instruct." Similarly, issues of decorum must be kept in mind, as when holy "texts command us to speak the truth: but to whom?" (*CPW* 6: 760). If not seen in such rhetorical context, Milton's view may appear shocking, as they did to Perez Zagorin to whom "Milton's allowance for lying [...] was so wide that it bordered on laxity" (Zagorin 240n).

6 These qualities bear close resemblance to those of Crassus (Cicero 1.45–68).

Aphorisms[7] appear to them the highest points of wisdom" (*CPW* 2: 375–6). Therefore, children should be won "early to the love of vertue and true labour, ere any flattering seducement, or vain principle seise them wandering" (383).

The "right path of a vertuous and noble Education" (376) was to a large extent a curriculum for an orator. It included "famous Political Orations,"[8] which, after being read, memorised and "solemnly pronounc't with right accent, and grace," could endue the students "with the spirit and vigor of Demosthenes or Cicero, Euripides, or Sophocles." They were followed by "those organic arts which inable men to discourse and write perspicuously, elegantly, and according to the fitted stile of lofty, mean, or lowly" (*CPW* 2: 401). And finally, the "gracefull and ornate Rhetorick taught out of the rule of Plato, Aristotle, Phalereus, Cicero, Hermogenes, Longinus" (402).

Plato and Cicero also feature in the list of "morall works" (396) discussing vices and virtues, but it is notable that of the two of them, only Cicero is raised as an example of the aforementioned "spirit and vigor." By omission, it can be argued that although Plato's works were suitable for learning morality and rhetoric, on the political level he did not represent the republican ideal as well as Cicero. In fact, Milton later attested in *Areopagitica* that Plato was "a man of high authority indeed, but least of all for his Commonwealth" (*CPW* 2: 522).[9]

Earlier, in *The Reason of Church-government Urg'd against Prelaty*, Milton had also used Plato, but only as an authority to promote the use of rhetoric in a

7 Paul Rahe has used this part in an argument that Milton opposed Machiavelli's ideas, as these ideas were "the sort first propagated by the author of The Prince." Yet it could also be argued that similar examples or "points of wisdom" could have been found from many classical authors as well, for example from Tacitus or Sallust (Rahe 260).

8 This would most likely include such democratically oriented speeches of Pericles' funeral oration, although as Hobbes had showed, opposing allusions to Thucydides could also be made. Yet it can be assumed that Milton did not share Hobbes's view, as David Norbrook has argued that the depiction of London in "Areopagitica" (*CPW* 2: 554) as an imitation of ancient Athens, was "a pointed counter to Hobbes's doubts about Athens in his Thucydides" (Norbrook 60, 130).

9 Jonathan Scott has argued for the influence of Plato's *Laws* in *Of Education* (Scott 173), but from the political viewpoint it is notable that the work itself does not appear in Milton's list of "grounds of law" (*CPW* 2: 398), although many figures of republican canon do.

society – a role rarely attributed to Plato.[10] According to Milton, Plato saw that "persuasion certainly is a more winning, and more manlike way to keepe men in obedience then feare."[11] This persuasion followed the ideals of rhetoric, as "there should be us'd as an induction, some well temper'd discourse," "utter'd with those native colours and graces of speech, as true eloquence the daughter of vertue can best bestow upon her mothers praises." Thus, rhetorical persuasion could "incite, and in a manner, charme the multitude" into seeing "how good, how gainfull, how happy it must needs be to live according to honesty and justice" (*CPW* 1: 746–7).

The utility of such learned persuasion was present again in *A Treatise of Civil Power in Ecclesiastical Causes*. To Milton, "force is no honest confutation, but uneffectual, and for the most part unsuccessful," and instead the "sound doctrine, diligently and duly taught" would be "always prevalent against seducers" (*CPW* 7: 261–2). Milton remained adamant, that "surely force cannot work perswasion" (266), and what was needed was the rhetorical approach: dialogue, discussion and argument (Achinstein 141).

This approach of persuasion should also be taken into account in interpreting Milton's professed intolerance in *Areopagitica*. For the *locus classicus*, "I mean not tolerated Popery and open superstition," is followed by such a proviso: "provided first that all charitable and compassionat means be us'd to win and regain the weak and the misled" (*CPW* 2: 565). The same approach of persuasion with proper decorum was advocated in dealings with "schismaticks." It involved "gentle meeting and gentle dismissions," debate and examining "the matter throughly with liberall and frequent audience" (567).

Nevertheless, in order to tell the difference between persuasive, beneficial rhetoric and seditious demagogy, one had to be properly educated. In *Areopagitica* Milton gave the example of Romans, who were "so unacquainted with other learning, that when Carneades[12] and Critolaus, with the Stoick Diogenes comming Embassadors to Rome, tooke thereby

10 Annabel Patterson has pointed out how although Milton used Plato's authority, it was to serve notions incompatible with Plato's (Patterson: 33–34).

11 This bears close resemblance to the words of Jesus in *Paradise Regained* (*Complete Poems* 1.222–3):

"By winning words to conquer willing hearts,
And make persuasion do the work of fear;

12 On Carneades as the symbolic rhetorical hero: Skinner, "Reason and rhetoric" 9–10, 98.

occasion to give the City a taste of their Philosophy, they were suspected for seducers by no lesse a man then Cato the Censor, who mov'd it in the Senat to dismisse them speedily, and to banish all such Attick bablers out of Italy." (497)

This showed how even the most virtuous of men could make bad decisions without the help of learning, just as learned men without virtuous upbringing could succumb to flattery or demagogy. On the latter point, Milton reiterated in the *Second Defence of the English People* how "nothing can be more efficacious than education in moulding the minds of men to virtue" (*CPW* 4: 1.625).

In promoting humanistic education Milton also asserted his republicanism. For Thomas Hobbes, it was precisely because of the way how "in these westerne parts of the world, we are made to receive our opinions concerning the Institution, and Rights of Common-wealths, from Aristotle, Cicero, and other men, Greeks and Romanes" that "men from their childhood have gotten a habit (under a false shew of Liberty,) of favouring tumults and of licentious controlling the actions of their Soveraigns" (*Leviathan* 149–50). Milton saw the same learning from a republican angle, as in *In Defence of Himself*, where he wrote how "we who as youths under so many masters are accustomed to toil at imaginary eloquence, and think that its rhetorical force lies in invective no less than in praise, do at the desk bravely strike down, to be sure, the names of ancient tyrants" (*CPW* 4: 2.795).

For Hobbes, the rhetorical redescription allowed by such education was especially dangerous, as it was "from the reading, I say, of such books, men have undertaken to kill their Kings, because the Greek and Latine writers, in their books, and discourses of Policy, make it lawfull, and laudable, for any man to do so; provided before he do it, he call him Tyrant" (*Leviathan* 225–6).[13]

But for Milton, this laudable practice was unfortunately restricted "in the debating room or in the school of rhetoric," since "in the state for the most part we adore, or rather worship such men, and call them most mighty, most powerful, most august" (*CPW* 4: 2.795).[14] Such flattery of

13 On the paradiastolic rediscriptions and Hobbes: Skinner, "Reason and rhetoric" 339–42.

14 Joad Raymond has argued that Milton's "Tenure of Kings and Magistrates" of 1649 was "perhaps one of the linguistically slippery works that Hobbes condemned in Leviathan": perhaps this was Milton's answer (Raymond 71).

tyrants, rising from abused rhetoric and neglected education, rather than rhetoric and humanistic education as such, was the true danger.

Clearly, Milton's views on rhetoric and education conformed well with his republican ideals, but they did not imply an inclination towards full democracy. In the republican arrangements of *The Readie & Easie Way to establish a Free Commonwealth*, Milton reiterated the importance of mending the "corrupt and faulty education" by teaching the people to appreciate the classical virtues and "to hate turbulence and ambition" (*CPW* 7: 443), but as in his other works, Milton's educational programmes were mainly designed for the propertied classes – nobles, gentry, wealthier citizens (Lewalski 209, 215).[15] In Milton's republic "only those of them who are rightly qualifi'd" would, after many rounds of choosing from those of "better breeding," elect "the worthiest" (*CPW* 7: 449) to rule his meritocratic republic of humanists.

In comparison to James Harrington's scheme, where a lower chamber of the republic would not be allowed to debate (Harrington 226, 251, 266–8), Milton attacked it as voting "without reason shown or common deliberation" (*CPW* 7: 441). But Milton would not suffer decision-making by "the noise and shouting of a rude multitude" (442) either. It seems, that although Milton had a positive view of the role of rhetoric in a republic, it was bound within the limits of propriety.

Conclusion

Rhetoric was a crucial element in Milton's political thought. In many ways, his view of freedom of speech, toleration, and rhetoric itself was based on the rhetorical approach: there are number of negative aspects, but also many positive ones. Rhetoric may be prone to abuse as flattery or demagogy, as well as toleration may benefit heresy and schisms, but through persuasion and education they would both be beneficial for the republic on the whole. Like for James Harrington and Marchamont Nedham, rhetoric in

15 See also Patterson 55–56, where it is also pointed out that although access to this education was never explicitly restricted, social distinctions were affirmed implicitly by the terms used.

republicanism is a balancing act: between demagogy in a chaotic democracy, and flattery in a tyranny, there is the virtuous eloquence of an ideal Commonwealth.

Works cited

Achinstein, Sharon. *Literature and dissent in Milton's England.* Cambridge: Cambridge University Press, 2003.

Aristotle. *The Art of Rhetoric.* Cambridge, MA: Harvard University Press, 1926.

Peter Burke. *The Art of Conversation.* Cambridge: Cambridge University Press, 1993.

Cicero, Marcus Tullius. *De Oratore.* Cambridge, MA: Harvard University Press, 1959.

Fontana, Benedetto, Cary J. Nederman and Gary Remer, eds. *Talking Democracy: Historical Perspectives on Rhetoric and Democracy.* University Park, PA: Pennsylvania State University Press, 2004.

Harrington, James. "The Commonwealth of Oceana." *The political works of James Harrington.* John G. A. Pocock, ed. Cambridge: Cambridge University Press, 1977.

Hobbes, Thomas. *A briefe of the art of rhetorique: containing in substance all that Aristotle hath written in his three bookes of that subject, except onely what is not applicable to the English tongue.* London: 1637.

–. *Leviathan.* Richard Tuck, ed. Cambridge: Cambridge University Press, 1991.

–. "Of the life and history of Thucydides." *Eight Bookes of the Peloponnesian Warre.* London: 1629.

Lewalski, Barbara K. "Milton and the Hartlib Circle. Educational Projects and Epic Paideia." *Literary Milton: Text, Pretext, Context.* Diana Benet and Michael Lieb, eds. Pittsburgh: Duquesne University Press, 1994.

McKnight, Laura Blair. "Crucifixion or apocalypse? Refiguring the Eikon Basilike." *Religion, Literature, and Politics in Post-Reformation England, 1540–1688.* Donna B. Hamilton & Richard Strier, eds. Cambridge: Cambridge University Press, 1996.

Miller, Jeff. "Warning the Dêmos: Political Communication with a Democratic Audience in Demosthenes." *History of Political Thought* 23/3 (2002).

Milton, John. *Complete Prose Works.* 8 vol. Don M. Wolfe, gen. ed. New Haven: Yale University Press, 1953–1982.

–. *The Complete Poems.* John Leonard, ed. London: Penguin Books, 1998.

Nedham, Marchamont. *Certain Considerations Tendered in All humility, to an Honorable Member of the Councell of State, Aug. I 1649.* London: 1649.

Norbrook, David. *Writing the English Republic: Poetry, Rhetoric and Politics, 1627–1660.* Cambridge: Cambridge University Press, 1999.

Patterson, Annabel. *Reading between the lines.* Madison, Wis.: University of Wisconsin Press, 1993.

Rahe, Paul. "Classical republicanism of John Milton." *History of Political Thought* 25/2 (2004).

Raymond, Joad. "The King is a Thing," *Milton and the Terms of Liberty*. Graham Parry and Joad Raymond, eds. Cambridge: Brewer, 2002.

Scott, Jonathan. *Commonwealth Principles: Republican Writing of the English Revolution*. Cambridge: Cambridge University Press, 2004.

Skinner, Quentin. *Reason and Rhetoric in the Philosophy of Hobbes*. Cambridge: Cambridge University Press, 1996.

–. *Visions of Politics*, vol. II. Cambridge: Cambridge University Press, 2002.

Smith, Nigel. *Literature and Revolution in England, 1640–1660*. London: Yale University Press, 1994.

Zagorin, Perez. *Ways of Lying: Dissimulation, Persecution, and Conformity in Early Modern Europe*. Cambridge, MA: Harvard University Press, 1990.

Kemmer ANDERSON

Those Tenured Tyrants: How Milton's *Tenure of Kings and Magistrates* Influenced Jefferson's *Declaration of Independence*

If the *Tenure of Kings and Magistrates* and the *Declaration of Independence* were an equation, then certain elements in this political word problem would have to be factored out. The variable elements of this hypothetical calculus depend on the time and distance of these human events as well as the purpose of each document. The function "to depose a King and put him to death for Tyranny" (TKM 20) is differentiated from the function "to dissolve the political bands" (TJ 315). Timing determines the course for each argument. Since Milton writes after the event of the English Civil War and the trial of Charles I, his focus is on the execution of a king. On the other hand, because Jefferson writes during the American Revolution and the reign of George III, his language concentrates on the act of separation. However, the common denominator in this political science centers on the word "tyrant."

Both Milton and Jefferson walked a Socratic divided line in framing the preamble of their declarations. Their abstract ideas create the Platonic ideal for a state. Each abstract form raises the mind of man toward the level of light and liberty in the call to throw off the chains of a despot and illusions spawned by living under such a system. The first sentence of the *Tenure* draws a Socratic distinction to the epistemological levels of thought: "If men within themselves be govern'd by reason, and not generally give up their understanding to a double tyranny, of Custom from without, and blind affections within, they would discerne better, what it is to favor and uphold the Tyrant of a Nation" (*TKM* 3). Milton's appeal to "understanding" and "reason" elevates the audience to the level of invisible objects in an effort to free the mind from its slavery to a double tyrant within the mind and the state in order to contemplate the idea of justice. His Socratic ladder distinguishes "custom" and "affection" from Plato's "opinions" and "imagination." Both states of sensory reality reap doubt and fear as the

Presbyterian party backed away from the charge of tyrant "under which Name they themselves have cited him in the hearing of God..." (*TKM* 5). Lydia Dittler Schulman points out in *Paradise Lost and the Rise of the American Republic*: "Both are built on Milton's Platonic understanding of the complementarity between tyranny in the state and bondage to passions in the individual" (Schulman 95). In Socratic terms, Milton tries to connect his reluctant Glaucons to "the ascent into the upper world and the sight of the objects there with upward progress of the mind into the intelligible region" (Plato 260) – a region represented by Freedom. Milton does not divide reason and revelation, but establishes virtues for the republic by uniting reason and freedom: "For indeed none can love freedom heartilie, but good men; the rest love not freedom, but licence; which never hath more scope or more indulgence then under Tyrants" (*TKM* 3). Milton recognizes the conflict between liberty and tyranny by reversing the passions that enslave the citizen with the hearty love of freedom. To be free or not be free is established by the action verb to love freedom or not love freedom. To use Stanley Fish's term "backsliders" (Fish 50) for the Presbyterians, the backsliders wish to slide back into their old and more secure chains of monarchy and tyranny.

Using the same Socratic forms, Jefferson created a "new identity" (Erikson 7) as Erik Erikson emphasized in his Jefferson Lecture. Jefferson begins with "a decent respect for the opinions of mankind" (TJ 315). His line of reason is established under the title, "the laws of nature and nature's god" (TJ 315), thus avoiding the seventeenth century argument concerning divine law – an argument invoked by Charles I. As for "Nature's God," Milton is more concerned about the "wrath of God" (*TKM* 8) or the "intent of God" (*TKM* 3). But both Jefferson and Milton, in the words of Albert Camus' Rebel, "derived [their] coherence from [their] Creator" (Camus 51). In his second paragraph Jefferson transforms the abstract forms of "life, liberty, and pursuit of happiness" (TJ 315) into rights – "inalienable rights" (TJ 315). This shift from Socratic idea into the action of rights distinguishes the document as piece of political science that shapes an actual Republic. However, proving the case of "absolute Tyranny" (TJ 316) is the objective of both documents.

In his *Politics*, Aristotle provides the common compass to direct Milton and Jefferson in demonstrating the despotism of Charles I and George III. Milton establishes an Aristotelian definition: "Aristotle and the best of Political writers have defin'd a King, him who governs to the good and profit of his People and not for his own ends..." (*TKM* 11). In concrete language, Aristotle presents the characteristics and methods of the tyrant: "tyranny aims at three things, one to keep its subjects humble, second to have them continually distrust one another; and the third is lack of power for political action" (1314a15–25). Jefferson sums up his investigation on tyranny: "A prince whose character is thus marked by every act which may define a tyrant is unfit to be the ruler of FREE people" (TJ 318). The *Tenure* and the *Declaration* present the case and call for political action for dissolving the partnership between the King and people.

Hannah Arendt affirms this definition in *On Revolution*: "Since the end of antiquity, it had been common in political theory to distinguish between government according to law and tyranny, whereby tyranny was understood to be the form of government in which the ruler ruled out of his will and in pursuit of his own interests, thus offending the private welfare and the lawful, civil rights of the governed" (Arendt 126). But Arendt frames the conflict of the problem in archetypal proportions. Before the human mind organized epistemological problems by forms, categories, and definitions, myth provided the language to explain these struggles for dominance. At the genesis of narrative, Arendt seems to choreograph this drama of power: "No cause is left, but the most ancient of all, the one, in fact, that from the beginning of our history has determined the very existence of politics, the cause of freedom versus tyranny" (Arendt 1). Based on this paradigm, the "Charge against the King" and the "Sentence of the High Court of Justice" affirm this description of a tyrant in a language that applies classical definitions and primal struggles to a particular time and person:

> [...] Charles Stuart, being admitted King of England, and therein trusted with a limited power to govern by, and according to law of the land, and not otherwise; and by his trust, oath, and office, being obliged to use the power committed to him for the good and benefit of the people, and for preservation of their rights and liberties; yet, nevertheless, out of wicked design to erect and uphold in himself an unlimited and tyrannical power to rule according to his will, and to overthrow the rights and liberties of the people (Gilbert 371–2, 377).

From these official terms, Milton constructs his argument for the execution of the King as one citizen who calls "to account a tyrant, or a wicked King" (*TKM* 7). He does not claim the voice of a magistrate when he writes:

> But who is a Tyrant cannot be determin'd in general discourse, otherwise then by supposition; his particular charge, and the sufficient proof of it must determin that: which

> I leave to Magistrates, at least to the uprighter sort of them, and of the people though in number less by many, in whom faction least hath prevaild above the Law of nature and right reason, to judge as they find cause (*TKM* 7).

Like Jefferson 127 years later, Milton establishes his case in the "laws of nature" (TJ 315). Milton must use right reason to argue through scripture as a proof text that the divine right of kings, a prerogative claimed by Charles I, does not excuse his crimes against the people; consequently, "that turning to Tyranny they may bee as lawfully depos'd and punish'd, as they were first elected…" (*TKM* 8). Again the argument focuses on deposing the king who occupies the same land boundaries as his citizens while the colonists occupy a new world – literally "another World," (*PL*, II, 1004) described by the Anarch as "Hung ore my realm, linked in a golden Chain" (*PL*, II, 1005). While Milton must deal with factions of people split by civil war, Jefferson must form "one people to dissolve the political bands which have connected them to another" (TJ 315).

In the *Declaration* Jefferson must prove the charge of "an absolute tyranny over these states" (TJ 316) by presenting specific facts "to a candid world" (TJ 316). Milton builds his case by articulating the effects of power and will: "And because his power is great, his will boundless and exorbitant" (*TKM* 16). With epic strokes of boundless space the polemist paints Charles I with the shadowy lines of Satan. Finally, Milton moves from definition to action: "Against whom the people lawfully may doe, as against a common pest, and destroyer of mankind" (*TKM* 17). Again Milton returns to an epic epithet of "destroyer of mankind" to rouse the people to their duty to execute this tyrant. Using an emotional appeal, Milton encourages the people to accept their duty to depose and punish a tyrant.

Unlike Milton, Jefferson cannot juxtapose "free people" and slave. But in submitting his facts to "a candid world" (TJ 316), Jefferson in his original draft attempts to turn the mirror of the slaveholder to reflect the King: "He has waged cruel war against human nature itself, violating its most sacred rights of life and liberty in the persons of a distant people who never offended him, captivating & carrying them into slavery in another hemisphere or to incur miserable death in thir transportation thither" (TJ 318). When the committee strikes this line, Jefferson is denied in his rhetoric a Miltonic step toward life and liberty for all. Milton, however, is free to construct his argument to demonstrate how a subject may become the King's slave: "Secondly, that is to say, as usual, the King hath as good right to his Crown and dignitie, as any man to his inheritance, is to make the Subject no better than the kings slave, his chatttell, or his possession that may be bought and sould" (*TKM* 11).

In 1628 the King began his own *Declaration* by stating: "However princes are not bound to give account of their actions but to God alone" (Gilbert 83). In 1646, the King claimed his birth right in his "Answer to the Propositions Presented at Newcastle" when he stated: "His Majesty assures them, that as he can never condescend unto what is absolutely destructive to that just power which, by the laws of God and the land, he is born unto" (Gilbert 306). For Jefferson just power was not determined by one's station at birth, but "just powers were derived "from the consent of the governed" (TJ 315). But in "The King's Second Answer to Propositions Presented at Newcastle," he used all the necessary words to improve his station as a just man when now "he will be most willing to condescend unto them in whatsoever shall be really for their good and happiness" (Gilbert 309). But the good and happiness was predicated on maintaining "the power of the Crown" (Gilbert 309). Milton, more than "the party calld Presbyterian" (*TKM* 34), knows that kings are never powerless. Milton also seemed to know already another characteristic of kings and tyrants: "To do ought Good will never be our Task" (*PL*, I, 159). The King, however, had no understanding of how the definition and eventual charges of tyranny might apply to his behavior as he limits the meaning to his reciprocal right to speak: "To conclude, 'tis your King who desires to be heard, the which if refused to a subject by a King would be thought a tyrant for it" (Gilbert 309). During the civil war of words between the King and Parliament, "tyranny and servitude" became the common vocabulary for describing the condition of the nation. In his essay on "John Milton and the Politics of Slavery," Quentin Skinner points out: "Milton indicates with particular clarity what might be described as the conditional character of unfreedom" (Skinner 11). In the *Tenure* Milton has a free conscience to reinforce this language with a passion for liberty: "Without which natural and essential power of a free Nation though bearing high thir heads, they can in due esteem be thought no better then slaves and vassals born, in the tenure and occupation of another inheriting Lord" (*TKM* 32). Milton affirms that just power must be natural in origin and not inherited by a Sovereign at birth.

Milton, along with Algernon Sidney, authors a language of natural rights that others may follow in the path of liberty. Referring to the "undeniable truths" (Sidney 8) of politics, Algernon Sidney in *Discourses Concerning Gov-*

ernment states the foundations have been laid for "man is naturally free; that he cannot justly be deprived of that liberty without cause" (Sidney 8).

Knowing his audience of Royalist leaning Presbyterians, Milton refers to Martin Luther's statement that a Pope or an Emperor may be deposed: "If Luther, or whoever els thought so, he not stay there; for the right of birth or succession can be no privilege in nature to let a Tyrant sit irremoveable over a Nation of free born, without transforming that Nation from the nature and condition of men born free, into natural, hereditary, successive Slaves" (*TKM* 37). Milton frames his demonstration for natural law firmly on the foundation of a Reformation proof rather than in the "self-evident principles" (Aquinas 58) of Aquinas' *Treatise on Law*.

By the time Jefferson writes the *Declaration*, the intellectual steps that lead through natural law have already been bridged. Without the previous work of Milton, Sidney, Locke, and others, Jefferson might have been paralyzed with a "migraine" (Erikson 23). But because he could follow the sublime arguments of natural law already prepared by other thinkers, he could gracefully write the self-evident truths of liberty. Before Jefferson is able to claim "certain inalienable rights" (TJ 315), Milton encourages the timid with the fact that "we have the honour to precede other Nations who are now labouring to be our followers" (TKM 32). We too have the honor here in Grenoble to question and debate to what extent Milton cleared the way for France and America to remove a tyrant. In the *Tenure* Milton frames the problem: "For as to this question in hand what the people by their just right may doe in change of government, or of governour, we see it cleerd sufficiently" (*TKM* 32). It is from this document and others that Jefferson derives his language of "just powers." Milton states: "to be a free Nation and not have in themselves the power to remove or to abolish any governour supreme, or subordinat, with the government it self upon urgent causes, may please their fancy with a ridiculous and painted freedom" (*TKM* 32). By 1776 Jefferson is able to affirm: "it is the right of the people to alter and abolish it and to institute new government" (TJ 315). Although worried about the power of the Anglican Church in his home state of Virginia, Jefferson writes from a vocabulary excised from the ecclesiastical fury of the English Civil War. "Laying its foundation on such principles" (TJ 315) found in the *Tenure*, Jefferson smoothly presents a case in a focused language free from the biblical language sown among the thorns of Presbyterians, who shrunk from executing the King.

Jefferson avoids prophetic utterance with the injunction that "under absolute despotism it is their right, it is their duty to throw off such government, & to provide new guards for their future security" (TJ 315–16). Milton reminds his audience: "How much more justly then may they fling off tyranny, or tyrants; who being once depos'd can be no more then privat men, as subjects to the reach of Justice and arraignment as any other transgressor" (*TKM* 33). Whether the action is "to throw" or "fling," both writers move to a velocity of language that centers on justice. Jefferson concludes: "We have appealed to their native justice and magnanimity [...]. They have been deaf to the voice of justice" (TJ 432). In this appeal to reason, justice is the rational Socratic virtue that coherently centers the natural law argument. Milton concludes his step-by-step argument by emphasizing the just rights that the people possess: "To teach lawless Kings, and all who so much adore them, not mortal man, or his imperious will, but Justice is the onely true sovran and supreme Majesty upon earth" (*TKM* 33). In these words Milton becomes the voice of justice. How ironic that the British were deaf to that voice during the American Revolution.

Although Milton does not sign the death warrant of Charles I, his logic supports and joins the "hands and seals" (Gardiner 380) of Bradshaw, Grey, and Cromwell. With courage and conviction Milton stands against tyranny. As author and patriot, Jefferson fixes his signature against "absolute Tyranny" (TJ 316). The other signers of the Declaration of Independence were good Patriots, unlike Milton's bad men who "would seeme good Patriots" (*TKM* 3). "Endu'd with fortitude and Heroick vertue" (Id.) of the *Tenure*, the Founders "with a firm reliance on the protection of divine providence, mutually (pledged) to each other our lives, our fortunes, and our sacred honor" (TJ 319). Thus Washington, Adams, Jefferson, Henry find their match in Milton's angelic band of Michael, Gabriel, Raphael, and Abdiel until faction and party measure them by Jacobin yardstick and provide them with other names from a Pandemonium of fear and envy. For the Federalist propagandists, Jefferson "Springs upward like a Pyramid of fire / Into the wild expanse" (*PL*, II, 1013–14) of French politics to become Milton's Satan.

As for the *Tenure of Kings*, Jefferson may have had a copy of Milton's *Works* in Philadelphia if apocryphal stories could be believed. It is my belief that he took the same extensive notes on the *Tenure* that he did for his "Notes on Episcopacy" when he examined *The Reason for Church Government* and *Of the Reformation in England* for the "Bill for Religious Freedom." But the fire at Shadwell on February 1, 1770 (Malone 125) destroyed this intellectual record. Yet from these fires Thomas Jefferson, the phoenix of the American dream, rose with that same Miltonic spirit of prose and reason that served England during its time of revolution and dissolution of monarchy. Though his own country not unkinged, John Milton "lit the torch of liberty for nations yet unborn" (BCP 190).

Works Cited

Aquinas, Thomas. *Treatise on Law (Summa Theologica, Questions 90–97).* Intro. Stanley Parry. South Bend: Gateway Editions.

Aristotle. *Politics.* Trans. & Ed. Ernest Baker. London: Oxford UP, 1958.

Arendt, Hannah. *On Revolution.* New York: Viking Press, 1963.

Book of Common Prayer. New York: The Church Hymnal Corporation, 1979.

Camus, Albert. *The Rebel.* Trans. Anthony Bower. New York: Vintage International, 1991

Constitutional Documents of the Puritan Revolution 1625–1660. Ed. Samuel Rawson Gardiner. 3rd ed. Oxford: Clarendon Press, 1906.

Erikson, Erik. *Dimensions of a New Identity: The Jefferson Lectures in Humanities.* New York: W. W. Norton & Co., 1974.

Fish, Stanley. *How Milton Works.* Cambridge: Harvard UP, 2001.

Jefferson, Thomas. *The Papers of Thomas Jefferson.* Ed. Julian P. Boyd. Princeton: Princeton University Press, 1951.

Malone, Dumas. *Jefferson the Virginian.* Boston: Little Brown & Co., 1987.

Milton, John. *John Milton: Complete Poems and Major Prose.* Ed. Merritt Hughes. Indianapolis: Odyssey Press, 1957.

–. "Tenure of Kings and Magistrates." *Milton: Political Writings.* Ed. Martin Dzelzainis. Cambridge: Cambridge UP, 1991.

Plato. *The Republic.* Trans. Desmond Lee. 2nd ed. London: Penguin Books, 1974.

Schulman, Lydia Dittler. *Paradise Lost and the Rise of the American Republic.* Boston: Northeastern UP, 1992.

Sidney, Algernon. *Discourses Concerning Government.* Ed. Thomas West. Indianapolis: Liberty Classics, 1990.

Skinner, Quentin. "John Milton and the Politics of Slavery." *Prose Studies* 23:1 (2000): 1–22.

Danièle FRISON

Droits et Libertés dans *The Tenure of Kings and Magistrates* de John Milton

Introduction

La première édition de *The Tenure of Kings and Magistrates* date de la mi-février 1649, soit moins de deux semaines après la mort de Charles Ier, exécuté le 30 janvier. La seconde édition, «revue et augmentée»,[1] fut publiée en 1650. Les spécialistes ont beaucoup polémiqué sur le fait de savoir si Milton avait déjà commencé à écrire *The Tenure* pendant le procès du roi, à la fin du mois de janvier 1649, c'est-à-dire du vivant du roi, ou s'il l'écrivit après que le roi eut été exécuté. La majeure partie des critiques conviennent qu'une première mouture fut probablement rédigée pendant le procès, puis complétée après l'exécution de Charles Ier, et qu'enfin d'autres ajouts vinrent enrichir la seconde édition. Le titre complet de l'œuvre explicite le propos du pamphlet, à savoir:

> démontrer qu'il est légitime, et qu'il a été considéré comme légitime depuis toujours, pour tous ceux qui en ont le pouvoir, de demander des comptes à un tyran, ou à un mauvais roi, et, après que celui-ci a été dûment déclaré coupable, de le déposer et de le mettre à mort; si les MAGISTRATS ordinaires ont négligé ou ont refusé de le faire.[2]

Le titre complet continue et se termine par: «Et que ceux qui, depuis peu, blâment la déposition du roi sont ceux-là même qui l'ont décidée».[3]

Il est clair que *The Tenure* fut écrit par Milton principalement afin de tenter de justifier le régicide. Mais lorsqu'on lit le texte, il apparaît tout aussi clairement que celui-ci constitue également une réponse et une réfutation

1 L'édition anglaise dit *"with improvements"*.

2 *"Proving that it is lawfull, and hath been held so through all ages, for any, who have the Power, to call to account a Tyrant, or wicked King, and after due conviction, to depose, and put him to death; if the ordinary MAGISTRATE have neglected, or deny'd to doe it."*

3 *"And that they, who of late so much blame Deposing, are the Men that did it themselves."*

des théories politiques récentes avancées par Filmer et Hobbes pour défendre la monarchie absolue, le premier (Filmer) démontrant que le pouvoir des rois est de droit divin, tandis que le second (Hobbes) présentait l'absolutisme comme étant conforme au plan divin.

Ainsi, dans *Pro Patriarcha*, dont des versions manuscrites circulaient dès 1641, Filmer affirmait non seulement la nécessité d'un souverain suprême doté d'un pouvoir personnel (théorie qu'il reprenait presque mot pour mot de Jean Bodin), mais également sa conviction que «Charles Ier d'Angleterre était héritier d'Adam en ligne directe».[4] Filmer ajoutait que les rois de son époque avaient hérité de la «suzeraineté qu'Adam, lorsque Dieu l'avait créé, avait sur le monde entier et que les Patriarches qui descendaient de lui possédaient de droit».[5]

Filmer défendait encore cette même idée qu'il était nécessaire que le pouvoir soit concentré dans les mains d'un souverain suprême dans un pamphlet publié moins d'un an avant la parution de la première édition de *The Tenure*, en avril 1648, et intitulé *L'anarchie d'une monarchie limitée ou partagée*[6], et à nouveau dans un autre pamphlet publié en août de la même année et intitulé *De la nécessité du pouvoir absolu de tous les rois: et en particulier des rois d'Angleterre.*[7] Le titre du premier pamphlet, *L'anarchie*, est parlant: tout partage du pouvoir, toute séparation des pouvoirs, conduit à l'anarchie et au chaos.

La nécessité d'un souverain suprême jouissant d'un pouvoir personnel était également affirmée par Hobbes, que ce fût dans son *De Cive*, publié à Paris en 1642, ou dans ses *Eléments de Droit, naturels et politiques*[8], œuvre qui circulait sous forme manuscrite dès 1642, avant qu'elle ne fût publiée en 1650 et qu'elle ne fût finalement incorporée au *Léviathan*.

Ainsi, lorsqu'il écrivit *The Tenure*, Milton n'était pas simplement en train de justifier le régicide. Même si la seconde partie de l'œuvre consiste en une réfutation des arguments – tant religieux que politiques – des presbytériens qui condamnaient l'exécution de Charles Ier, dans un premier temps, Milton s'avère principalement préoccupé de réfuter, dans une démonstration ra-

4 "That Charles I was a direct heir of Adam" (*Pro Patriarcha*, *in: Patriarcha and Other Political Works of Sir Robert Filmer*, éd. Peter Laslett, Oxford, 1949, p. 21).

5 "The lordship which Adam by creation had over the whole world, and by right descending from him the Patriarchs did enjoy" (*Pro Patriarcha*, ed. Laslett, p. 58).

6 *The Anarchy of a Limited or Mixed Monarchy.*

7 *The Necessity of the Absolute Power of All Kings: and in Particular of the Kings of England.*

8 *Elements of Law, Natural and Political.*

pide et néanmoins magistrale, les arguments des défenseurs d'un souverain suprême doté d'un pouvoir personnel, et particulièrement les théories de Filmer et de Hobbes. Il réfute, en particulier, l'un de leurs principaux arguments (ou, du moins, l'un des principaux arguments de Hobbes), à savoir qu'un pouvoir souverain suprême et personnel est nécessaire en raison de la Loi de Nature. Milton démontre également que, contrairement à ce qu'avance Filmer dans *L'anarchie*, la division du pouvoir, loin de mettre en danger les institutions existantes, assure, au contraire, leur protection.

Des prémices identiques, mais des conclusions distinctes

Partant des mêmes prémices que Hobbes, à savoir d'une vision identique de l'état de Nature et de la Loi de Nature, Milton arrive à un contrat social d'une essence totalement différente du contrat hobbesien. Par ailleurs, tout en se fondant sur la Bible (plus précisément sur la Genèse) comme le fait Filmer, Milton en vient à prouver le contraire de la théorie de Filmer.

A priori, Hobbes et Milton, du moins le Milton de *The Tenure*, semblent partager la même vision de la Loi de Nature et du premier corollaire de celle-ci, à savoir la nécessité, pour les hommes, de conclure un contrat social. Cependant, les deux schémas de société civile auxquels ils aboutissent sont à l'opposé l'un de l'autre. Pour les deux théoriciens, la nature humaine après la Chute, ou état de Nature, est dangereuse pour la survie de l'Homme. Hobbes décrit l'état de Nature comme une «guerre de tous contre tous»[9]; et, selon Milton, les hommes succombèrent à la force et sombrèrent dans la violence de la minute où Adam commit la transgression originelle:

> Jusqu'à ce que, à partir de la transgression d'Adam, victimes entre eux du Mal et de la violence, et prévoyant que de tels agissements allaient nécessairement entraîner la destruction de tous [...][10]

9 "Such a warre, as is of every man against every man." (*Leviathan*, I, xiii, ed. Everyman, p. 64)

10 "Till from the root of Adam's transgression, falling among themselves to doe wrong and violence, and foreseeing that such courses must needs tend to the Destruction of

Mais, si Hobbes et Milton tombaient d'accord sur la nature déchue et corrompue de l'homme dans l'état de Nature, leurs opinions divergeaient quant au statut originel de l'homme dans cet état de Nature. Et de leurs divergences de vues quant au statut de l'homme découlait, nous allons le voir, une vision différente du statut présent de l'homme, de ses droits et de ses devoirs.

Selon Filmer, les hommes naissent des sujets: ils font partie de l'héritage, du patrimoine, que les rois ont hérités d'Adam. Cependant que, selon Hobbes, même si les hommes naissent libres et égaux, une fois qu'ils ont renoncé à leur liberté pour adhérer au contrat social, ils ne peuvent plus revendiquer leur liberté. En revanche, selon Milton, non seulement les hommes naissent libres et égaux, mais ils le demeurent: le contrat social ne leur retire pas le droit fondamental et inaliénable de disposer d'eux-mêmes et de leurs gouvernants. Bien qu'ils défendent des points de vue totalement différents, les trois penseurs ont tous trois recours à des arguments religieux et chacun justifie son point de vue comme étant conforme au plan divin.

Comme il a déjà été dit, pour Filmer, les rois de son époque ont hérité de «la suzeraineté qu'Adam, lorsque Dieu l'avait créé, avait sur le monde entier et que les Patriarches qui descendaient de lui possédaient de droit»[11] et «Charles Ier était l'héritier d'Adam en ligne directe».[12] La théorie de Filmer avait pour corollaire que l'autorité royale se trouvait placée au-dessus des lois humaines ou d'«une élection arbitraire par le peuple»[13] et qu'il était impossible qu'aucune puissance humaine pût limiter, ou modifier, ou détruire, l'autorité du souverain. A l'appui de sa théorie, Filmer cite un certain nombre de précédents tirés des Ecritures qui prouvent que, dans les temps bibliques, il n'a jamais existé une institution qui fût une «monarchie limitée» et que les monarchies anciennes n'étaient aucunement tenues de reconnaître les prétentions de l'aristocratie ou du peuple à un quelconque partage du gouvernement. Ainsi, Filmer exclut la possibilité d'un contrat social qui lierait le souverain et le peuple.

Hobbes, au contraire, justifie l'existence de la monarchie et son caractère absolu par le contrat social que le peuple conclut avec le souverain. Contrai-

---

them all [...]." (*TKM*: *The Tenure of Kings and Magistrates*, in: *Complete Prose Works of John Milton*, vol. III (1648–1649), New Haven, CT, Yale University Press, 1962, p. 199.)

11 "The lordship which Adam by creation had over the whole world, and by right descending from him, the Patriarchs did enjoy." (*Pro Patriarcha*, ed. Laslett, p. 58)

12 "Charles I was a direct heir to Adam." (*Pro Patriarcha*, ed. Laslett, p. 21)

13 "An arbitrary election of the people." (*Pro Patriarcha*, ch. 22, ed. Laslett, pp. 95–96)

rement au contrat féodal en vertu duquel chacune des parties avait ses droits et ses devoirs propres, en vertu du contrat social hobbesien, qui est un contrat unilatéral, le peuple renonce à tous ses droits: afin d'éviter de périr de la main les uns des autres, les sujets se mettent sous la protection et la domination absolue du souverain. Le pouvoir de ce dernier en vertu de ce contrat social est si total qu'il ne peut même pas y renoncer lui-même, pas plus que ne le peuvent ses héritiers, et ce pouvoir ne peut en aucune manière être limité par ses sujets. Ainsi, pour Hobbes, il n'y a pas de contrat social entre le roi et ses sujets qui limite le pouvoir du souverain:

> Il ne peut y avoir aucune rupture du Contrat, de la part du Souverain, et par conséquent aucun de ses sujets, sous aucun prétexte de forfaiture, ne peut être libéré de sa sujétion.[14]

Pour l'auteur du *Léviathan*, la liberté du sujet ne limite en aucune façon le pouvoir du souverain: «Néanmoins nous ne devons pas comprendre que, par une telle Liberté, le pouvoir de vie et de mort du Souverain est soit aboli, soit limité.»[15] Une telle conception du pouvoir royal était exactement la théorie prônée par les souverains Stuart et proclamée par Jacques Ier dans son ouvrage publié en 1598 et intitulé *The Trew Law of Free Monarchies.*

Hobbes ne se contente pas de justifier ce pouvoir absolu des rois par une démonstration de la cohérence interne de sa doctrine: il l'appuie également de références à la Bible, en particulier à l'épître aux Romains (Romains 13, 1–3) et à un passage du Livre de Samuel (1 Samuel 8, 11–14) qui traite des exactions auxquelles les Juifs devaient s'attendre de la part de n'importe lequel des rois qui les gouverneraient:

> Il prendra vos fils, et il les mettra sur ses chars [...] et à récolter ses moissons, [...] et vos filles [...] pour en faire des cuisinières, et des boulangères. Il prendra [...] vos champs, vos vignes et vos oliviers, et les donnera à ses serviteurs [...] Il prendra la dîme de vos troupeaux, et vous-mêmes serez ses esclaves.[16]

14 "There can happen no breach of Covenant, on the part of the Soveraigne; and consequently none of his subjects, by any pretence of forfeiture, can be freed from his Subjection." (*Leviathan*, II, xviii, ed. Everyman p. 91)

15 "Neverthelesse we are not to understand, that by such Liberty, the Soveraign power of life, and death, is either abolished, or limited." (*Leviathan*, II, xxi, ed. Everyman, p. 112)

16 "He shall take your sons, and set them to drive his chariots [...] and gather in his harvest [...] and your daughters [...] to be his cooks, and bakers, and your fields and olive-yards, and give them to his servants [...] He shall take the tithe of your flocks,

La Loi de Nature telle que définie par Hobbes avait pour objet de neutraliser les conceptions selon lesquelles il existait une loi de Nature primaire et une loi de Nature secondaire, conceptions sur lesquelles était fondée la théorie selon laquelle il existait un contrat social entre le peuple et ses gouvernants, avec les corollaires qu'une telle théorie impliquait: une monarchie limitée, des souverains élus susceptibles d'être déposés par les magistrats de rang inférieur ou par le peuple lui-même, et le droit du peuple de changer de forme de gouvernement.

Loi de Nature primaire et Loi de Nature secondaire: le droit du peuple de changer de gouvernement

La conception selon laquelle il existait deux lois de Nature: une primaire et une secondaire avait été formulée dès 1643 par les porte-parole du Parlement. Selon cette conception, il y avait eu, avant la Chute d'Adam, une Loi de Nature primaire et parfaite qui était l'expression naturelle de la «raison juste» que Dieu partageait avec les hommes. Ainsi, à Putney, pendant les discussions qui avaient opposé, au sein de l'armée, les officiers et les simples soldats, les Niveleurs avaient identifié la Loi de Nature avec la Loi de la Raison. Selon eux, la première Loi de Nature était encore en partie visible: elle sous-tendait la seconde Loi de Nature et constituait le fondement des nations diverses qui existaient de par le monde. La meilleure forme de la première Loi de Nature, qui avait presque entièrement disparu, était le code divin que Dieu avait prescrit de manière directe à Moïse sur le Mont Sinaï: les Dix commandements et les lois mosaïques qui en étaient dérivées, les unes de nature religieuse, mais les autres de caractère séculier (ces mêmes lois dont Milton fait l'éloge dans le *Paradis Perdu*[17]).

Milton soutenait cette conception d'une Loi de Nature primaire et d'une Loi de Nature secondaire. A l'instar de Filmer et de Hobbes, il a recours à des arguments religieux et à des citations tirées de la Bible; mais il s'en sert pour prouver le contraire des vues avancées par Filmer et Hobbes. Ainsi, il

---

and you shall be his servants." (I Samuel 8: 11–14, cité par Hobbes dans *Léviathan*, II, xx, éd. Everyman, p. 108)

17 *Paradis Perdu*, Livre XII, vers 230–231.

se réfère à la Genèse pour souligner que les hommes sont nés libres et égaux, car ils ont tous été créés à l'image de Dieu:

> Aucun homme sensé ne peut être assez stupide pour nier que tous les hommes, par nature, sont nés libres, car ils sont l'image et la ressemblance de Dieu lui-même, et qu'ils ont été créés, par privilège au-dessus de toutes les autres créatures, pour commander et non pour obéir.[18]

De cette liberté et de cette égalité originelles de tous les hommes il découle, écrit Milton, que tous les hommes continuent à être libres et égaux, et que, par conséquent, ils ont le droit de disposer d'eux-mêmes.

Mais Milton ne se contente pas d'avancer des arguments tirés de la Bible. Il réfute les références bibliques fournies par Filmer et par Hobbes, non seulement au moyen d'autres citations tirées de la Bible, mais également au moyen de passages tirés d'Aristote et de Tertullien. C'est ce qu'il fait, par exemple, pour étayer sa définition d'un roi, définition qui est essentielle, car elle lui permet de justifier le droit du peuple anglais de déposer Charles Ier. Ainsi, à l'appui de sa définition d'un roi comme étant «celui qui gouverne pour le bien et le profit de son Peuple, et non pour ses propres fins»[19], par opposition au «tyran [...] qui, au mépris des Lois et du bien commun, règne uniquement pour son propre profit et celui de sa faction»[20], il cite Aristote en ces termes:

> [...] étant donné que, dès lors, Aristote et les meilleurs écrivains sur la Politique ont défini un Roi comme étant celui qui gouverne pour le bien et le profit de son Peuple, et non pour ses propres fins, il s'ensuit des causes nécessaires que les titres de Seigneur Souverain, de Seigneur naturel, et autres, sont soit des arrogances, soit des flatteries, que les Empereurs et les Rois les plus réputés ont refusées, et que l'Eglise, tant des Juifs (Isaïe 26. 13) que des premiers Chrétiens détestait, ainsi qu'il apparaît chez Tertullien et d'autres.[21]

18 "No man who knows ought, can be so stupid to deny that all men naturally were born free, being the image and resemblance of God himself, and were by privilege above all creatures, born to command, and not to obey." (*TKM*, *op. cit.*, 198).

19 *TKM*, 202.

20 *TKM*, 212.

21 "[...] seeing that from hence Aristotle and the best of Political writers have defined a king, him who governs to the good and profit of his People, and not for his own ends, it follows from necessary causes that the titles of Sov'ran Lord, natural Lord, and the

Après une longue démonstration des raisons pour lesquelles les hommes en vinrent finalement à instituer une société civile, Milton, dans une sorte de résumé de l'histoire politique mondiale, en commençant par la Grèce antique et en terminant par l'histoire politique de l'Angleterre, explique la véritable signification du contrat social et en définit la portée et les limites. Selon lui, les rois et les magistrats détiennent le pouvoir uniquement parce que le peuple leur a confié ce pouvoir en dépôt:

> Il est ainsi manifeste que le pouvoir des Rois et des Magistrats n'est rien d'autre qu'un pouvoir dérivé, qui leur a été transféré et confié en dépôt par le Peuple, pour le bien Commun de tous, et que, Fondamentalement, le pouvoir reste entre les mains du Peuple, et ne peut lui être retiré sans violer ce qui lui appartient Naturellement de droit.[22]

Le passage cité ci-dessus présente un double intérêt. Il offre un intérêt d'abord parce qu'il réfute l'argumentaire de Filmer: tandis que pour Filmer ce sont les rois qui possèdent un héritage, un patrimoine («[...] Charles Ier était l'héritier d'Adam en ligne directe»[23]), pour Milton, au contraire, c'est le peuple qui possède un patrimoine et un héritage. Ainsi, Milton réfute l'affirmation de Filmer et d'autres penseurs selon laquelle la monarchie est de nature héréditaire, les rois ayant un droit patrimonial sur leur royaume.

En second lieu, le passage précité offre l'intérêt de souligner le fait que le contrat social repose sur le concept de *«trust»*, c'est-à-dire à la fois de dépôt et de confiance. Il est frappant que le terme *«trust»* apparaît de manière récurrente dans le texte de *The Tenure*. Or, le *«trust»* était (et demeure) un concept important et une institution fondamentale en droit anglais. L'*equity* appliquée par la Cour de la chancellerie donnait à ce concept force de loi et le *«trust»* constituait un instrument juridique très utilisé en Angleterre: en fait, l'importance vitale du *«trust»* pour la société anglaise fut probablement une des raisons pour lesquelles la Cour de la Chancellerie, qui

---

like, are either arrogancies, or flatteries, not admitted by Emperours and Kings of best note, and dislikt by the Church both of Jews (Isai. 26. 13) and ancient Christians, as appears by Tertullian and others." (*TKM*, 202)

22 "It being thus manifest that the power of Kings and Magistrates is nothing else, but what is only derivative, transferr'd and committed to them in trust from the People, to the Common good of them all, in whom the power yet remaines Fundamentally, and cannot be taken from them, without a violation of their Natural birthright." (*TKM*, 202)

23 "[...] that Charles I was a direct heir of Adam." (*Pro Patriarcha*, ed. Laslett, p. 21)

protégeait ce concept et le rendait exécutoire, ne fut pas abolie pendant la Révolution anglaise et lors de l'instauration du Commonwealth.

Selon un *«trust»*, le propriétaire d'origine d'un bien ou d'un droit confie son bien ou son droit à une personne de confiance, appelée *«trustee»*, qui a pour obligation de gérer ce bien ou ce droit au profit du propriétaire originel ou d'un autre bénéficiaire. Or, cette définition correspond exactement à la nature du contrat social tel qu'il est défini par Milton, qui réfute totalement le contrat social unilatéral de Hobbes. La définition du contrat social en termes d'un *«trust»* justifie, en soi, la déposition de Charles Ier et lui donne une base légale. Dans le passage qui précède le dernier passage cité ci-dessus, c'est-à-dire dans le résumé de l'histoire politique mondiale[24] qui se termine par un gros plan sur l'histoire politique de l'Angleterre[25], Milton donne les raisons pour lesquelles la conduite des rois et des gouvernants avait rendu nécessaire d'imposer des limites à leur pouvoir au moyen de lois et de serments qui leur étaient imposés lors de leur couronnement afin de s'assurer qu'ils respecteraient les lois en vigueur. Ensuite, après avoir défini l'essence de ces serments et du contrat social qui lie le roi et son peuple en termes de *«trust»*, Milton s'emploie à démontrer de quelle manière les rois d'Angleterre, et en particulier Charles Ier, ont violé le contrat social et le pouvoir qui leur était confié. Sa démonstration repose précisément sur le fait que tous les hommes sont nés libres et égaux et que leur liberté et leur égalité autorisent le peuple à infliger au roi le même traitement que celui qui est infligé au peuple au nom de la loi.

Ainsi, dans un premier temps, Milton réfute l'argument de Filmer selon lequel «le Roi a un droit sur sa Couronne et son rang comme si ceux-ci étaient son patrimoine» en ces mots:

> Deuxièmement, dire, comme il est habituel, que le Roi a autant droit à sa Couronne et à son rang, que n'importe quel homme à son patrimoine, c'est rabaisser les Sujets au rang d'esclaves, de cheptel, ou de biens du Roi, que ce dernier peut acheter ou vendre.[26]

24 *TKM*, 199.

25 *TKM*, 201.

26 "Secondly, that to say, as is usual, the King has as good right to his Crown and dignitie, as any man to his inheritance, is to make the Subject no better then the Kings slave, his chatell, or his possession that may be bought and sould." (*TKM*, 203)

Dans un second temps, Milton proclame que dans la mesure où tous les hommes sont égaux, tous, y compris le roi, sont également soumis à la règle de droit:

> Mais supposons qu'elle [la Couronne] soit, de droit, héréditaire, que peut-il y avoir de plus juste et de plus conforme au droit, si un sujet, pour certains crimes, doit se voir privé, lui-même et ses héritiers, de la totalité de son patrimoine, au nom de la Loi, au profit du Roi, que de même un Roi, pour des crimes semblables, se voie confisquer par le peuple, tout son titre et son patrimoine.[27]

Or, précisément, quelques pages plus haut, Milton venait de dresser la liste des crimes perpétrés par Charles Ier, dénonçant:

> [...] des massacres en masse ont été infligés à ses fidèles Sujets, ses Provinces ont été mises en gage ou aliénées, comme données en salaire à ceux à qui il avait demandé de venir et de détruire des Villes et des Régions entières.[28]

Puis, dans une sorte de parenthèse, Milton écarte l'argument des royalistes selon lequel les rois ne doivent rendre de comptes qu'à Dieu seul:

> Troisièmement, il s'ensuit que de dire que les Rois ne doivent rendre de comptes qu'à Dieu seul, est la subversion de toute Loi et de tout gouvernement. Car, s'ils refusent de rendre compte, alors tous les pactes faits avec eux lors de leur Couronnement, tous les Serments sont vains et sont de pures moqueries et toutes les Lois qu'ils jurent de préserver sont inutiles.[29]

Car, continue Milton, que se passe-t-il si un roi ne craint pas Dieu, rompt son serment et se comporte comme un Dieu et non comme un magistrat mortel. Une fois de plus, Milton se réfère à Aristote pour soutenir son point de vue:

27 "But suppose it [the Crown] to be of right hereditarie, what can be more just and legal, if a subject for certain crimes be to forfet by Law from himself, and posterity, all his inheritance to the King, then that a King for crimes proportional, should forfet all his title and inheritance to the people." (*TKM*, 203–204)

28 "[...] whole massachers have been committed on his faithfull Subjects, his Provinces offered to pawn or alienation, as the hire of those whom he had sollicited to come in and destroy whole Citties and Countries." (*TKM,* 197)

29 "Thirdly it follows, that to say Kings are accountable to none but God, is the overturning of all Law and government. For if they refuse to give account, then all cov'nants made with them at Coronation; all Oathes are in vaine, and meer mockeries, all Lawes which they sweare to keep, made to no purpose." (*TKM*, 204)

> Aristote [...] écrit dans le quatrième livre de sa Politique, chapitre 10, qu'une Monarchie qui n'est pas contrainte de rendre compte, est la pire des Tyrannies; et la plus insupportable pour des hommes nés libres.[30]

Puis, après quelques digressions supplémentaires, Milton en vient à la conclusion de sa démonstration:

> Il s'ensuit enfin que puisque le Roi ou le Magistrat tient son autorité du peuple, à la fois originellement et naturellement pour le bien du peuple avant tout, et non pour son propre bien, alors le peuple peut, aussi souvent qu'il le jugera bon, soit le choisir, soit le rejeter, le garder ou le déposer, même s'il ne se conduit pas en tyran, simplement au nom de la liberté et du droit qu'ont des Hommes nés libres d'être gouvernés de la manière qui leur convient.[31]

Par cette phrase, Milton ne se contente pas de justifier le régicide comme étant la juste punition d'un tyran. Il va beaucoup plus loin. Du fait, précisément, que le contrat social miltonien n'est pas un contrat mais un *«trust»*, il adopte un point de vue très moderne, à savoir que non seulement le peuple peut déposer son gouvernant ou ses gouvernants s'il n'est pas satisfait de la conduite de celui-ci ou de ceux-ci, mais que le peuple peut décider de changer son mode de gouvernement et ses institutions et les remplacer par d'autres qui lui semblent mieux convenir à ses besoins.

Conclusion

Je conclurai donc cette lecture de *The Tenure* en soulignant la modernité de Milton. De la même manière qu'il avait défendu la liberté d'expression et condamné la censure dans *Areopagitica* (1644), et de la même manière qu'il avait défendu la pratique du divorce dans *Of the Doctrine and Discipline of*

30 "Aristotle [...] writes in the fourth of his politics chap. 10 that Monarchy unaccountable, is the worst sort of Tyranny; and least of all to be endured by free born men." (*TKM*, 204)

31 "It follows lastly, that since the King or Magistrate holds his authoritie of the people, both originally and naturally for their good in the first place, and not his own, then may the people as oft as they shall judge it for the best, either choose him or reject him, retaine him or depose him though no Tyrant, meerly by the liberty and right of free born Men, to be govern'd as seems to them best." (*TKM*, 206)

Divorce (1643), dans *The Tenure*, Milton explique la nature du contrat social, ou plutôt du «*trust* social», qui lie les gouvernants et les gouvernés, en des termes très modernes. Non content de rendre le contrat social contraignant pour les deux parties, à l'opposé du contrat hobbesien, il va jusqu'à définir le contrat social comme imposant plus d'obligations au roi qu'au peuple, dans la mesure où il affirme le droit du peuple de choisir et de modifier son mode de gouvernement, même si le souverain n'est pas un tyran, simplement sur le fondement de la liberté et de l'égalité de tous les hommes.

Certes, on connaît les limites de l'égalitarisme de Milton. On sait que, bien qu'il proclamât l'égalité fondamentale de tous les hommes, dans la pratique, il se conduisait de manière élitiste. Il convient de se souvenir que pour lui «le peuple» signifiait un corps limité d'hommes éclairés qui étaient plus intelligents et plus instruits que les autres. Le fait même que Milton ait continué de soutenir Cromwell, au point de devenir son «Secrétaire latin», c'est-à-dire son ministre des Affaires étrangères, prouve suffisamment qu'il était plus proche des élites que des Niveleurs. Ces réserves faites, il convient néanmoins de reconnaître que Milton a contribué à montrer la voie d'une vision plus démocratique du gouvernement selon laquelle les gouvernants sont simplement les «*trustees*» ou fidéicommissaires auxquels le peuple confie le pouvoir en dépôt.

Références

Filmer, Robert. *The Anarchy of a Limited or Mixed Monarchy*, April 19, 1648; E 436 (4); *in: Robert Filmer, Patriarcha and Other Writings*, ed. J. P. Sommerville. Cambridge: Cambridge UP, 1991. 131–71.

–. *The Necessity of the Absolute Power of All Kings: and in Particular the King of England*, August 21, 1648; E 460 (7); *in: Robert Filmer, Patriarcha and Other Writings*, ed. J. P. Sommerville. Cambridge: Cambridge UP, 1991. 172–183.

–. *Patriarcha, The Naturall Power of Kinges Defended against the Unnatural Liberty of the People*, Cambridge University Library MS Add. 7078; *in: Patriarcha and Other Political Works of Sir Robert Filmer*, ed. Peter Laslett, Oxford, 1949.

Hobbes, Thomas. *De Cive* (Paris, 1642); English version (1651), *in: De Cive or The Citizen*, ed. New York: S. P. Lamprecht, 1949.

–. *Elements of Law, Natural and Politic* (1650), ed. F. Toennies. London: Simpkin, Marshall & Co., 1889; Cambridge: Cambridge UP, 1928.

–. *Leviathan* (1651), ed. K. R. Minogue. London: Everyman, 1973.

James I, King of England. *The Trew Law of Free Monarchies* (1598). *The Political Works of James I*, ed. Ch. H. McIlwain. Cambridge, Mass.: Harvard UP, 1918.

Milton, John. *The Doctrine and Discipline of Divorce* (1643). *Complete Prose Works of John Milton*. Vol. II (1643–45), New Haven: Yale UP, 1959, p. 222 sq.

– *Areopagitica* (1644). *Complete Prose Works of John Milton*. Vol. II (1643–45), New Haven: Yale UP, 1959, pp. 480–570.

– *The Tenure of Kings and Magistrates* (1649). *Complete Prose Works of John Milton*. New Haven: Yale UP, Vol. III, 1962, pp. 189–258.

– *Paradise Lost* (complete ed. 1674); Paris: Aubier (2 vols), 1965.

Yuko Kanakubo NORO

On Milton's Proposal for a "Communitas Libera" Reconsidered – from *Defensio Prima*, through *The Readie and Easie Way*, to *Paradise Lost**

In October 1658,[1] one month after Cromwell's death caused extensive political anxiety in the minds of many English people, Milton published a revised edition of *Pro Populo Anglicano Defensio* (hereafter *Defensio Prima*). He added significant phrases to the 1651 version and republished it, thereby encouraging English republican minds and reminding them of their cause in the establishment of the ideal government. In the concluding part of the new version, he added the following phrase, which is important in terms of the writing of *PL*, whose oral dictation, it is reported, Milton had also begun in 1658.[2]

> [...] to the cause of Christendom above all – that I am pursuing after yet greater things if my strength suffice (nay, it will if God grant), and for their sake meanwhile am taking thought, and studying to make ready.[3]

Some surmise that while he dictated *PL*, the entire contents of *Defensio Prima* sometimes recurred and resounded in his mind, and greatly influenced the writing of *PL*. We encounter relevant parallels between the de-

* This paper is the revised version based on my oratorical presentation delivered at the Eighth International Milton Symposium held at Grenoble University on the 9th of June, 2005.

1 Robert W. Ayers presents this date: *Complete Prose Works of John Milton,* Vol. IV, Yale U. P., p. 295, pp. 1140–44; Martin Dzelzainis asserts that "the Defensio was … followed by … the corrected and enlarged 1658 duodecimo edition," commenting on one of Milton's additions in Chapter V of *Defensio Prima* that "this addition may reflect the uncertain state of affairs following the recent death of Cromwell": *John Milton Political Writings* (Cambridge UP, 1991), p. viii, and p. 151.

2 Cf. Christopher Hill says "Aubrey dated Milton's resumption of work on *Paradise Lost* to two years before the King came in…" and develops his discourse according this line: *Milton and the English Revolution* (Faber & Faber, 1977), p. 143.

3 *The Works of John Milton*, Vol. VII, eds Frank A. Patterson et al., Columbia U. P., p. 559, hereafter cited as *CE*.

scriptions in *PL* and *Defensio Prima*.[4] However, the 1658 edition of *Defensio Prima* seems to have enjoyed much less attention by Milton critics than other tracts of this period critical of English Republicanism. The 1658 edition of *Defensio Prima* plays an important role in relation with *PL*, and simultaneously, with the second edition of *The Readie and Easie Way to Establish a Free Commonwealth*. My aim in this paper is to reassess the 1658 edition of *Defensio Prima* in relation to the second edition of *Readie and Easie Way* and *PL*.

***

The first edition of *The Readie and Easie Way to Establish a Free Commonwealth* was published in the last week of February 1660. In that edition, Milton asserts that each county of England should be reorganized as a small commonwealth governed by "nobility and gentry", and that "[a] Grand or General Council" based on those political units, should be established. Moreover, its members were to be the "Rump members." However, on February 21 – just before the publication of the first edition – "the Secluded Members" conspiring with General Monck annulled the resolution of the Rump, and resolved the opening of new parliament on April 25, excluding the Rump members. Thus, Milton hurriedly revised the tract and published it in early April 1660.[5] It is noteworthy that at this time Milton continued to dictate *Paradise Lost* as he had stated in the concluding part of the 1658 edition of *Defensio Prima*.

The revised version of *The Readie and Easie Way* preserves his proposal for the establishment of "the Grand or General Council," while differing fundamentally from the first edition in other areas. Those expressions supporting the Rump members are eliminated (the recalled Rump Parliament itself no longer existed). The name of Sulla, the tyrannical Roman dictator,

4 Cf. Joan S. Bennett elaborately argues this problem in her "God, Satan, and King Charles: Milton's Royal Portraits," *PMLA* (1977), pp. 441–457; Yuko Kanakubo Noro, "The Making of Satan, Milton's Old Enemy – from *Pro Populo Anglicano Defensio* to *Paradise Lost*," *Bulletin of College of Humanities & Sciences, Nihon University* No. 65 (College of Humanities & Sciences, Nihon University, 2003), pp. 43–48. This paper of mine is based on the script delivered by the authoress at the Seventh International Milton Symposium held at South Carolina University, Beaufort on the 7th of June, 2002.

5 As for the publication dates of both editions, I follow the opinion of Robert W. Ayers in *CPW*. Vol. VII, pp. 343–344, and pp. 398–400.

appears on the title page, further clarifying Milton's reproach of General Monck.

As for the idiosyncratic features found in the second edition, Thomas N. Corns proves that "[t]he first edition contains rather more imagery than other late Miltonic pamphlets and the distinction is sharpened in the second edition, in which Milton introduces new material supercharged with imagery."[6] Keith W. Stavely discusses Milton's "coordinate, linear style" and "his more structured style ... alternate throughout the tract and create a pattern of futile but heroic political struggle."[7] Kevin Gilmartin analyses, in minute detail, Milton's fundamental political conceptions particularly in the second edition of *The Readie and Easie Way*. (He compares them to earlier writings such as *Areopagitica* and *The Tenure of Kings and Magistrates*.[8]) Reuben Sanchez elucidates the similarity (and difference) of *The Reason of Church Government* and *The Readie and Easie Way* based on the way Milton utilized Jeremiah.[9]

Most other critical attention seems to concentrate on Milton's prose works prior to *The Readie and Easie Way* (except *Defensio Prima*). According to Corns, "*The Readie and Easie Way* deserves comparison with Milton's more successful early political writings." It is therefore appropriate to examine the relation between *Defensio Prima* and *The Readie and Easie Way*, as well as the relation between *The Readie and Easie Way* and *PL*. It is noteworthy that Stanley Stewart compares, in minute detail, the first and second editions, and points out a link between the second edition and *PL*. He further affirms that it is important, in understanding *PL*, to remind us of the distinction between the "ordained" and "permissive will" of God.[10] Stewart refers to the links between the additional parts in pages, 449–450, and *PL*

6 *The Development of Milton's Prose Style* (Clarendon Press Oxford, 1982), pp. 44–45.

7 "The Style and Structure of Milton's *Readie and Easie Way*," *Milton Studies* Vol. 5, (University of Pittsburgh Press, 1968), pp. 269–287.

8 "History and Reform in Milton's *Readie and Easie Way*," *Milton Studies* Vol. 24 (University of Pittsburgh Press, 1989), pp. 17–41.

9 "From Polemic to Prophecy: Milton's Uses of Jeremiah in *The Reason of Church Government* and *The Readie and Easie Way*," *Milton Studies* Vol. 30, (University of Pittsburgh Press, 1993), pp. 27–44.

10 "Milton Revises *The Readie and Easie Way*", *Milton Studies* Vol. 20 (University of Pittsburgh Press, 1984), p. 217.

III, 665, 685; 183–84, and XII, 112–12, where Milton's concept that "God ordained the commonwealth for his 'peculiar people'" is presented.[11]

***

When the second edition of *The Readie and Easie Way* appeared, almost all of Milton's political expectations were overturned. Therefore, the whole atmosphere of the second edition is completely different from that of the first edition. While its content is said to be more pessimistic and more tragic, Milton's idealistic conceptions which have run through his political tracts are brought into clearer relief. They will subsequently converge into the ideal form of government in *PL*. Five years before the publication of Stewart's paper, Akira Arai, a prominent Japanese Miltonist, focused his attention on this point, and closely compared the first and the second editions of *The Readie and Easie Way*. Arai demonstrates the important link between the second edition and *PL*. In his paper, he points out the three main sweeping additions in the revised edition. The first part is on the law of nature (*CPW* 7: 409, ll. 14–420), the second on the society of ants (427, ll. 24–29), and the last is on "the Grand Council constituted to perpetuitie" (437, ll. 14–444). Arai asserts that all of changes merge into the ideal republican government presented in *PL*.[12]

The first added part shows Milton's assertion that "the Parliament of England…justly and magnanimously abolished" monarchy, "turning regal bondage into a free commonwealth," based on "the law of nature only, which is the only law of laws truly and properly to all mankinde fundamental," which are "beginning and the end of all Government." The councillors abolished "mere positive laws, neither natural nor moral." As is clear from the quotation above, "nature" and "moral" are closely interwoven in Milton's philosophy of politics. The second part is added at the point where Milton criticizes the Royalists, citing Proverbs 6:6–8 as follows:

11 It is noteworthy that the paragraph Stewart quotes from the second edition of *The Readie and Easie Way* resounds the paragraph from *Defensio Prima*; "Upon this argument verse 18 is in point: 'And ye shall cry out in that day because of your king which ye shall have chosen you; and the Lord will not hear you in that day.' Yea, that punishment awaited them for obstinately persisting to desire a king against God's refusal." (*The Works of John Milton*, Vol. VII, p. 101)

12 "Milton to Ouseihukko – Milton & the Restoration," *Milton Ronkou – Studies on Milton*, (Tokyo, Chukyo Publishing Company, 1979), pp. 53–66. As for my discussion in Section IV of this paper, I owe much to Arai's ideas presented in this book.

> Go to the Ant, thou sluggard, saith Solomon; consider her waies, and be wise; which having no prince, ruler, or lord, provides her meat in the summer, and gathers her food in the harvest. which evidently shews us, that they who think the nation undon without a king, though they look grave or haughtie, have not so much true spirit and understanding in them as a pismire;

Milton continues in the second edition, saying:

> [...] these diligent creatures [ants]... are set the example to impudent and ungoverned men, of a *frugal and self-governing democratie or Commonwealth*; safer and more thriving in the joint providence and counsel of many industrious equals, then under the single domination of one imperious Lord. [Emphasis mine]

It is clear that the society of ants symbolizes Milton's ideal republican government, and the moral features recommended in the quotation – industry, frugality, self-governance, equality, and preparation for the future – are repeatedly demonstrated with variations in his republican theories.[13]

Concerning the phrase, *"democratie or Commonwealth"*, we must keep in mind that Milton adopts the word, "commonalty" in addition to the "freedom" of the community members, juxtaposing the word in question with key terms like "Commonaltie or Commonwealth", "commonalties or [...] more general assemblies," and "other counties or commonalties."[14] Moreover, Milton declares "nobilitie and chief gentry" to be the constituents of the community. In the same paragraph, Milton clarifies his idea about the construction of "the Grand Council," which was rather ambiguous in the first edition. Considering this in light of the other addition on page 444, we grasp the three-layered governmental system proposed by Milton: First, "ordinary assemblies" constitute the main cities of each county. Secondly the representatives elected from the assemblies organize the "general assembly," and the representatives elected from this "general assembly" con-

13 Also, in the closing part of *Defensio Prima,* we remember, Milton admonishes his "countrymen", maintaining their moral features and maintaining their liberty: "[...] so ye shall prove that unarmed and in the midst of peace ye of all mankind have the highest courage to subdue [...] faction, avarice, the temptations of riches, and the corruptions ... and in maintaining your liberty shall show as great justice, temperance, and moderation as you have shown courage in freeing yourselves from slavery." (*The Works of John Milton*, Vol. VII, p. 553) It is apparent that in Milton, the moral features represented by virtues such as "industry, frugality, self-governing, equality, and preparation for future" are indispensable for the constituents in constructing and maintaining an ideal, free commonwealth.

14 *CPW* 7: 458–9.

stitute the "Grand or General Council". Here we recall the three-layered system of church government proposed by Milton in *The Reason of Church Government.* In this work "a general assembly" is based on the gathering of "little synod[s]" consisting of all "parochial consistor[ies]."[15] Arai therefore justly asserts that the origin of the three-layered governmental system in the second edition of *The Readie and Easie Way* is rooted in *The Reason of Church Government.* The third, significant addition in the second edition of *The Readie and Easie Way* is the paragraph proposing the "perpetual senate", which designates the "Grand or General Council".[16] The distinctive feature of Milton's idea is situated in the notion that this governmental system is supported only by "nobility and chief gentry" with "magnanimitie", which "govern[s] without a maister." (*CPW* 7: 448)

***

There is a significant link between the second edition of *The Readie and Easie Way* and *PL.* We encounter lines 24–32 of Book XII, where Nimrod, the first tyrant of "proud ambitious heart," "dispossess / Concord and *law of Nature*" being "not content / With fair *equality*, *fraternal state*" (Emphasis mine). Secondly, we notice lines 484–9 of Book VII, describing the "*Parsimonious emmet*, *provident* / *Of future*, in small room *large heart* (i.e., magnanimity) enclosed, / Pattern of just *equality* perhaps / Hereafter, join'd in her popular Tribes / Of *Commonalty*" (Emphasis mine). It is significant that the distinctive features of ant society depicted in the second edition of *The Readie and Easie Way* – magnanimity, frugality, equality, and preparation for future – are represented in these lines. Moreover, "commonalty", one of the most significant key words in Milton's republicanism, appears here only once in the epic. It is manifest that Milton depicts an emmet as the symbol of the representative member of his free commonwealth of three-layered government. Moreover, the Creation of Adam belongs immediately after

15 *CPW* 1: 789. None of the critics cited in my paper refers to the link between the three-layered governmental systems in *The Reason of Church Government* and *The Readie and Easie Way* except Akira Arai.

16 The similar proposals are offered by Sir Henry Vane and Henry Stubbe (*CPW* 7: 181). Laura L Knoppers refers to Milton's idea of establishing the Senate, which will produce an ideal community. "*The Readie and Easie Way* and the English Jeremiad," eds David Loewenstein and James G. Turner, *Politics, Poetics, and Hermeneutics in Milton's Prose* (Cambridge UP, 1990), p. 220.

this scene, where our ancestral father is "endu'd / With Sanctity of Reason [...] *Govern the rest, self-knowing [...] Magnanimous* to correspond with Heav'n" (ll. 505–11; emphasis mine) Adam in this scene represents the ideal governor as one of "nobility and chief gentry" advocated in *The Readie and Easie Way*.[17] For the third link between the second edition of *The Readie and Easie Way* and *PL*, Arai introduces lines 224–6 of Book XII, "there they shall found / Their *government*, and their *great Senate* choose / Through the twelve Tribes, to rule by Laws ordain'd." (Emphasis mine) On top of it, the word, "Senate", appears only once in the epic.[18] Milton here uses "Senate" instead of "Elders" because he casts a stern glance towards the Presbyters (meaning "elders") since they connived with Royalists, in promoting the Restoration.

***

My first aim in this section is to show that Milton's fundamental republican ideas, clarified in the significant links between the second edition of *The Readie and Easie Way* and *PL*, existed in *Defensio Prima* to some extent. I then affirm that the revision of *Defensio Prima* influenced the second edition of *The Readie and Easie Way*. These fundamental republican ideas are produced, elaborated and weave their way from *Defensio Prima*, through *The Readie and Easie Way* to *PL*.

In the first place, Milton tempers and elaborates the law of nature in his controversy with Salmasius. Quite a few arguments on the law of nature develop (with variations) in *Defensio Prima*. In *Defensio Regia*, Salmasius insists that the "law of kings arises from...the law of nature" (*CE*, VII, 73) while Milton asserts that "[w]hen people are bound by such an oath, a king turned tyrant or rotted with cowardice releases them by breaking his oath; *justice* herself releases them; *the very law of nature* releases them" (*CE*, VII, 267, emphasis mine). Here we are reminded of the phrase, "mere positive laws, neither natural nor moral" (*CPW* 7: 413) because "nature" and "justice" are regarded as a set phrase equivalent in meaning here. Milton then

17 Arai also refers to the line 557 of Book VIII, where Adam's eye catches "Greatness of mind and nobleness" in Eve. Therefore, it is safe to state that Milton admits woman to be the governor of her community as well as man at least before the Fall.

18 Eleven years after Arai, David Loewenstein also elucidates this link between the second edition of *The Readie and Easie Way* and *PL*. *Milton and the Drama of History* (Cambridge UP, 1990), p. 123.

declares that "the law of God does exactly agree with the law of nature," and assures us that the "law of nature is a principle implanted in all men's minds, to regard the good of mankind in so far as men are united together in societies." The law of nature for Milton is the law of the people. It defends their welfare and punishes those (even kings) who encroach the rights of the people. This assertion agrees with the description of the natural law in the second edition of *Readie and Easie Way* and the depiction of Nimrod in *PL*.

Secondly, the metaphor of ants in the second edition of *Readie and Easie Way* and *PL* is a kind of convergence of Aristotle's and Virgil's descriptions, biblical depictions (*Proverb*. vi, 6; xxx, 25) and the information of the common encyclopaedists of Milton's day. Milton adds one more feature, "magnanimity," to the ant imagery, and makes it the model of the ideal member of his free commonwealth.

On the other hand, the bee imagery recalls the metaphor of bees in *Defensio Regia* presented by Salmasius as the symbol of "commonwealth" with harmless kings. Milton exposes his adversary's incoherence, citing *Apparatus ad Primatum Papae*, where Salmasius mentions some divines of the Council of Trent who utilize the bees' image as the symbol of the Popish supremacy (*CE,* VII, 87). According to the notes of John Carey and Alastair Fowler, the bee exemplifies civil merits as well as the ant.[19] In Milton's case, however, the commonalty of ants presents a striking contrast to the ill-governed gathering of bees, where the "swarming" female bees feed their husbands, and drone them (*PL*, VII, ll. 484–490). Their system of governing is a reversed form of tyranny, where female and male bees are unequal, confronting head-on the ideal community advocated by Milton, where male and female support each other on equal terms. Significantly, Delilah in *Samson Agonistes* proposes this satanic wife-and-husband relation and tempts Samson. The bee imagery in *PL* closely links the image of "Satan and his peers" and the word, "swarm" (I, l. 767; l. 776) with its sibilant sound, "the hiss of rustling wings" (l. 768). In the middle of Book X, Satan, after succeeding in the temptation of our first ancestors, triumphantly gives a victory speech (though illusory) over God in front of his fellow fiends in Hell. Finishing his hyperbolical speech, Satan awaits "Universal applause". Instead, he is forced to exit from the stage of *PL* forever by "A dismal universal *hiss*, the sound of public scorn" (Emphasis mine). Simultaneously he is metamor-

19 *The Poems of John Milton* (Longmans, 1968), p. 804.

phosed into "A monstrous Serpent." Hissing re-echoes hissing. The whole of Hell resounds with the hissing sounds uttered by all kinds of fiendish serpents.[20] We understand "hiss" in line 573 in two ways: first as the harsh noise of serpents and as in hissing an actor off the stage. Oddly, Le Comte makes no mention of this second meaning in his *A Dictionary of Puns in Milton's English Dictionary* (1981).

In the third place, the word "senate" appears a number of times in *Defensio Prima.* However, I will cite only one example to demonstrate the relation between the senate and the magistrates – including kings, because the king is only a nomination when one magistrate governs the community, Milton asserts,

> What is certain [...] is that the Consul both, and all other magistrates, were bound to obey the Senate, whenever the Senate and the people decided that the interest of the commonwealth so required.

Milton inserted the following passage, after revising the 1651 folio[21]:

> For this point I have abundant authority in Marcus Tullius's oration for Sestius [...]. "Our ancestors, when *they had thrown off the power of the kings*, created offices to last one year, but in such wise that *over the commonwealth they set the deliberative assembly of the Senate to last forever*; *that the members were to be elected into this assembly by the people as a whole*; and *that entrance into that exalted body should stand open to the industry and virtue* [my translation from the Latin, 'virtuti'] of all the citizens. They stationed the Senate as the guardian, protector, and champion of the State. This body's authority it was that they would have the magistrates employ, and would have them be, as it were, servants of *this most weighty assembly* [*gravissimi consilii*]" (*CE,* VII, 371–3; emphasis mine).

Cicero is always Milton's chief mentor in *Defensio Prima,* always encouraging him and showing "the ready and easy way to establish a free commonwealth." The situation where Milton and his countrymen found themselves is strikingly similar to the time when Cicero wrote *Pro Sestio.* The idea of the perpetual senate, elected by the community members, clearly appears here. The elected should be of "industry and virtue", and the assembly is called "the grandest council" *[gravissimi consilii]*.

20 Yuko K. Noro, "The Making of Satan, Milton's Old Enemy," p. 44. In this paper, I discuss the link of imageries between Satan & Milton's political adversaries, Salmasius, Alexander More, and Charles I.

21 Dzelzainis, p. 187.

As for the three-layered governmental system, no mention or hint is made in the quotation above. In other place of *Defensio Prima* Milton develops his idea of political society in verbal retort with Salmasius, utilizing three Latin words, "civitas" (county), "communitas" (city) and "municipium" (town), as *The Manner of Parliament* advocates (*CE,* VII, 446–7). They are not used merely as the scales of certain administrative division of regions, but reveal Milton's concepts of community. All of the concepts connote the idea of a "self-governing" body politic regardless of their size. The most important point for Milton is not the visible grandeur of the communities, but the spirit.

Salmasius says that one of a king's offices is to develop villages into towns, and towns into cities. *(Regis est, de vico municipium, de eo civitatem facere, ergo illos creat qui constituunt domum inferiorent.)* In response to this, Milton declares, *"etiam agris populus est populus"* (*CE,* VII, 428), meaning that people are people even in the fields. Here Milton awakens his audiences obsessed by the outward shaping of communities, and reminds them of the original spirit of communities.

It was not yet time for Milton to combine the two different governmental systems – Ciceronian "grandest council" standing perpetual, and the system advocated in *The Manner of Parliament* with the Presbyterian three-layered system of church government outlined in *The Reason of Church Government.* It took two more years, and more serious situations for Milton to establish the concept of the "Grand Council or the Senate" firmly founded on the multi-layered system.

It is clear that the 1658 revision of *Defensio Prima* directly influenced the second edition of *The Readie and Easie Way,* and the creation of *Paradise Lost,* and indirectly did so through the second edition of *The Readie and Easie Way.* When there was some probability for Milton to change reality, he was preoccupied with how discourse adapted itself to the political process of real world. However, after he realized all of his expectations for reality had disintegrated, his ideals moved him to revise *The Readie and Easie Way.* He employed all the knowledge and wisdom he acquired through diligent industry to express himself in Latin, his second language. Milton advocates establishing a free commonwealth, "communitas libera" towards his audience repeatedly in various styles and structures of arguments: twice in 1651, in 1658, February and April in 1660, and 1667, in Latin and in English, in oratorical style, in prose, and in epic. His voice has reached us beyond the "Fire Walls" of space and time.

Georgi VASILEV

Philosophie et figures dualistes dans les pamphlets de John Milton

Milton, les sectes dualistes (bogomiles, cathares, vaudois, lollards) & la Réforme protestante

De nombreuses études ont été consacrées au caractère spécifique des vues religieuses de Milton. Nous pouvons citer l'une des plus récentes, celle d'A. D. Nuttall, *The Alternative Trinity: Gnostic Heresy in Marlowe, Milton and Blake* (1998): l'auteur utilise le terme «quasi-gnostique»[1] pour décrire la pensée religieuse de Milton; or, nous savons qu'au Moyen-âge, le gnosticisme s'est répandu à travers le bogomilisme et les courants qui en sont dérivés.[2] La même année, dans le recueil *Milton and Heresy* (1998), Stephen M. Fallon voyait chez Milton un arminien calviniste («unmistakable Arminianism [...] complicated by Calvinist vestiges»).[2] Le titre de la monographie de Neil Forsyth sur le *Paradis perdu*, *The Satanic Epic* (2002), accentue aussi l'aspect

1 A. D. Nuttall, *The Alternative Trinity: Gnostic Heresy in Marlowe, Milton and Blake*. Oxford, Oxford UP, 1998, p. 127.

2 Le terme bogomilisme provient du prénom du prêtre Bogomil (du bulgare «Bog», Dieu, et «mil», gentil, d'où *Bogomil*: «celui qui est cher à Dieu»; cf. Théophile), fondateur d'une secte dualiste néomanichéenne au Xe siècle. Les Bogomiles propageaient l'idée que l'Univers avait deux principes: le bien et le mal, Dieu et le diable, la lumière et les ténèbres. Le monde céleste et l'âme représentent le principe du bien, le monde extérieur et le corps humain, celui du mal. Nos corps représentent une prison pour l'âme divine, il est nécessaire de les faire périr par le travail et le jeûne pour la délivrance des âmes. Les Bogomiles niaient les institutions politiques et religieuses. Le tsar, les boyards et le clergé étaient considérés comme le diable et le servant fidèlement. C'est pourquoi le peuple ne devait pas se soumettre à ceux-ci. Ils niaient aussi tous les symboles et les rituels de l'église, ne respectaient pas la croix, car, d'après leur doctrine, elle servait le déshonneur et la mort du Sauveur.
Par «ses courants dérivés», l'auteur pense surtout aux Cathares et aux Vaudois.

hétérodoxe de la théologie de Milton: «*Paradise Lost* is not an orthodox poem and it needs to be rescued from its orthodox critics.»[3]

Certains auteurs ont approché intuitivement la présence de la philosophie dualiste dans le poème de Milton sans la nommer directement, comme S. H. Gurteen, à la fin du XIXe siècle, dans *The Epic of the Fall of Man: A Comparative Study on Caedmon, Dante and Milton.*[4] Il y a soixante-dix ans, Arthur Lovejoy formulait la thèse de l'heureuse faute dans un article demeuré célèbre, "Milton and the Paradox of the Fortunate Fall,"[5] thèse reprise récemment par Hugh White: «La participation de Milton en une tradition ancienne d'après laquelle la Chute est une *felix culpa*, un événement finalement heureux, puisqu'il rapporte plus de bien que nous aurions eu sans lui.»[6] Cependant cette «tradition ancienne» reste inexpliquée. Nous pouvons encore énumérer d'autres recherches, d'autres trouvailles partielles, d'autres analogies vagues. Il ne faut pas omettre les efforts de Maurice Kelley, l'un des miltoniens les plus éminents du XXe siècle, éditeur du *De Doctrina Christiana*, ni les publications de Barbara Lewalski.[7]

Mais ne vaut-il pas mieux remplacer la recherche intuitive en répondant à deux questions concrètes:

- Quelles sont les sources historiques de cette hérésie?
- Quelles sont ses expressions directes dans les traités de John Milton?

Notre travail deviendra plus productif quand les faits seront jugés d'une précision sociologique. Encore ne faut-il pas négliger les autodéfinitions du poète lui-même – peut-être même faut-il commencer par là. Elles sont présentes dans *Areopagitica* et dans *Eikonoklastes* où le poète, tout en rejetant l'institution épiscopale, annonce sa sympathie et son admiration pour les églises hérétiques des vaudois et des cathares:

> I add that many Western Churches Eminent for thir Faith and good Works, and settl'd above four hundred years agoe in *France*, in *Piemont* and *Bohemia*, have both taught and practis'd the same Doctrin, and not admitted of Episcopacie among them.

3 "*Paradise Lost* is not an orthodox poem and it needs to be rescued from its orthodox critics." Neil Forsyth, *The Satanic Epic*. Princeton: Princeton UP, 2002, p. 1.

4 New York. 1896.

5 ELH4 (1937): 161–79.

6 Hugh White, *Langland, Milton and felix culpa*. *The Review of English Studies*, New Series, Vol. 45, No. 179 (Aug., 1994): 336–356. P. 336.

7 Voir, dans *Studies in English Literature* Vol. 32, 4 (1992), les articles de Barbara Lewalski, Christopher Hill et de Maurice Kelley.

> And if we may beleeve what the Papists themselves have writt'n of these churches, which they call *Waldenses*, I find it in a Book writt'n almost four hundred years since, and set forth in the *Bohemian* Historie,[8] that those Churches in *Piemont* have held the same Doctrin and Goverment, since the time that *Constantine* with his mischeivous donations poyson'd *Silvester* and the whole Church.[9]

Cette citation atteste que Milton connaissait bien l'histoire des églises dites hérétiques des XIIe-XIVe siècles, et l'allusion à «un livre publié il y a quatre cents ans» pourrait laisser penser qu'il a travaillé à partir de documents originaux. Mentionnant expressément l'Eglise vaudoise, pour laquelle il avait une affection particulière,[10] Milton évoque indirectement l'Eglise cathare quand il parle de «d'Eglise de France»; il cite encore l'Eglise de Bohême, c'est-à-dire l'Eglise hussite. De cette manière, le poète devient un historien audacieux, car il établit un lien, il crée une continuité historique entre la Réformation anglaise et les vaudois (dernier quart du XIIe siècle), sans oublier l'influence des cathares et l'affiliation des hussites.

Avec le respect particulier qu'il a pour John Wycliffe, Milton dévoile une autre source d'idées importante. De cette façon, il trace un contexte intégral, embrassant vaudois, cathares, hussites et Wycliffe (cela veut dire aussi les lollards). Son affinité pour l'héritage de Wycliffe est nettement exprimée. *Areopagitica* décrit Wycliffe et Hus comme les initiateurs du premier conflit important avec la papauté:

> for about that time *Wicklef* and *Husse* growing terrible, were they who first drove the Papall Court to a stricter policy of prohibiting.[11]

S'il place Wycliffe au fondement de la Réforme anglaise, cela veut dire qu'il se voit lui-même, en tant que réformateur, comme son héritier: "our *Wicklefs* preaching at which all the succeeding *Reformers* more effectually lighted their *Tapers*."[12] Il se livre à une vraie apologie de Wycliffe, en le proclamant

8 NDR: Selon l'éditeur de *CPW* 3 (Merritt Y. Hughes), Milton fait référence à *The history of the Bohemian persecution, from the begining of their conversion to Christianity in the year 894. to the year 1632. Ferdinand the 2. of Austria. Reigning. In which the unheard of secrets of policy, consells, arts, and dreadfull judgements are exhibited* (Londres, 1650).

9 *Eikonoklastes*, *CPW* 3: 513–14.

10 Voir William B. Hunter, "Milton and the Waldensians", *Studies in English Literature, 1500–1900*, SEL Vol. 11, No. 1 (1971), pp. 153–164

11 *CPW* 2: 502: "for about that time *Wicklef* and *Husse* growing terrible, were they who first drove the Papall Court to a stricter policy of prohibiting.".

12 *Of Reformation*, *CPW* 1: 525–26.

à l'origine de la Réformation européenne. Selon Milton, une réalisation plus heureuse de l'œuvre de Wycliffe sur l'île d'Albion aurait été la gloire de la nation anglaise, au point qu'elle serait connue comme le centre névralgique de la Réformation de l'Europe entière:

> And had it not bin the obstinat perversenes of our Prelats against the divine and admirable spirit of Wicklef, to suppresse him as a schismatic and innovator, perhaps neither the Bohemian Husse and Jerom, no nor the name of Luther, or of Calvin had bin ever known: the glory of reforming all our neighbours had bin compleatly ours.[13]

Milton, dans son zèle réformateur, lui qui appelle de ses vœux «une réforme de la Réformation»,[14] se reconnaît pleinement dans l'esprit et la pratique des églises hérétiques, il se voit clairement dans la lignée de Wycliffe.[15] En glorifiant son «esprit divin et admirable», Milton rend à Wycliffe l'un des hommages les plus appuyés à l'un de ses compatriotes. Cela signifie que le lien de parenté spirituelle entre Wycliffe et Milton, que William Summers[16] est le seul à relever au début du XXe siècle, révèle une source essentielle de l'idéologie spécifique miltonienne.

Expressions doctrinales

Cet engagement de Milton en faveur des mouvements hérétiques (bogomiles, cathares, vaudois, lollards) culmine, cette fois de manière complètement ouverte et passionnée, dans son poème *On the Late Massacre in Piemont.* Le poète dénonce, l'année même où elles sont perpétrées, les cruelles représailles catholiques à l'encontre des vaudois du Piemont le 24 avril 1655:

13 *CPW* 2: 552. Milton reconnaît l'influence des réformateurs européens en Angleterre, tout en faisant l'effort de ne pas négliger la contribution propre de la Réformation anglaise: "we have looked so long upon the blaze that Zuinglius and Calvin hath beaconed up to us, that we are stark blind." (Id., 550)

14 *Areopagitica*, *CPW* 2: 553.

15 Voir Jean Duvernoy, «Cathares et Vaudois sont-ils des précurseurs de la Réforme?», *Etudes théologiques et religieuses*, Montpellier 1987 (3), pp. 377–384.

16 Summers, William H. *Our Lollard Ancestors*. London. 1904, p. 29.
Comparés à Summers, les autres auteurs, admettant une relation Wycliffe-Milton, sont beaucoup plus hésitants. A. L. Rowse mentionne une influence possible de Wyclif dans son livre *Milton the Puritan. Portrait of a Mind* (Londres, Macmillan, 1977; Lanham, MD: University Press of America, 1985).

Avenge O lord thy slaughter'd saints, whose bones
Lie scatter'd on the Alpine mountains cold
Ev'n them who kept thy truth so pure of old
When all our fathers worshipp'd stok and stones
Forget not: in thy book record their groans.[17]

Certains spécialistes des hérésies médiévales pourraient objecter que les victimes au Piémont ont été des vaudois et que, par conséquent, le poète s'est déclaré ami d'une Eglise qui n'est pas dualiste. Les choses prennent un tour différent si nous en venons aux faits. Il semble que Milton fasse la distinction entre vaudois et cathares. Il est le champion d'une Eglise où le Verbe de Dieu sera prêché en langue vernaculaire, l'Evangile sera à la portée des croyants et ils n'auront pas besoin des évêques. C'est l'usage commun des vaudois et des cathares et, pour être fidèle à la vérité, il faut préciser que les cathares ont été les premiers à traduire, avant Valdo, le Nouveau Testament en provençal, et que c'est plutôt Valdo qui prête et adopte pour sa communauté le modèle de l'Eglise cathare. Cette vue d'organisation, plutôt de la réorganisation de l'Eglise, propre aux cathares et aux vaudois, devient une ligne de développement dans l'histoire de la Réformation anglaise, visible dans la vie et l'activité de Wycliffe (et des lollards), Tyndale et Milton. Seulement, Milton y ajoute des arguments strictement dualistes, particulièrement nombreux.

1. Par exemple dans le poème déjà cité, il dit: "When all our fathers worshipp'd stocks and stones," ce qui est la locution connue des lollards – les dualistes anglais – qui, suivant les croyances bogomilo-cathares, s'attaquaient par ces mots aux icones.[18]
2. Il célèbre, à sa manière, le principe fondamental du dualisme, quand il parle de la connaissance du bien et du mal: "the knowledge of good and

17 John Milton: *Selected Shorter Poems and Prose*. Ed. Tony Davies. London, New York, Routledge, 1988/9, p. 137.
NDR: Comme l'atteste son *Commonplace Book* (*CPW* 1: 379), Milton s'appuie sur l'*Histoire ecclésiastique des églises réformées, recueillies en quelques vallées de Piedmont, et circonvoisines, autrefois appelées Eglises vaudoises, commençant dès l'an 1160 de nostre seigneur, et finissant en l'an 1643; par Pierre GILLES, pasteur de la Tour. Genève, chez Jean de Tournes, 1644.*

18 Expression, mise par écrit au 8 août, l'an 1511, au procès contre les lollards de Kent. *Heresy Proceedings 1511–12*. Edited by N. Tanner. Kent. 1997, p. 85. Sur la base d'une étude comparée ("Bogomils and Lollards. Dualistic motives in England during the Middle Ages," *Etudes Balkaniques*, Vol. 29.1 (1993): 97–111), je décris la parenté entre cathares et lollards.

evill as two twins cleaving together leapt forth into the World."[19] Cela rappelle sans équivoque le concept primordial des cathares, enregistré par le fameux inquisiteur Bernard Gui: «La secte, l'hérésie et les partisans dévoyés des Manichéens reconnaissent et confessent deux Dieux ou deux Seigneurs, à savoir un Dieu bon et un Dieu mauvais.»[20]

3. Les comparaisons pourraient être plus détaillées. La négation des icônes et de la croix est un trait connu des dualistes, comme en témoigne Euthymius Zigabenus, dans *Panoplia dogmatica* (XIe siècle): «Ils méprisent les saintes icônes et les appellent idoles des païens, argent et or, œuvres des mains humaines.»[21] La formule «œuvre des mains humaines» est enregistrée au procès contre les lollards de Kent, pendant les années 1511–12.[22] Milton aussi attaque les icônes, les définissant comme des idoles ("images and idols"), il qualifie leur adoration de déviation du vrai devoir chrétien. Il écrit: "stones & Pillars, and Crucifixes have now the honour, and the almes due to *Christs* living members."[23] Le poète rejette les louanges iconiques offertes au Christ comme autant d'actes d'idolâtrie.[24] Il fait preuve d'une connaissance approfondie de l'histoire quand il étaye son attitude iconoclaste avec une allusion aux empereurs byzantins Léon III (717–741) et Constantin V Copronyme (741–775). Milton revisite l'histoire de l'Eglise officielle pour en extraire des précédents soutenant la thèse dualiste, d'ailleurs finissante, et il félicite de l'audace de ces empereurs byzantins prompts à abattre les images superstitieuses.[25]

19 *CPW* 2: 514.

20 Bernard Gui, *Manuel de l'inquisiteur*. Vol. I, éd. G. Mollat. Paris, 1926, «Les classiques de l'histoire de France au Moyen Age», 8/9, p. 10: «Manicheorum itaque secta et heresies et ejus devii sectatores duos Deos aut duos Dominos asserunt and fatentur, benignum Deum videlicet et malignum…»

21 Ἀτιμάζουσι και τας σεβασμίος εικονας, ταε ιδωλα λέγοντες των εθνων, αρύριον και χρυσιον, ἐργα χειρων ανθρωπων. In: *Euthymii Zigabeni de haeresi bogomilorum narratio*. Gerhart Ficker, *Die Phundagiagiten*, Leipzig: Barth, 1908, p. 97.

22 "… made with many hands." In: *Heresy Proceedings 1511–12*. Edited by N. Tanner. Kent. 1997, p. 85.

23 *Of Reformation*, *CPW* 1: 547.

24 Id., 523: "pageanted about, like a dreadfull Idol."

25 *Eikonoklastes*, *CPW* 3: 343: Alors que Charles Ier avait été «L'Image du roi» *(Eikon Basilikè)*, Milton propose «L'Iconoclaste», *Eikonoklastes*, "the famous Surname of many Greek emperors, who in thir zeal to the command of God, after long tradition of Idolatry in the Church, took courage, and broke all superstitious Images to peeces."

4. Un vestige du dualisme transparaît dans l'opinion compliquée et distante de Milton à l'égard de la croix. L'objection des bogomiles contre la croix est bien connue; citons, par exemple, le prêtre Cosmas: «ils parlent de la croix de cette manière: comment la vénérer? Parce que les juifs ont crucifié sur elle le fils de Dieu, elle est très détestable à Dieu.»[26] On retrouve cette exclamation bogomile transplantée chez les lollards anglais – le couturier William Hardy de Mundham exprime le même sentiment: "and no more worship ne reverence oweth be do to the crosee than oweth be do to the galwes whiche men be hanged on."[27] Le prêtre bulgare Cosmas dans sa polémique contre les bogomiles nous rappelle aussi que les hérétiques «coupent les croix et en font des outils».[28] Milton de nouveau témoigne d'une compétence remarquable en histoire en nous signalant qu'il connaît bien «ces énormités du vulgaire» en Angleterre et son information est évidemment l'une des plus anciennes sur la pratique des lollards.[29] Les mêmes manifestations lollardiennes sont documentées par le tribunal qui juge les lollards à Norwich. L'un des accusés se prononce pour la destruction systématique des images: "all ymages owyn to be destroyed and do away."[30]

Le poète évite ces opinions extrêmes, il transforme la négation dualiste de la croix en une critique plus ou moins rationaliste de l'adoration aveugle de la croix, qui était un lieu commun de la vie ecclésiastique avant la Réformation. Il avertit qu'une vénération exagérée du crucifix pourrait être nuisible, par exemple, au moment du baptême, quand le prêtre «gratte» de manière mécanique une croix sur le front de l'enfant.[31] Il décoche une flèche aussi contre Constantin et sa mère Hélène, percevant comme un acte de fétichisme le fait que l'on ait fixé un des clous

26 Презвитер Козма. Беседа против богомилите – in: Стара българска литература 2. София. 1982, p. 34.

27 Norman P. Tanner, *Heresy Trials in the Diocese of Norwich, 1428–31*. London, Royal Historical Society, 1977, p. 154.

28 Презвитер Козма, op. cit., p. 33.

29 *Eikonoklastes*, *CPW* 3: 535: "Not to justify what enormities the Vulgar may committ in the rudeness of thir zeal, we need but onely instance how he bemoanes *the pulling down of Crosses* and other superstitious Monuments, as the effect *of a popular and deceitful Reformation*. How little this savours of a Protestant, is too easily perceav'd."

30 Norman P. Tanner, op. cit., p. 86.

31 *Eikonoklastes*, *CPW* 3: 523: "Then was baptism, changed into a kind of exorcism and water, sanctified by Christ's institute, thought little enough to wash off the original spot, without the scratch or cross impression of a priest's forefinger."

ayant servi à la crucifixion de Jésus sur l'heaume de Constantin ou sur la bride de son cheval en guise d'amulette.[32] Finalement, il ne croit pas que la découverte de la croix de Jésus par Constantin et Hélène soit un exploit. Cette distance miltonienne envers la croix est confirmée par ses mots, que si cette découverte était vraiment importante, elle aurait été faite encore par les disciples du Christ.[33]

5. Une autre influence dualiste évidente sont les expressions employées par Milton qui parle des «bons hommes» *(good men)*[34], plus particulièrement, des «bons hommes et saints» *(good men and Saints)*,[35] des «milliers de bons hommes» *(thousands of good men)*.[36] Dans la structure des bogomiles, des cathares et des lollards, c'est le nom de leurs leaders, autrement appelés «les parfaits». Le contexte dualiste est confirmé par l'opposition entre les «good men» de «l'évêché» et le langage mordant, adressé à l'Eglise officielle. Tandis que les cathares qualifient leur Eglise d'«Eglise bonne», d'«Eglise de Jésus-Christ», ils traitent l'Eglise catholique comme la «mère de fornications, grande Babylone, courtisane et basilique de diable, synagogue de Satan».[37] C'est avec de tels mots enflammés que Milton attaque les évêques quatre cents ans plus tard:

> They are not *Bishops*, GOD and all *good Men* (my emphasis) know they are not, that have fill'd this Land with late confusion and violence; but a Tyrannicall crew and Corporation of Impostors, that have blinded and abus'd the World so long under that Name.[38]

John Milton et le transfert des manuscrits vaudois-cathares

Notre liste des preuves et des analogies pourrait être largement augmentée. Mais il est temps de poser une autre question: est-il possible de supposer des contacts réels, documentés, de Milton avec des traditions, des fonds de

32 Ibidem, 556.
33 Ibidem.
34 *The Reason of Church-governement*, *CPW* 1: 795.
35 Id., 805.
36 Ibidem, 792.
37 Gui, B., op. cit., p. 10
38 *Of Reformation*, *CPW* 1: 537.

l'hérésie dualiste et ses ramifications? Puisqu'il exalte le nom de Wycliffe et surtout son activité réformatrice, nous devrions accepter les œuvres de John Wycliffe, son héritage, comme une source importante, bien connue du poète.

Il y a encore une autre aventure plus ouverte, plus saillante, qui mérite d'être présentée, plutôt rappelée au public miltonien. Revenons au moment où Milton écrit son poème *On the Late Massacre in Piemont* (1655). On sait bien que Cromwell a mené une intense campagne diplomatique pour arrêter les persécutions contre les vaudois au Piémont, ce qui lui a valu le titre de «capo e prottetore» du protestantisme dans certaines relations vénitiennes, comme le dit ce grand critique russe du 19ème siècle sur le catharisme, Nikolay Osokin.[39] Les documents de cette mission ont été préparés par le secrétaire des langues étrangères (Latin Secretary), Milton; il existe même une estampe du XIXe siècle, intitulée «O. Cromwell et J. Milton protestant contre le massacre des vaudois» *(O. Cromwell and J. Milton protesting against the massacre of the Waldensians)*. Samuel Morland, qui a été envoyé en Europe pour accomplir cette tâche, a réalisé encore une autre mission importante: il a reçu des mains de Jean Léger, pasteur de la vallée de Lucerne et modérateur du Piémont, une collection des manuscrits vaudois,[40] qui sera léguée à l'Université de Cambridge en 1658. Les connaissances approfondies de Morland en cette matière sont visibles dans son livre *History of the Evangelical Churches in the Valleys of Piedmont* (1658).

Cette histoire est complétée par une découverte du 20e siècle, que l'on doit au philologue belge Théo Venckeeler: celui-ci a découvert un texte cathare dans une collection similaire, arrivée en Angleterre à la même époque, cette fois-ci de Dublin. Il s'avère que le manuscrit, connu sous la référence A.6.10 (aujourd'hui MS 269), contient deux traités cathares d'origine provençale, le premier dédié à l'organisation de l'Eglise cathare, le deuxième présentant une glose sur la prière cathare principale «Pater Noster».[41] La conclusion de Théo Venckeeler est étayée par Anne-Claire Jolliot-

39 Осокин, Н. История альбигойцев и их времени. Москва. 2000, p. 183.

40 Brenon, A. *Localisation des manuscrits vaudois*. Turin, Centro studi piemontesi, 1978, p. 196.

41 Théo Venckeleer, «Un recueil cathare: le manuscrit A.6.10 de la ‹Collection vaudoise› de Dublin. I. Une apologie», *Revue belge de philologie et d'histoire* 38 (1960), 815–834. «Un recueil cathare: le manuscrit A.6.10 de la ‹Collection vaudoise› de Dublin. II. Une glose sur le Pater», *Revue belge de philologie et d'histoire* 39 (1961), 759–793.

Brenon.[42] D'ailleurs, de tels mélanges des manuscrits vaudois et cathares, correspondant aux jonctions partielles tardives des deux communautés pendant les persécutions, sont signalées par Nikolay Osokin et Jean Duvernoy.

Ainsi, l'Angleterre au XVIe siècle s'est-elle procurée des collections vaudoises cathares essentielles et il est logique de supposer que Milton ait pu avoir un contact immédiat avec ces sources, d'autant qu'il était partie prenante dans la défense des vaudois. L'activité du trio Milton / Cromwell / Morland sur ce point-là est bien documentée.

Cependant, il est nécessaire de formuler une nuance: tout en empruntant le langage polémique des dualistes, Milton a gardé un respect pour certaines figures importantes de l'Eglise officielle. Son but n'est pas de créer une contre-église, imitant la vie clandestine des bogomiles, des cathares, des vaudois ou des lollards; il veut une Eglise nationale, un foyer spirituel social, mais elle doit être réformée conformément à la pratique simplifiée des dualistes, qui d'ailleurs reproduisent la communauté primitive de Jésus et de ses apôtres. Il s'agit de changer l'Eglise nationale en adoptant le potentiel réformateur des dualistes. Cette tactique nous fait voir Milton non comme un crypto-hérétique, mais comme un réformateur radical qui récupère l'humilité organisationnelle et la richesse spirituelle des communautés hérétiques du Moyen-âge.

Références

Cyrillic

Презвитер Козма. "Беседа против богомилите". *Стара българска литература.2. Ораторска проза.* София. 1982.

Осокин, Николай. *История альбигойцев и их времени.* Москва. 2000. First edition in 1869, Казань.

42 Anne-Claire Jolliot-Brenon, *Les livres des Vaudois. Catalogue.* Ecole pratique des hautes études. Thèse. V-e section – sciences religieuses. Annuaire. Tomes LXXX-LXXXI. Extraits du fascicule II, p. 71.

Latin

Döllinger, Ignaz von. *Dokumente vornehmlich zur Geschichte der Valdesier und Katharer herausgegeben.* T. II. Munich, C. H. Beck, 1890, repr. Darmstadt, Wissenschaftliche Buchgesellschaft, 1968.

Duvernoy, Jean. «Cathares et Vaudois sont-ils des précurseurs de la Réforme?», *Etudes théologiques et religieuses*, Montpellier 1987 (3), pp. 377–384.

"Euthymii Zigabeni de haeresi bogomilorum narration." In: Ficker, G. *Die Phundagiagiten.* Leipzig, 1908

Fasciculi Zizaniorum magistri Johannis Wyclif cum tritico. Ed. by Walter W. Shirley. London. 1858

Gui, Bernard. *Manuel de l'inquisiteur.* T. I. Paris, 1926.

Hudson, Ann. *Selections from English Wycliffite Writings.* Cambridge, Cambridge UP, 1978.

Hunter, William B. "Milton and the Waldensians," *Studies in English Literature, 1500–1900*, SEL Vol. 11, No. 1 (1971), pp. 153–164.

Kent Heresy Proceedings 1511–12. Edited by Norman Tanner, Maidstone, Kent Archaeological Society, 1997.

Lovejoy, Arthur. "Milton and the Paradox of the Fortunate Fall," *A Journal of English Literary History* 4 (1937): 161–79.

Milton and Heresy. Cambridge, Stephen B. Dobranski and John P. Rumrich, eds, Cambridge, Cambridge UP, 1998.

Nuttall, Anthony D. *The Alternative Trinity: Gnostic Heresy in Marlowe, Milton and Blake.* Oxford, The Clarendon Press, 1998.

Milton, John. *Complete Prose Works of John Milton.* General Ed. Don Marion Wolfe. New Haven, Conn.: Yale UP, 1953–82.

Rowse, A. L. *Milton the Puritan. Portrait of a Mind.* London: Macmillan, 1977.

Summers, W. *Our Lollard Ancestors.* London. MCMIV-1904.

Vasilev, G. *Dualist Ideas in the English Pre-Reformation and Reformation (Bogomil-Cathar Influence on Wycliffe, Tyndale and Milton*, Sofia, Bulkoreni, 2005.

–. *The "Secret Book" of the Bogomils and "Paradise Lost": Toward a Definition of Spiritual Kinship*, presented at *SPACES, GAPS, BORDERS*, 8th Conference of the Bulgarian Society for British Studies, Sofia University, Sofia, Bulgaria, 24–26 October 2003. Available online at: *http://www.geocities.com/bogomil1bg/MiltonBSBS.html*

Part III

The Great Poems

1. Paradise Lost

Matt DOLLOFF

Urania, Antidote to Tyranny

"Urania," the word for Milton's peculiar muse of *Paradise Lost*, appears only twice in his publications, both in the grand invocation at the beginning of Book VII. Yet perhaps no single signifier in all of Milton's works encapsulates such a broad and sweeping set of meanings; and Milton is surely aware of this. He performs his famous sleight of hand by declaring, "Descend from heav'n Urania, by that name / If rightly thou art called," followed closely by, "The meaning, not the name I call" (1–2, 5). Some critics have taken this as ambiguity to dismiss "Urania" as some kind of quirky afterthought or inadequate substitute for a Christian muse of epic poetry. "Milton called her Urania for want of a more appropriate or lovelier word," declares Scott Elledge; while Harold Bloom, with some justification, claims, "Milton has no name for her." But Milton's choice cannot be random and it is incumbent upon us to meditate his muse and explore the possibilities of her genealogy, or genealogies, in earnest.

One perverse fact about historical usages of "Urania" is that they are consistently abstruse. She experiences numerous protean transformations and seems subject to the vicissitudes of ever-changing times and tastes and the idiosyncrasies of individual authors and readers. Therefore my on-going research has taken me across the ages and literary genres. While it is fair to surmise that Milton wants us first to think of Hesiod's Muse of Astronomy, she is so much more. She is an aspect of Aphrodite as defined in Plato's *Symposium*. She is an agent of generation in authors, such as Macrobius and Bernardus Silvestris, from Late Antiquity to the Middle Ages. She is protector of chastity and friendship in Sidney's *Arcadia*, an inspiration to the poet in Dante's *Purgatorio*, a consoler to the forlorn in Tennyson's *In Memoriam*, a defender of homosexuals in Karl Heinrich Ulrichs's late-Victorian sexological studies, and an hermaphroditic American circus acrobat in Joris-Karl Huysmans's *Against Nature*. But because I wanted to tailor my research to the general political theme of this conference, I revisited many texts that contained her in one sense or another and noticed that, of or beyond the muses nine, Urania seemed most qualified to oppose tyranny and the sexual licentiousness of kings, even as she remained the vehicle for relating heavenly truths and divinely inspired poetry. The Book VII invocation is both poetical and political in nature ("still govern thou my son" (7.30)), for with Urania Milton will be "more safe" not just in the content of the poem, but also in his own historical situation. "With dangers compassed round," she will protect him from the notoriously prodigious Charles II and his vile rout, who like a "Bacchus and his revelers" have caused him to fall "on evil days."

From their earliest times, the Muses were the unwarranted victims of tyranny. In Book V of Ovid's *Metamorphosis*, Minerva visits Helicon, where, having been greeted by Urania, one of the muses relates to her their sad history.

> We are happy, or would be, were we only safe. So far, it seems, no outrage ever is forbidden, our maiden souls are frightened; we remember, too well, the look of that fierce king Pyreneus. His Thracian soldiery had captured Daulis, he ruled that land, unfairly won, and saw us, once, on our way to Parnassus (115).

Then, with false obeisance, the king tricked them into his house to avoid a rainstorm, whereupon he tried to rape them. They fled; he pursued, jumped, and fell to his death – quite literally a "salacious" demise.[1]

What appalled the Muses was not just the king's political tyranny, but also his sexual incontinence, which is symbolic of that tyranny. Simply put, the tyrant wishes to possess and consume everything – material goods as well as others' bodies and sexuality. As Caligula says, "Omnia mihi, & in omnes licere" (Suetonius 217), or roughly, "All things belong to me and in all things I am allowed."[2]

But it seems that by the time of Caligula's Roman Empire, the Muses had forgotten their troubled past, at least all but Urania. Consider this passage from a poem often cited as Milton's source, Du Bartas' "Urania, Or the Heavenly Muse," translated by Joshua Sylvester (1605):

1 I mean for this to be a pun based on an etymological transference noted in the *Cassell's Latin Dictionary* under the entry for "salio, salire…": to spring, leap, or jump. According to the editors, "sal *or* mica (salis) saliens, *sacrificial salt, which* (as a good omen) *leapt up when thrown into the fire*: farre pio et saliente mica, Hor."

2 The Antwerpian commentators of the 1591 edition of Suetonius, where I found this quotation, reckoned that Caligula substituted "mihi" for "homini," meaning that all things to be enjoyed by every man were now his – a clear affirmation of the shift from republic to empire (217).

> I [Urania] cannot (griefless) see my Sisters' wrongs
> Made Bawds to Lovers, in deceitptfull sayings
> In forged sighs, false tears, and filthy songs,
> Lascivious shows, and counterfeit complainings.
>
> Alas, I cannot, with dry eyes, behold
> Our holy songs sold, and profaned thus
> To grace the graceless; praising (too too bold)
> Caligula, Nero, and Commodus (531).

Here again we see not only the inevitable juxtaposing of bawdiness and tyrants, but also the distancing of Urania from her sisters. Moreover Milton, in proclaiming her "nor of the muses nine" (7.6), will separate his Urania entirely in a new but not so distinct meaning.

This passage from Du Bartas and Milton's nominal exclusion of the Muse of Astronomy resemble the *Consolation of Philosophy*, written while Boethius, himself fallen on evil days, was imprisoned, eventually to be executed by the tyrant and Arian heretic Theodoric the Ostrogoth. In this work, Lady Philosophy visits Boethius in prison:

> Now when she saw the Muses of poetry standing by my bed, helping me find words for my grief, she was disturbed for a moment, and then cried out with fierce blazing eyes: "Who let these theatrical tarts in with this sick man? Not only do they have no cures for his pain, but with their sweet poison they make it worse" (135).

Here Lady Philosophy chastises the Muses in a tone not unlike Du Bartas' Urania's. The traditional commodities of the Muses are somehow no longer sufficient to oppose tyranny, especially as history moves away from the classical towards the Christian. In *European Literature and the Latin Middle Ages*, E. R. Curtius writes, "the rejection of the Muses by Christian poets is scarcely anything but a badge of conventionally correct ecclesiastical thought" (240).

Nevertheless, pondering this transition from the Muses' "golden times" to the Christian era, Robert Aylett, whose *Urania, or the Heavenly Muse* (1654) has been largely overlooked as one of Milton's sources, has his Urania remark:

> But Satan since another pattern set,
> Which he would have all his to imitate;
> And like the Fowler draweth to his Net
> Poor Birds with merry note and pleasing Bait.

But thou that seek'st God's Glory, not thine own,
And striv'st to quench, not quicken lustful Flames;
Chuse these divine ensamples I have shown,
And guild not with fair words the foulest shame (88).

Of course, his power-grab in heaven having been defeated, in *Paradise Lost* it is the tyrant Satan himself who suffers most from unrelieved lust, especially when he sees the innocent bliss of Adam and Eve:

I to hell am thrust,
Where neither joy nor love, but fierce desire,
Among our other torments not the least,
Still unfulfilled with pain of longing finds (4.508–11).

Therefore he is compelled to seduce them and all mankind thereafter.

While the other muses might appear reflexively in Renaissance texts, they seem little more than curious vestigia; meanwhile, Urania, in Aylett's text and *Paradise Lost*, somehow maintains viability as a distinct, if awkward, Christian muse. Like Lady Philosophy, she is the bridge between heavenly truths and personal ethics; and those ethics are based on chastity, friendship and love – three qualities that stand in stark opposition to tyrannical behavior. Sydney's Claius and Strephon opine:

> Hath not [Urania] thrown reason upon our desires, and, as it were given eyes unto Cupid? Hath in any, but in her, love-fellowship maintained friendship between rivals, and beauty taught the beholders chastity? (7–8)

Granted, the *Arcadia* is set in pagan times, but the Christianizing of Urania by means of what E. R. Curtius calls "harmonistics," or the attempt to fuse Christian and Pagan influences in the Renaissance, is apparent, although more so in Du Bartas' poem. To Urania, Du Bartas pleads, "Let Christ (as Man-God) be your double mountaine, / Whereon to muse" (538). Formerly Pagan Urania now serves as heaven's ambassador and promotes Christian chastity and sexual continence.

But aside from general lasciviousness, Urania is prepared to oppose an important subset of lewd behavior that is causally linked to tyrannical behavior. Perhaps the worst sex crime among the wretchedly dissolute tyrants in classical and medieval texts is sodomy. This astonishingly commonplace evil underscores the tyrant's belief in his right to possess all bodies and sexualities, regardless of gender, and serves to remind readers of philosophy and history that nothing is beneath a tyrant who believes he is above all. For example, in his *Nicomachean Ethics*, on which Aquinas comments, Aristotle discusses the incontinence of the tyrant Phalaris, who had sex with boys – if he didn't eat them first (Aristotle 186; Aquinas 643). Gildas writes of the supposed King of Cornwall, Constantine, who disguised himself as an abbot in order to slay two royal youths. Thereafter he abandoned his wife, and God implanted in his heart the "bitter scion of incredulity and folly, taken from the vine of Sodom" (315). Geoffrey of Monmouth recounts the history of Mempricius, who, after killing his brother to obtain the crown, also deserted his wife "and abandoned himself to the vice of sodomy, preferring unnatural lust to normal passion" (78). In all cases, these accusations of sodomy occur as the last stone in an avalanche of wicked behavior.

John of Salisbury in his *Policraticus* blames this depravity on the court itself:

> [I]t is a frequent occurrence that a court either receives or creates vicious men, among whom transgressions increase in audacity since their vices are indulged by reason of their intimacy with the powerful. [...] For this reason, the court has been compared to the infamous fountain of Salmacis, which is notorious for weakening virility (90).

Again, the source is Ovid's *Metamorphosis*, where the waters of this "evil fountain [...] make men weak and feeble" and anyone who enters them is turned into a hermaphrodite (90).

Milton is of course aware of this tradition. Both Gildas and Geoffrey are sources for his own *History of Britain*, and it is with the very phrase "unnatural lust" that Milton describes Mempricius (CE 16). Moreover, at the very end of Milton's history, the great men of the court were given over to gluttony and "spent all they had in Drunk'ness, attended with other Vices which effeminate mens minds" (CE 316). Reflecting on the poor judgment of those who support a tyrant, Milton in *Eikonoklastes* writes, "they live and dye in such a strook'n blindness, as next to that of *Sodom* hath not happ'ned to any sort of men more gross, or more misleading" (CE 67). It is no coincidence that when Milton resorts to ad hominem in calling Salmasius a hermaphrodite in the "Second Defense," he situates Salmasius in the court of Christina, Queen of Sweden. Salmasius' Latinized name is of course a near homophone of the infamous fountain.

This type of name-calling perhaps also appears in *Paradise Lost.* In Book 6, Satan baits Abdiel by suggesting that those who continue to serve God are lazy sycophants:

> I see that most through sloth had rather serve,
> Minist'ring Spirits, trained up in feast and song;
> Such hast thou armed the minstrelsy of heav'n,
> Servility with freedom to contend,
> As both their deeds this day shall prove (6.166–70).

Milton plays on the similarity between "minstrel" and "minister," a pun noted in the OED. However, "minstrel" could have another meaning related to a passage from Shakespeare's *Romeo and Juliet*:

> Tybalt: Mercutio, thou consortest with Romeo –
> Mercutio: Consort! What, dost thou make us minstrels?
> And thou make minstrels of us, look to hear nothing
> But discords [...] 'Zounds, consort! (3.1.45–49)

Inasmuch as this exchange has been interpreted as Mercutio's sexual joke, founded on Tybalt's suspicions about the close friendship between Romeo and Mercutio[3], Milton's Satan may be following suit. Abdiel's angry response bolsters this definitional nuance: "Thyself not free, but to thyself enthralled; / Yet lewdly dar'st thou our minist'ring upbraid" (6.182–83). "Lewdly" is often glossed in accordance with the OED with a word like "ignorantly" or "foolishly," but it could equally mean "lasciviously." This linguistic game continues in *Paradise Regained* after Satan tempts the Son with two youths "of fairer hue/ Than *Ganymede* or *Hylas*" (PR, 2.351-2), the former cupbearer to Zeus, the latter water fetcher for Heracles. Including those two youths in the "these" of the following passage, Satan says.

> All these gentle Ministers, who come to pay
> Thee homage, and acknowledge thee thir Lord:
> What doub'st thou Son of God? sit down and eat. (PR, 2.374-6)

3 Mercutio's bisexuality is more apparent in the DaPorto original; and in texts from Late Antiquity, the sphere of Mercury (Hermes) is the realm of hermaphrodites, justified astronomically by the fact that the planet Mercury sometimes appears above the sun and sometimes below, and always near Venus (Aphrodite).

To chide Satan, the Son replies,

> I can at will, doubt not, as soon as thou,
> Command a Table in this Wilderness,
> And call swift flights of Angels ministrant
> Array'd in Glory on my cup to attend. (PR, 2.383-6)

It certainly seems as if Milton is comparing the cup-bearing Ganymede to the cup-bearing ministrant Angels. While it is not necessarily the case in *Paradise Lost*, Terry Eagleton reminds us that there is a "long tradition of Satan as hermaphrodite" (63), and Foucault that in Milton's day, "hermaphrodites were criminals, or crime's offspring" (38), as were the Sons of Belial. Thus Satan, overcome by his own insatiable lust, hypocritically impugns the only court in the cosmos that is not lascivious, where courtiers are not drunken louts or murderers, let alone Sodomites.

Therefore Urania, as an aspect of Aphrodite defined by Plato in his *Symposium* and others ensures the sanctity of the angels' consorts, as well as Adam and Eve's before the fall, and any chaste person's thereafter. In the Socratic scheme, Dionian love, though blessedly hopeful of attaining immortality, is heterosexual, fertile, fleshly, and therefore inferior to Uranian male, homosocial, intellectual and spiritual love. The former is pregnant in body and produces children, the latter pregnant in soul and produces poetry and all the arts (209a, paraphrasing Benjamin Jowett). Of course, in Milton's imagination the angels in heaven do have sex, but theirs is heavenly love by definition, unencumbered by lust or reproduction. That the angels could be hermaphrodites is allowed not only in the cosmographies of Late Antiquity, but also in medieval Christian revisions such as Bernardus Silvestris'. Interestingly, the passage where Milton claims that angels "can either sex assume, or both" (1.424) is followed closely by an indictment against Astarte and the Sidonian Virgins as if to ask why they would ever choose to be female. Moreover, Astarte is the eastern proto-Aphrodite[4], whom Macrobius names "Venus Architis" in the *Saturnalia.* In his commentary on the "Pervigilium veneris,"[5] Cecil Clementi argues con-

4 Milton wants us to make this association since he also brings up Thammuz, the Phoenician Adonis.

5 Curiously, of the three surviving manuscripts, one is the "codex salmasianus" named after Milton's arch-enemy. It was translated into English by the royalist Thomas Stanley complete with commentary including some from Salmasius himself.

vincingly that this goddess would become Dionian Aphrodite in the Greek pantheon.

In order to clarify, rather than cite Plato, I'll provide John Evelyn's commentary on the first book of Lucretius' *De Rerum Natura* (1656):

> Plato in his *Banquet* reckons up two [Venuses]; the one very ancient, daughter of the Heavens, Urania, or Caelestis, intimating the brightness and refulgency of the Divinity, together with a most secret affection[6] which she produceth, endeavoring to attract our souls, and unite them to the essence of God. But the second and younger, daughter of Jupiter and Dione, whom he names Pandemia,[7] [is] popular, carnal and voluptuous (98–9).

I should note that it was, as here, a commonplace in the mid-seventeenth century to shorten "Uranian Aphrodite" to simply "Urania." See, for example, Samuel Sheppard's *The Loves of Amandus and Sophronia* (1650), Thomas Shipman's *Red Canary* (1677), as well as Robert Aylett's *Urania, or the Heavenly Muse* (1654). But to continue, this version of Urania will become patroness of a young group of Oxford poets from the 1890s, including Oscar Wilde's consort Alfred, Lord Douglas, who practiced, for want of a better term, Platonic love and called themselves "Uranians." Urania had already been resuscitated as a defender of same-sex civil rights against discriminatory tyranny in Germany by Ullrichs, Kertbeny, and Kraft-Ebing. I see no reason why Milton's Urania would not also exist on this philosophical continuum ranging from Plato to the *fin de siècle*. But this claim must come with a firm caveat: what is permissible to the angels is not necessarily permissible to us. Theirs is angelic, heavenly love; ours must be chaste, as *Comus* makes patently clear.

At the beginning of this paper, I claimed that Milton published the word "Urania" only twice, but he did also write it in a very odd place – one of his outlines for tragedy:

> Sodom.
> the Scene before Lots gate
> the title Cupids funeral pile. Sodom Burning.

6 Notice how this "secret affection" replaces homosexuality.

7 Here as an aside, I introduced a triple pun. "Pandemonium" or "demons everywhere;" "Pandemia" patroness of the wrong sort of love; and "pandemic," the first written appearance of which the OED cites from Harvey's *Morbus Anglicus* 1666. Thus you get: "a plague of lusty demons."

If we are not already astounded by Cupid's presence in Sodom, then we will be when "the Gallantry of the town passe by in Procession with musick and song to the Temple of Venus Urania or Peor" (CE 233). Peor appears in *On the Morning of Christ's Nativity* and again in *Paradise Lost* 1.412; as a hermaphroditic false god from the general vicinity of the wicked city, he seems the viable choice. But for Milton even to consider Venus Urania as the goddess of Sodom is truly extraordinary. Later in the outline he writes,

> at the preists inviting the Angels to the Solemnity the Angels pittying thir beauty may dispute of love & how it differs from lust seeking to win them in the last scene (CE 234).

The angels attempt to turn the sinners away from lust with the rhetoric of Uranian Venus even as she is herself the goddess of Sodom. I suspect that when Milton wrote this outline, that choice was based on her patronage of male-male love, which was the root of Sodom's evil; but by the time he wrote *Paradise Lost*, Urania, minus "Venus," had come to signify a heavenly, chaste, Christian love. But at least the connection between kings and sodomy remains consistent, for he adds one embellishment to the very end of the outline that does not appear in Genesis 19:

> to the king & nobles when the firce thunders begin aloft the angel appears all girt with flames which he saith are the flames of true love & tells the K[ing] who falls down with terror his just suffering the fire and brimstone "of true love" rain on the court of Sodom as a "warning to all other nations.

Presumably, this "true love" would be the kind of love the Angels preach in the final scene before the destruction – Uranian love – but here a punitive force expressed with morbid irony.

Moreover, it is clear from his commentary that John Evelyn understands Urania to be a mirror to the essence of God. How Venus arrives at this function might best be explained by Macrobius' elaboration on the allegory behind the birth of Uranian Aphrodite. In the *Saturnalia*, written not long before Boethius' *Consolation*, Macrobius reminds us that in this myth, Saturn, as Cronos or "Time,"

> having cut off the privy parts of his father, Heaven [ouranos], threw them into the sea and that from them Venus was born and received the name Aphrodite from the foam [aphros] out of which she was formed – a myth from which we are meant to understand that, while chaos lasted, times and seasons did not exist, since time has fixed

> measurements and those are determined by the revolution of the heavens.[8] [...] And...the seeds of all things which were to be created after the heavens flowed from the heavens [...] However, the power of generating an everlasting succession of living creatures passed from the heavenly fluid to Venus (64–5).

It is no coincidence that Milton finally introduces Urania in Book 7, the book that recounts the story of creation. Seven is also the number of man for other authors who feature Urania – Macrobius, Bernardus Silvestris, and Alan of Lille. If this mediation is Urania's special function, then a Caesar or divine right monarch, who believes himself to be the mediator between the divine and the earthly, is an imposter. So it was with Nimrod, the first tyrant to "arrogate dominion undeserved / Over his brethren," (12.27–8), who falsely claimed "second sovranty" from heaven. This autocrat's Tower of Babel vainly attempted to bridge physically the distance that Urania has made irrelevant spiritually.

But Urania has her revenge against tyranny also as a muse of poetry. At the beginning of *Eikonoklastes*, Milton provides an epigraph from Sallust: *"Quidlibet impune facere, hoc scilicet regnum est."* Roughly, "to do what you will with impunity, that apparently is what a king is." Borrowing from Shakespeare, I have translated "quidlibet" as "what you will;" and another declension of this word, "quodlibet," was understood in Milton's day as a disputation, often theological, and later as a musical medley (OED). Philip Sidney appropriates quodlibet for his own purposes. In his *An Apology for Poesy*, he declares that the "[poets'] matter is quodlibet indeed [...] never marshalling [poetry] into an assured rank, that almost the readers cannot tell where to find themselves" (159). It is the poet's prerogative to do what he will, not a king's; and "of all sciences," says Sidney, "is our poet the monarch" (150). The meaning of Urania will probably never be marshaled into an assured rank, but today I hope to have shown that in many respects, and aspects, Urania embodies what Caligula's own family desperately pleads for in Suetonius' passage on Caligula – an "antidotum adversus caesarem" (217).

8 An inscription I spotted on a former navigation building in Barcelona shortly after our conference read: "Uranie coeli motus scrutatur et astra."

Works Cited

Aquinas, Thomas. *Commentary on the Nicomachean Ethics.* Trans. Litzinger. Chicago: Henry Regnery. 1964.

Aristotle. *Nicomachean Ethics.* Trans. Irwin. Indianapoolis: Hackett. 1985.

Aylett, Robert. *Divine and moral speculations in metrical numbers,* London: Abel Roper. 1654.

Boethius. *The Consolation of Philosophy.* Trans. S. J. Tester. Cambridge: Loeb Classical Library (Harvard). 1918.

Cassell's Latin Dictionary. New York: Macmillan. 1959.

Clementi, Cecil. *Pervigilium Veneris, The Vigil of Venus.* Oxford: Basil Blackwell. 1936.

Curtius, E. R. *European Literature and the Latin Middle Ages.* Princeton: Princeton. 1990.

DuBartas (Guillaume de Sallust). *Bartas: His Devine Weekes and Workes.* Trans. Joshua Sylvester. Gainesville, Fl: Scholars' Facsimiles & Reprints. 1965.

Eagleton, Terry. *The Rape of Clarissa.* Minneapolis: Univ. of Minnesota Press. 1982.

Evelyn, John. *An Essay on the First Book of T. Lucretius Carus De Rerum Natura.* London: Gabriel Bedle and Thomas Collins. 1656.

Foucault, Michel. *The History of Sexuality.* Vol. 1. Trans. Hurley. New York: Vintage. 1978.

Geoffrey of Monmouth. *Geoffrey's British History.* Trans. Lewis Thorpe. London: Penguin. 1966.

Gildas. *The Works of Gildas and Nennius.* Trans. Giles. London: J Bohn. 1841.

John of Salisbury. *Politicraticus.* Trans. Nederman. Cambridge: Cambridge UP. 1990.

Macrobius. *The Saturnalia.* Trans. Davies. New York: Columbia UP. 1969.

Milton, John. *Complete Poems and Major Prose.* Ed. Hughes. Indianapolis: The Odyssey Press. 1957.

–. *The Works of John Milton.* New York: Columbia UP. 1931–42.

Ovid. *Metamorphoses.* Trans. R. Humphries. Bloomington: Indiana Univ. Press. 1955.

Plato. *Symposium.* Trans. Jowett. In *The Collected Dialogues of Plato.* Ed. Hamilton. Princeton: Princeton Univ. Press. 1961.

Shakespeare, William. *Romeo and Juliet.* Boston: Houghton – Mifflin (Riverside). 1974.

Sidney, Philip. "Apology for Poetry." In *Critical Theory Since Plato.* Ed. Adams. New York: Harcourt Brace Jovanovich. 1992.

–. *The Complete Works of Philip Sidney.* Cambridge: Univ. of Cambridge Press. 1922.

Suetonius. *De vitae caesarum.* Antwerp: Plantiniana Antwewrpiae. 1591.

T. ROSS LEASURE

Spenser's Diabolical Orator and Milton's "Man of Hell"

In one of the opening sequences to Kevin Smith's film, *Dogma*, we find a principal character, the angel in exile, Loki, in the process of convincing a nun that she abandon her vocation of selfless charity in favor of the pursuit of personal fulfilment:

> [G]o get yourself a nice dress. You know, fix yourself up and find some man – find some woman – that you can connect with, even for a moment, 'cause that's all life is, sister, it's a series of moments. Why don't you seize yours? (Smith 5)

In pressing his case, Loki draws upon the textual authority of Carroll's *Through the Looking Glass*, arguing from seemingly compelling premises that what the nun had formerly regarded as the most noble of lifestyles was actually a misguided capitulation to the will of an unsympathetic monolith called "organized religion." Instead, he proposes that self-indulgence (purportedly ignoble) is indeed the only path to happiness, and therefore, is not only justified, but laudable. Loki proves himself an accomplished sophist – one that may be more precisely defined as an adoxographer (from the Greek, *adoxos*, meaning "ignoble") who, by rhetorical means, convincingly inverts the presumed categories of noble and ignoble action. It should come as no surprise that the practitioner of such rhetoric here is an angel fallen from grace since, traditionally, those sophists who constitute adoxographers are frequently of the demonic ilk. From certain of those "sons of Belial" in the Old Testament, to the original Loki of Norse mythology, to the devil of Cynewulf's *Juliana*, and beyond, these "men of hell" ply their rhetorical arts to the detriment of those unfortunates unable to see through their sophistical adoxography.

I term these rhetors "belialists" because they find their epitomization in the devil of Milton's infernal synod of Book II of *Paradise Lost*, a figure with a rich literary history extending back to its ancient roots in such scriptural texts as Judges 19 and 1 Kings 21.

Among those fictional rhetors that share an especial relation to Milton's Belial is Spenser's allegorical character, Despayre, from Book I, canto ix of *The Faerie Queene.* Their connaturality runs far deeper than the often mentioned association of each with the deadly sin of Sloth (in Latin, *acedia*). Indeed, the key to their affinity is more profound than the patently valid observation that each character constitutes an accomplished rhetorician. Rather, the relationship between Belial and Despayre rests in certain specific rhetorical strategies each employs as adoxographer that ultimately link both figures to a traditional characterization of the lesser demon as something of a litigator or legal advocate. One finds Belial most notably so portrayed in a Latin treatise of 1382, known commonly as the *Consolatio Peccatorum*, penned by the Italian cleric, Jacobus Palladinus (or alternately, in its fifteenth-century French translation by Pierre Ferget, entitled *Le Procès de Belial*).[1]

Like that in the *Consolatio*, the "*parliament* of devils" convened in Book II of *Paradise Lost*, of course, grows out of literary convention, and there can be no doubt that its designation as a "parliament" (or synod) identifies it with the deliberative and legislative processes of court politics.[2] Redcrosse's encounter with Despayre, on the other hand, would seem a far cry from such a venue, and indeed, there is no body of debaters, but rather only one embodied debate – Despayre himself. Nevertheless, Spenser explicitly posits this encounter between knight and ghoul as a "tryall" (I.ix.31:3). Trevisan makes clear to Redcrosse, warning the latter of Despayre's "charmed speaches" (30:9), that he and his companion, Terwin, have undergone a trial, the like of which the surviving knight hopes never to repeat. Despayre's "subtile tong, like dropping honny," according to Trevisan, melts into the heart, and searches every vein of the unwary; "O never Sir," he warns, "desire to *try* [Despayre's] guilefull traine" (31:9). Heedless, Redcrosse promises never to rest until he in fact has "that treacherous art [...]

1 See my articles on the matter, "Jacobus Palladinus, the Belial Tradition, and Milton's Lesser Demon" (*Cithara* 43 [2003]: 37–45), and "The Belial Tradition Revisited: Situating the Lesser Demon in the Works of Palladinus, Salandra, Vondel, and Milton" (*Cithara* 44 [2005]: 3–15).

2 Milton, of course, refers to Satan's assembly explicitly as a "synod" (2.391 and 6.156), but the synonymity of these terms is evident. The tradition to which I refer includes, but is not limited to, the medieval "song," *Þe Develis Perlament* (or *Parliamentum of Feendis*), of 1430 (see Frederick Furnivall's 1867 edition in volume 24 of the Early English Text Society [old] series).

heard and *tryde*" (32:2). The scene is set; the court, convened; and Redcrosse foolishly plans to defend himself against Despayre's "idle speach" (31:1) in a trial for his very soul.

In Despayre's subterranean, hellish, and ultimately sheolic dwelling, Redcrosse finds himself in something of a court-like crucible where pure justice, untainted by divine mercy or grace, is to be meted out. In this trial, Despayre constitutes the prosecuting attorney, akin to the "sober lawyer" identified by William Empson (52) in Milton's Belial of the infernal synod. Of necessity, Despayre must then play the "self-respecting Sophist," a fitting epithet that Neil Forsyth confers upon the lesser demon of *Paradise Lost* (109).[3] The conflation of these two figures is not only made possible by virtue of Despayre's association with the "unthrifty" vice of sloth, but also, and more importantly, because he justifies that vice through the deployment of sophistical adoxography.[4] Beyond each orator's espousal of "ease," Belial and Despayre share a "rhetorical virtuosity" in the language they use to question divine purposes and manipulate their auditors through a variety of strategies often aimed at inverting the natural relationship of the "noble" and the "ignoble" – the very definition of adoxography. What Una recognizes as Despayre's "vaine words," and what Spenser himself identifies as "subtile sleight" (53:2 and 54:3) is the sophistical medium that facilitates adoxographical argumentation in canto ix of the *Faerie Queene*, as does the "false and hollow" speech of Belial whose tongue "droppt [not honey but sweet] Manna" (2.113–4).

As Spenser observes in an editorial comment in Book III regarding Cymoent's attempt to circumvent the slaughter of her son, Marinell, at the hands of Britomart,

3 Forsyth may base this epithet in part on Alastair Fowler's note concerning Belial's prevaricative capacity in the latter's own edition of *Paradise Lost* (2.113–114).

4 "Unthrifty" may seem to modern readers a peculiar lexical choice. However, at least since Chaucer's age, the word could function as a particularly exact rendering of the Hebrew *beli ya'al* from which Belial's name derives. According to the *Oxford English Dictionary*, "unthrifty" had been understood to mean both "[p]roducing or bringing about no advantage, profit, or gain," and "[l]oose or lax in respect of conduct, morals, or virtue" (*s.v.* 1 and 3 respectively). "Unthrifty" then does double-duty first as a literal translation of the Hebrew word for "worthlessness," Belial's namesake, and as a term which qualifies one attribute commonly ascribed to this particular demon and those who follow him, namely *acedia*, or sloth.

> So ticle [or uncertain] be the termes of mortall state,
> And full of subtile sophismes, which doe play
> With double sences, and with false debate,
> T'approve the vnknowen purpose of eternall fate. (3.4.28:6–9)

The "termes" referred to here designate not only the duration of life, but also the inherent capacity of language to deceive, and especially in this particular context, the attempt to prove the purpose of eternal fate which, because it remains only within the purview of the Deity, must of necessity be wholly inscrutable.[5] Despayre and Belial, however, claim to be able to divine God's will themselves, and impart to their auditors this supposed truth.

Of course, Desypayre's big "trick" (as Ernest Sirluck put it) is his neglecting to mention the supersedence of the Old Testament Covenant of the Law by the Covenant of Grace as expressed through the Gospels; but the subtlety Despayre employs in doing so attests to the "consummate skill and artistry" (also noted by Sirluck) that ultimately allies the allegorical figure with that of Milton's lesser demon.[6] More specifically, however, both Belial and Despayre go about establishing a false identification with their respective interlocutors not merely, as Belial does, by addressing the other devils as "peers," but surreptitiously by their appropriation of their auditors' own use of language. In addition to modeling the exposition of his argument after Moloch's call for "open Warr," Belial echoes the previous orator's repeated use of the comparative adjective, "worse." In like fashion, Despayre immediately latches on to Redcrosse's invocation of the justice that spurs him on to take vengeance for the fallen Terwin. As a consequence of these verbal echoes, each demonic attorney (etymologically speaking, "one appointed or ordained to act [or speak] for another") effec-

5 I contend also that these terms are the words through which we hope to make sense of our circumscribed existence, the purpose of which remains "vnknowen" due at least in part to language's capacity to fashion a reality rather than define it.

6 The "basic device governing Despair's rhetoric," writes Sirluck, "consists quite simply in the suppression of one of a pair of essential terms (mercy) in the Christian equation of judgment, and the representation of the other (justice) as constituting the whole relation of God to human conduct" (8). It is intriguing to note that, although the term "mercy" is indeed absent in the exchange between Despayre and Redcrosse, Merci, as another allegorical character, does appear in canto x in the house of Holinesse (as does Speranza). The placement of these figures in the episode immediately following the encounter with personified despair highlights the prior absence of mercy's mention.

tively goes about the business of evacuating his gulls of their own will – each employing the faculty of reason through the use of subtle sophisms in order (to borrow a bit of current critical terminology) to colonize the volition of the other. In this evacuation of others of their will, both Despayre and Belial effect an economy of "de*moral*ization" designed to bring the will (and hence the behavior) of the other into line with his own ignoble character.

Despayre initially (and very cunningly) reproduces Redcrosse's own language (37:8–9), echoing the knight's rhetorical question ("What iustice can but iudge against thee right, / With thine owne blood to price his blood[?]" [37:8–9]) with his own query: "What iustice euer other iudgement taught, / But he should dye, who merits not to liue?" (38:1–2). Despayre appropriates Redcrosse's principle term, "justice," in order "to play subversively" upon it, and then misappropriates another closely related term, "grace," tellingly not invoked by the knight who seems to have forgotten the role of Grace in personal salvation: "Is not great grace to helpe him ouer past, / Or free his feet, that in the myre sticke fast?" (39:4–5). In this manner, Redcrosse's interlocutor becomes a mirror to the knight – the adversary-advocate posits himself as a falsely analogous figure; as such, he can then proceed more effectively to give eventually, as Harold Skulsky describes it, "a lulling impression of rightness to his equation of spiritual suicide or defection with bodily rest."[7] As a result, the knight literally and metaphorically

7 According to Skulsky, Despayre's argument "unfolds in five principal stages" (213). The first is essentially the trick to which Sirluck refers – taking "advantage of Redcrosse's ill-chosen emphasis on justice and vengeance rather than mercy" (38). The second stage is Despayre's accusation that Redcrosse envies Terwin's newfound ease, and that Redcrosse harbors a misplaced joy in his own objectively woeful existence (39). In the third stage, Despayre's contention that "all deeds ostensibly done by human beings are really done by God and could not have failed to occur (41–2)" (213) is sufficiently persuasive to stun Redcrosse into silence for the remainder of the canto. Taking advantage of Redcrosse's muteness, Despayre then moves in for the kill, calling to the knight's attention his own supposedly irredeemable sinfulness – a function of his continued existence, since the longer one lives, the more crimes one is able to commit whether through "bloud-shed" and "avengement" (the daily fare of knighthood), or through succumbing to other temptations born of pride or lust. Finally, Despayre delivers his *coup de grace* (pun intended), returning to the notion of divine justice – best to suffer just punishment now than delay the inevitable (47). In short order, as Skulsky writes, "Spenser has given [Despayre] rhetorical cunning to match the terrible ensnarement he represents."

"identifies" with Despayre, in a way far more devastating than any presumed identification he might experience with the deceased Terwin.

Despayre's initial questions are by no means the end of his interrogative onslaught, but rather, only a prelude to his pervasive use of the rhetorical strategies of *anthypophora* and *anacoenosis*.[8] The first both poses and answers questions, raising and presumably settling potential objections. The latter (very closely related) tactic seems implicitly to ask the auditor's judgment, presuming a common interest between the inquisitor and the gull. Both act as part of a program of systematic interrogative destabilization. By means of the deployment of these two rhetorical strategies, Despayre plays the role of a prosecuting attorney whose case relies heavily upon the inversion of noble and ignoble goals – in other words, adoxography.

Despayre eventually invokes the concept of "ease" like a mantra five times in the three stanzas that constitute his initial rhetorical volley; and these stanzas happen to contain nine anthypophoratic or anacoenotic figures. Furthermore, if one infers the reiteration of "ease" through the rhyming of "seas" and "please," then Despayre successfully integrates his key term, closely associated with the sin of sloth, five times within the single concluding stanza of that preliminary argument which also contains two of his anthypophoratic formulations:

> [Terwin] there does now enioy eternall rest
> And happie ease, which thou doest want and craue,
> And further from it daily wanderest:
> What if some litle paine the passage haue,
> That makes fraile flesh to feare the bitter waue?
> Is not short paine well borne, that brings long ease,
> And layes the soule to sleepe in quiet graue?
> Sleepe after toyle, port after stormie seas,
> Ease after warre, death after life does greatly please. (40:1–9)

"Ease after warre," not surprisingly, is also that course of inaction promulgated by Milton's Belial with comparable verbal intrepidity. In addition to co-opting Moloch's mantric usage of "worse," and his exhortation to "open Warr," Belial, like Despayre, attempts to dissuade his audience from any plans of revenge (the final term in Moloch's own peroration). He acknowl-

8 Skulsky enumerates many more such strategies than are necessary to cover within the scope of the present article since only these two relate directly to inquisitorial processes.

edges the justice of God's ire at their angelic insurrection, and advocates ultimately what amounts to a suicidal impulse – their acceptance of divine retribution that might result in, if not the subsidence of the infernal "raging fires," at least the fallen angels' inurement to the conditions of hell. In counseling "ignoble ease," Belial deploys "words cloath'd in reasons garb," and in true adoxographical fashion, "make[s] the worse appear / The better reason, to perplex and dash / Maturest Counsels" (2.226–227; 113–115). And what John Steadman says of Belial applies equally to Spenser's Despayre; each counsels "in the name of honor," and appeals "paradoxically to fortitude in arguing a course of inaction dictated by fear" (253). Each "exhorts to vice in the name of the contrary virtue." This abuse of rhetoric – made possible by what Steadman refers to as the "moral ambivalence of eloquence" (257) – establishes the figure of Milton's Belial as a quintessential sophist, and why the poet must warn his readers as Trevisan warns Redcrosse of Despayre's charmed speeches. These caveats, on the part of each poet, fundamentally betray the *ethos* of their diabolical orators, and assert that *dianoea* (can and) will destroy you.[9]

Likewise, what Skulsky observes of Spenser may also be said of Milton, that each "is aware that rhetoric is as dangerous a resource as it is subtle and potent; [and that] in his art, he has made the enemy of hope an evil virtuoso" (214). As such an "evil virtuouso," Belial, like Despayre, makes use of anthypophora and anacoenosis as a means to supplant the will of his demonic counterparts with his own. After addressing his "peers," and thereby side-stepping any of the hierarchical implications of his terminal (and therefore superior) position among the devils in the procession of Book I, and after affecting agreement with his audience by claiming to be "not behind in Hate," Belial casts aspersions upon Moloch's soundness of mind; his fellow devil, Belial claims, has grounded "his courage on despair / And utter dissolution" (126–8). It is at this point that the demonic orator commences his anthypophoratic interrogation: "First, what Revenge?" he asks (129). Subsequently demonstrating the futility of Moloch's "sad cure," and considering its deleterious ramifications, Belial asks the second of an

9 *Dianoea* (from the Greek) literally means "a revolving in the mind," and is in some instances indistinguishable from *anthypophora.* It is "the use of animated questions and answers in developing an argument" (see *Silva Rhetoricae*). *Ethos*, on the other hand, "names the persuasive appeal of one's character, especially how this character is established by means of the speech or discourse."

estimated thirteen questions over the course of the following fifty lines.[10] Like Despayre's anacoenotic peroration, Belial's apposite rhetorical strategy here cunningly effects his auditors' identification with him and his point of view, destabilizing reasonable objection, and in a sense, demoralizing Satan's diabolical army. Neither Belial nor Despayre gives their gulls much, if any, time to think. These rhetorical strategies, akin to legal examination or interrogation are performed before a jury of sorts – in Belial's case, the infernal synod, and in Despayre's, a jury of one, Redcrosse himself, who is ultimately not only the defendant, but acts as his own defense attorney, the judge, and of course, potential self-executioner, as well.

Each prosecutor, in his appeal to the justice of God's doom on sinners, must of necessity, as Steadman notes of Belial, be a practitioner of Aristotelian deliberative oratory; Steadman, however, rather than acknowledge the lesser demon as a sober lawyer (as Empson does), prefers to see him as "a politician" (242) who "adapts the commonplace of justice to the demands of deliberative oratory" (244), and who uses "rhetorical proofs designed to win or seduce his companions to accept the policy most congenial to his own temperament" (243). There is, I think, very little difference (especially in this case) between a politician and a prosecutor, and there is no question that Spenser's Despayre operates in precisely the same manner. Furthermore, as Steadman goes on to explain, Belial's Aristotelian rhetoric rests largely upon the principle of "the maximization of good and the minimization of evil" (249). Here we find the intersection of Milton's orator-advocate and the adoxographer *par excellence*, for he espouses "ignoble ease" and "peaceful sloath" in the name of a positive end, and eschews the prospect of renewed hostile action as only capable of bringing down a greater evil upon the heads of the already fallen. Despayre's own Aristotelian rhetorical flourishing is likewise couched in the presumption that Redcrosse, following Terwin's lead, will effectively reduce *in toto* the evil he is bound to commit by doing the honorable thing now of committing suicide.

Despayre's argument, unlike Belial's, however, is interrupted by his victim who, realizing that the Everlasting has indeed "fix'd / His *canon 'gainst self-slaughter*" (*Hamlet* 1.2.131–2), objects,

> [...] The terme of life is limited,
> Ne may a man prolong, nor shorten it;

10 I say "estimated" because one might consider some questions to be compound or multipartite, rather than discrete queries.

> The souldier may not moue from watchfull sted,
> Nor leaue his stand, vntill his Captaine bed. (41:2–5)

This *un*-sustained objection only gives the prosecution an opportunity once again to co-opt and pervert the knight's dogmatic defense:

> Who life did limit by almightie doome,
> Quoth [Despayre] knows best the termes established;
> And he, that points the Centonell his roome,
> Doth license him depart at sound of morning droome. (6–9)

Redcrosse's "term" has expired; the drum has sounded, claims the ghoul, as the latter embarks upon the second and final round of anthypophoratic and anacoenotic assault, the first question of which adoxographically transmutes the sense of the *Pater Noster*. Matthew's "Thy kingdom come. Thy will be done on earth as it is in heaven" (6:10) becomes Despayre's "Is not his deed, what euer thing is donne, / In heauen and earth?" (42:1–2). This question, like seven of the eleven remaining interrogatives that round out his oration, strategically deployed, can only be answered by the simple binary, "yes or no." While creating the illusion of forensic complexity, Despayre actually "leads the witness," as it were, by a series of relatively simplistic questions.

In like fashion, though uninterrupted, Belial leads his auditors to those conclusions that coincide with his own designs, making it seem as though, under the circumstances, discretion really is the better part of valor. The irony is that both Belial and Despayre bank upon their auditor's lack of discretion, the ability to judge rightly, so that they mistake the ignoble end to which each diabolical orator has painstakingly led them as the better reason, the honorable deed. Certainly, the strategies considered here as they are deployed by the figures of Milton's Belial and Spenser's Despayre do not exhaust the stock and store of rhetoric, and there remains work to be done on other potentially productive points of comparison between the two. Further study, I suspect, will serve to confirm not only the nature of the relationship between these diabolical orators as litigious figures that exalt ease and sloth over struggle and enterprise, but perhaps demonstrate the tradition out of which both emerge.[11] The roots of that tradition extend

11 This is not to discount the impressive and useful work already done by scholars not specifically considered here, like Gretchen Bohach and Todd H. Sammons, to whose respective dissertations I owe a great deal. Both Bohach's *Desperate Measures: Spenser,*

back to the scriptural instantiation of a prevaricating and pernicious demon allied with Jezebel in 1 Kings, and span the literatures of both Continental and Insular medieval Europe. In the hands of such accomplished rhetoricians as Milton and Spenser themselves, it should come as no surprise that the seventeenth-century Belial and sixteenth-century belialist alike deploy such cunning and compelling terms as each presses his case in one infernal chamber or other; nor subsequently should the contemporary recrudescence of an equally shrewd (and still fallen) angel in *Dogma* at the hands of an astute director and screenwriter like Smith, who admits the influence of Milton upon the film.

Works Cited

Burton, Gideon. "Silva Rhetoricae." 24 September 2005. Brigham Young University. 1996–2003 <http://humanities.byu.edu/rhetoric/silva.htm>.

"Þe Develis Perlament" in *Hymns to the Virgin and Christ.* Ed. Frederick Furnivall. London: EETS (o.s.) 24: 41–57.

Empson, William. *Milton's God.* Norfolk: New Directions, 1962.

Forsyth, Neil. *The Satanic Epic.* Princeton: Princeton UP, 2003.

Milton, John. *Riverside Milton.* Ed. Roy Flannagan. Boston: Houghton Mifflin, 1998.

–. *Paradise Lost.* Ed. Alastair Fowler. London: Longman, 1998.

Shakespeare, William. *Hamlet.* Ed. G. R. Hibbard. Oxford: Oxford UP, 1998.

Sirluck, Ernest. "A Note on the Rhetoric of Spenser's 'Despair.'" *Modern Philology* 47 (1949): 8–11.

Skulsky, Harold. "Despair." *Spenser Encyclopedia.* Ed. A. C. Hamilton. Toronto: University of Toronto Press, 1990.

Smith, Kevin. *Dogma: A Screenplay.* New York: Grove Press, 1999.

Spenser, Edmund. *The Faerie Queene.* Ed. A. C. Hamilton. London: Longman, 2001.

Steadman, John. "'Semblance of Worth': Pandaemonium and Deliberative Oratory." *Milton's Epic Characters.* Chapel Hill: University of North Carolina Press, 1968.

Shakespeare, Milton and the Renaissance Man of Hell (UC-Irvine 1996), and Sammons' *Stylistic Variation in Milton's* Paradise Lost (Stanford 1980), informed the writing of my own dissertation. Similarly, I must credit Patrick Cullen's *Infernal Triad: The Flesh, the World, and the Devil in Spenser and Milton* (Princeton UP 1974), and Susan Snyder's "The Left Hand of God: Despair in Medieval and Renaissance Tradition" (*Studies in the Renaissance* 12 [1965]: 18–59).

Martin DAWES

Adam's Co-creation of Eve: Taking Liberties with Milton's Ironic God

Greeting "the sociable Spirit" Raphael, Adam is deferential enough at first, "bowing low" (5.360). Courtesy tempers curiosity; after Raphael's makeshift account of the War in Heaven, Adam elicits the story of Creation with a winning combination of humility and flattery: "Deign to descend now lower, and relate … How first began this Heaven" (7.84–6). It may then seem impertinent of Adam to take over the storytelling with an imperative: "now hear mee relate / My Storie" (8.204–5). Yet the Archangel claims to be "Pleas'd" (8.248). My contention is that Adam takes the liberty of recounting his own creation and his co-creation of Eve not simply to detain his visitor but mainly because he has learned important lessons from wrestling in dialogue with his maker – some of the same lessons that Raphael would have learned from the dramatic Council in Heaven. In daring to negotiate for "Collateral love" (8.426), Adam learns that healthy growth is dialogical, and that often by means of irony God invites his creatures to trial, rewarding not unquestioning obedience but "embold'nd" response (8.434).[1] More generally, I submit that reading Milton's God as characteristically wielding what Linda Hutcheon calls "irony's edge" reveals him as a kind of Lord Protector, a caretaker-king challenging his subjects to become fully-fledged citizens, or in other words co-creators. To learn with Adam how to read the Father's irony, its harshness and its humour, is to begin to gauge the republicanism – and the humanism – of *Paradise Lost.*

1 Dennis Danielson has hinted at this conception: God presents "a limited view of reality" so that "questions are raised" (107). Similarly, Hugh MacCallum observes a "process of education by disputation with God" (100). Martin Kuester, focusing on Raphael's pedagogy, describes irony as a "pedagogical strategy" (266), while Brian Johnson relates God's irony to "the death of the Author." See also E. M. Good on the irony of the Old Testament God. Quotations are from the Riverside edition, with the exception of *On Christian Doctrine* (see Works Cited).

While Christopher Hill and others have proposed that we apprehend Milton's Heaven in contrast with the absolutism that led to revolution in the 1640s, the contrast remains in doubt. William Empson's portrait of a celestial Stalin who engineers the Fall still strikes a chord with many readers, and other critics have struggled with God's apparent incoherence. Victoria Silver, for example, has recently argued that the poet is an ironist who gives us two Gods, one harsh and the other tender, in order to impress upon us the mystery of a distant God. But this is to dismiss the possibility of a coherent character with purposes of his own, and thus to disregard the internal drama. Milton's readers aside, what about God's readers within the dramatic frame? What if God too were an ironist?

My argument is that harsh provocations such as God's charge of "ingrate" (3.97) – often considered the epic's "most persistent problem" (Christopher 114) – or more humorous ones such as his suggestion that Adam "Find pastime" with the animals (8.375), are not falsehoods or cruelties but ironies. As *On Christian Doctrine* has it, "the various uses of irony … are calculated not to deceive but to instruct" (761). By means of instructive irony, signalled by "conflictual textual or contextual evidence" (Hutcheon 37), God enlists our aid as co-creators without short-circuiting our education with total knowledge or compromising our "freedom to choose" (*Areopagitica* 1010) with monological commands.[2] God's irony primes the engine of history by inviting us to engage freely in its trials, for better or for worse. What is more, trial-by-irony seems to nurture God as well, enabling him by our ascension (cf. 5.469–503) to transcend the absolute monarchy that he once inhabited "alone / From all Eternitie" (8.405–6).

Readers alert to irony in Milton have tended to see it as a strategy of "dual terms" (Kuester) beneath which lies the one true meaning. But Hutcheon suggests that irony can be inclusive as well as differential; it involves an "interaction of perspectives" (a phrase of Kenneth Burke's). Thus, ironic meaning is not a ready-made opposite *behind* God's testing words, but rather a joint effort with his interpreters that "happens in the space *between* (and including) the said and the unsaid" (Hutcheon 12; italics in original). If God's irony were merely oppositional, the irony of *antiphrasis*,

2 In several of his pamphlets, Milton argues that God "gives no full comments" (*Divorce* 969) but rather "deal[s] out by degrees his beam" (*Areopagitica* 1023) – hence his ironies' partial truths. The "shortcircuiting" to which I refer would amount to apocalypse (from *apokalyptein*, 'disclose').

his tests would have all the subtlety of propaganda.[3] Instead, this is an irony dialectically pregnant insofar as it typically presents nothing but the truth while stopping so provocatively short of the whole truth, or steering so pointedly clear of the most telling truth, as to serve God's creatures with a hermeneutical challenge. Adam, for example, can indeed "find pastime" among the animals, whose "language" he knows (8.373), yet God leaves unsaid the full mutuality that Adam must strive to define. Barbara Lewalski has described this method of instruction or trial as Socratic (123). Unlike Socrates, however, God does not make fools by playing the fool; his nurturing has little use for dissimulation. Crucially, ironic meaning is less the achievement of the divine ironist than it is the product of his interpreters. This is why genuine irony is such an apt instrument for a Father bent on diffusing power (e.g., "all Power / I give thee" [3.317–18]; cf. n. 4 below). As J. Hillis Miller observes, such irony "cannot be used as an instrument of mastery" (105). Trusting to its provocative "edge," irony hails, but must depend upon, the other.

The poet of irony owes much to the radical pamphleteer who had insisted that "Christ meant not to be tak'n word for word" (*Divorce* 950), and that only such hermeneutical "trial ... by what is contrary" (*Areopagitica* 1006) confirms us in virtue as grown-up reader-citizens. As David Loewenstein observes, there is a striking "imaginative continuity between these two stages of Milton's literary career" (1). Born out of a political maelstrom, Milton's ironic God can thus be read historically not just as the antithesis of Charles I or II but as a caretaker-king differing also from the Lord Protector whom Milton once had hoped would "save free Conscience" ("To ... Cromwell" 291). Whereas Cromwell and other "ambitious leaders in the armie" (*Readie and Easie Way* 1140) had let down the republican cause for the promise of personal power, God promises to help us put an end to power. As the Father of "self-limitation" (Danielson 49) tells his Son, "thy regal Sceptre shalt lay by, / For regal sceptre then no more shall need" (3.339–40). Milton's concept of an abdicating ironist has further analogues in contemporary politics, as he was able to draw not only upon the pam-

3 Sharon Achinstein finds antiphrastic irony (meaning "'the opposite of what is actually said'" [161]) to be typical of the propaganda of the pamphlet wars. While Achinstein here quotes Quintilian, Cicero distinguishes between antiphrastic irony and that of "saying something *other* than one means" (N. Knox 10; my emphasis), the latter being the way of Milton's God. On classical and Renaissance theories of *ironia*, see Norman Knox and Dilwyn Knox.

phlets and the Lord Protector but also upon Parliament's Self-denying Ordinance (1645), which transformed a lacklustre Parliamentary army led by its own aristocratic Members into an effective meritocracy in which leadership could be earned. Analogously, Milton's self-denying God invites and rewards the taking of liberties for the sake of "Rational Libertie" for all (12.82). The ultimate goal of communion in godhead, when "God shall be All in All" (1 Cor. 15 / 3.341), awaits those who dare to talk back to their maker.[4]

Although Milton's ironist evidently prefers contentious co-creators to slavish servants, when it comes to commissions the initiator is normally God. It therefore speaks volumes of Milton's humanism that Adam should dare to commission his maker as matchmaker. In Genesis, of course, Eve is entirely God's idea: "It is not good that the man should be alone; I will make an help meet for him" (2:18). But Milton's dramatization raises our special status as *imago,* and clearly *amor, dei* to startling heights, as Adam goes beyond his biblical counterpart (not to mention other "wrestlers" with God such as Abraham and Moses) in taking the liberty of petitioning God to create for him a partner. Milton's Adam comes to realize that "Expressing well the spirit within [him] free" means exercising well his creative capacities for reasoning and choosing (8.440). In order to live up to these endowments, Adam must take the liberty of disputing, no matter who is speaking, just as Milton in *Eikonoklastes* dares to dispute the "martyred" monarch of *Eikon Basilike.* And Adam's performance in this pedagogical drama is all the more impressive for its being his debut. For Milton, humankind is always already Israel, a contender or wrestler with God.[5]

Yet this is not to deny that the Father goes some way towards commissioning Adam's commission, courageous as it is. God's dialogical method of trial-by-irony invites precisely this kind of liberty-taking. Moreover, if

4 Milton's *Doctrine* affirms that "All in All" signifies communion rather than dissolution: "each man will rise [to God] with the same identity that he had before" (620–1). Those readers who have gathered before me a political narrative of abdication include Empson (137), Hill (303), Johnson (68), and David Norbrook (475). However, I disagree with Johnson's view that "[God] does not risk much by abdicating" (68). Loving irony, as we shall see, promotes genuine freedom. In Prolusion VII, Milton had argued suggestively that, "when universal learning has completed its cycle," it will be "as if indeed some god had abdicated the throne of the world and entrusted its rights, laws, and administration to [humankind] as governor" (869).

5 *On Christian Doctrine* likewise stresses human freedom and high status: "God made no absolute decrees about anything which he left in the power of men" (155).

Eve will need some persuading but no coercing to enter into partnership, Adam too is formed as a dialogical being who craves the company of equals. In fact, God's "youngest Sons" appear to be not just inquisitive social animals but "naturally, instinctually republican" (Norbrook 463), as Adam later reacts with vehement anti-monarchism to Michael's talk of Nimrod (12.64–5). Even so, the liberties that Adam takes with his maker, whom he reasons must be far above his equal ("some great Maker, then, / In goodness and in power praeeminent" [8.278–9]), rival those taken by the Son in the Council in Heaven (cf. 3.150–66).[6] Just as the Son challenges the Father to make "Mercy collegue with Justice" (to recall God's later challenge to the Son [10.59]), so Adam challenges his maker to fulfil the human need for reciprocity – i.e., for the spirit of republicanism in the microcosm of the domestic.

Although Adam's drama will be "imbued with humour," as Kristin Pruitt points out (25), no sooner has God introduced himself "mildely" (8.317) than he is warning "Sternly" of "The Pledge of thy Obedience and thy Faith" (8.333, 325). God thus allows for Adam's immaturity as he does for that of the angels upon the exaltation of the Son (cf. 5.600–15), spelling out in similar terms the consequences of faithlessness rather than of misinterpretation: "Remember what I warne thee, shun to taste, / And shun the bitter consequence" (8.327–8). With the imperative driven home by repetition, this smacks of the infamous "Dye hee or justice must" (3.210). Indeed, the reporting phrase that follows the warning, "pronounc'd / The rigid interdiction" (8.333–4), recalls the stern demand to "pay the rigid satisfaction" (3.211–12). Thus, while God at this stage eases the interpretive challenge with an unambiguous warning, Adam's moral challenge is already underway. From day one, his Eden is defined both by the "harmonie" that now exists and by the horror that could be. Harshly as well as humorously, Milton's ironic God nurtures human freedom by providing the stuff of moral choices. No sooner has Eden received its governors than a certain salutary knowledge of good and evil is born and nurtured with them – through Adam's trial, through Eve's dream, and through the debate with Raphael. Pre- and postlapsarian worlds are in this respect not so divided,

6 While a discussion of the Council is beyond my scope here, the challenging and challenged Father of Book 3 is evidently the same provocateur who tests Adam in Book 8. Irony is characteristic of God, notwithstanding Stanley Fish's curious sense of the "atonal formality of God's abstract discourse" (88).

and *Areopagitica* will be increasingly relevant to Eden: "the knowledge … of vice is … necessary to the constituting of human vertue" (1006).

Adam's inaugural trial then develops variations on this theme of "harmonie" with the world and its maker, offering him further "freedom to choose." Having already mentioned "men innumerable" (8.297), God hints again that something is missing: "all the Earth / To thee and to thy Race I give" (8.338–9). That "each Bird and Beast" approaches "two by two" to be named (8.349–50) also puts Adam on his mettle:

> […] but in these
> I found not what me thought I wanted still;
> And to the Heav'nly vision thus presum'd (8.354–56).

Adam's "thought" derives partly from innate need yet mainly from his ability as a Miltonic hunter-gatherer of truth to put two and two together in a way familiar to us from the Son's piecing together God's intentions in Book 3 and Abdiel's interpreting the exaltation of the Son in Book 5.[7] However, that Adam "presumes" to raise the issue of partnership – "with mee / I see not who partakes" (8.363–4) – has as much to do with his daring as with his reason. In God's obvious delight at this contentiousness, we glimpse Milton's vision of a leader quite unlike the Stuarts or the Cromwells, who "could not endure the beings [they] had created to dispute with [them]" (Norbrook 486). For it is "with a smile more brightened" (8.368) that God "disputes" with Adam, reminding him that the animals are no puppets either: "knowst thou not / Thir language and thir wayes, they also know / And reason not contemptibly" (8.372–4).

Here, God's smile contributes to the "conflictual evidence" that for Hutcheon signals irony. Yet Adam arguably fails this part of the test by dismissing relationships with "unequals" as "Tedious" (8.383, 389). The directive to "Find pastime" with the animals, Adam decides, is not both an ironic, partial truth and a teasing goad but only a goad: "Among unequals what societie / Can sort?" (8.384–5), he pleads, punning on the true "consort" for whom he longs. God's subsequent reaction need not be read as "leaden" irony "on the subject of women," as Georgia Christopher con-

7 It is in the divorce tracts that Milton first elaborates the image of the "skilful and laborious gatherer" (*Divorce* 969), the type of bold interpreter crucial to the progress of the good in *Paradise Lost*.

tends (117), so much as a wry comment on the subject of the disparaged "societie" of "unequals":

> A nice and suttle happiness I see
> Thou to thy self proposest, in the choice
> Of thy associates, *Adam*, and wilt taste
> No pleasure, though in pleasure, solitarie (8.399–402).

Adam will not (rather than cannot) take pleasure in other "associates," so his "solitarie" state is partly his own fault. After all, to say "with these / Find pastime" is hardly to say "among these find a wife." But God clearly approves of this Miltonic creature who seems to want heaven on earth and is not afraid to "propose" so. Indeed, Adam's creative elaboration of "his like" as one "fit to participate / All rational delight" (8.418–33) – a definition that echoes Milton's own formulations of companionate marriage in the divorce tracts – brings God to commend him for "Expressing well the spirit within [him] free" (8.440). This commendable spirit is not simply that of human reason but also the same "[Old Testament] spirit of contentiousness" that Michael Lieb finds in the Council in Heaven ("Celestial Dialogue" 233).

Still more astonishing than Adam's "freedom us'd / Permissive" (8.434–5), however, is God's apparently hinting at his own need for mutuality, possibly his very motive for creating in the first place:

> What thinkst thou then of mee, and this my State,
> Seem I to thee sufficiently possest
> Of happiness, or not? who am alone
> From all Eternitie, for none I know
> Second to me or like, equal much less.
> How have I then with whom to hold converse
> Save with the Creatures which I made, and those
> To me inferiour[?] (8.403–10)

These questions certainly succeed in prompting Adam to elaborate on his desire, as a "defective" and quite different being, for the solace of "Collateral love" (8.425–6). And the Father goes on to praise Adam and even to explain the pedagogical approach: "Thus farr to try thee, Adam, I was pleas'd"; "for trial onely brought, / To see how thou could'st judge of fit and meet" (8.437, 447–8). Juggling and judging irony's interplay of said and unsaid, the plucky Adam has indeed co-realized his Eve. But the reader is left to wonder whether what is supposedly no more than strategic irony ("for trial onely") does not in fact speak to God's own "defective" condition as a dynamic being caught up, like his creatures, in dialogue and in narrative.[8]

Such bold engagement in trial both strengthens Adam's "direct, intimate, and dynamic" relationship with God (Pruitt 39) and wins him the "rational delight" of true partnership with Eve. It might then seem obvious that Adam has passed his test with flying colours. Yet his understanding has its limits: "pastime" with unequals should be distinguished from "all rational delight," but "harmonie," God implies, need not be restricted to human mutuality. While Adam's conclusions must remain partial truths, trial in *Paradise Lost* does allow for provisional verdicts; and this time, at least, Adam succeeds. Admittedly, irony "potentially excludes: … there are those who 'get' it and those who do not" (Hutcheon 54). But the trials of Milton's God are inclusive insofar as 'success' and 'failure' alike will lead to further trial. The existence of hell may seem to argue a point beyond which further trial is useless because all freedom has been given over to enthrallment; yet even the fallen Satan suffers the activity of conscience (e.g., 4.42–3), as if he were not conclusively fallen but continually falling. In any case, God's trial of Adam exemplifies his characteristic mode of relation with those creatures who remain free, a mode marked by what Hutcheon calls "aggregative" irony. By virtue of its powerful "affective charge," aggregative irony has the potential to create "'amiable communities' … between ironist and interpreter" (54–5), as we find in Adam's budding intimacy with his creator.

Evidently, being a "fully human" co-creator need not depend on transgression, as the *felix culpa* school would have it. To insist with John Ulreich and others that the Fall is "a necessary – and fortunate – step in humanity's evolution" (78) would be to forget that the "amiable community" of prelapsarian humankind was evolving rather nicely. The dialogue in Book 8 demonstrates that human beings were already, in God's words, "Authors to themselves in all / Both what they judge and what they choose" (3.122–3)

8 Further speculation on this point is perhaps, as Milton might say, fruitless. But the epic's *telos* and the argument for irony suggest that, by creating other minds and risking trial-by-irony, the God who once was "All" seeks to raise his creatures to "Union or Communion, deifi'd" (8.431), and ultimately to escape from fruitless solipsism into the fruitful relationship of "All in All." See D. Bentley Hart on God's "story."

before being seduced into satanic self-authorship.[9] Adam's taking over the storytelling from Raphael only confirms the power of prelapsarian human authorship. Moreover, if Adam's dialogical daring can be traced to the encounter with his maker, his generic invention, as Lewalski has made clear, owes much to Eve's authorship of her own story. Like Adam's, Eve's creativity and curiosity are "fully human" even in innocence – as when she assures her husband that "to know no more / Is womans happiest knowledge" (8.637–8), only to anticipate in her next breath his eager interrogatives: "But wherefore all night long shine these [stars], for whom/ This glorious sight, when sleep hath shut all eyes?" (8.657–8).

Adam may have been his partner's co-creator, but initially, then, their "fully human" relationship is "defined by exchange and transformation, not by hierarchy" (Peczenik 260). To be sure, Milton's and Adam's elevation of Eve above the misogynistic traditions undergoes a reversal with the Fall. Adam's shifting images of Eve "chart the course of his Fall" (Peczenik 250), bottoming out in misogyny and literalism with Eve as nothing more than "a Rib / Crooked by nature" (10.884–5). What has yet to be realized, however, is the full extent of Raphael's unwitting influence on this process. For it may justly be objected: if Adam and Eve are evolving so nicely as co-creators with God, how is it that they are about to succumb to Satan? Anne Ferry gestures towards an answer in pointing out that "Raphael preaches St. Paul's [fallen] view of woman's relation to man," a view which Adam does his best to "correct" by praising his partner's "thousand daily decencies" (8.601; Ferry 123).[10] Both Adam's growing "sense of his own stature," gained in part from the debate with his maker (Lieb ["Adam's Story"] 35), and Adam's corresponding sense of Eve's individuality, which is what leads him to correct Raphael – both of these, I shall conclude by suggesting, are seriously undermined by the "sociable Spirit's" authoritarianism, which Adam will echo just before the Fall.[11] It is from within another trial – the testing debate with Raphael, himself merely a creature on trial – that Adam grapples with the lessons of his first trial.

9 For a summary of the *felix culpa* controversy, see Danielson (202–27).

10 The *Doctrine* confirms that "neither Man nor Angel" is exempt from perspectival limitations: "there are many things of which [the angels] are ignorant. [...] Dan. 8:13" (348).

11 Adam's echoing of Raphael ranges from the indirect (9.265–6, 357–8) to the direct (9.375).

Despite the example of Satan's fall, Raphael still celebrates the warrior's ethos of exaltation through force, as opposed to God's way of exaltation through humility: "behold the excellence, the power / Which God hath in his mighty Angels plac'd" (6.637–8), he trumpets to the impressionable couple. This will lead his rapt listeners to the dangerous conclusion that evil has been "Driv'n back" (7.57). Worse still, Raphael's mistrust of human mutuality brings him to urge Adam to take charge of Eve and her moral welfare. As Kuester observes, "knowledge of coming human disobedience makes [Raphael] insist even more firmly on automatic obedience" (271). The Archangel's well-meaning attempt to impose a moral chain of command from himself to Adam and on 'down' to Eve perverts the essence of freedom, as his own words suggest: "how / Can hearts, not free, be tri'd whether they serve / Willing or no[?]" (5.531–3). Because of Raphael's incoherent paternalism, which throws out the baby of freedom with the bathwater of evil and error, it will be up to Eve to repair human liberty in the separation scene, even at the cost of enabling the Fall.

Yet God's "self-denying ordinance" must entrust even the most important missions to limited creatures such as Raphael. Otherwise, agency or judgment would be God's alone, and we would be unable to earn the devolution of power that his great goal of communion requires. If the co-operative ways of Milton's ironic God are *necessarily* flawed in their dependence on flawed interpreters, such is the cost of genuine co-operation.[12] By the same token, if in his own words the Father rations truth, or departs from the most telling truth, for the sake of trial, then the "departures" of mistaken and/or malicious creatures can serve ironically as another source of trial – an abundant source not just for themselves but for all those who encounter them or otherwise come to "read" them. The faithful Raphael, as we have seen, is invited to put Adam and Eve and their relationship to the test with his limitations, just as Satan is given leave to put Eden to a still sterner test with his perversions. And yet, for all of the ironic education potentially derived from error, we may still miss the ironies and choose the Devil's ways instead of God's. Good creatures may become good for nothing and fail to exercise their right to citizenship, fail to take liberties with the powers that be.

12 The *Doctrine* excludes from God's "general decree" those "things [...] which God performs *in co-operation with others*, to whom he has granted, by nature, freedom of action" (153; italics added).

The evolution of Adam and Eve in *Paradise Lost* reflects Milton's own political experience in its fragility, its destructibility. Human evolution is fragile precisely because it is dialogical, and hence dependent, like God himself, on fallible others. The Father can extend the measured hand of irony, but must depend upon flawed co-authors to read and to write back. That the poem nevertheless proclaims the ultimate triumph of "Libertie," albeit "with wandring steps and slow," bespeaks Milton's humanistic faith in political dialogue. More important than the horror of history or the guilt of original sin is the learning process modelled in Adam's dialogue with his maker as well as in the final books. This is the process of awakening, often through error, to our capacity as co-creators, our ability both to learn from history and to intervene in it – even if, as Milton had evidently realized by 1660, "we may be forc'd perhaps to fight over again all that we have fought, and spend over again all that we have spent" (*The Ready and Easie Way* 1138).

Works Cited

Achinstein, Sharon. *Milton and the Revolutionary Reader.* Princeton: Princeton UP, 1994.

The Holy Bible. 1611. Authorized Version. New York: Ivy Books, 1991.

Christopher, Georgia B. *Milton and the Science of the Saints.* Princeton: Princeton UP, 1982.

Danielson, Dennis R. *Milton's Good God: A Study in Literary Theodicy.* Cambridge: Cambridge UP, 1982.

Empson, William. *Milton's God.* London: Chatto & Windus, 1965.

Ferry, Anne. "Milton's Creation of Eve." *Studies in English Literature, 1500–1900* 28 (1988): 113–32.

Fish, Stanley E. *Surprised By Sin: The Reader in Paradise Lost.* London: St. Martin's Press, 1967.

Good, E. M. *Irony in the Old Testament.* London: S.P.C.K., 1965.

Hart, D. Bentley. "Matter, Monism, and Narrative: An Essay on the Metaphysics of *Paradise Lost.*" *Milton Quarterly* 30 (1996): 16–27.

Hill, Christopher. *Milton and the English Revolution.* New York: Viking Press, 1977.

Hutcheon, Linda. *Irony's Edge: The Theory and Politics of Irony.* London & New York: Routledge, 1995.

Johnson, Brian. "Sacred Silence: The Death of the 'Author' and *Paradise Lost.*" *Milton Quarterly* 29 (1995): 65–76.

Knox, Dilwyn. *Ironia: Medieval and Renaissance Ideas on Irony.* Columbia Studies in the Classical Tradition, Vol. XVI. Leiden: E. J. Brill, 1989.

Knox, Norman. *The Word 'Irony' and Its Context, 1500–1755.* Durham, NC: Duke UP, 1961.

Kuester, Martin. "The End of Monolithic Language: Raphael's Sematology in *Paradise Lost*." *English Studies in Canada* 15 (1989): 263–76.

Lewalski, Barbara K. *Paradise Lost and the Rhetoric of Literary Forms.* Princeton, NJ: Princeton UP, 1985.

Lieb, Michael. "Adam's Story: Testimony and Transition in *Paradise Lost*." *Living Texts: Interpreting Milton.* Ed. K. A. Pruitt and C. W. Durham. Selinsgrove: Susquehanna UP, 2000. 21–47.

–. "Milton's 'Dramatick Constitution': The Celestial Dialogue in Book III." *Milton Studies* 23 (1987): 215–40.

Loewenstein, David. *Milton and the Drama of History.* Cambridge: Cambridge UP, 1990.

MacCallum, Hugh. *Milton and the Sons of God: The Divine Image in Milton's Epic Poetry.* Toronto: University of Toronto Press, 1986.

Miller, J. Hillis. *Fiction and Repetition: Seven English Novels.* Cambridge, Mass.: Harvard UP, 1982.

Milton, John. "On Christian Doctrine." *Complete Prose Works of John Milton.* Vol. 6. Ed. Maurice Kelley. Trans. John Carey. New Haven, CT: Yale UP, 1973. 8 vols. 1953–82.

–. *The Riverside Milton.* Ed. Roy Flannagan. Boston & New York: Houghton Mifflin, 1998.

Norbrook, David. *Writing the English Republic: Poetry, Rhetoric and Politics, 1627–1660.* Cambridge: Cambridge UP, 1999.

Peczenik, Fannie. "Milton on the Creation of Eve: Adam's Dream and the Hieroglyphic of the Rib." *A Fine Tuning: Studies of the Religious Poetry of Herbert and Milton.* Ed. M. A. Maleski. Binghamton: Medieval and Renaissance Texts and Studies, 1989. 249–72.

Pruitt, Kristin A. *Gender and the Power of Relationship: 'United as One Individual Soul' in Paradise Lost.* Pittsburgh: Duquesne UP, 2003.

Silver, Victoria. *Imperfect Sense: The Predicaments of Milton's Irony.* Princeton, NJ: Princeton UP, 2001.

Ulreich, John C. "'Argument Not Less But More Heroic': Eve as the Hero of *Paradise Lost*." *'All in All': Unity, Diversity, and the Miltonic Perspective.* Ed. C. W. Durham and K. A. Pruitt, Selinsgrove: Susquehanna UP, 1999. 67–82.

Virginie ORTEGA-TILLIER

Qualités plastiques de l'évocation poétique & caractéristiques des illustrations du *Paradis perdu* de Milton

Il s'agit de mettre en évidence les éléments de rupture et de continuité qui caractérisent les qualités plastiques de l'évocation poétique et les illustrations du *P.p.*, thèmes et motifs replacés dans le cadre plus général de recherches sur l'iconographie du Paradis terrestre.[1] Il conviendra de souligner les apports de Milton dans les représentations d'un sujet vénérable, traditionnel, qui engage un passionnant dialogue entre les arts visuels et la littérature, entre la lettre et la figure.

Le Paradis terrestre, lieu biblique, littéraire et poétique se situe durant l'époque moderne au centre d'une culture: plus de cent cinquante ouvrages littéraires ont été composés entre 1540 et 1700 par des auteurs de confession catholique ou protestante sur ce thème. Comme le *P.p.*, ces textes appartiennent à la poésie chrétienne dans laquelle, en ces temps de Réformes, les entreprises de conversion se mêlent aux célébrations de la gloire de Dieu dans les merveilles de la Création; à la poésie érudite, où les connaissances permettent de renouveler et d'enrichir le répertoire poétique, de susciter l'émotion par la multiplication des évocations sensuelles: visuelles, olfactives, musicales. Il s'agit bien d'instruire et de plaire, de séduire l'œil pour toucher l'esprit; à la poésie naturelle, voire scientifique, à laquelle appartient notamment la *Semaine* de Du Bartas. Ils participent, au même titre que des ouvrages d'inspiration ou de forme moins littéraires à la pérennité d'un thème biblique millénaire. Les poètes y mêlent habilement certains des aspects fondamentaux de l'Humanisme de la Renaissance, fondé sur les enseignements bibliques, les préceptes néoplatoniciens et l'érudition moderne. La nostalgie du *locus amœnus* proche de celui de la littérature antique se caractérise essentiellement par l'esthétique de la variété, le caractère

1 Virginie Ortega-Tillier, *Le jardin d'Eden. Iconographie et topographie (XVe-XVIIIe siècles)*, Dijon, Editions de l'Université de Dijon, 2006.

amène et harmonieux, la proximité de l'humain et du divin. Les considérations morales sur la Chute de l'homme et sa relation au divin teintent alors fréquemment la narration de perspectives eschatologique et sotériologique. La paraphrase biblique et la fidélité au texte de la Genèse, auquel s'adjoignent des références aux Psaumes, au Livre de la Sagesse et aux *Héxamérons*, n'excluent cependant pas certaines originalités narratives et descriptives. Les questions théologiques et scientifiques sur l'origine du monde et de la vie, la perception de l'espace, la vision du Monde sublunaire et les questionnements géographiques ne sont pas absents de la verve descriptive. La description empreinte de louanges de l'Œuvre de Dieu se traduit par celle de la Nature originelle féconde, berceau de l'humanité et de l'Homme perçu à la fois comme microcosme et chef-d'œuvre du Créateur.

Tous ces éléments traditionnels se retrouvent dans le *P.p.* (1667). Milton demeure généralement fidèle au texte de la Genèse et à la tradition exégétique dans les descriptions du Paradis. Il adjoint à cette source le *locus amœnus* de la littérature antique et les débats érudits sur la localisation et la pérennité du Jardin d'Eden, qui ne constituent cependant pas son intérêt premier. Par exemple, lorsque le poète évoque le cours des quatre fleuves, il se garde bien de précision (IV, 223–235) ce qui est original dans son époque. En effet, du Xe au XIVe, des «mappemondes» ou des «descriptions du monde», héritières des *Etymologies* d'Isidore de Séville (VIIe) ou de la *Topographie chrétienne* de Cosmas Indicopleutès (IXe), signalent l'emplacement oriental du Paradis, souvent rendu inaccessible par l'océan circulaire qui entoure l'œkoumène, le monde connu habité. En 1553 apparaît dans l'édition française du *Commentaire de la Genèse* de Calvin une carte géographique qui devient dès la décennie suivante une illustration répandue dans des Bibles européennes, catholiques ou protestantes, jusqu'à la fin du XVIIe. Parmi de nombreux exemples, citons la carte d'une Bible (Lyon, 1569)[2] gravée par Eskrich où le Paradis est marqué par le Péché originel, celle d'une Bible parisienne (XVIIe)[3] avec Eden en Chaldée et une publiée à Amsterdam en 1669[4] avec Eden près de Bagdad. En 1691 paraît à Paris le *Traité de la situation du Paradis terrestre* de Huet, où Moïse est représenté comme le père de la Géographie et le jardin localisé précisément, dans une région nommée Eden, au sud-est de la Babylonie.

2 Dijon, BM Est146.
3 Dijon, BM 17735.
4 Dijon, BM 18750.

Rien de tout cela ne se découvre dans le poème, même au Livre IV, le plus précis sur ce sujet (208–214). Milton situe cependant le Paradis sur une montagne, évoque «le jardin d'Assyrie» (IV, 285), fait allusion aux localisations de l'Eden en Ethiopie ou près de l'équateur (IV, 280–287), intègre la légende des Iles Fortunées. Ces caractéristiques se retrouvent par exemple dans la planche du Livre IV de l'édition de 1688 du *P.p.*[5], l'une des plus complètes pour la caractérisation du jardin originel. Signifiant à la fois l'aménité et l'éloignement, la situation orientale, exotique du Paradis, un palmier et un éléphant sont nettement mis en évidence par l'artiste au centre du second plan, entre les deux anges. Ces deux éléments sont traditionnels dans l'iconographie édénique comme dans les transpositions poétiques de la Genèse.

Egalement traditionnelle, l'esthétique de la *varietas* qui participe à la beauté de la langue de Milton et qui se retrouve dans de nombreuses illustrations du *P.p.*, comme avec Westall[6] qui figure Eve auprès d'une végétation exotique, variée et foisonnante. Doré tire aussi admirablement parti de l'exotisme de la végétation paradisiaque.[7] Cette esthétique de la *varietas* est très courante dans l'iconographie du Paradis: la nature originelle reflète la grandeur des œuvres de Dieu et en célèbre la diversité: la faune et la flore composent les motifs les plus à même de le souligner. La nature originelle est perçue comme un livre, un miroir, à la fois source de délectation et lieu de méditation. Il s'agit, pour les écrivains et les artistes, de la découvrir, de l'observer, de la parcourir et de la faire connaître. Ce goût de la description et de la figuration des choses de la nature s'intègre dans une vision nouvelle de l'environnement de l'homme et dans une perception moderne de la place de ce dernier au sein de la Création divine, dont la variété ordonnée présente le Créateur en artiste, en grand architecte.

Ainsi, ni Lens ni Milton ne s'éloignent de lieux communs sur le sujet. Mais les quatre fleuves mentionnés par la Bible – le Phison, le Gihon, le Tigre et l'Euphrate – sont tout aussi essentiels, figurés sous une forme naturaliste, celle de rivières serpentant d'un plan à l'autre de la composition, ou sous l'aspect d'une fontaine plus ou moins architecturée, héritière de modèles médiévaux. Les exemples abondent, dans les images comme dans les textes: ces fleuves ne sont-ils pas de précieuses indications géogra-

5 Voir par ex.: http://myweb.stedwards.edu/georgek/milton/lens/lensindex.htm

6 Voir par ex.: http://myweb.stedwards.edu/georgek/milton/westall/westall8.html

7 Voir par ex.: http://myweb.stedwards.edu/georgek/milton/dore/doreindex.htm

phiques pour les érudits s'aventurant dans le débat de localisation de l'Eden? La discrétion de Milton à ce sujet est suivie par Lens. Le fait que ce ne soit pas un cas isolé dans les illustrations du *P.p.* indique clairement que les artistes ont suivi avec attention le texte du poète. Voyons aussi les œuvres de Doré ou celles de Martin. L'élément aquatique est présent mais sous la forme d'une paisible étendue d'eau, un lac miroitant.[8]

Il n'y a guère que Martin qui s'autorise une traduction moderne de la fontaine traditionnelle avec la cascade[9], élément naturel qui apparaît très tardivement dans l'iconographie édénique et coïncide avec la sensibilité romantique. Plusieurs passages suggèrent clairement cette caractéristique topographique (par ex. IV, 260–263). Le motif de la cascade apparaît progressivement dans l'art du paysage européen, à partir de la seconde moitié du XVIIe. Avant le XIXe cependant, avant les sensibilités romantiques et réalistes, la cascade est utilisée pour deux raisons principales. La première raison est de marquer l'exotisme d'un paysage comportant une scène biblique, comme avec cette représentation du repos pendant la Fuite en Egypte peinte par Francesco l'Albani (v.1650, Fontainebleau).[10] La cascade et le palmier participent à l'évocation de l'exotique Egypte. La seconde raison est de signifier le caractère sauvage de la nature, comme le feront les peintres romantiques et naturalistes. Il Domenicano utilise à plusieurs reprises ce motif de la cascade, certainement avec le souvenir des jardins italiens: par exemple pour une représentation de la Fuite en Egypte (v.1620, Louvre)[11], ou dans un paysage avec un ermite dans lequel se remarquent d'étroites ressemblances dans la structure avec la gravure de Martin.[12] Certains aspects sont liés à l'esthétique classique et à la conception du paysage historié. Mais la diagonale ascendante qui structure l'image, la situation au premier plan à droite de la narration et la forme de la cascade se jetant dans un petit lac sont des éléments particuliers qui se retrouvent dans les deux œuvres. Il existe plusieurs versions de la peinture du Domenicano, qui de plus a été vite gravée; Milton a peut-être vu, durant son voyage en Italie en 1638, ce genre de paysages qui ont peut-être influencé ses descriptions de l'Eden. L'influence italienne vient peut-être seulement du graveur lui-même,

8 Voir par ex.: http://myweb.stedwards.edu/georgek/milton/martin/martinindex.htm

9 Voir par ex.: http://myweb.stedwards.edu/georgek/milton/martin/martin18.htm

10 Voir le site de la base Joconde: http://www.culture.gouv.fr/documentation/joconde/fr/pres.htm

11 Ibid.

12 Ibid.

mais en tout cas, elle existe et fait bien le lien avec le poème miltonien. Dans tous les cas, la cascade est un élément original de l'iconographie du Paradis, que Milton décrit et que ses illustrateurs représentent. Le seul autre exemple rencontré appartient à un recueil de *Figures de la Bible* publié à La Haye en 1728.[13]

Pendant son voyage italien, Milton est allé à Florence, Rome et Naples, où des jardins «réels» ont sans doute marqué son imagination et sa mémoire, des lieux dont il s'est sans doute souvenu lors de la rédaction du *P.p.* Les caractéristiques du jardin de la Renaissance ont été fixées dès le milieu du XVe; trois principes essentiels ont été mis en place: la géométrisation des formes et des structures, l'omniprésence de l'eau et la référence aux usages des Anciens. L'art et la nature ne font plus qu'un; la Renaissance définit une «troisième» nature, dans la lignée de Cicéron qui en distinguait deux (sauvage ou transformée par la main de l'homme). En cette époque où la perspective passionne artistes et théoriciens, le jardin offre une large pyramide visuelle à l'observateur, le regard plonge dans des plans dégagés, le parcours visuel s'anime de verticales et d'horizontales. Dans ce contexte, la disposition du sol en terrasses permet de jouer sur les dénivellations et d'accentuer la priorité donnée aux cascades et aux jeux d'eau. Ces aspects se retrouvent par exemple dans les jardins de la Villa Lante à Bagnaia, à la Villa d'Este de Tivoli, à la Villa Buonvisi à San Pancrazio. Ces conceptions sont en rupture avec la fontaine médiévale, comme l'iconographie du *P.p.* l'est avec la représentation traditionnelle des quatre fleuves d'Eden.

Autre élément des jardins italiens de la Renaissance présent dans la poésie de Milton: les grottes. Vinci, dans ses études pour un Traité sur l'eau en 15 parties, évoque le double sentiment que le visiteur a à l'approche des grottes artificielles: un sentiment partagé entre la crainte d'y pénétrer et la curiosité d'en découvrir le mystère. Très présente dans les jardins italiens de la Renaissance, comme dans le Sacro Bosco de Bomarzo, la grotte fait référence à l'amaltheum des jardins antiques décrits par Cicéron dans nombres de ses lettres. L'auteur y célèbre à travers la grotte la parfaite union de la nature et la culture. Cependant, les grottes du Paradis de Milton sont bien différentes. Le poète les évoque à plusieurs reprises, par exemple aux Livres IV (257–258 et 453–455) et V (229–233).

13 Paris, B.N.F. Ra51pet.fol.

Une gravure de Medina[14] traduit plastiquement ces grottes naturelles, ces berceaux de verdure décrits par Milton; elle synthétise trois épisodes qui font suite au mauvais rêve d'Eve, son péché. Elle raconte son rêve à Adam, puis «ils sortirent de dessous la voûte de leur berceau d'arbres» (1er plan, à droite; V, 137) et «ils s'inclinèrent profondément, adorèrent, et commencèrent leurs prières» (V, 144–145). Un détail lie le poème aux écrits de Palissy par exemple: Milton évoque l'»ouvrage champêtre du matin» (V, 211). La sensibilité protestante du poète rejoint celle de Du Bartas et de Palissy qui ne conçoivent pas le lieu sans un minimum d'activité: après une prière, le premier couple «s'empresse à leur ouvrage champêtre» (V, 211) et à leurs «fraîches occupations» (V, 125) «leur croissant ouvrage» (IX, 202). Ce travail effectué au paradis par Adam et Eve est le plus souvent figuré par les artistes comme une conséquence de la Chute, et suit donc l'Expulsion.

Dieu envoie Raphaël pour exhorter l'homme à l'obéissance (2e plan à gauche): «Raphaël s'avançait dans la forêt aromatique; Adam l'aperçut; il était assis à la porte de son frais berceau [...] Eve, dans l'intérieur de son berceau, attentive à son heure, préparait pour le dîner des fruits savoureux» (V, 298–304). Adam mène l'ange à sa demeure et lui offre les fruits cueillis par Eve (3e plan, au centre): «Cependant notre premier père pour aller à la rencontre de son hôte céleste, s'avance hors du berceau» (V, 350–351); «ils arrivèrent à la demeure sylvaine» (V, 377–378); «leur table était un gazon élevé et touffu, entouré de siège de mousse» (V, 391–392).

Ces berceaux de verdure peuvent faire penser à certaines constructions du jardin que Poliphile et son aimée Polia traversent au cours de leur songe initiatique.[15] On sait à quel point l'ouvrage de Colonna – traduit en anglais dès 1592 – a marqué les esprits et l'art du jardin. Mais le jardin de Poliphile est un jardin où l'art et la nature se rencontrent sans fusionner: or, l'Eden de Milton est cette beauté «sauvage au-dessus de la règle et de l'art» (V, 297). La nature édénique que Milton décrit et que ses illustrateurs représentent est bien cette nature sauvage, certes harmonieuse et ordonnée, mais une nature qui ne porte pas d'empreinte visible d'une création autre que celle de Dieu. Selon de nombreux auteurs de l'époque, comme Palissy ou Du Bartas, la nature est le livre de la création, l'autre livre de Dieu, avec la Bible. Cette particularité fait de Milton un précurseur de l'esthétique des

14 Voir par ex: http://myweb.stedwards.edu/georgek/milton/medina/medina296.htm

15 Voir par ex le site Gallica: http://gallica.bnf.fr/scripts/ConsultationTout.exe?O=02200005 (fig. 41 et 42, éd. Venise, 1499).

jardins telle qu'elle se développe notamment en Angleterre dès le début du XVIIIe.

«Je ne doute pas que lorsqu'un Français lit une description du jardin d'Eden, il se le figure à l'image de Versailles, avec ses haies bien taillées et ses treillages» écrit en 1782 Walpole dans *History of the Modern Taste in Gardening*.[16] En retour, l'Eden de Milton est à l'opposé des jardins dits «à la française», «réguliers» ou «formels», et les Anglais ont élaboré un art du jardin dans le même esprit. D'ailleurs, le *P.p.* est l'une des rares épopées modernes citées dans les traités sur les jardins: ainsi les théoriciens du XVIIIe, époque du triomphe du jardin dit à l'anglaise, se figurait ce lieu de plaisir à la manière l'Eden miltonien. Ces jardins sont bien connus: de nombreux châteaux ou *country houses* des XVIe, XVIIe et XVIIIe subsistent ou ont été restaurés. Ils sont les témoins de la coexistence, au XVIIe, de plusieurs traditions: l'esprit médiéval avec le jardin clos de murs; l'influence italienne, c'est-à-dire maniériste, avec ses grottes, sculptures et jeux d'eau; la présence d'éléments classiques, comme les parterres de broderies, les allées, les miroirs d'eau. Cela est en partie dû à la présence en Angleterre, à la demande de Charles II, du Français Mollet. Il travailla au parc Saint James et publia en 1651 *Le jardin de plaisir*. On constate avec ses dessins le raffinement décoratif des éléments structurant, de manière rigoureuse et symétrique, ses jardins.

D'ambitieuses réalisations furent aussi menées pour Jacques Ier, par exemple, avec les frères de Caus. Le premier a travaillé à Hatfield House, en collaboration avec le botaniste Tradescant; le second a notamment réalisé, pour le comte de Pembroke, le jardin de Wilton. Mais dans le même temps, les *Essais* de Bacon soulignent que les jardins sont devenus une forme d'art et un fait de civilisation. L'auteur souligne le souci de bannir tout ce qui relève d'un art trop visible et affirme déjà, comme Milton, certains traits du style qui prévaut au XVIIIe dans le jardin «dégéométrisé», dit «à l'anglaise». Il débute le chapitre 46 consacré au jardin par un rappel de celui planté par Dieu, fondement de son opinion sur l'art des jardins: "and indeed, it is the purest of the human pleasures. It is the greatest refreshment to the spirits of man." Même s'il avoue un peu plus loin sa préférence pour une structure traditionnelle du jardin ("the garden is best to be square"), Bacon souligne que les parterres en broderie polychromes sont des futilités qui n'ont leur

16 *Anecdotes of Painting in England*, 5 vol., 2e éd, Londres, 1782, t. 4, p. 235.

place que sur les pâtisseries: "you may see as good sights, many times, in tarts."

Cette mode des berceaux de verdure sera mentionnée en France beaucoup plus tard, dans *La théorie et pratique du jardinage* de Dézallier d'Argenville (1709). Son chapitre VIII porte sur les portiques, les berceaux et les cabinets de treillage, éléments évoqués un demi-siècle plus tôt par Palissy et Milton. Ils sont «assurément quelque chose de beau et magnifique» et «relèvent et rehaussent infiniment la beauté naturelle des jardins». Les berceaux de verdure de Milton et de ses illustrateurs appartiennent à la catégorie dite des «berceaux naturels» définis ainsi: «ils sont simplement formés de branches d'arbres entrelacées avec industrie, et soutenues par de gros treillages, cerceaux, perches, etc., ce qui compose des galeries, des portiques, des salles et des enfilades de verdure couvertes naturellement.» La même année, une lettre de John Vanbrugh à la duchesse de Marlborough marque un tournant dans l'histoire des jardins. La lettre traite des travaux du palais de Blenheim et du parc de Woodstock. Vanbrugh définit l'effet recherché: le jardin doit être comme une peinture, il doit être pittoresque et respecter le caractère sauvage de la nature.

Ainsi durant la première moitié du XVIIIe, on assiste à un vaste mouvement qui a dégéométrisé les jardins anglais, a «paysagé» le jardin alors que les Français «enjardinaient» le paysage. Les acteurs de cette évolution sont Vanburgh, Bridgeman, Burlington, Brown et Kent; ils travaillent à Blenheim, Castel Howard, Claremont, Stowe, Rousham ou Chiswick. Tout cela se précise avec la vague du palladianisme: désormais, outre la référence à l'antique avec les architectures aux volumes sobres et les péristyles, les jardins se font irréguliers, souples et sinueux et se fondent dans le paysage. A la même époque, Newton, alors président de la Royal Society de Londres, menait ses attaques contre le cartésianisme et la méthode des géomètres. Il faut aussi souligner l'importance du *Traité sur l'entendement humain* de Locke où l'accent est mis sur les sensations, les sentiments, les sens, la psychologie: autant d'éléments dont Milton est aussi le précurseur.

En effet, une autre caractéristique présente dans le *P.p.* et ses illustrations est l'union du sensible au spirituel: l'intimité, la tendresse et la sensualité qui se dégagent de l'évocation de la vie d'Adam et Eve au Paradis, élément clairement en rupture au regard de la tradition. Le portrait que Milton dresse du premier couple est empreint de «stature héroïque» et atteint une nouvelle profondeur psychologique. Adam et Eve sont en effet présentés tels des héros tragiques à l'origine de l'épopée humaine: ils ne sont pas des types, mais des prototypes. Tous deux sont évidemment très beaux: Adam, «patriarche de l'humanité» (IX, 376), fut «formé pour la contemplation et le courage» (IV, 297), Eve, «pour la douceur et la grâce séduisante» (IV, 298), «belle, divinement belle, faite pour l'amour des dieux» (IX, 489). Les relations du premier couple sont décrites avec tendresse et sensualité, dans une union du sensible et du spirituel qui rappelle certaines œuvres majeures de l'art baroque, au premier rang desquelles l'*Extase de sainte Thérèse* du Bernin. Dans le *P.p.*, l'ange évoque le «plaisir pur» qu'Adam goûte «dans [son] corps» (VIII, 622). Après la Chute, s'allume «pour la première fois le désir charnel» (IX, 1011–1013), les regards d'Adam sont «lascifs» (IX, 1013–1014), et «ils brûlent impudiques» (IX, 1015).

Mais Milton évoque aussi avant le Péché l'union amoureuse et charnelle d'Adam et Eve (IV, 738–751). Flatters sut à merveille transposer la tendre et charnelle intimité qui unit Adam et Eve avant la faute, enlacés dans un épais berceau de verdure.[17] Un même élan sensuel caractérise une gravure de Fuseli.[18] Schiavonetti choisit de représenter l'émerveillement amoureux d'Adam se penchant avec un geste de délicate retenue vers la femme encore endormie.[19] Comme la majorité des œuvres fondées sur le *P.p.*, la gravure accentue le naturalisme exotique de l'environnement dans lequel l'intimité du premier couple est mise en scène. Une scène proche, tout aussi sensuelle et tendre, fut gravée par Westall.[20] On remarque les mêmes caractéristiques dans une planche de Blake.[21] L'artiste a souligné l'intimité du couple par cette couronne de feuillages qui forme comme une auréole autour d'eux. Hayman représente d'une autre manière l'union d'Adam et Eve: assis sous deux arbres aux troncs enlacés.[22]

L'amour unit Adam et Eve, y compris lors de la fatale désobéissance. Milton présente l'aspect psychologique et amoureux de l'épisode: Adam imite le geste d'Eve par amour et fidélité, «follement vaincu par le charme d'une femme» (IX, 999). La scène fut représentée avec une grande justesse de ton dans une gravure d'après Melin.[23] Assis sous un bananier, Eve soutient délicatement la main d'Adam qui porte le fruit défendu. Notons la

17 Voir *Adam et Eve de Dürer à Chagall. Gravures de la B.N.F.*, Paris, 1992, n° 87a.
18 Voir par ex: http://myweb.stedwards.edu/georgek/milton/fuseli/fuseli20.html
19 Voir *Adam et Eve de Dürer à Chagall. Gravures de la B.N.F.*, Paris, 1992, n° 54.
20 Voir par ex: http://myweb.stedwards.edu/georgek/milton/westall/westall5.html
21 Voir par ex: http://www.pitt.edu/~ulin/Paradise/images/PL04a.JPG
22 Voir par ex: http://myweb.stedwards.edu/georgek/milton/hayman/hayman4.htm
23 Voir *Adam et Eve de Dürer à Chagall. Gravures de la B.N.F.*, Paris, 1992, n° 87.

discrète présence du serpent, dans l'angle inférieur gauche de la composition, alors que l'iconographie traditionnelle en fait un acteur majeur.

Cette dimension psychologique et charnelle est absente du texte biblique; le talent de Milton a été ainsi d'insister sur un aspect particulier de l'aventure humaine, aspect novateur, original, qui n'est cependant pas en contradiction avec la tradition. Mais avant le *P.p.*, les artistes osaient rarement figurer une telle intimité. Quelques exemples antérieurs existent, mais ils concernent la Chute, non la vie d'Adam et Eve au jardin d'Eden, par exemple une gravure de Baldung[24] ou une planche de Jean de Gourmont.[25] Généralement, les œuvres où se ressent une telle atmosphère appartiennent aux XVIIIᵉ et XIXᵉ, et témoignent d'une sensibilité romantique, comme une gravure de Janinet.[26]

Les conséquences immédiates de la transgression se font d'abord sentir dans la nature qui pousse un «gémissement», la terre tremble «jusque dans ses entrailles», le ciel se couvre fait «entendre un sourd tonnerre, pleura quelques larmes tristes» (IX, 1000–1004). De météorologiques, les tempêtes deviennent intérieures et touchent Adam et Eve (IX, 1123–1126). Le désespoir d'Adam fut transposé avec talent dans une planche gravée d'après Flatters.[27] Seul, assis sur un rocher, le premier homme, conscient de son acte, se prend la tête entre les deux mains. L'harmonie paradisiaque brisée est suggérée par l'agave épineux, la découpe du rocher, la silhouette inquiétante et sombre des sapins. Surtout, la violence de l'éclair lumineux – présage du courroux divin – et l'aigle emportant un mouton solidement tenu entre ses serres achèvent de composer ce tableau du Paradis désormais perdu.

Le lecteur habitué aux versions poétisées du récit de la Genèse peut être surpris de la discrétion de la figure du Créateur dans l'œuvre de Milton. Le *P.p.* est avant tout le récit de l'épopée humaine, tragique et dramatique, composante psychologique du poème et de ses illustrations tout à fait nouvelle. De plus, Milton considère la Nature comme œuvre de Dieu, faite par lui et de lui, une Création qui porte les signes, les vestiges de cette origine divine; mais, dans le texte comme dans les images, Dieu est extérieur à la Création: il n'est pas dans le jardin et intervient rarement auprès de ses créatures. Par exemple, et contrairement à l'iconographie dominante, Dieu

24 Ibid, n° 5.
25 Ibid, n° 59.
26 Ibid, n° 73.
27 Ibid, n° 87b.

ne crée pas Adam en deux temps, le modelage et l'insufflation. Selon Gn II, 7, Adam est «modelé avec de la poussière prise du sol» avant d'être installé au Paradis. Cette première création est souvent davantage suggérée que clairement représentée: cette rareté iconographique s'explique en grande partie par les considérations théologiques refusant de mettre en valeur la figure divine en deus artifex, dans une activité qui rappelle immanquablement le travail de la terre, conséquence du Péché. Quelques artistes l'adoptent cependant, à travers des solutions plastiques parfois habiles qui soulignent l'origine terrestre de l'homme, le caractère matriciel de la Terre et donc de la nature, plus que le geste de Dieu s'adonnant tel un potier au modelage d'une matière première. On le voit par exemple dans les gravures de bibles luthériennes allemandes.[28] Adam est le héros du *P.p.*, car sa destinée et celle de la race humaine sont le sujet du poème. Il faut attendre le Livre VIII pour découvrir le récit de la Création de l'homme. Adam lui-même raconte son réveil (VIII, 253–256). Medina a traduit de façon simple et efficace cette scène, ajoutant uniquement le Soleil souriant et bienveillant, symbole de la présence divine.[29]

Aussi, les jours de la Création seront évoqués à travers la narration de l'ange à Adam, au Livre VII. Cet agent intermédiaire, essentiel dans le poème, est représenté avec habileté par Medina.[30] L'ange désigne des médaillons dont les compositions sont inspirées des fresques de Raphaël (Loggia du Vatican) largement diffusées par la gravure: Medina n'est pas original dans le choix de son modèle, mais la référence à Raphaël est choisie parce que Milton lui-même la suggère dans son poème.

Les commentateurs ont souvent souligné le «matérialisme visionnaire» de Milton lorsqu'il évoque d'une façon éloquente la *Création des animaux* (VII, 453–466). De nombreux artistes figurèrent, à la suite de Raphaël dont les fresques ont certainement inspiré le poète, les animaux sortant de terre, pleinement formés. Milton a sans doute découvert à Rome en 1638 ces peintures, dont il a gardé longtemps le souvenir, qui rejaillit lors de la rédaction du *P.p.*

Fidèle au texte biblique, Milton évoque la «garde de chérubins» placée «à l'orient du jardin» pour garder le chemin de l'arbre de vie (XI, 118–122). Michel est ensuite chargé d'expulser le couple, ce qui n'est pas dit dans la

28 Augsbourg, 1534 et Wittenberg, 1572.

29 Voir par ex: http://myweb.stedwards.edu/georgek/milton/medina/medina428.htm

30 Voir, par ex: http://myweb.stedwards.edu/georgek/milton/medina/medina390.htm

Genèse mais presque toujours figuré par les artistes, autre témoin de l'importance de la culture visuelle et artistique de Milton. Michel conduit Adam et Eve sur «une montagne, la plus haute du Paradis» pour y recevoir «des Visions de Dieu» (XI, 377–378). Enfin, l'ange leur annonce l'alliance nouvelle et la naissance du Messie et ses dernières paroles à Adam sont les suivantes: «Ayant appris ces choses, tu as atteint la somme de sagesse. [...] ajoute la foi, la vertu, la patience, la tempérance; ajoute l'amour dans l'avenir nommé Charité, âme de tout le reste. Alors tu regretteras moins de quitter ce Paradis, puisque tu posséderas en toi-même un Paradis bien plus heureux.» (XII, 575–587) Adam et Eve partent main dans la main, dans des termes évoquant la longue marche de l'humanité à travers l'histoire de l'errance des Israelites dans le désert avant l'entrée dans la Terre Promise, retour au Paradis originel: «l'ange les prit par la main, les conduisit droit à la porte orientale [...]. Ils regardèrent derrière eux, et virent toute la partie orientale du Paradis, naguère leur heureux séjour, ondulée par le brandon flambant: la porte était obstruée de figures redoutables et d'armes ardentes [...]. Main en main, à pas incertains et lents, ils prirent à travers Eden leur chemin solitaire.» (XII, 636–649)

Dans le poème de Milton, la Chute du genre humain paraît à la fois comme acte de transgression qui marque le refus de soumission de la créature à son créateur et comme acte tragique qui n'est toutefois pas irréparable. L'ange apprend aussi à Adam que «Dieu n'attache la sainteté à aucun lieu». L'homme, cultivant son âme et sa foi, possédera en lui-même «un Paradis bien plus heureux» (XII, 587). La mort ouvrira l'accès à un paradis céleste qui est conçu à l'image du Paradis terrestre, au climat tempéré, d'une «agréable vicissitude». La reconquête est annoncée et sera effective dans le *Paradis reconquis*:

> Moi qui chantais jadis le bienheureux jardin
> Perdu par la désobéissance d'un seul, je chante maintenant
> Le paradis recouvré par tous les humains
> Par la ferme désobéissance d'un seul, pleinement éprouvé
> A travers toutes les tentations, et le Tentateur déjoué
> Dans toutes ses ruses, défait et repoussé,
> Et le jardin d'Eden dressé dans la stérile étendue (I, 1–7).

Luis Fernando Ferreira SÁ

Notes on a Postcolonial Fall in Milton's Paradise

Milton's imperial epic, in the words of Martin Evans, seems to transform itself into an imperious epic in relation to post-colonial matters in the post-modern moment. Evans (1996) begins to discuss his overall thesis in the following ways: the texts linked to the literature of colonialism treat recurrent themes – of the colony itself, of the status of the colonized, of colonizers and their reasons – and share a common object whose lineaments are figured and delineated from linguistic practices, descriptive tropes, narrative organization, and conceptual categories. Departing from a supposedly shared discursive practice found in colonialist texts, Evans proceeds to connect these same practices to the grand argument of *Paradise Lost*: in justifying the ways of God to men Milton would appeal to an imperial discourse. This imperial discourse, however, is reworked as an ambivalent practice in the epic and is redressed in empyreal overtones. David Quint's *Epic and Empire* (1993) is another seminal volume whose beginnings are a rejection in *Paradise Lost* of imperialism and of the imperial epic tradition traced down to Virgil. Quint introduces a different critical moment when he proposes that the epic is transformed into adventurous romance, and that, finally, *Paradise Lost* is an epic that put an end to all other epics; Milton is a poet against empire. On the way that traverses empire and post-colony, Samuel Johnson is cited in an epigraph to *Milton's Imperial Epic* and sheds light on the notes to come: "[t]he subject of an epick poem is naturally an event of great importance. That of Milton is not the destruction of a city, the conduct of a colony, or the foundation of an empire" (1996: 1). This privileged reader of Milton's text understood that *Paradise Lost* would not found an empire, would not promote the empire, but maybe would initially de-stabilize the epic genre in its negotiations with (u)empire (agency and practice).

As long as negotiations are at stake, Homi Bhabha in his Afterword to the volume *Milton and the Imperial Vision* sets out on "an ironic act of courage" when he comments on Balachandra Rajan's propositions on Milton's epic as suffering from an imperial temptation. *Pace* Bhabha, "Milton earns the authority to speak in our time, to become part of the postcolonial conversation, because of the deep ambivalence that exists in his 'imperial voice''' (1999: 317). This earned authority associated with deep ambivalence is the Miltonic terrain *par excellence* and one on which I will not fear to thread. Milton's imperious epic will be read in its ambivalence and in its various negotiations.[1]

The choice of images in *Paradise Lost* for a crucial moment in one of the Western grand narratives of human history – the Fall – challenges the informed reader or critic to consider the relation between the acquired condition of Adam and Eve and the discourses of power and colonization in face of the New World. The surprising passage in the epic, with the images related to Adam's and Eve's loss of their "first naked glory" (9. 115)[2], reveals the extent to which this narrative of the Fall is associated with the loss of liberty of the colonized peoples of the New World. *Paradise Lost* exposes both histories as one possible history of human life. In addition, at the moment of re-dressing themselves, Adam and Eve symbolize the Fall also in terms of civility and civilization. In what follows, I will discuss this passage in particular with a view to understanding how the narrative eye/I (the authorial epic narrator) over these images and characters is less imperialist and much more likely to be linked to a political thinker exploring an instance of temporal and cultural difference. This bi-focal narrative outlook into politics and cultural difference will be thought out in relation to postcolonial assumptions.

Paradise Lost represents the acquired state of things through which Adam and Eve had to transit after the Fall: a fall into language (a postlapsarian one), and a fallen language that evokes a vast complex of contingencies and conflicts, complexities and paradoxes, that which also emerges in any postcolonial reading. The temporary center of discussion gravitates round the idea that the New World was habitually described in terms of a new Eden and that Milton's paradise is filled with images of this baiting New World. The implication is not a simple one, of course, since the Fall in *Paradise Lost* is first introduced through a satanic admiration of this new world that is God's "latest" creation; superimposed upon this first narrative, the reader is presented with the epic narrator's admiration upon the creation

1 On Milton and Imperialism see also Paul Stevens's "*Paradise Lost* and the Colonial Imperative" (1996) and Pompa Banerjee's "Milton's India and *Paradise Lost*" (1999).

2 *John Milton: Complete Poems and Major Prose*, ed. Merritt Y. Hughes (New York, 1957). Parenthetic Book and line references to Milton's *Paradise Lost* are to this edition.

and the subsequent loss by humankind of God's new world in relation to the New World. One of the forms Satan finds in order to tempt Eve, for instance, is a corruption of Adam's and Eve's sovereignty over the created "things" in the Garden of Eden: "Me thus, though importune perhaps, to come / And gaze, and worship thee of right declared / Sovran of creatures, universal dame" (9. 610–12). This corrupting stare, this gaze previously negotiated in Pandemonium, will subvert natural sovereignty into imperial domination. The next step of the serpent, as in a *stare decisis* inside out, will be to induce Eve to eat of the forbidden fruit after having openly declared that the "mother of mankind," "Sovran of creatures" and "universal dame," is to become "Empress of this fair World, resplendent Eve, / Easy to me it is to tell thee all" and still, "Empress, the way is ready, and not long" (9. 568–9, 626). This eye-straining imperial topos and eye-stained satanic trope will become more and more evident in the representation of fallen human subjectivity in *Paradise Lost.*

The allusive structure of the scene of the Fall impels the reader to understand this very Fall through the t(r)opological optics of imperialism, that is, the convocation, or even recruitment, of Adam and Eve to the contemporary "problematics" of opposition, conflict, and difference initiates with the loss of "innocence" of the autochthonous subject or the aborigine.[3] Such state of affairs is complicated still more if the reader take into consideration that the Fall is narrated in the register of shame and naturalized through a surprising and adventurous ethnographic comparative admiration:

> And girded on our loins, may cover round
> Those middle parts, that this newcomer, Shame,
> There sit not, and reproach us as unclean
> [...] there soon they chose

3 In relation to vision, optics, and the eyes/I's that see and are seen I side myself with Jean Starobinski through Martin Jay (1994) in their prefatory remarks on the judiciousness of reading: "[t]he complete critique is perhaps not one that aims at totality ... nor that which aims at intimacy (as does identifying intuition); it is the look that knows how to demand, in their turn, distance and intimacy, knowing in advance that the truth lies not in one or the other attempt, but in the movement that passes indefatigably from one to the other. One must refuse neither the vertigo of distance nor that of proximity; one must desire that double excess where the look is always near to losing all its powers" (19–20). It is such ambivalent desire, a willingness to risk this loss that guides and empowers my critical entrance in the labyrinths of *Paradise Lost.*

> The fig-tree, not that kind for fruit renowned,
> But such as this day to Indians known
> In Malabar or Decan spreads her arms
> Branching so broad and long, that in the ground
> The bended twigs take root, and daughters grow
> About the mother tree, a pillared shade
> High overarched, and echoing walks between;
> There oft the Indian herdsman shunning heat
> Shelters in cool, and tends his pasturing herds
> At loop-holes cut through thickest shade. Those leaves
> They gathered, broad as Amazonian targe,
> And with what skill they had, together sewed,
> To gird their waist, vain covering if to hide
> Their guilt and dreaded shame, O how unlike
> To that first glory! Such of late
> Columbus found the American so girt
> With feathered cincture, naked else and wild
> Among the trees on isles and woody shores.
> Thus fenced, and as they thought, their shame in part
> Covered (9. 1096–98, 1100–20).

There seems to be nothing new in the analogy between Milton's Eden and the New World, or between Adam and Eve and the ab-original inhabitants of this New World. What is "new" in the aforementioned passage focusing on the Fall is that the epic narrator makes representation equivalent to loss, an autochthonous loss.

The colonization of Adam and Eve by Satan, or the imperialism of Satan in regard to the "original" couple, asserts, with direct references, the interdependence between universal Fall and historical fall (for example, the fallen subjects of seventeenth-century England that submitted themselves to a "corrupt tyranny" of a Charles I or even to an-other "corrupt tyranny" of an Oliver Cromwell). In *Paradise Lost,* the postlapsarian "universal" subject of Scripture equalizes, in an ambivalent fashion, the dispossessed native subjects of the New World; the beginning of history is, in such transactional manner, the chosen first moment of colonialism and imperialism. Again, the aforementioned passage seems to sway both under a colonialist vision of history and up the mast that gives away postcolonial vistas into histories. Which vision of history is played out? What textual tradition of this history is a yoke critiqued out in the open or "yoked out" deconstructively? Before being described as the natural inhabitants of America, of the New World, Adam and Eve chose the "banyan:" an East Indian family tree that sends out shoots which grow down to the soil, roots that form secondary trunks, and whose leaves look like the leaves of the fig tree. As the epic narrator makes clear, the ab-original couple did not choose the well-known fruit derived from that tree, nor did they choose the blossoms of that same tree, they chose instead the leaves of a similar, but not equal, tree that grows in India. From India, the epic narrator next takes the readers, from lines number 1102 to 1108 of Book 9 of *Paradise Lost,* to the noun "Indians" and "Indian." At this exact moment, the informed reader and critic are faced with the superimposition of East (India, Indian, Indic) and West (Indian-American, indigenous), and also confronted with a linguistic slip whose posterior ab-use has rectified, recrudesced, at fault and to a fault, the forms and the structures of imperialism. Nonetheless, if Adam and Eve cover themselves up with the leaves of this Indian/indigenous tree, they do it out of shame and as the consequence of an error. Again, this linguistic slip, an isomorphism at best, indicates a re-vision of the registers of discovery of the New World. The fault/the fall and shame of Adam and Eve are represented and can be read thus: as a deviation of Columbus (a detour from the sea-routes that would lead to the East-Indies), as a defalcation of the discoveries (they failed to meet the European promises and expectations), as the defacement of colonization (erasure of any previous subjectivity), as the defaults of imperialisms, and even as a possible defeasance of postcolonialisms (thinking them in terms of a general theory of resentment or simply as trivial acritical generalizations). All those mis-takes, as if posed in relation to an interdependent universal Fall and a historical fall, are still to be confirmed in the next corrective evidence in the same passage of the epic.

Fault, falls, superimposition and interdependence of ideas are also to be found in the reference in the epic to the "Amazonian targe" or light Amazonian shield. At this point, what is ambivalent, and not ambiguous, is what "Amazonian" in the poem refers to. Would there be a reference to the "recently" discovered warriors that inhabited the riverbank, or their textual prototypes, fierce female combatants that inhabited the classical antiquity? In case the reader opts for the first possibility, the Amazonian peoples, the poem asserts soon after that that Columbus found(ed) these peoples "recently" discovered in America girt in the "first naked glory" before their fall. Another point of inferential interest: would this lineament be a pronouncement, forfeiture, prefiguration that the Amazonian peoples, until then as much innocent as pre-fallen Adam and Eve, should be corrupted by discovery and then from this point on be dis-covered in a linguistic slippage, a shaking soil of signification, or be re-discovered from a blurred eye? If the answer to this (un)rhetorical question is a "positive" one, would not the text be linking, definitely, the European (or English, to be more specific) imperial project to the satanic imperial prospect in *Paradise Lost*? And yet: in making such connection, could the epic still be read in its proto- or pro-colonial/imperial affiliations? In a localized sense, by reading these textual aporias, by mis-reading them, I intend to open up the epic toward a postcolonial conversation, that is, I recover the poem from a critical arena full of insidious interpretations, and redeem the text, redirect its foreclosed contents, toward a critical battlefield fulfilled with readings and mis-readings. The colonial/imperial avatars in Milton's paradise may then submerge, for there to emerge postcolonial questionings.

On this very route, following the theological line of thought that takes the Fall and the participation of Satan in this fall as a better good, that is, as *felix culpa*, I would add that a reader, any reader, may understand the discovery and colonization of the American peoples by the Europeans also in terms of a devious "fortunate fall." Bearing the biblical text in mind, one cannot recuperate a lost innocence, one cannot recuperate the Garden of Eden, one cannot know good by good, but, one has to opt and recoup salvation, or losses, with great labor on the (in)fertile soils of signification. In relation to the colonized peoples, and according to the negotiable prospects I read in the text, one would be confronted with the following: there is no way to recuperate, let alone regain, one's lost and found origins, there is no way to recuperate one's "nation"/notion of "purity," there is no way one can know the civilizational "good" as being simply a "good." Notwithstanding, one may reach back/toward "salvation" in the ways of subjectivity, laboring on the side of re-cognition and on the strife of negotiation. We, readers of the epic, cannot deny the founding violence – there is complicity between violence and discourse –, in the same way we cannot retaliate, the text in question, with violence:

> [t]he point is not to recover a lost consciousness, but to see, to quote Macherey, the itinerary of the silencing. [...] So from that point of view, our view of history is a very different view. It is also cumulative, but it's a view where we see the way in which narratives compete with each other, which one rises, which one falls, who is silent, and the itinerary of the silencing rather than the retrieval (Spivak 1990: 36, 31).

Curious as it might appear, the mis-reading of epistemic violence – to mention just one, and one associated with European imperialism – as a fortunate fall or *felix culpa* for the peoples who suffer(ed) the evils of colonization should be plentifully linked to the itinerary of the silencing as Macherey and Spivak see it. Excuses masked as *ex-culpas*,[4] happy or misshapen ones, in the strategic time and place of postcolonial discourse would not, some way or another, retrieve much, or retrial, rescue or salvage anything worth the while. These *ex-culpas*, obliterative or oblivious of responsibility, cannot, once again, correct any state of affairs, once the matter is not related to correction or the like. Put in a different manner, "the aftermath of colonialism is not only the retrieval of the colonial history of the past but the putting together of a history of the present" (Spivak 1991: 139), this very same reading/re-reading that I am now putting forth in my misreading of the epic. And yet, "[t]he most frightening thing about imperialism, its long-term toxic effect, what secures it, what cements it, is the benevolent self-representation of the imperialist as savior" (Spivak 1992b: 781). Nothing better than strategic and (in)felix (ex)culpas of negotiation, the misreading that I am now briefly proposing, to deconstruct "benevolence" in any salvage.

Imperial benevolence and postcolonial ambivalence are to be found on the Amazonian targe of Milton's epic. The second possibility of reading the passage, the allusion to the classical female combatants, would bring about one more layer of complication and complexity, since the complicity of this text with the imperial project is getting ever and ever more remote. If the informed reader reflects on the reference to the combatants, s/he would be surprised by the correspondent attractions and repulsions: the Amazons, as members of a female warrior race that would repeatedly fight against the Greeks, would be combating, now in a mythological intertext, the (proto)–

4 I use the term *ex-culpa* in the following accumulations: first, as an improper derivation from the verb to exculpate: "to clear from alleged fault or guilt." Second, as an ironic derivation from the usage of the verb to exculpate, implying "a clearing from blame or fault often *in a matter of small importance*." Third, as a means to call attention to the fact that *ex-culpa* is a term associated with the itinerary of silencing in the sense that what is of great importance in this process is the (un)blameworthy violence perpetrated both in practice and in discourse. Fourth, *ex-culpa* is a term related to the itinerary of silencing less as an attempt at retrieval and more in its attempts at negotiation. Fifth, the term *ex-culpa* also denotes a discursive/rhetorical maneuver that attempts to release one either from an obligation that binds the conscience (straightens the eye/I) or from the consequences of committing an act of grave (ir)responsibility.

imperialist and patriarchal projects of the classical antiquity. A referential system of such magnitude and (dis)order, placed at a crucial moment of the text, serves, at least, to corroborate the suggestion that the politico-colonialist alliances of the epic are ambivalent to a discredit. "A nice bit of controlled indeterminacy there, resting upon one of the most firmly established European conventions: transition from Christian psychobiography to Romantic Imagination. [...] The problem of irrational faith is interiorized into allegory in the narrowest possible sense" (Spivak 1991b: 146). Even though Spivak does not refer to Milton's epic, this same romantic imagination is to be found in the passage in question in terms of mythology/ ideology. In addition, if faith is irrational or not extrapolates the scope of these short notes on Milton's *Paradise Lost*, but in *lato sensu*, this very same faith is allegorized in the epic to the extent it becomes aporetic. The fall of Adam and Eve and the immediate consequences of this fall are textual movements where the ab-original couple dress themselves up in combat and repeat a battle at times mythological, at times theological, at times cultural and ideological. Religion, seen as a cultural allegory, permitted the epic narrator and author to produce an-other (text) immediately assessable by grinding and superimposing the attendant problems related to race, exploration, conquest, and colonization.

Once more,

> [i]ndeed, literature might be the best complement to ideological transformation. The successful reader learns to identify implicitly with the value system figured forth by literature. Through learning to manipulate the figures, rather than through (or in addition to) working out the argument explicitly and literally, with a view to reasonable consent. Literature buys your assent in an almost clandestine way and therefore it is an excellent instrument for a slow transformation of the mind (Spivak 1992a: 278).

In the present case, this transformation takes place less as a consenting to the figures of speech or as a forgetting to read them, and more as a critical maneuver within the textual allegories that I presume to have refined to the point of being capable of reading them as aporias. There are yet many questions looking for their answers: how then is my assent given to this epical narrative? How am I, or indeed how was I, historically constituted as its implied reader so that I am now able to read it with pleasure within my cultural self-representation? Returning to the first point, I would say that my assent was given to the narrative of *Paradise Lost* in terms of acknowledgement. To the second, I would presume to be a well-informed reader of the epic, and that my misreading of the text is a "jouissance" because I sight the textual ambivalences and see the valences (fall, loss, lack) within Milton's paradise.

Works Cited

Banerjee, Pompa. "Milton's India and *Paradise Lost.*" *Milton Studies* 37. Labriola, Albert C. (Ed.). Pittsburgh: University of Pittsburgh Press, 1999. 142–165.

Bhabha, Homi. "Afterword: An Ironic Act of Courage." In: Rajan, Balachandra and Sauer, Elizabeth (Eds). *Milton and the Imperial Vision.* Pittsburgh: Duquesne UP, 1999. 315–322.

Evans, J. Martin. *Milton's Imperial Epic:* Paradise Lost *and the Discourse of Colonialism.* Ithaca: Cornell UP, 1996.

Jay, Martin. *Downcast Eyes: The Denigration of Vision in Twentieth-Century French Thought.* Berkeley: University of California Press, 1994.

Milton, John. *John Milton: Complete Poems and Major Prose.* Hughes, Merritt Y. (Ed.). New York: Odyssey Press, 1957.

Quint, David. *Epic and Empire: Politics and Generic Form from Virgil to Milton.* Princeton: Princeton UP, 1993.

Spivak, Gayatri Chakravorty. "The Burden of English." In: Rajan, Rajeswari S. (Ed.). *The Life of the Land: English Literature Studies in India.* New Delhi: Oxford UP, 1992a. 275–299.

–. "Acting Bits/Identity Talks." *Critical Inquiry*, n. 18, 770–803. Summer 1992b.

–. "Feminism in Decolonization." *Differences*, v. 3, n. 3, 139–170. Fall 1991.

–. *The Postcolonial Critic: Interviews, Strategies, and Dialogues.* New York: Routledge, 1990.

Stevens, Paul. "*Paradise Lost* and the Colonial Imperative." *Milton Studies* 34. Labriola, Albert C. (Ed.). Pittsburgh: University of Pittsburgh Press, 1996. 3–21.

Charlotte CLUTTERBUCK

The Sinner's View of God in the Invocations and Book III of *Paradise Lost*[1]

Milton's double voice: the Poet and the Believer in the Invocations

In *Paradise Lost*, Milton articulates two intentions: to write an "adventurous song" that will pursue "Things unattempted yet in prose or rhyme," and to "justify the ways of God to men" (I.11–26). Both are problematic.

First, Milton constructs a persona who is outside his story rather than within it, and who (unlike the personae of Dante, Donne, or Langland) is more concerned with his poetry than with his search for God. Some critics, noting the hubris of writing an epic about the Fall, suggest that the persona is in danger of falling, but finally avoids "blasphemous pride" by a humble "dependence on God" shown in the invocations (Riggs, 63; McMahon, 1; Schindler, 47–50). However, I believe that the invocations dramatize an increasing distance between God and the persona who secures his poem at the cost of endangering his relationship with God.

Secondly, unlike any other major English poet, Milton makes God the Father a character in his poem; many readers, finding his Father repellent, have considered the poem flawed as a result. However, this paper argues that Milton creates these "flaws" deliberately, writing in "fallen language" (Kinney, 134; Ricks, 109): his repellent Father is the projection of a sinful, vainglorious poet who has "wisdom at one entrance quite shut out" (III.50).

Milton's persona has two distinct roles: the bombastic "Poet" who stands outside the story's action and overtly uses the first person to discuss his own poetry; and the Believer who does not use first person pronouns,

1 These ideas are explored in greater detail in my subsequently published book, *Encounters with God in Medieval and Early Modern English Poetry* (Aldershot: Ashgate, 2005).

but is covertly in the story. It is sometimes necessary to read the poem on two levels, as a public expression of faith in God and the Poet's own prowess, and as a private expression of fear that this prowess may alienate the Believer from God.

The first invocation represents the Fall as already past, while Redemption lies in the future:

> Of man's first disobedience, and the fruit
> Of that forbidden tree, whose mortal taste
> Brought death into the world, and all our woe,
> With loss of Eden, till one greater man
> Restore us, and regain the blissful seat,
> Sing heavenly Muse [...] (I.1–6).

But historically speaking, the Fall and the Redemption had both occurred already; within the narrative, neither has yet occurred. This suggests that *Paradise Lost* concerns, not only the history of Man's Redemption, but also the future possibility of the Poet's salvation.

As soon as the Poet appeals to the Muse, foregrounding literary rather than moral matters, the tight focus of the opening blurs. He clutters the text with names of places (Schindler, 49–50) where he might find inspiration – Oreb, Sinai, Sion, Siloa. There is thus no firm location for his statement:

> I thence
> Invoke thy aid to my adventurous song,
> That with no middle flight intends to soar [...]
> [...] while it pursues
> Things unattempted yet in prose or rhyme (I.12–16).

The passage suggests the adventurous Satan who tempts Mankind (Schindler 49–50) and the pride of Icarus, who refused to take a middle way and fell to his death (McMahon, 28–33). The language here is objectified rather than personal: the Poet invokes "aid," not for himself, but for a song that pursues not God, but "Things".

The language changes completely when he requests instruction from the Holy Spirit:

> And chiefly thou O Spirit, that dost prefer
> Before all temples the upright heart and pure,
> Instruct me, for thou know'st; thou from the first

> Wast present, and with mighty wings outspread
> Dove-like sat'st brooding on the vast abyss
> And madest it pregnant: what in me is dark
> Illumine, what is low raise and support (I.17–23).

The repeated "thou" and the four imperatives ("instruct," "illumine," "raise," "support") place the persona and Spirit in the intimate connection of plea-prayer. The Believer asks humbly for spiritual help: his confession of darkness and lowness suggests that he does not think he has an "upright heart and pure". He makes the Spirit the subject of all the verbs, and honours his creative role of making the abyss "pregnant".

However, this humility disappears as soon as the Poet speaks of his poem:

> That to the highth of this great argument
> I may assert eternal providence,
> And justify the ways of God to men (I.24–6).

Who is the Poet to justify the ways of God to men? Here he makes himself into the grammatical subject and asks to rise, not to heaven, but to the "highth of this great argument". Ironically, the Poet does not "soar" at all, but plummets directly into hell, going on to make the abyss "pregnant" with the foul pregnancies of Satan and Sin.

In the second invocation, the Poet is more distant from God: "Smit with the love of sacred song" rather than love of God; relating to the "holy Light" in which God dwells rather than to the Spirit himself. He asks uneasily, "May I express thee unblamed?" and nervously reiterates that he has returned safely from Hell to revisit the Light; instead of aspiring to be like Moses, he now prays to equal pagan poets "in renown". His loss of intimacy with the Spirit becomes more poignant when he humbly admits that the Light does not revisit him, but that he has "wisdom at one entrance quite shut out". But again, he promptly abandons humility, wishing to "see and tell / Of things," not to relate to God (III.1–55).

He has moved further from intimacy with the Spirit in the third invocation (VII.1–40) when he invokes the "goddess" Urania and with her help presumes to enter "the heaven of heavens". Comparing himself to the pagan figures of Bellerophon and Orpheus, he asks the Muse to return him to earth "with like safety… Lest… I fall," and claims that on earth

> More safe I sing with mortal voice [...]
> [...] though fallen on evil days,
> On evil days though fallen, and evil tongues;
> In darkness, and with dangers compassed round,
> And solitude; yet not alone, while thou
> Visit'st my slumbers nightly [...] (VII.24–9).

But how can he be safe if he is encompassed with dangers? The repetition of "fall" (Schindler, 53–4) and the stress on his "solitude" suggest Adam and Eve's "solitary" journey to exile.

Schindler argues that in the last invocation the Poet has overcome his hubris, and is secure in his inspiration, for the Muse now visits him without being invoked (55–5; see also McMahon, 59). However, I believe that his spiritual state is worse than before. He begins bluntly:

> No more of talk where God or angel guest
> With man, as with his friend, familiar used
> To sit indulgent [...] (IX.1–3).

Now he cannot even talk about God, let alone to him. Words describing sin and alienation from God fall like blows: "foul distrust, and breach / Disloyal [...] revolt / And disobedience"; "alienated, distance and distaste, / Anger and just rebuke, and judgment"; "a world of woe, / Sin and her shadow Death, and Misery / Death's harbinger" (IX.6–13).

Although the Poet "now must change / Those notes to tragic," he embraces this "sad task" with relish: it is a "more heroic" topic than Achilles, a "higher argument" that can "raise" the renown of the epic form; instead of asking for spiritual illumination, he asks his "celestial patroness" for "answerable style". He chooses his topic, not because it will bring him closer to God, but because it will enable him to write a better epic than anyone else (IX.13–43).

> Yet he doubts his success,
> [...] if all be mine,
> Not hers who brings it nightly to my ear (IX.46–7).

The idea of the Muse dictating nightly to the ear of the Poet suggests corruption. Satan, as a toad, poured into Eve's sleeping ear "Illusions [...] phantasms and dreams [...] Vain hopes [...] inordinate desires [...] engendering pride" (IV.800–809). The resonance between the two images is reinforced when the Poet immediately relates Satan's return to Eden for the final temptation.

The movement of the invocations from closeness to distance suggests that the hubris of the Poet's undertaking has distanced him from God, a distance that is reflected in the way that he writes about God, especially in Book III.

Division in the Godhead in Book III

In depicting God, Milton makes three key linguistic choices: he uses narrative about God rather than the focused dialogue of plea-prayer; he then shows God speaking within that narrative; and finally, he depicts two persons of the Godhead speaking to each other.

Dialogue allows a poet to relate to God without having to describe or explain him. It favours personal pronouns that establish connection and verbs (often imperatives and interrogatives) that articulate desire for God in the present tense or urgent-future, allowing a sense that the relationship with God is outside time. In contrast, narrative is rich in nouns that describe things and their place in the world, and verb tenses relating past and sometimes future actions. A narrative about God inevitably represents him as operating within space and time.

One of the problems with writing speeches for God is that the sense of God operating in time is magnified when God himself uses tenses. Even more seriously, Milton's construction of a debate on the merits of justice and mercy suggests that there is division within the Godhead, and that the Son, albeit with the Father's approval, wins this argument.

Although many critics have of course discussed various aspects of Milton's language in Book III, there has not been, so far as I know, any extensive analysis of the interplay between the Father and Son and the differences in their style. The Father uses syntax and judgemental modifiers to distance Man and first-person pronouns to assert himself. The Son uses vigorous verbs and all the personal pronouns to offer himself and restore connections. However, at times, both seem more interested in power than in love, and remote from Man. This coincides with a use of the predictive-future, an increase in empty modifiers and words expressing time or space, and a change from true dialogue to narrative or explanation.

In Book III, the absence of the Spirit suggests that this vision of God is neither raised nor illumined. God appears to the unfallen Adam as a single divine presence (VIII.314); it is perhaps only from the sinner's viewpoint that God has conflicting aspects such as justice and mercy, or even Father and Son. God's speeches need to be read on two levels: the complex use of tenses suggest, both that all times are present to God, and that sinners can only see God's actions from the warped viewpoint of time; God's repellent aspects create a tension between theological truths about the salvation of Man and the Believer's internal debate about whether or not he personally can be redeemed.

From the outset, the Father views Adam and Eve "From the pure empyrean" (III.57), that is, from a distance. He draws the Son's attention to Satan's journey:

> Only begotten Son, seest thou what rage
> Transports our adversary, whom no bounds
> Prescribed, no bars of hell, nor all the chains
> Heaped on him there, nor yet the main abyss
> Wide interrupt can hold (III.80–4).

Here the Father merely observes and interprets what is happening: he does not use the first person or justify himself, and his verbal adjectives and participles ("Prescribed," "Heaped," "interrupt") create a compressed and vigorous syntax. As soon as the speech moves into the future tense he begins to justify himself:

> [...] and [Satan] shall pervert
> For man will hearken to his glozing lies,
> And easily transgress the sole command,
> Sole pledge of his obedience: so will fall,
> He and his faithless progeny: whose fault?
> Whose but his own? Ingrate, he had of me
> All he could have; I made him just and right,
> Sufficient to have stood, though free to fall (III.92–9).

His tone becomes hostile as he piles up judgemental modifiers: "glozing," "easily," "faithless," "Ingrate". The term "faithless progeny" draws attention to the doubtful justice, in human terms, of punishing the sinner's progeny. The Father seems to gloat over this prospect, even to command it with his use of "shall pervert" (Peter, 11. Emma, 102), and it seems that, even before the Fall, Man is not independently capable of acting well, only of sinning (Mitchell, 76). Yet the Father holds Man responsible for his sin: when Man was virtuous, he was passive, "placed" (by God) in the garden (III.90), the object of the verbs "destroy" and "pervert" (III.90–2); when he sins, he becomes active, the subject of the verbs "hearken," "transgress," "fall".

The Father's syntax places Man in relationship with sin rather than God: "they themselves decreed / Their own revolt [...] Till they enthral themselves [...] they themselves ordained their fall." The only present, positive indicative verbs he applies to Man in this whole speech are "they trespass" and "man falls deceived" (III.122, 130). Thus, for the Father, Man's virtue is already past, and his sin dominates the eternal present: and this is before Man has actually sinned within the narrative.

The Father seems egotistical, speaking at the Son rather than to him; he does not show any love for Man: it appears that his sole reason for creating him was to gain "pleasure [...] from [...] obedience paid". His repeated assertions ("I made him just and right [...] Such I created [...] I formed them free") suggest self-righteous certainty, as do his judgemental and tautological modifiers ("false guile [...] useless and vain [...] high foreknowledge [...] high decree"). Yet there is a querulousness in his rhetorical questions, and in the way he makes himself the subject of negative or hypothetical constructions: "What pleasure I from such obedience paid [...] they themselves decreed / Their own revolt, not I [...] if I foreknew [...] I else must change / Their nature" (III.103–28).

After this hostility, coldness, and even uncertainty, his final announcement of mercy seems unconvincing, intended to make his "glory excel" rather than to rescue his creatures (III.129–34). But if the debate is read as the Believer's inner debate, then the Father's hostile tone and his suggestion that sin has already occurred may mask the Believer's abhorrence of his own sin, while the Father's offer of mercy represents the Believer's hope that in his case mercy will prevail.

Such a reading seems the more likely because the Son's reply unmakes the Father's speech. Rather than mirroring "all his Father," he reflects only mercy, "Love without end, and without measure grace" (III.139–42). His urgent brevity contrasts strongly with the Father's uncertain wordiness;

while the Father spoke coldly of Man, the Son speaks warmly, engaging in dialogue, speaking to the Father without any use of first-person pronouns:

> For should man finally be lost, should man
> Thy creature late so loved, thy youngest son
> Fall circumvented thus? (III.150–2)

The effect of representing the issue dramatically is to suggest that the Son wins the Father over, even dictates to him with the repeated imperative, "that be from thee far / That far be from thee, Father"; he points out that in exercising justice against Man the Father would abolish his creation, allow his goodness and greatness to be "questioned and blasphemed" and give Satan the victory (III.153–66). His insistence that the Father cannot deny mercy without denying his own nature suggests the Believer's own desire that this should be true. In response, the Father declares that it is, affirming their essential harmony, using the second person:

> All hast thou spoken as my thoughts are, all
> As my eternal purpose hath decreed [...] (III.168–72).

Disconcertingly, the Father immediately reverts to self-justification and hostility, a change that again occurs with a change to the future tense, subjecting God to time:

> Man shall not quite be lost, but saved who will,
> Yet not of will in him, but grace in me
> Freely vouchsafed; once more I will renew
> His lapsed powers, though forfeit and enthralled
> By sin to foul exorbitant desires;
> Upheld by me, yet once more he shall stand
> On even ground against his mortal foe,
> By me upheld, that he may know how frail
> His fallen condition is, and to me owe
> All his deliverance, and to none but me (III.173–82).

The Father's assertion that Man can be saved if he wills is immediately undercut when he says, "Yet not of will in him, but grace in me". The grammar removes any free agency: Man is the subject of the passive verbs "lost," "saved," "upheld"; his powers are "forfeit and enthralled [...] to foul exorbitant desires" until God renews them. Man is the subject of "shall stand," but this action is only possible if he is "Upheld by me [...] by me upheld," so that he may know his frailty and owe all his deliverance to God. No human effort seems possible.

It may be theologically true that without God's grace all that Man can do is sin, but for the Father to say so with a constant insistence on first-person pronouns makes him sound tyrannical and egotistical. Instead of showing the Father watching with compassion while Man does sin (which would be the logical way of suggesting that all times are present to God), Milton shows him foretelling Man's sin. This begs the question: why does the Father create Man and then set a test of obedience that he knows Man will fail?

The question becomes more urgent when the Father discusses predestination (III.183–202). He speaks of offering grace, of clearing dark senses and softening stony hearts, of placing his "umpire conscience" in the soul as a guide. But he mentions grace and mercy only in the context of limiting them: he has chosen some for "peculiar grace [...] such is my will"; sinners are warned "to appease betimes / The incensed Deity, while offered grace / Invites"; sinners will "never taste" the "day of grace" as the Father will "exclude" them from mercy. Most serious is his statement that neglectful men will be "hardened, blind be blinded more, / That they may stumble on, and deeper fall" (III.200–1). It seems that the Father hardens and blinds sinners so that they may fall deeper into sin and justify their punishment.

The Father next speaks of Man's inability to "pay" satisfaction for his sin:

> But yet all is not done; man disobeying,
> Disloyal breaks his fealty, and sins
> Against the high supremacy of heaven,
> Affecting Godhead, and so losing all,
> To expiate his treason hath nought left,
> But to destruction sacred and devote,
> He with his whole posterity must die,
> Die he or justice must; unless for him
> Some other able, and as willing, pay
> The rigid satisfaction, death for death (III.203–12).

The active verbs again stress that Man can act only for evil: "disobeying," "breaks," "sins," "affecting Godhead," "losing all". As a result, Man becomes passive, "to destruction sacred and devote," capable of only one action – dying. The Father destroys the grammatical connection between himself and Mankind, using no verbal processes in which Man and God are both participants: Man breaks his fealty, sins against heaven, affects Godhead, loses all, has nothing left to expiate his treason, and must therefore die.

In his speeches, the Father speaks of his past gifts to Man, of Man's future fall, and future redemption or damnation, but never describes himself in harmony with Man in the present. This is problematic: from a narrative point of view, Man has not yet sinned; from the eternal point of view, Redemption rather than sin should be the strongest present reality. The dilemma is resolved, once again, if the passage is read as reflecting the Believer's anguished concern that for him the helplessness of sin is the present reality, while redemption is only a future possibility.

Again, the Father's speech ends with a sudden reversal, as he asks (knowing the answer) whether anyone has the charity to redeem Man (III.213–16):

> And now without redemption all mankind
> Must have been lost, adjudged to death and hell
> By doom severe (III.222–4).

As Kinney notes the lines demonstrate that, rather than Man being condemned before he has sinned, Man is redeemed before he has sinned (143).

The Son offers to die for Man:

> Behold me then, me for him, life for life
> I offer, on me let thine anger fall;
> Account me man; I for his sake will leave
> Thy bosom, and this glory next to thee
> Freely put off, and for him lastly die
> Well pleased (III.236–41).

In these lines a prayer is interleaved with a promise. The grammar neatly reinforces both the Son's obedience to the Father, and his action on behalf of Man: he is the object of clauses in which the Father is the subject: ("Behold me"; "on me let thine anger fall, / Account me man") and the subject of clauses in which Man is the beneficiary ("life for life I offer"; "I for his sake will leave"; "and this glory […] put off, and for him lastly die"). Here the Son uses the first person for the first time, to offer himself to the Father on behalf of Man.

This is a moment of intensely focused dialogue. The imperatives ("Behold," "let […] fall," "Account"), with their unexpressed subjects, speed up and intensify the action. Lines 236–8a are very high in pronouns (expressed and understood): the Son's action grammatically restores the connection between God and Man "[Do thou] behold [...] me for him"; "[my] life for [his] life I offer [thee]").

However, as soon the syntax moves into the future tense (III.238b), the connections weaken. Pronouns are replaced with noun phrases that make the language more wordy and remote: the Son does not speak of leaving thee, but "Thy bosom, and this glory next to thee". Milton minimizes Christ's human suffering: the human reality implied by "die" is quickly distanced by the change to a personified "Death". The passage changes from the demand to the information-giving function of dialogue, from plea to spoken narrative, as the Son goes on to describe, not his rescue of Man, but his victory over Death in the predictive-future:

> Under his gloomy power I shall not long
> Lie vanquished [...]
> [...] that debt paid,
> Thou wilt not leave me in the loathsome grave [...]
> Death his death's wound shall then receive, and stoop
> Inglorious [...]
> I through the ample air in triumph high
> Shall lead hell captive [...]
> [...] Thou at the sight
> Pleased, out of heaven shall look down and smile [...]
> Then with the multitude of my redeemed
> Shall enter heaven long absent, and return,
> Father, to see thy face, wherein no cloud
> Of anger shall remain, but peace assured (III.242–63).

Again the poetry weakens, with auxiliary verbs, empty modifiers, and words that suggest time and space: "Shall lead [...] shall look [...] shall enter"; "[Death's] gloomy power," "loathsome grave," "stoop / Inglorious," "triumph high"; "not long," "then," "long absent"; "through the ample air," "look down". Here the Son uses first person pronouns to revel in his future temporal triumph. The Father will be pleased, not by Man's Redemption, but by the defeat of the enemy, smiling while the Son ruins his foes. Anger is again associated with the Father: it has clouded his face, and the peace that fills his presence is brought there by the Son.

However, if the speech is read as the Believer's appropriation of the Son's voice, it has a completely different ring: the future tense now expresses the Believer's faith in his own salvation; the objectification of "Death" indicates that his fear of dying has been replaced by confidence in Christ's victory over death; the concrete details and empty modifiers suggest that he is carried away by his enthusiasm; finally, under cover of the Son's voice, he allows himself to address the Father, stressing that anger is past and peace present.

The Father responds with his warmest speech of the poem:

> O thou in heaven and earth the only peace
> Found out for mankind under wrath [...]
> [...] well thou knowest how dear,
> To me are all my works, nor man the least
> Though last created, that for him I spare
> Thee from my bosom [...]
> [...] be thou in Adam's room
> The head of all mankind (III.274–86).

This passage is true dialogue: for the first time, the Father uses second-person more frequently than first-person pronouns; for the first and only time, he applies a positive modifier, "dear," to Man, and uses Adam's name.

However, this mood does not last long: the Father casually declares that the Son will restore "As many as are restored, without thee none" (III.289), as if it does not much matter how many will be restored. He follows his brief account of the Son's love with an extensive account of his future glory that makes it hard to believe his assertion that "in thee / Love has abounded more than glory abounds". The Father, again concerned with divine status, closes by asking the angels to "honour him as me" (III.305–43). It sounds unpleasantly smug for the Father and Son to talk to each other about the Son's future glory. They repeat each other, telling the story twice and prolonging it beyond the climax of the Son's offer to redeem Man.

Overall, the heavenly conversation sets up tensions between the Father and Son: the Father's lexis and syntax emphasize sin and alienation, the Son's connection; the Father takes the side of justice and death, the Son the side of mercy and life; the Father appears self-asserting, the Son self-denying; the Father can sound uncertain, the Son always speaks with assurance. When either speaks in the predictive-future tense, contradicting the idea that all times are present to God, they sound self-concerned.

These dilemmas can be resolved if the episode is read on two levels: as Milton's public account of Redemption of Mankind; and as the Believer's anguished but private debate about his own spiritual status. Whereas Mankind is already redeemed, the Believer's sin continues as he continues to narrate the poem. The future passages then can be read as the Believer's over-enthusiastic expressions of faith and hope that God's mercy, already granted to Mankind, will, in the future, be granted to him as an individual.

The Believer's covert encounter

At the end of the Parliament, the angels sing a hymn to both Father and Son, which Milton reports in indirect speech:

> Thee Father first they sung omnipotent,
> Immutable, immortal, infinite,
> Eternal king; thee author of all being,
> Fountain of light, thy self invisible
> Amidst the glorious brightness where thou sit'st
> Throned inaccessible (III.372–7).

The pronoun "Thee" is the object of "sung". However, the angels must actually have used the vocative and sung, "Thou, Father omnipotent [...] thou author of all being," and later, "Thou [...] of all creation first, / Begotten Son" (III.383–4). It is thus the persona who addresses the Father (and later the Son) directly, telling him that the angels "sung thee".

This puts the whole hymn in the Believer's own mouth, but humbly: he does not use the first-person pronouns that would clearly place himself in the text, but slips unobtrusively into the song. There is a compelling tension between the intimacy implied by his use of second-person pronouns and the distance implied by his failure to use first-person ones. In contrast with the Poet's ambitious prayers for poetic inspiration in the invocations, the Believer here is concerned only with God's glory, asking nothing for himself.

The hymn stresses that the "brightest seraphim / Approach not, but with both wings veil their eyes" (III.381–2). However, as soon as the voice leaves simple praise and returns to narrative, he associates God with physical violence, relating in the past tense how the Son drove his flaming chariot, "o'er the necks [...] of warring angels" (III.390–9). He looks at the very face of the Father, describing it as contorted with "the strife / Of mercy and justice" (III.406–7), and represents the Son as appeasing the Father's wrath and ending the strife. This makes the Father subject to time and unable to resolve the conflict between mercy and justice without the Son's help.

At the end of this time-bound passage, the Poet returns, using the first person to draw attention to his artistic endeavour:

> Hail, Son of God, saviour of men, thy name
> Shall be the copious matter of my song
> Henceforth, and never shall my harp thy praise
> Forget, nor from thy Father's praise disjoin (III.412–15).

He immediately breaks this promise by returning to the activities of Satan (III.417ff.)

Milton depicts three unfallen encounters with God: Adam and Eve's "unanimous" prayer (IV.720–36); the Father's commendation of Abdiel (VI.29–43); and Adam's meeting with his creator (VIII.311–499). All are reported in direct speech. Direct dialogue with God is lost when Adam prefers God's creature to God himself. Adam and Eve's repentant prayer is reported in indirect speech (X.1098–104), demonstrating that direct dialogue with God is only possible for unfallen creatures. Yet the Poet "reports" what the conversation between the divine Persons in Heaven, depicting the Father as hostile, concrete, and time-bound – the view of the unregenerate sinner.

In four lengthy invocations, the Poet shows more concern with his own creation than with his Creator. At the end of the poem, however, Milton silences him completely as Adam and Eve leave the garden in resignation to God's will, with "providence their guide," following a "solitary way" (XII.637–49) that harks back to the Poet's solitude (VII.28). It is as if the Believer, having finally ousted the Poet, sees his own sinfulness in Adam and Eve, accepts and understands it, but also takes comfort that as their sin was redeemed, so too his sinfulness may also find redemption.

Works Cited

Kinney, Clare Regan. *Strategies of Poetic Narrative: Chaucer, Spenser, Milton, Eliot.* Cambridge: Cambridge UP, 1992.

McMahon, Robert. *The Two Poets of Paradise Lost.* Baton Rouge and London: Louisiana UP, 1998.

Ricks, Christopher. *Milton's Grand Style.* Oxford: Oxford UP, 1963.

Riggs, William, G. "The Poet and Satan in *Paradise Lost*," *Milton Studies* 2 (1970): 59–82.

Schindler, Walter. *Voice and Crisis: Invocation in Milton's Poetry.* Hamden, Connecticut: Archon, 1984.

Margaret Justice DEAN

Martyrdom Reconsidered: Adam's Profit from Abdiel's Example

Citing Cyprian in *Of Reformation*, Milton inveighs against idolatry of bishop martyrs (*YP* I.534–5). Later he derogates the false martyrdom of "Romish priests" (*YP* III.575–6). In 1649 he expands upon this work in *Eikonoklastes* by attempting to topple "The Royal Martyr." While many scholars note Milton's engagement with martyrdom in *Eikonoklastes*, Laura Knoppers (1994) and John Knott (1993) trace this concern through Milton's major poetry, but no scholar has yet noted the prominence of this issue in *Paradise Lost.* Most agree with Knott in asserting that *Paradise Lost* does not fulfil its promise of extolling "Patience and Heroic Martyrdom" (IX. 32).[1] However, Milton's lifelong concern with martyrdom, especially his desire to forestall idolatry of martyrs, manifests itself in his depiction of Adam's education beginning in Book V.[2]

As I argue elsewhere, given that most of his contemporaries, as well as Milton himself, acknowledge competing martyr claims, how were the "false" to be discerned from the "true"? Historian Brad Gregory cites numerous examples of exemplary demeanor of supposed "false" martyrs at their executions as detailed by writers who assert that these same individuals are now suffering in Hell. The behavior, words, and pathos of these "false" martyrs at the stake as reported by their detractors are often indistinguishable from those of the "true" martyrs as described by their own advocates. Gregory explains this phenomenon by citing the pervasive *ars moriendi* tradition, which valued steadfastness in suffering and death; most

1 See Knott, pages 168–170.

2 This brief essay does not attempt to trace the martyrological controversy that raged in Europe after the publication of Foxe's *Actes and Monuments.* Readers should consult Brad Gregory's *Salvation at Stake: Christian Martyrdom in Early Modern Europe* (Harvard, 1999). Rather, this essay links Milton's definition of martyrdom from *De Doctrina Christiana* with his depiction of Abdiel and his discussions of false martyrs, such as Charles I and Mary Queen of Scots, with Adam.

of the martyrs of whatever doctrinal perspective suffered patiently and steadfastly in order to buttress their doctrinal perspective with their demeanor (313–341). Because of their inability to distinguish false martyr from true on the external bases of appearances and behavior, even final words, controversialists resolved this polemical problem by examining doctrine. Gregory notes that this also constituted, "the same criterion by which they identified their martyrological communities" (320). The relevant doctrine is most clearly delineated by Augustine of Hippo. According to Gregory (320) and Knott (155), Christian controversialists of all major confessions relied on Augustine's criteria to discern true from false martyrs: "[N]ot the punishment, but the cause, makes a martyr"[3] came to serve as the most reliable and universally accepted method of discrimination.[4]

This touchstone of Augustine's appeared in the early print controversies of the Reformation. I summarize Gregory here and elsewhere. In response to the executions of Lutherans in the 1520's and the subsequent publication of martyrologies about them, controversial tracts arose denouncing the status of some as "false martyrs" while extolling others as "true martyrs." These tracts are termed "antimartyrologies" by Gregory because unlike martyrologies, which memorialize and praise dying witnesses without much discrimination, antimartyrologies discriminate. Rather these define the "true martyrdom" of their own by denouncing the "false martyrdom" of those of the opposing camp. This inclusion of antimartyrology within martyrologies served to polarize confessional camps throughout Europe, but it also helped forge a doctrinal consensus concerning what constituted Christian martyrdom and what did not (340).[5]

Milton applies Augustine's touchstone in *Eikonoklastes*, which attempts to shatter the king's image as martyr in order to release the English from their idolatry of him. In doing so, Milton is employing antimartyrology to expose a false martyr with an idolatrous cause. While some scholars read *Eikonoklastes* as a reluctant and distasteful foray into such controversy in the

3 See "Letter LXXXIX" (374), *"Martyrem non facit poena, sed causa,"* quotation translated by Knott (155). This essay does not attempt to describe the entire history of Christian martyrology, but to apply Augustine's touchstone to Adam's motive for choosing what he stages as martyrdom, disobedient death with Eve rather than obedient life with God.

4 See my article in *Milton Studies* 46 (2007).

5 Generally, the two genres (antimartyrology and martyrology) appear together in the same work. This paragraph is extracted from my article in *Milton Studies 46*.

service of the Commonwealth, I read it as the most prominent example of Milton's engagement with antimartyrology, an engagement that is intensified and refined in *Paradise Lost*.[6] As it is in much of his controversial prose, a major portion of Milton's epic is devoted to antimartyrology, which develops a stark contrast between the false martyrdom of Adam the First and the true martyrdom of Adam the Second.

This essay focuses on one aspect of a longer article, to appear in *Milton Studies 46*;[7] that article traces the development of Adam's false martyrdom. Here, I present Adam's introduction to martyrdom via Abdiel's defiance of Satan in the context of Raphael's history of the War in Heaven in Books V and VI of *Paradise Lost*. The prominence of Abdiel's example, the foil Abdiel provides for Satan, and the lesson Raphael urges from his narration, when viewed in the light of martyrological controversy and Adam's subsequent words and actions, suggest that Adam's developing notion of martyrdom diverges significantly from Milton's ideal as delineated in *De Doctrina Christiana*.

***

The prominence of Abdiel's example, that of the first just individual among many depicted in *Paradise Lost*, suggests its importance in Milton's epic. "Attentive" Adam is entranced by Raphael's account of the War in Heaven, but when he urges Adam to "profit [from the] terrible Example … Of [Satan's] disobedience" (VI.909–911), Raphael neglects the attraction of other examples included within his history. The most obvious example is Abdiel, whose extra-biblical episode comprises some twenty-five percent of this history of the War in Heaven.[8] Why does this seemingly minor character, who never reappears in the epic, or elsewhere in Milton's oeuvre, occupy so many lines? As Knott has observed, Abdiel is one of Milton's examples of martyrdom in the epic (169). Abdiel is the exemplary individual, who resists the crowd of Satan's followers and "suffers for Truth's sake," as do later heroes of faith (especially Enoch and Noah) in the visions Michael presents to Adam. However, Abdiel is an angel, not a human; he is not subject to

6 See for instance, Merritt Hughes' introduction to *Eikonoklastes* (*YP* III.166–7). Flannagan's introduction in *The Riverside Milton* generally tracks Hughes.

7 The article referred to here has since appeared as "Choosing Death: Adam's Temptation to Martyrdom in *Paradise Lost*." *Milton Studies* 46 (2007): 30–56.

8 See my calculation of this percentage in *Milton Studies 46* (2007).

death, so he does not quite fit the "one just man" paradigm usually applied to him. Milton may have inserted this episode to emphasize his contention that the true martyr need not suffer death; he need only "suffer for Truths sake."

Abdiel's martyrdom is the first example of heroism ever presented to Adam, who seems at least as impressed with Abdiel's positive example as he is awed by Satan's negative one. Raphael, the narrator, seems impressed with the fortitude of the lower-ranking angel. He labels him, "fervent," "faithful," "unmov'd," "constant," "single," "dreadless," as well as noting his "Loyaltie, Love, Zeal" (V.849–903 and VI.1).

Most notably, Abdiel's commendation by God the Father is the highest praise afforded any created being in the epic, specifically situating it within Milton's definition of martyrdom.

In *De Doctrina Christiana*, Milton defines martyrdom as a subspecies of zeal; his definition omits the usual requirement that the martyr suffer death for his profession, adding "imprisonment, torture, disgrace" to the list of wrongs sufficient to mark martyrdom.[9] Milton denotes the term as, "[The] firm and, when necessary, open profession of true religion and of our worship of [God] [...]. This profession, when it leads to death or imprisonment or torture or disgrace, is called MARTYRDOM" (*YP* VI.701).[10] An examination of the Father's praise for Abdiel in Book VI, lines 29–43, demonstrates his status as a martyr in Milton's mold. The Father commends Abdiel's approach: his verbal and spiritual resistance to satanic rhetoric and peer pressure are superior to armed resistance. He notes that Abdiel has "fought / The better fight." Furthermore, employing Augustine's touchstone, the Father emphasizes Abdiel's open and "single … [maintenance of] the Cause / Of Truth." He contrasts the force of Abdiel's words with the force of the rebel angels' arms. He acknowledges that Abdiel's suffering is "worse to beare / Then violence." He reiterates Abdiel's godly motive, obedience: "for this was all thy care / To stand approv'd in sight of God." Even as he assigns Abdiel a place among the warrior angels preparing for the War in Heaven, the Father consistently prefers Abdiel's use of words to his use of force, calling the later "the easier conquest." As Raphael's ac-

9 Interestingly, this definition allows Milton himself the status of martyr.

10 For the sake of brevity, Milton's prooftexts and opposite extremes are omitted here. While Milton's definition of martyrdom in *De Doctrina Christiana* may seem relatively weak, it is utilized effectively by Knott and Knoppers in developing their arguments about Milton's engagement with martyrdom.

count and the Father's commendation emphasize, Abdiel is a martyr according to Milton's standards; the seraph suffers disgrace in order to "open[ly] profess[ ] the true religion and ... worship [of God]."

***

Raphael's heroic narrative presents Abdiel's obedience as a foil for Satan's disobedience, but it also highlights Abdiel's fortitude in the context of war. Abdiel, whose name means "Servant of God,"[11] is initially obedient to his commanding officers. As a member of Lucifer's legions, Abdiel follows them to "the limits of the North" to "The Palace of great Lucifer." Once there, upon hearing Satan's argument and intention of rebellion against the supreme head, Abdiel challenges him. The commander fires back, accusing Abdiel of heresy (V.855–856), to which Satan later adds sedition (VI.152), ambition (VI.159), and "Servilitie" (VI.169). Abdiel's zealous speeches (V.809–848 and 877–895) contrast Satan's cause with his own. He condemns Satan's ingratitude (for his high position assigned him by God), hypocrisy (in placing himself above his peers, when He condemns God for doing so), forgetfulness (in neglecting God's bounty to the angels), and creaturely presumption (in condemning as unjust God's decrees and refusing to acknowledge him as Creator). According to Roy Flannagan, Abdiel "reinstates the value of the orders of angels, which Satan had debased" (502, note 240). His initial speech exemplifies the "open profession of true religion and worship"; Abdiel's subsequent actions demonstrate Milton's requirement that the "profession, ... lead [ ] to ... disgrace." Flannagan describes Abdiel as "run[ning the] gauntlet through the hostile fallen angels" (504, note 254) while returning to God, thus Raphael highlights Abdiel's courage, as well as his constancy in suffering. Raphael's history mentions Abdiel's adherence to true doctrine, his devotion to "truth," against the multitudes who side with Satan. Raphael seems to emphasize the cause for which Abdiel suffers, his obedience, but the audience is impressed with the contrast between Abdiel's raw courage and Satan's politic wiles. Satan's cowardice in awaiting the response of his legions before responding to Abdiel contrasts with the seraph's ready adherence to Truth. Abdiel may be too effective a foil for Satan because his fortitude seems to overshadow his cause in Raphael's account.

11 See *The Riverside Milton* (Flannagan), 508, note 13.

Furthermore, the Father's commendation of Abdiel's cause and martyrdom is obscured by the heroic action of the narrative. Abdiel fades briefly into the pre-battle mobilization and muster. Later, the seraph re-emerges as a courageous warrior, engaged in single combat with Satan. After his initiation of the War of Heaven when he strikes the first blow in a duel with Satan, the last we hear of him is in the midst of battle "annoy[ing] / The Atheist crew" (VI.369–370). Our final view of Abdiel presents him as God's champion rather than as suffering martyr. This view is the one Adam internalizes as he conflates notions of warrior and martyr to construct his own notion of chivalrous crusader, one firm in loyalty and love, zealous in his cause, who resists his opponent no matter the cost. Adam focuses on the martyr's armed resistance, but neglects his motive.

***

The primary lesson Raphael urges from his history of the War in Heaven is that Adam shun the "terrible example" of Satan's rebellion and disobedience (VI.894–912). Raphael reiterates the threats of satanic seduction and disobedience (VI.900–912; VIII.634–643). However, by choosing to insert the memorable martyrology of Abdiel into his history, he risks its misinterpretation because of the notorious difficulty of separating appearances and actions from beliefs in the context of martyrdom. Since Augustine's touchstone indicates that the motive for choosing death must be the only means of discerning the true from the false martyr, in order for Adam to discern the truth of Abdiel's martyrdom, he must focus on the motive behind Abdiel's actions, not the courage displayed in them. According to Gregory, sixteenth and seventeenth-century antimartyrologists, such as Martin Luther, Thomas More, Hugh Latimer, Nicholas Harpsfield, John Foxe, Robert Southwell, Philipp Melanchthon and others struggled with the problem of misleading, but impressive, fortitude in the face of death among those they designated false martyrs because of their heretical beliefs (330–337). While Abdiel's example is a positive one, Raphael's use of it in the context of heroic narrative, allows Adam to fix on Abdiel's obvious fortitude and neglect his less obvious cause.

Additionally, Raphael's evident admiration for Abdiel's fortitude impresses Adam, whose subsequent actions and words in Books IX and XII demonstrate that he extracts more from the attractive example of Abdiel's heroic martyrdom than the "dire example" of Satan's rebellion. Adam seems incapable of imagining any personal attraction to satanic rebellion. Once Raphael concludes his war history, Adam's response is "admiration and deep Muse"; he is amazed, but unsure how this history applies to his situation; he requests to know, "What nearer might concern him" (VII.62). Both Adam and Raphael seem ignorant of the notion that false martyrdom is itself a form of satanic rebellion, but martyrologists of the sixteenth and seventeenth centuries frequently note this distortion (Gregory 335–336).

***

Adam's profit from Abdiel's example is presented in Books IX and XII, where Adam's focus on the externalities of martyrdom becomes evident.[12] Adam's "profit" becomes his distortion of martyrdom to his own ends. At his temptation scene, when he should have reconsidered the Father's commendation of Abdiel, Adam attempts to replicate the seraph's spectacular fortitude and zeal. By employing these virtues in the service of a false cause, Adam distorts martyrdom from godly obedience to satanic rebellion.

According to Gregory, antimartyrologists of the era complained that credulous onlookers were frequently swayed by appearances, such as victims' patience and fortitude in the face of death, rather than adhering to Augustine's touchstone to determine the validity of the martyrdom (334–338). Adam joins this credulous crowd.

Swayed by the heroic presentation of Abdiel, rather than convinced of the justice of his cause, Adam presents himself as a hero of Abdielian mold during Book IX. His actions and words display fortitude, loyalty, love, and zeal, but omit crucial obedience. Fortitude is the primary virtue he displays. His ambition to fortitude is evident in his words to Eve during the Separation Scene, he wishes to "shade" and "protect" Eve; "her Husband [will] guard[ ] her, or with her the worst endure[ ]" (IX.266–269). He pleads that his fortitude is enhanced by Eve's presence (IX.309–316). Later during Adam's temptation by Eve, his words and actions evince the fortitude to which he has earlier aspired. He speaks of his choice to act on his convictions, "for with thee / Certain my resolution is to Die" (906–7).[13] Suitably

12 Raphael himself notes Adam's penchant for focusing on externals when Raphael comments near the end of his visit about Adam's fixation on Eve's "outside, fair no doubt" (*PL* VIII.568).

13 See also his subsequent lines: "I with thee have fixt my Lot, / Certain to undergoe like doom, if Death / Consort with thee, Death is to mee as Life" (*PL* IX.952–954).

impressed with what she sees as Adam's "perfection" in virtue (964), but what the reader knows is disobedience, Eve is

> [...] much won that he his Love
> Had so enobl'd, as of choice to incurr
> Divine displeasure for her sake, or Death (991–993).

Once Adam displays his fortitude by eating the deadly fruit and realizing the consequences of the Fall, he reminds Eve of his "Immutabl[ity]" when she was subject to death, but he was not (1165). Adam's display meets Milton's stated standards for fortitude, "[It] is chiefly apparent when we repel evils or stand against them unafraid" (*De Doctrina Christiana*, *YP* VI.738), but fortitude in the cause of disobedience cannot transform Adam into an Abdielian martyr.

His loyalty to Eve is evident in his previously mentioned assertions and actions. Additionally, he refuses to live without her, even if God should create another woman (908–912); such another creation is clearly a possibility (Danielson 123). He affirms their marriage as "The Link of Nature," "The Bond of Nature" (914 and 956) that binds them together.

His love of Eve is affirmed throughout his temptation scene and afterward; both Adam and Eve comment upon it. Eve encourages his martyr-like resolution to die, "O glorious trial of exceeding Love" (960). She comments that they are "linkt in Love so deare" (970). After the Fall, Adam complains of Eve's failure to fully reciprocate his love.[14]

Finally, Adam's zeal is on full display in Book IX. Martyrdom is one legitimate expression of "Zeale," as Milton defines it in his treatise (*YP* VI.697–703). If, as Flannagan observes, "Abdiel is the embodiment of zeal,"[15] Adam is the embodiment of its distortions. Aping Abdiel's zeal, he hopes to replicate the angel's heroism. He risks disgrace; he even exceeds the angel by risking death for his relationship with Eve. His evident zeal in defending his marriage is that which Milton labels "Ignorant and imprudent" (*YP* VI.698) because it opposes true zeal, like Abdiel's, which expresses "an eager desire to sanctify the divine name, together with a feeling of indignation against things which tend to violation or contempt of relig-

14 "Is this the Love, is this the recompence / Of mine to thee" (*PL* IX.1163–4), Adam complains.

15 See Flannagan 501, note 232.

ion" (*YP* VI.697).[16] Instead of indignation against such violation, Adam's disobedience endorses it.

Just as Adam's misconstruction of Abdiel's martyrdom becomes an avenue of disobedience in Eden, Adam's misconstruction of the Son's martyrdom threatens his future obedience. Even after he has repented of violating the sole command, suffered some of the consequences of the Fall, and submitted to Michael's lessons, Adam continues to misconstrue martyrdom. This is most evident in his joyful reaction to Michael's explanation of the work of the Son in Book XII. Adam responds with the militaristic notion that the Son will engage the Serpent in single combat, "say where and when / Thir fight, what stroke shall bruise the Victors heel" (384–5). Michael must correct Adam's notion of the Son's final battle with Satan as single combat, like Abdiel's or Michael's with Satan in Book VI, "Dream not of thir fight, / As of a Duel" (XII.386–7). Michael goes on to explain the cause of the Son's coming martyrdom:

> Obedience to the Law of God, impos'd
> On penaltie of death, and suffering death,
> The penaltie to thy transgression due (XII.397–399).

Adam must not be allowed to assume that his personal punishment can satisfy "high Justice," that he now can live as he likes, though banished from Eden. He must learn what he failed to learn from Raphael's story, how to accurately read and obediently follow the best example of martyrdom, that of the Son. In Book XII, Michael must correct Adam with sermons and repetitive exempla, which emphasize the Son's example to teach Adam that the cause alone makes the martyr.

As a genre, Raphael's heroic narrative fails to properly instruct Adam because of the attractive excitement of acts of fortitude and "things so high and strange, / So unimaginable as … Warr so neer the Peace of God" (VII.53–55). Within his history the centrality of the cause for which the martyr suffers is obscured. In Book IX Adam sees no connection between Satan's rebellion and his own developing concept of martyrdom. Adam's notion of martyrdom increasingly resembles the false zeal and false martyrdom of Promethean rebellion rather than obedient resistance to false doctrine. Adam's fallible understanding of martyrdom in Book IX is superfi-

16 Instead of "sanctify[ing] the divine name," Adam speaks evil of it by asserting that God will break his own word rather than punish the humans (IX.938–951).

cially based on Abdiel's example, but learned from Satan via idolatry of Eve.

Like the credulous English of Milton's time, who persisted in viewing Charles I and Archbishop Laud as martyrs, Adam's understanding of martyrdom is distorted by his uncritical "reading" of martyrology, his heroic ambitions, and his tendency to judge the validity of martyrdom on the basis of the martyr's behavior. Adam extracts all the wrong lessons from Abdiel's example in his effort replicate it.

Works Cited

Augustine. "Letter LXXXIX." Trans. J. G. Cunningham. *The Confessions and Letters of St. Augustin*, Vol. 1. Nicene and Post-Nicene Fathers. 1886. Grand Rapids: Eerdmans, 1988.

Bible, Authorized Version. Philadelphia: Holman, 1942.

Danielson, Dennis. "Through the Telescope of Typology: What Adam Should Have Done." *Milton Quarterly* 23.3 (1989): 121–127.

Gregory, Brad S. *Salvation at Stake: Christian Martyrdom in Early Modern Europe.* Cambridge: Harvard UP, 1999.

Knoppers, Laura Lunger. *Historicizing Milton: Spectacle, Power, and Poetry in Restoration England.* Athens, Georgia: Georgia UP, 1994.

Knott, John R. *Discourses of Martyrdom in English Literature, 1563–1694.* Cambridge: Cambridge UP, 1993.

Milton, John. *Complete Prose Works of John Milton, Volumes I-VIII.* Ed. Don Wolfe. New Haven: Yale UP, 1953–1982.

–. *The Riverside Milton.* Ed. Roy Flannagan. Boston: Houghton Mifflin, 1998.

Antonella PIAZZA

Milton and Galileo: The Astronomical Diet of *Paradise Lost*

> To ask or search blame thee not, for Heav'n
> Is as the *Book of God* before thee set,
> Wherein to read his wondrous Works, and learn
> His Seasons, Hours, or Days, or Months, or Years
> (*Paradise Lost,* VIII, 64–69, *emphasis mine*).[1]

The idea of Nature as a book written by God is, I think, the most meaningful Galilean allusion in Milton's sacred poem. Galileo's most revolutionary and long lasting 'contribution' to modernity was, in fact, his differentiation between the two books: Holy Scripture and the book of Nature, both written by God and aiming at the same truth. The great astronomer contended that they were both written by God, both aimed at one and the same truth, but with diverse languages and for different readers. Though the formulation of that distinction was Galileo's defensive move against the Inquisition, it was to prove the origin of a dangerous aporetic dichotomy between the sciences of man and those of nature, a split which was to cause a painful feeling of deprivation of meaning in the modern individual who found that his passionate, impulsive psychic internal organization was irreducible to a rationally ordered external world.

What I would like to argue is that, by including three times Galileo in *Paradise Lost,* Milton, though ambivalently, ambiguously, sometimes latently, was attempting a cultural, poetic reparation. He tried – as an extreme defence of his poetic monistic materialism – to keep together ethics and science, the ways of God and the ways of nature, the heaven of God and the sky of astronomy. There is no doubt that in the poem the attitude towards the Copernican revolution is not of a simple nature: "The universe is unmistakably terracentric; we look through the telescope of Galileo (the only contemporary mentioned in the poem) at the universe of Ptolemy," is Wil-

1 All the quotations from Milton are in Merritt Y. Hughes ed. *John Milton. Complete Poems and Major Prose*, Indianapolis: The Odyssey Press, 1971.

liam Kerrigan's synthetic formulation of the contradiction (196). Milton, as Kerrigan recognizes, chose the Bible as his epic subject to respond to an attack contemporary science was moving against poetry and religion. The Bible had, in fact, been long considered the authority on both ethical and scientific wisdom; by rewriting it, Milton meant to Christianize (keeping together and going beyond) both the classical heroism of Homeric and Virgilian epics (poetry) and the Lucretian epic of matter (science). Moreover, in Kerrigan's view, the presence of Lucretian materialism in the cosmic setting of *Paradise Lost* would clearly demonstrate that in the early modern scientific revolution physiology – the transition from alchemy to chemistry and physics – had prime place over the transition from astrology to astronomy. The critic posits in the poem the centrality of the body, food, nutrition, matter, and the subordination, the peripheral location of the sky, a sort of repression of "thinking in astronomy."[2] Which would explain the choice of a 'terracentric', Ptolemaic system.

But in the space of *Paradise Lost*, crossed by ultra-rapid angelic flights, pervaded by Satanic leaps into infinite chaotic elementary dimensions, the idea of a sort of astronomical anorexia founded on Milton's opting for a deprived, closed, traditional cosmology sounds, at the very least, problematic. In order to clarify Milton's creative venture, the distinction between the attitude of Adam and that of the poet towards Galilean astronomy, between what I call their different astronomical diets, has now to be considered and interpreted.

Adam and Eve's astronomical diet

Milton's choice of a geocentric cosmos as the setting for Adam and Eve symbolically points to the centripetal focus of the poem on a private, domestic dimension. As the foundation for his wisdom and happiness, in fact, Adam is offered the physiological coincidence of a healthy mind in a healthy body which he can achieve through a temperate diet, an obedient

2 In *Areopagitica* Milton – recalling his visit to the blind scientist prisoner of the Inquisition though in his own house, presents the tragic case of Galileo's limitation of freedom for 'thinking in astronomy'.

limitation (the apple is presented as 'that sole command / So easily obey'd amid the choice / Of all tastes, VII.47–49). In the pre-fallen world, Adam is allowed a physiological rather than an intellectual aspiration. During their discourses at table in Book V Raphael promises him:

> Time may come when men
> With angels may participate, and find
> No inconvenient Diet, nor too light Fare;
> And from these corporeal nutriments perhaps
> Your bodies may at last turn all to spirit,
> Improv'd by tract of time, and wing'd ascend
> Ethereal, as wee, or may at choice
> Here or in Heav'nly Paradises dwell (V.493–500).

In this way Milton establishes a sacred bond between body and soul: in a move which spiritualizes the body while materializing the soul. He hints at a new anthropology which posits the mind and the soul in the body. That is why both body and mind need a diet, as Raphael teaches.[3]

The exhilarating possibilities served to Adam's body shrink radically when his intellectual curiosity is answered back:

> Such Commission from above
> I have receiv'd, to answer thy desire
> Of knowledge within bounds; beyond abstain
> To ask, nor let thine own inventions hope
> Things not reveal'd, which th'invisible King
> Only Omniscient, hath suppresst in Night,
> To none communicable in Earth or Heaven:
> Enough is left besides to search and know (VII, 118–125).

It serves little purpose for Adam – Raphael admonishes – to choose between the two competing cosmological systems ("Whether the Sun predominant in Heav'n / Rise on the Earth, or Earth rise on the Sun … leave them to God above," VIII.161–2, 169). Suffice that he enjoy his Eve in Paradise: "Heav'n is for thee too high / To know what passes there; be lowly wise" (VIII.172–173). Adam's diet of astronomical speculation seems

3 "But knowledge is as food, and needs no less/Her temperance over appetite, to know/In measure what the mind may well contain, /Oppresses else with surfeit, and soon turns/Wisdom to folly, as nourishment to wind" (VII, 126–130).

rigorously strict, bordering on anorexia. Milton seems here to follow Galileo's dictate aimed at excluding common man from astronomical learning.

Galileo's distinction between the Book of God and the Book of Nature had ultimately delegitimized the authority of the Scriptures on scientific questions and it was for this reason that he was first denounced to the religious authorities. The Bible – Galileo had argued in one of his Copernican letters – does not investigate nature, it merely mentions the sun and the moon, leaving out all the other planets. The metaphorical language of the Bible, radically different from the mathematical language of astronomy, aims, according to Galileo, to convey a moral, rather than an intellectual wisdom accessible to common people who can then transform it into virtue. In short, common man could be spared the 'thinking in astronomy', leaving it to the astronomers, the scientific artists (Galileo himself had used this definition, 'artisti scientifici', which is echoed in Milton's 'Tuscan artist' 1.288).

While the 'lowly flight', which Adam's astronomical investigation was granted in Eden, seemed to move, in any case, within the debating context of the new science, after the Fall the authority of the Bible on scientific questions is literally and definitively restored. In the meta-narrative move of Book XII, when Michael sums up the Biblical narrative for Adam, the archangel says:

> the rest
> Were long to tell
> [...]
> Or how the Sun shall in mid Heav'n stand still
> A day entire, and Night's due course adjourn,
> Man's voice commanding, 'Sun, in *Gibeon* stand,
> And thou moon, in the vale of *Aialon*,
> Till *Israel* overcome (XII.260–1, 263–7).

The passage from Joshua 10.12 is quoted literally, and not by chance. It might be a clear demonstration that the Bible maintains that the sun moves, and this is why the passage was, as is well-known, repeatedly and obsessively quoted as the crux of the matter in the Copernican dispute between the defenders and opponents of the astronomical competence of the sacred text. Here Milton seems to take sides and endorse the anti-Copernican stance of the religious dogma by offering Adam the Scripture as *the only* authority on scientific investigation.

However, if both the prelapsarian education to happiness and the post-lapsarian preoccupation with salvation of the edenic couple seem to leave out intellectual curiosity and freedom of investigation, the so-called Galilean question keeps being hauntingly formulated throughout the poem. It is Eve who daringly introduces it: "But wherefore all night long shine these, for whom / This glorious sight, when sleep hath shut all eyes?" (IV.655–656).

Eve formulates her question at the end of a tense lyrical speech to her loved husband connotated by a repetitive mirroring structure. "With thee conversing I forget all time," then ten lines follow in which Eve praises the rich variations of a day, 'the breath of the morn', 'the grateful evening mild', 'the silent night', 'the glittering starlight', a catalogue she *verbatim* repeats in order to declare to Adam that all firmament is nothing to her if he is not with her. After such a soothing, hypnotic tone her question, introduced by an adversative 'But' ("But wherefore all night long shine these, for whom / This glorious sight, when sleep hath shut all eyes?"), comes as a disturbance in the relationship between the inner and the outer perspective, as a disruption, in a critic's words, in the "linking … of the erotic and the speculative" (Judith Scherer Herz, 154).[4]

Although the woman's curiosity is exploited by Satan in her temptation, the 'Galilean question' is not demonized, up to the end it is left open as a sign of Milton's ambiguity towards Adam and Eve's astronomical diet. The question to and about nature is posited again and again, it is even obliquely suggested to the couple, after the fall in the end, as part of a reparative consolation in Michael's final discourse:

> To whom thus also th'Angel last repli'd:
> This having learnt, thou hast attain'd the sum
> Of wisdom; hope no higher, though all the Stars
> Thou knew'st by name, and all th'ethereal powers,
> All secrets of the deep, all Nature's works,
> Or works of God in Heav'n, Air, Earth, or Sea,
> And all the riches of this World enjoy'dst,
> And all the rule, one Empire; only add
> Deeds to thy knowledge answerable, add faith, … then wilt now not be loth

4 Similarly – though by means of an opposite device – in the dialogue between Adam and Raphael, when Adam reformulates Eve's Galilean question the restrictive advice for a reductive astronomical low flight is followed by a rich and satisfying answer on the sex of the angels.

> To leave this Paradise, but shalt possess
> A paradise within thee happier far (XII, 574–582, 585–587).

The implications of the last line on our discourse-that is a re-reading of the 'paradise within' will be discussed further on, in the last section

The poet's astronomical diet

So Adam and Eve's astronomical diet consists in keeping the new astronomy at bay, pretending there is no use for them to penetrate the secrets of the cosmos, no reason to choose one of the two competing systems. Intellectual speculation, the exploration of the sky – as Galileo had suggested – seems inaccessible to common man and is left to scientists. But the lowly horizon suggested to Adam by Raphael sounds absolutely not negotiable for the blind epic poet whose 'advent'rous song" "with no middle flight intends to soar / Above th'Aonian mount, while it pursues / Things unattempted yet in prose or rhyme" (I.1–16).

Another kind of diet, another symbolic relationship is to be established in the text between the poet and astronomy, ultimately between the blind poet and the blind Tuscan Artist.

In the poet's dimension the intellectual drive is no longer repressed, peripherally marginalized, decentred, as it were, indeed it becomes the ground for an agonistic confrontation.

The physiology of aspiration – based on 'One First Matter All' – proved, in the end, for Adam and Eve, to be one of those poetic fables which, though ridiculed by scientists (Galileo included), powerfully embodied a configuration of desire: a yearning for 'a loved object', be it another human being, an angel, a landscape. That fable, in fact, mirrors Milton's monistic idea of matter, a materialistic kind of physics consistent with the premises – including the Galilean ones – of the new science.

Against the Aristotelian distinction between a sublunary matter, imperfect, because subjected to change and motion, and a superlunary space, perfect, because immutable, the new science grounded the new epistemology on the principle of a 'non solution' of continuity in the natural structure of the earth and of the sky. It is that material continuity which allows for the angels' speedy flights, grants Satan's 'pontific' structures able to join Hell and Earth, and even accords the human body the possibility of taking on an angelic form. In spite of the diabolical presence, there is one light, one truth, both for Milton and Galileo which – in contrast with the medieval world still operative in Faustus' cosmology – divinizes nature. The new physics is the necessary premise for the new astronomy.

Donald Friedman opposes the idea widely shared by critics, by Northrop Frye as an example, who maintain that Milton introduced Galileo to symbolize 'the gaze outward [...], the speculative reason that searches for new places, rather than the moral reason that tries to create a new state of mind' (Frye, 58). On the contrary, Friedman believes that this is only partly the truth reflected in the several images of the philosopher. The speculative reason represented by Galileo and that Milton implicitly praises in *The Doctrina Christiana* is, for the critic, indeed parallel to the moral reason above all in 'its desire to create a new state of mind' (Friedman, 170).

Now, on the three occasions in which Galileo is evoked in the text, he is always associated with his telescope ('optic glass', 'glazed optic tube', 'the glass / Of Galileo').[5] The insistence on that instrument, which was able to magnify the sense of sight, could be interpreted as a sign of the blind poet's feeling of loss or of envy. On the contrary, the telescope hints at the limitations and uncertainties of the senses ('less assured', 'to descry') rather than at the increase of their power.

Hans Blumenberg is excellent – Donald Friedman maintains – on the ambivalent impact of the telescope, which at the same time extended the capabilities of the senses and revealed the existence of a reality that escaped those capabilities. He characterizes this as a challenge to the 'postulate of visibility', the traditional view according to which the intelligible must be present to the senses, which are reason's only access to reality (Friedman, 171).

5 "... his ponderous shield, / Ethereal temper, massy, large, and round, / Behind him cast; the broad circumference /Hung on his shoulders like the moon, whose orb / Through *optic glass* the Tuscan artist views / At evening from the top of Fesole, / Or in Valdarno, to descry new lands, /Rivers or mountains in her spotty globe" (I, 284–291).
"There lands the Fiend, a spot which like perhaps / Astronomer in the sun's lucent orb / Through his *glazed optic tube* yet never saw" (III, 588–594).
"... as when by night *the glass / Of Galileo*, less assured, observes / Imagined lands and regions in the moon" (V, 261–271) *(emphasis added).*

In an analogous way in order to reach out for the sky and the heav'n, the poet's astronomical impulse is not dieted on admiration or optic glasses, but on an inward sight which overcomes the senses, a different 'art of seeing' and visibility. The blind poet, in fact, laments:

> But cloud instead, and ever-during dark
> Surrounds me, from the cheerful ways of men
> Cut off, and for the Book of knowledge fair
> Presented with a Universal blanc
> Of Nature's works to me expung'd and ras'd,
> And wisdom at one entrance quite shut out.
> So much the rather thou Celestial Light,
> Shine inward, and the mind through all her powers
> Irradiate, there plant eyes, all mist from thence
> Purge and disperse, that I may see and tell
> Of things invisible to mortal sight (III, 45–55).

The poet is here competing with that particular art of seeing with which Galileo had endowed the astronomer, the privileged reader of the book of Nature. In *Il Saggiatore* (1623) speaking of the book of the universe Galileo said:

> This grand book cannot be understood unless one first learns to comprehend the language and read the letters in which it is composed. It is written in the language of mathematics, and its characters are triangles, circles and other geometric figures without which it is humanly impossible to understand a single word of it; without these, one wonders about in a dark labyrinth (qtd in Friedman, 171).

Furthermore Milton, always careful to police and curb excessive freedom, would have subscribed to a distinction Galileo had advanced in the *Dialogo su i Massimi Sistemi* (a distinction which brought about his final incrimination by the papal commission). In the *Dialogo* Salviati maintains that although the human mind is radically inadequate to understand 'the multitude of intelligibles' (what he refers to as *extensive* understanding), it can be thought to grasp a proposition with the assurance normally attributed to 'Divine intellect'. These propositions – mainly mathematical and geometrical forms – are understood by the human mind, Galileo wrote, *'intensively'*.

The poet's astronomical diet was, then, based on his enthusiastic reliance on a divine mind which, although 'intensive', was capable of reading prophetically both into the Book of God and that of Nature.

Eve's reflection and the paradise within

Milton, however, did not mean to limit that intellectual gift – the 'intensive' gaze – to a scientific aristocracy as the astronomer himself intended. He spoke not in mathematical formulae, but in poetical figures, and his domestic epic was intended for the new common men and women.

In the genetic moment of Eve's awakening after her birth, Milton encoded his 'enfolded sublime' (Kerrigan, 231), there available for any reader to decode:

> That day [...]
> [...] much wond'ring where
> And what I was, whence thither brought, and how.
> Not distant far from thence a murmuring sound
> Of waters issu'd from a Cave and spread
> Into a liquid Plain, then stood unmov'd
> Pure as th'expanse of Heav'n; I thither went
> With unexperienc't thought, and laid me down
> On the great bank, to look into the clear
> Smooth Lake, that to me seemed another Sky.
> As I bent down to look, just opposite,
> A Shape within the wat'ry gleam appear'd
> Bending to look on me, I started back,
> It started back, but please'd I soon return'd,
> Pleas'd it return'd as soon with answering looks
> Of sympathy and love (IV.449, 451–465).

This image has very often been interpreted as an expression of Eve's primary narcissism. But she does not share the destructive narcissism of Satan (R. Britton), whose self-centred and circuitous mind auto reflexively projects solely his hell ('a Mind is its own Place'). She first wonders where she is and then who she is ('much wond'ring where / And what I was'); the lake then mirrors 'th'expanse of Heav'n', 'another Sky' together with Eve's beautiful face. Thus in the mirror image Eve catches sight, not of an undifferentiated self, but of a self in relation: she is in nature, a part of it, and with it. I believe that Eve's erotically charged relation with nature, reflected in the water, is the most effective and moving representation of a recoverable 'paradise within'. Eve as part of the heavenly sky, part of nature, is the subject of an irresistible attraction and that bond is the genetic promise of an inextricable alliance. It is no longer a problem of boundaries, of astronomical diets, but the promise of a 'good object relation'.

The image in the liquid plain reflects a duality – woman and nature – whose tragic split (threatened both by the fallen nature of man and by the new science) needs continuous and temperate reparations: new beginnings, new genesis, new nativities (which, as Hannah Arendt claimed, is the most fertile of Christian legacies.) Eve's nativity as a proleptic figure of the paradise within, is another way to look at both *Paradise Lost* as a domestic psychic epic and at the creative prophetic nature of poetry. So, in the end, the inclusion of the astronomer in the Sacred epic warranted a still possible compromise between the Book of God and the Book of Nature and revealed the superiority of poetry over a divisive new science, the triumph of the monist Milton. The last epic venture to imagine both how 'vada il cielo' [how the sky works] and how 'si vada al cielo' [how to go to heaven], according Galileo's famous formulation.

Works Cited

Britton, Ronald. *Belief and Imagination. Explorations in Psychoanalysis*, London and New York: Routledge, 1998.

Friedman, Donald. "The Art of Seeing" in Mario A. Di Cesare (ed.). *Milton in Italy. Contexts Images Contradictions.* New York: Binghamton, 1991.

Fry, Northrop. *The Return of Eden*, Toronto: Toronto UP, 1965

Galilei, Galileo. *Dialogo dei Massimi Sistemi,* Milano: Mondatori, 1996.

–. "Lettere copernicane (1613–15)" in *Opere di Galileo Galilei*, Torino: Utet, 1999.

Herz, Judith Scherer. "'For whom this glorious sight?': Dante, Milton, and the Galileo Question" in Mario A. Di Cesare (ed.). *Milton in Italy. Contexts Images Contradictions.* New York: Binghamton, 1991.

Kerrigan, William. *The Sacred Complex. On the Psychogenesis of* Paradise Lost. Cambridge, Massachussets and London, England: Harvard University Press, 1983.

Part III

The Great Poems

2. Paradise Regained

Daniele BORGOGNI

"Real or Allegorical I Discern Not": *Paradise Regained* and the Problem of Representation in Early Modern England

Ever since Northrop Frye's definition of *Paradise Regained* as "a technical experiment that is practically *sui generis*" (Frye 235), the 'brief epic' has always represented a problem for miltonists[1], puzzled by its much deprecated plainness[2] and its elusive and liminal textuality that, on the contrary, offers great potentialities to its interpreters because it requires different and sometimes contradictory approaches that frustrate any attempt to fix its meaning.[3] What makes *Paradise Regained* so interesting, in other words, is not necessarily its thematic or stylistic elements traditionally analysed by critics, nor the patterning of the content[4], but precisely its heterologic nature, its multiple, de-centered and centrifugal character that unfolds different, even syncretistic, interpretative possibilities.

1 As Babcox aptly summarises: "*Paradise Regained* has a history of troubling its readers" (36).

2 For a historical survey of the critical reception of *Paradise Regained* see Shawcross ("Critical Heritage") and MacKellar.

3 This difficulty is demonstrated by the fact that, apart from single articles, critical contributions on *Paradise Regained* are mainly found in chapters or parts of books centred on *Paradise Lost* or Milton in general, while there are only five book-length studies entirely dedicated to the brief epic: Pope, Lewalski ("Brief Epic"), Weber, and Shawcross ("Paradise Regained") and the more recent Borgogni. Stein is explicitly declared more a collection of essays than a monograph and Rushdy is more concerned with Milton's last phase in general than with the texts. Also the fundamental volumes by Rajan and Wittreich are collection of essays.

4 In 1983, S. E. Fish still felt obliged to criticise mainstream – and too traditional – studies on *Paradise Regained* such as the aforementioned 'classic' volumes by Pope or Lewalski: "the models that have been proposed as providing the structure of the poem always have the effect of dividing it up, of foregrounding some moments at the expense of others, of identifying climaxes, resolutions, and denouements, of declaring some scenes integral and others preliminary or ceremonial – the effect, in short, of giving the poem a plot" (176).

This paper, therefore, will not try to fix *Paradise Regained* in yet another 'new' interpretation, but rather to fuel the liveliness of the text analysing its dialogue with such a decisive cultural factor as the problem of representation in Early Modern England, not in order to account for the historical and cultural sources of the text (as some past studies already did) but to appreciate its inherently dialogic textual articulations, so that the historical and ideological contexts connected to the production of the 'brief epic' can be synergetically analysed in relation to its reception by the hermeneutic action of a participative reader.

The concept of representation became central in Early Modern Europe and especially in seventeenth-century England, where it played a primary role in aesthetics and hermeneutics but it also acquired a growing ideological weight. The Reformation had broken the medieval tie between words and images privileging the verbal element, yet language always ran the risk of becoming arbitrary and non-representative. It then became necessary to understand and to define clearly the nature, the scope and the possibilities of representation, in its double sense of representability (what could be represented in physical images) and representativity (what or who could be considered truly representative).

The emphasis laid on 'literalising' the world in the light of the Word, in order to understand God's signals to man, could not easily dispense with the parallel necessity of employing rhetorical 'colours' and images. The inherent compresence of literal and allegoric in the Scriptures had allowed religious writers to justify the use of different stylistic features and Calvin himself had in a way sanctioned all this by describing God's traces in the world[5] as having a representational rather than an immanent nature.[6]

This meant that the problem of interpretation became paramount: according to Luther (Loefscher 529), "The Holy Spirit is the very simplest writer and speaker there is in heaven and earth; therefore His words, too,

5 Of course the idea that man can get to know God and His love by reading His word in the Book of Scriptures and by detecting His presence in the book of Nature, can be traced back to such thinkers as Origen, Augustine, Bernard of Clairvaux, Hugh of St. Victor or St. Bonaventure. On this topic see obviously Migne but also Heffernan.

6 Calvin: "verum singulis operibus suis *certas gloriae suae notas insculpsit*" (I.V.1); "certa sunt divinitatis *insignia* in homine…in homine *impressa sunt immortalitatis signa*…Nempe ut *mundus* qui *in spectaculum gloriae Dei conditus est*" (I.V.5); "Ergo quanvis hominem serio oculos intendere conveniat ad consideranda Dei opera, quando *in hoc splendidissimo theatro* locatus est ut eorum esset spectator" (I.VI. 2), my emphasis.

cannot have more than one most simple sense, which we call the Scriptural or literal or tongue-sense". Tyndale (304) maintained that "the Scripture hath but one sense, which is the literal sense". Yet, when confronted with metaphorical expressions in the Gospels or in Pauline writings, the application of this notion became problematic: only the Spirit could be considered a trustful guide[7] and in the Protestant exegetical tradition the literal sense of any scriptural passage was held to be the sense gathered from the explication of metaphorical phrases, not the literal sense of the metaphorical figures themselves.

This ambiguity favoured a transformation of the term 'allegory' into an all-embracing ideologeme in the hands of radicals and institutions alike as hermeneutics was more and more invested with such compelling issues as politics and religion. As a consequence, the charges that Luther or Tyndale had levelled at the Pope, the Catholic Church, and in general at all those who recurred to allegorical readings in order to lock up the Word of God and wrap it in a series of opaque veils[8], acquired a new political and ideological flavour when Puritans, Republicans and Radicals (albeit for different reasons and with different emphasis) accused the Church and the Crown of being buttresses of absolutism, monopolising the Word of God for their political and economic purposes.[9]

All this triggered off stronger tensions as to the use of images and the concept of representation, and the hermeneutic anxiety became blatant when images began to be used to deal with spiritual matters: Calvin had clearly prohibited all forms of representation but authorised the painting or

7 Milton himself was explicit on this, considering the authority of the scriptures only an "external authority" whereas "the pre-eminent and supreme authority [...] is the authority of the Spirit, which is internal, and the individual possession of each man" (*CPW* 6: 587). He goes on stating that "I do not know why God's providence should have committed the content of the New Testament to such wayward and uncertain guardians, unless it was so that this very fact might convince us that the Spirit which is given to us is a more certain guide than scripture, and that we ought to follow it" (589).

8 For a thorough survey of the various issues in the Reformation controversy against Rome Evans and Christopher still provide useful insights.

9 As Norbrook has it: "During the 1630s and 1640s, however, the monarchy emerged ever more strongly as the central bulwark of those monopolies, and it was abolished" (14).

sculpting of things which could be presented to the eye[10] in order to preserve the didactic potential of representation. Yet, images could become an unlawful and dangerous union of material and spiritual, fostering idolatrous practices such as portraying spiritual truths or realities. In fact, the call for an inward religion and the new emphasis put on the inner self as a true repository of religion often turned out to be an outward bodily experience, culminating in the notorious blasphemy cases of such people as William Franklin, Thomas Tany, Lodowick Muggleton or James Nayler.[11]

True reality for orthodox Protestantism and Puritanism was absent and otherworldly, and allegory was taken to be the sign of equivocation; yet, figurality was the only way for each man to understand himself in this life, in his own material existence. Literalism and figurality had become so inextricably tied in Protestant hermeneutic that, as Thomas Luxon writes, "Since the truly real is everything on the other side of the 'things of this world', what this world understands as realism is, strictly speaking, allegory" (190). So, while trying to fashion the believer's life, Protestant typology apparently had to devalue the concrete carnal existence making it a metaphor, a shadow of the true spiritual, otherworldly life to come.

A similar strategy can be appreciated in Wither's *Collection of Emblemes*, whose "Preposition to this Frontispiece" shows an extremely interesting antiphrastic procedure. The elaborated design[12] and metaphorical richness of the image are contained and disclaimed by saying that, in compliance with the Puritan love for literality, the original design was to be a "plaine Invention":

> Insteed thereof, the *Workeman* brought to light,
> What, here, you see; therein, mistaking quite
> The true *Designe*: And, so (with paines, and cost)
> The first intended FRONTISPIECE, is lost.
> The AVTHOR, was as much displeas'd, as Hee
> In such adventures; is inclin'd to bee;
> And halfe resolv'd, to cast this PIECE aside,

10 In Calvin's words: "Deum effingi visibili specie nefas esse putamus [...]. Si ne figurare quidem Deo corporem effigiem fas est, multo minus ipsam pro Deo, vel Deum in ipsa colere licebit. *Restat igitur ut ea sola pingantur ac sculpantur quorum sint capaces oculi*" (I.XI.12), my emphasis.

11 On all these, and their feminine counterparts, see Hill ("Upside Down"), Mack and Luxon.

12 For a full analysis of the frontispiece see Bath (111–15).

> As nothing worth: but, having better ey'd
> Those *Errors*, and *Confusions*, which may, there,
> Blame-worthy (at the first aspect) appeare;
> Hee saw, they fitted many Fantasies
> Much better, then what *Reason* can devise;
> And, that, the *Graver* (by meere *Chance*) had hit
> On what, so much transcends the reach of *Wit*,
> As made it seeme, an Object of *Delight*,
> To looke on what MISFORTVNE brought to light:
> And, here it stands, to try his *Wit*, who lists
> To pumpe the secrets, out of *Cabalists* ("Preposition to this Frontispiece").

The image is wrong, unauthorised by the author, the work of misfortune, yet it can be useful and become an "Object of Delight." This rhetoric of indirection and repudiation is imposed as the general mode of the whole text as the only way to authorise the content of the book. It conforms to the normative literal interpretation of orthodox Protestant hermeneutics and to the traditional *topos* of *sprezzatura*, but it is also the only way to stress the necessity of a personal interpretation by the reader, because anything can have both a meaning and its opposite.

The whole book is characterised by contrasting tendencies: the refusal to give an interpretation of the image, in tune with the Protestant bias against the visual arts, must nevertheless come to terms with the necessity of a guide to avoid wrong interpretations, and this often becomes the ideological prerequisite of a subjugation practice or the fashioning of the reader.[13] Likewise, the Protestant refusal of mediation is made to coexist with the traditional, Neoplatonic idea of the symbol as mysterious and enigmatic, in order to stimulate the reader's interest.

Of course, being at the same time representer and represented, interpreter and interpreted meant that

> When allegorical personifications or figures interpret their surroundings, their own actions, and their positions in the world, they do so as characters in a play or a fiction might do, characters for whom the horizon of the fictional world in which they are staged remains finally opaque, a veil hardly even perceived as a veil, let alone seen through (Luxon 26).

13 This is even more true if one considers that every single feature of the *Collection of Emblemes* is discussed at length and so the moral drawn in the various *subscriptiones* often turns out to be an attempt to impose a univocal meaning and stop the dissemination of interpretations. On this problem see also Cavell (179–180).

According to continental theorists, emblems and *imprese* were exactly the forms that could tear this 'veil' apart, the necessary instruments to live a real life. Being allegorical, emblematics was homogeneous with true otherworldly existence, yet it was potentially dangerous because it could be mistakenly taken literally at its face value. As a consequence, the delegitimation of the frontispiece, of the narrating voice and of the author, is paradoxically the only way to dignify them; their authority resides exactly in their not being authorised.

Just as in continental emblems, especially after advent of the Jesuits, the figures in the *Collection of Emblems* are given an increasing relevance and what may be called scene accessories are invested with (or deliberately deprived of) new meanings. This means that the *pictura* shifts progressively from *mimesis* to *diegesis*, it has no more the purely symbolic function of alluding to something else in a transparent way but acquires an opacity that makes it significant in itself, becoming a visual clue that binds the reader to the material world.

Wither's emblem III.3, for example, shows a mace and a sword and defines them transparent symbols of authority that have to be honoured, since there is an essential continuity between them, the prince and God. And yet, if on the one hand the emblem seems to allude to a perfect world in which signifier and signified coincide, on the other hand the acknowledged, progressive loss of transparency of the symbols means that the thorough description of objects and their meanings cannot be but deceitful, and people who try to find a meaning in them are deluded, as emblem II.23 clearly states:

> In *Objects*, here on *Earth*, we seeke to finde
> That perfect sollidnesse, which is confinde,
> To things in *Heaven*, though every day we see,
> What emptinesse, and faylings, in them be (II.23).

The presence and the consequent possibility of achieving a solid, unitary and unifying meaning is destabilised and dislocated, and the symbolic features of the *pictura* can be no more understood according to the old paradigms, because they tend to refer to themselves betraying their total artificiality. Images are no more seen and interpreted according to a transcendent metaphysical perspective: if the providentialistic ideology appeared less and less applicable, and signs could not be interpreted unambiguously anymore, writers had to recur to different strategies capable of understanding the real and its functioning, thus making images and signs a concrete effect of power practices involving a reader who lives in a world of increasing fragmentation.[14]

This is confirmed by the political implications of that other problematic issue, the representativity of words and images. This had of course not only a hermeneutic significance but a clear ideological[15] and political relevance, which became paramount during "the mid-1640s, when the modern concept of Parliamentary representation was first formulated" (Norbrook 141).[16]

Despite the Reformers' emphasis on the verbal aspect as the true vehicles of representation, images could not be dismissed so easily and also in Protestant countries the visual often prevailed over the verbal for instrumental reasons: as Karen Pinkus suggests, "the individual-group interaction was mediated precisely through the symbol or visual sign" (45). After all, the attacks against visual representations were as common as the attacks against the arbitrariness of words, as the elaboration of various universal language schemes during the seventeenth century demonstrate (see Salmon).

If the traditional doctrine of the king's two bodies (see Kantorowicz) had allowed the Royalists to fuse together king and kingdom, as if the king's real body could be accounted for as a transparent representation of the kingdom's 'allegorical' body, in the pre-revolutionary years the process of political representation, as David Norbrook states, "was analogous to the exhilarating process of spiritual self-discovery once the external forms of the old religion had dropped away" (Norbrook 143) because the corrupt nature of Parliamentary representation was only another aspect of the more

14 Praz had already noted these features but with different ideological implications: "The picture eventually became animated with an intense, hallucinatory life, independent of the page. The eyes were not alone in perceiving it; the depicted objects were invested with body, scent, and sound: the beholder was no longer before them, but in their midst. He was no longer impressed only, but obsessed" (170).

15 One of the clearest examples in case is the famous polemic between Kepler and Fludd on the truthfulness of visual representations, which disguised an attack against alchemical and occult practices from the scientific establishment. On this see Westman and Vickers-Struever.

16 Norbrook continues "The Parliamentary leaders presented themselves as defenders and representers of the people's liberties against assault from absolutist courtiers and clerics, but their concept of representation remained vague" (141–142).

general corruption of signs and language, no more built on the tradition of resemblance but according to a principle of difference.

In 1647, the Leveller Richard Overton still resorted to the opposition between being and appearing in his *An Appeale from the Degenerate Representative Body*, stating that

> such as are the representers of *Free-men*, must be substantial and reall *Actors* for *freedome* and *liberty*, for such as is the represented, such and no other must the figure or representation be, such as is the proportion, countenance and favour of the man, such and so must be the picture of the man, or else it cannot be the picture of that man, but of some other, or of somthing else, as the picture of a grim, meager, frowning face is, not the picture of an amiable, friendly smiling countenance; so tyranny neither is nor can possibly be the Representor of Freedome (Wolfe 169).

The radical, polemic force of these words has a clear rhetorical flavour and reminds of the excited debates among Italian scholars concerning the definition and the composition rules of truly significant *imprese*, in particular the need to use the language of natural signs in order to be truly representative (i.e. the need to avoid both excessive obscurity and excessive plainness).

If it would be absurd to push these similarities too far, it is nevertheless interesting to point out that political, hermeneutic, and allegorical aspects of representation share a common rhetorical discourse that denounces the ideological nature of the rhetorics of the 'natural order' of things: religious, economic, social hierarchies run the risk of becoming all artefacts and not metaphysical entities inherent in the natural order of things, just "simulacra" in Baudrillard's sense. If this is true of objects, it must be even more true of people in charge: Wither declares that a king is such only if he is a transparent mirror of God's authority (in emblem I.32, the virtuous king is defined "*Gods* immediate *Bleßing*") and a few years later in the same concept is applied to Cromwell, since it is "that *Heavn'ly King,* / Whom, he but represents" ("Vaticinium" 15). These peremptory statements are not only a moral invitation to rulers, but reminders for anyone in charge of his purely representative essence. If a monarch, or a Lord Protector, lacks transparency and ceases to represent (as it is often the case), if signifier and signified get separated, then his power is illegitimate and unnatural.

In conclusion, from emblem writers (such as George Wither) to radical political leaders (such as Richard Overton), the problem of what was really representative – of how words (or symbols or politicians) could represent transparently what they expressed – was a crucial issue before the Civil

War, when the debate on the corrupt nature of symbols (linguistic but also political) joined literature and politics, aesthetics and religion, hermeneutics and ideology.

Two decades later, the same problems reappeared in a very different cultural climate, perhaps without the former historical urgency but with a deeper political and hermeneutic relevance, in *Paradise Regained.* David Loewenstein analysed the relationships between *Paradise Regained* and the Quaker idea of the kingdom within, stressing the continuities between the cultural climate of the 40's and of the 60's (see Loewenstein), but also the verbal skirmishes on the problem of representation in its double meaning (what can be represented and what is representative) are a legacy of the past and a relevant item in *Paradise Regained,* deserving a more in-depth analysis.

The first problem that the text addresses is what Jesus can represent. According to the narrator, he is first of all a man ("By one man's firm obedience fully tried", I, 4) who will demonstrate his legitimacy to the title of Son of God through a concrete proof ("By proof the undoubted Son of God," I, 11): according to the narrator, in other words, Jesus can represent the Son because his concrete actions will be a transparent (and thus representative) proof of his theological identity. Satan, on the other hand, is perplexed by him because the theological Son cannot in fact be represented concretely. The Son of God "late of woman born" (I, 65) has to be investigated in his eligibility to represent truly, transparently the celestial Son, the first-begot. Yet, if, according to Calvin and to orthodox Protestantism, this world is corrupt and deceitful and no more than a figure of Heaven (see Calvin III.IX.1–2), the Saviour rests precisely on this no-man's land between earth and heaven, allegory and reality, a *medium* that alludes and directs the reader to something else but that at the same time cannot be reduced to something worthless and purely instrumental.

While Jesus' concreteness, his being 'here and now' cannot be dispensed with so easily, Satan tries to dismiss the Saviour as someone whose presence in the world, that is whose materiality, is ambiguous and thus non-representative. He is not a transparent sign "although in his face / the glimpses of his father's glory shine" (I, 92–3). So Satan keeps on tempting[17]

17 The traditional meaning attached to this word is "to try to attract, to entice to do evil; to allure or incite to evil with the prospect of some pleasure or advantage" (*OED* II, 4), but it also signified "to try the quality, worth, truth of something" (*OED* I), as translation of the New Testament term *πειρα,* that in its proper sense meant "ex-

Jesus because according to him "Sons of God both angels are and men" (IV, 197)[18] but he wants to understand "whether in higher sort / Than these thou bear'st that title" (IV, 198–199). Again in book IV Satan repeats this concept stating that

> I thought thee worth my nearer view
> And narrower scrutiny, that I might learn
> In what degree or meaning thou art called
> The Son of God, which bears no single sense;
> The Son of God I also am, or was,
> And if I was, I am; relation stands
> All men are Sons of God [...] (514–20).

If Christ's representativity is doubtful, Satan claims for himself a perfect correspondence, "relation stands," between his heavenly and hellish identity. Satan cannot conceive of a material body which is the "True image of the Father"; he is still tied to the rigid, orthodox Protestant concept of representation that dismissed the figural aspect in favour of the verbal one. Satan's mixing of religious, political and hermeneutic items is aimed at denying Jesus' representativity. Satan, in other words, aims at deconstructing the Saviour's legitimacy to representation, trying to show either that he has a common identity that he shares with men and angels and that therefore "bears no single sense" (IV, 517), or that he has a single and non-representative identity because he is a man that cannot possibly represent the theological Son (for example he calls him "Then hear, o Son of David, virgin-born; / For Son of God to me is yet in doubt" IV, 500–01, using all the biblical names attributed to the Son of God, but not the theological one). In other words Satan tries "to allow the outer word to force an unambiguous revelation of – to fix – the Son's identity" (Lanier 201).

The danger inherent in Satan's approach to Jesus is now clear, and reminiscent of the great debates of the 40's on representativity: for Satan Jesus' nature is ambiguous, "Real or allegoric I discern not," and this allows him to claim the title of Son of God also for himself, thus making a political action aiming at deconstructing hierarchies and meanings to his own advantage. He even hints that the traditional roles between Jesus and him-

---

periment, proof". As history of Christ's temptations, *Paradise Regained* is also the history of how the Son of God is "experimented."

18 For a full discussion of the problems raised by the use of the term "Son of God" see E. E. Ericson, Jr. and Hill ("Experience of Defeat").

self can be inverted. In Book IV, Satan says that "The Son of God I also am, or was, /And if I was, I am," appropriating the Tetragrammaton, the covenant name of God's theophany on Mount Oreb, whereas immediately after he tells Jesus that

> Thou art to be my fatal enemy.
> Good reason then, if I beforehand seek
> To understand my adversary, who
> And what he is [...] (IV, 525–28).

To consider Jesus as one's adversary means to identify him with Satan (that etymologically means 'adversary, enemy'). Jesus is in fact Satan's Satan, his tempter, one who tries to pervert and lead him astray from his mission. So Satan tries to give the Saviour a single role, or even his own, or alternatively a myriad roles and meanings, easily deconstructable.

In other words, the impression that one gets while reading *Paradise Regained* is that it rehearses through concrete characters the past debates on the nature of representation, with the aim of understanding the past errors and making the reader aware of those problems, obliging him to respond personally to those solicitations, so that he can find a personal solution to this problem. In the past the steady invitation to the reader to become a protagonist of the meaning production of a text had also become the ideological instrument for the reification and re-materialisation of the reading subject, imposing on him a behavioural model (and this is also what Satan accomplishes through his glib rhetoric with the other devils[19]). In *Paradise Regained*, on the contrary, the materiality of an image (that is the Saviour's physical presence in the world) acquires different implications: the reader already knows how all the story will end, what the nature of the Son of God is and he knows (or at least he should believe) that the Son of God is the transparent representative of the Heavenly King.[20] To Satan, on the contrary, he has not a single and immediately perceptible meaning, because the Father of Lies cannot accept the very idea of a perfectly representative Son of God, nor does he accept to investigate and discover Jesus' richness of meaning in a progressive way. To use the well-known Barthesian terminol-

19 For a fuller discussion of this issue see Borgogni.

20 As Douglas Lanier puts it, "To a remarkable degree the poem focuses our attention not upon heroic deeds but upon presentational strategy, on *how* Jesus outmanoeuvres Satan's attempt to secure through the public declarations of the Son and Father a definite knowledge of the Son's identity and vocation."

ogy, Satan would like to consider Jesus a *lisible* and not a *scriptible* character, whereas for the reader it becomes progressively clearer that Christ's representativity has other forms and implications than the ones that Satan would accept.

In portraying Jesus torn by doubts on how to begin his mission and to perform significant or representative actions, but also assertive in his answers to Satan's temptations, *Paradise Regained* proposes a *scriptible* character, in the sense that Jesus deconstructs all the traditional paradigms that should 'legitimate' him and proscribes a passive reading of his own character, requiring, on the contrary, an active interpretation by the reader, who must unravel and build the connections between Jesus' visual and abysmal nature. The Son of God, in other words, requires a series of linguistic, rhetorical, religious and hermeneutic abilities fostering a layered reading, but at the same time he claims for himself a role of transparent, perfect representation that the reader has to evaluate, understand and apply to his own life. If the hope of a 'ready and easy way' is now collapsed, the same is true for the old ready-made, taken for granted ideas of representation. Interestingly enough, Jesus does not give any theoretical justification of his representativity, the only thing that he chooses to do is to "say and stay" on the pinnacle, a miraculous action that must become a paradigmatic example for the reader as well. True representation can be achieved only through transparent deeds in which words and actions (saying and staying) are again reconciled and genuine expressions one of the other.

In conclusion, *Paradise Regained* is a more multilayered and polymorphic text than it is usually recognised: from a narrative point of view it shows the 'historical' victory of Jesus over the temptations; from a theological point of view it celebrates Jesus' heavenly identity and his regaining of Paradise, whose consequences men are still experiencing; but from a political and ethical point of view it has an open ending, giving the reader the responsibility in the future to strive for the same form of representation that Jesus has not discussed but enacted[21]: Jesus overcomes temptations, but the solution to the political and hermeneutic problems raised by his identity and actions in the text is left to the reader in his own concrete historical situation.

21 After all, as Peggy Samuels maintains, "Far from representing a retreat to a place of private, otherworldly meditation, the kind of relationship to the world enunciated by the poem involves the reflection on or 'revolving' of events in the world: preparation for action in, even governing of, that world" (172).

Works Cited

Babcox, Emily. "Physical and Metaphorical Hunger: The Extra-Biblical Temptations of Paradise Regained", *Milton Quarterly* 26 (1992): 36–42.

Bath, Michael. *Speaking Pictures. English Emblem Books and Renaissance Culture*, London and New York: Longman, 1994.

Borgogni, Daniele. *"Pondering Oft": Lettura argomentativa del* Paradise Regained *di John Milton*, Napoli-Perugia: Edizioni Scientifiche Italiane, 1998.

Calvin (Cauvin, Jean). *Institutionis Christianae Religionis* [1559], in Calvini, Joannis. *Opera selecta*, Barth P. – Niesel G. (ediderunt), editio tertia emendata, voll. III–V, München: Ch. Kaiser Verlag, 1967–74.

Cavell, Richard. "Representing Writing: The Emblem as (Hiero)glyph," eds Scholz B. F. et al., *The European Emblem. Selected Papers from the Glasgow Conference 11–14 August, 1987*, Leiden: Brill, 1990. 167–90.

Christopher, G. B. *Milton and the Science of the Saints*, Princeton: Princeton UP, 1982.

Ericson, E. E., Jr. "The Sons of God in *Paradise Lost* and *Paradise Regained*," *Milton Quarterly* 25 (1991): 79–89.

Evans, G. R. *The Language and Logic of the Bible: The Road to Reformation*, Cambridge: Cambridge UP, 1985.

Fish, S. E. "Things and Actions Indifferent: The Temptation of Plot in Paradise Regained," eds R. S. Ide – J. A. Wittreich, Jr., *Composite Orders*, special issue of *Milton Studies* 17 (1983): 163–85.

Frye, Northrop. "The Typology of *Paradise Regained*," *Modern Philology* 53.4 (1956): 227–28.

Heffernan, Thomas. *Art and Emblem: Early Seventeenth-Century English Poetry of Devotion*, Tokyo: Sophia University, 1991.

Hill, Christopher. *The World Turned Upside Down. Radical Ideas during the English Revolution*, London: Temple Smith, 1972.

–. *The Experience of Defeat: Milton and Some Contemporaries*, New York: Viking, 1984.

Kantorowicz, E. H. *The King's Two Bodies: A Study in Mediaeval Political Theology*, Princeton: Princeton UP, 1957.

Lanier, Douglas. "'Unmarkt, Unknown': *Paradise Regained* and the Return of the Expressed," *Criticism* 37 (1995): 187–212.

Lewalski, B. K. *Milton's Brief Epic. The Genre, Meaning, and Art of "Paradise Regained"*, Providence R. I.: Brown UP, 1966.

Loefscher, F. W. "Luther and the Problem of Authority in Religion," *Princeton Theological Review* 15.4 (1917): 553–603.

Loewenstein, David. "The Kingdom Within: Radical Religious Culture and the Politics of *Paradise Regained*", *Literature and History* 3 (1994): 63–89.

Luxon, Thomas. *Literal Figures: Puritan Allegory and the Reformation Crisis in Representation*, Chicago: The University of Chicago Press, 1995.

Mack, Phyllis. "Women Prophets during the English Civil War", *Feminist Studies* 8.1 (1982): 18–45.

MacKellar, Walter (ed.). *A Variorum Commentary on the Poems of John Milton. Volume IV: Paradise Regained*, New York: Columbia UP, 1975.

Migne, J.-P. (accurante). *Patrologiae Cursus Completus, seu Bibliotheca universalis, integra, uniformis, commoda, oeconomica, Omnium SS. Patrum, Doctorum, Scriptorumque Ecclesiasticorum, sive Latinorum, sive Graecorum*, Paris: J.-P. Migne, 1844–79.

Milton, John. *The Poems of John Milton*, ed. John Carey and Alastair Fowler, London: Longman, 1968.

–. *The Complete Prose Works of John Milton*, gen. ed. Wolfe, D. M., New Haven: Yale UP, 1953–1982.

Norbrook, David. *Writing the English Republic. Poetry, Rhetoric and Politics, 1627–1660,* Cambridge: Cambridge UP, 1999.

Pinkus, Karen. *Picturing Silence. Emblem, Language, Counter-Reformation, Materiality*, Ann Arbor: The University of Michigan Press, 1996.

Pope, E. M. *"Paradise Regained". The Tradition and the Poem*, Baltimore: Johns Hopkins, 1947.

Praz, Mario. *Studies in Seventeenth-Century Imagery*, 2nd ed., Rome: Edizioni di Storia e Letteratura, 1964.

Rajan, B. (ed.). *The Prison and the Pinnacle. Papers to Commemorate the Tercentenary of* Paradise Regained *and* Samson Agonistes, Toronto and Buffalo: University of Toronto Press, 1973.

Rushdy, A. H. A. *The Empty Garden. The Subject of Late Milton*, Pittsburgh: University of Pittsburgh Press, 1992.

Salmon, Vivian. *The Study of Language in 17th-Century England* [1979], Amsterdam and Philadelphia: John Benjamins Publishing Company, 1988.

Samuels, Peggy. "Labor in the Chambers: *Paradise Regained* and the Discourse of Quiet", *Milton Studies* 36 (1998): 153–76.

Shawcross, J. T. (ed.). *Milton: The Critical Heritage*, London: Routledge & Kegan Paul, 1970.

–. *"Paradise Regained": Worthy T'have Not Remain'd So Long Unsung*, Pittsburgh: Duquesne UP, 1988.

Stein, Arnold. *Heroic Knowledge. An Interpretation of* Paradise Regained *and* Samson Agonistes, Minneapolis: University of Minnesota Press, 1957.

Tyndale, William. *The Obedience of a Christian Man*, in *Doctrinal Treatises and Introductions to Different Portions of the Holy Scriptures*, ed. Walter, Henry [1848–50], Cambridge: Cambridge UP, 1968.

Weber, B. J. *Wedges and Wings. The Patterning of* Paradise Regained, Carbondale: Southern Illinois University Press, 1975.

Vickers, Brian and Struever, N. S. *Rhetoric and the Pursuit of Truth. Language Change in the Seventeenth and Eighteenth Century*, Berkeley and Los Angeles: University of California Press, 1985.

Westman, R. S. "Nature, Art and Psyche: Jung, Pauli, and the Kepler-Fludd Polemic," ed. Vickers, Brian. *Occult and Scientific Mentalities in the Renaissance*, Cambridge: Cambridge UP, 1984.

Wither, George, *A Collection of Emblemes*, London, 1635.

–. *Vaticinium Causuale*, London, 1655.

Wittreich, Jr., J. A. (ed.). *Calm of Mind. Tercentenary Essays on* Paradise Regained *and* Samson Agonistes *in Honor of John S. Diekhoff*, Cleveland OH: Press of Case Western Reserve University, 1971.

Wolfe, D. M. (ed.). *Leveller Manifestoes of the Puritan Revolution*, New York: Thomas Nelson & Sons, 1944.

Part III

The Great Poems

3. Samson Agonistes

Suvi MÄKELÄ

"[E]xiled from light": Beauty, the Senses and Freedom in *Samson Agonistes*

Milton's interest in the idea of the beautiful can be seen informing a great many of his writings. For instance, the concept of beauty plays a decisive role in the loss of freedom of Milton's Samson. This paper focuses on the effects of Samson's understanding of beauty on his state. It is only a partial reading of Milton's text and is meant to provide yet another perspective on the text. It does not strive to be a final, all-inclusive reading.

Milton and St. Augustine share similar views on the aesthetic, moral and religious aspects of beauty. In this paper I will use Augustine's ideas about the perception of beauty in my reading of Milton's *Samson Agonistes.* I will also use Plato's description of the ascent from the apprehension of physical beauty to the beauty of spirit in my reading of Samson's state. I will show how his physical captivity can be argued to be caused by a wrong perception of beauty, and how the disorder of his mind destroys his capacity to judge correctly.

In *The City of God* St. Augustine discusses two different standards by which people can lead their lives: "There is, in fact, one city of men who choose to live by the standard of the flesh, another of those who choose to live by the standard of the spirit" (547). This simply means that "just as the spirit is quite appropriately called carnal when it is the servant of the flesh, the flesh will with equal propriety be called spiritual, when it serves the spirit" (533). Basically, there are two different ways of perceiving reality depending on what standards one lives by. If one lives by the standard of the world or the flesh, one has a carnal perception, if by the standard of the spirit, one gains an insight, a spiritual vision. This "inner gaze" (463) is an intellectual vision dependent on reason. Augustine writes: "There are [...] matters which are perceived by the mind and the reason: and such perception is rightly described as a kind of sense" (431). Augustine sets this intellectual sense above the carnal senses: "far more important than any bodily sense, [is] the sense of the inner man, by which we apprehend what is just" (462).

Augustine also describes both idolatrous and correct ways of seeing the world and the beauty in it:

> The life which we live in this world has its attractiveness because of a certain measure in its beauty and its harmony with all these inferior objects that are beautiful. [...] Yet sin is committed for the sake of all these things and others of this kind when, in consequence of an immoderate urge towards those things which are at the bottom end of the scale of good, we abandon the higher and supreme goods, that is you, Lord God, and your truth and your law (*Confessions* 29–30).

Hence, the sin of idolatry consists of an unbalanced vision. This means treating something like virtue or beauty as one's own properties, or properties of another created being, thus not recognising them as reflections of God's virtue and beauty. This disrespect for the proper hierarchy of beauty results in a wrong relation to God and to the object or person idolised because it causes servility to things of a lower order. This, in turn, results in debasement and loss of spiritual vision. The creature loses its rightful place in cosmic order. Augustine points out that what an idolatrous person has forgotten is that "[t]he good which you love is from him [God]. But it is only as it is related to him that it is good and sweet. Otherwise it will justly become bitter, for all that comes from him is unjustly loved if he has been abandoned" (53–64).

In other words, one must not forget the relationship between all good things and God if one is to have a balanced relationship with God and proper respect for the good things.

In the *Symposium* Plato writes that physical examples of beauty should guide a human being to discern beauties of higher orders:

> He uses them like a ladder, climbing from the love of one person to love of two; from two to love of all physical beauty; from physical beauty to beauty in human behaviour; thence to beauty in subjects of study; from them he arrives finally at that branch of knowledge which studies nothing but ultimate beauty. Then at last he understands what true beauty is (45–46).

It is extremely important for a creature to be properly aligned with beauties of different orders and degrees, and to have a well-organised, harmonious mind. By valuating beauty incorrectly, one defects from the harmony of the universe and disrupts that harmony. Just like the macrocosm, or the universe, should be in a state of ordered harmony, the happiest state of the microcosm, or the individual creature, is a state of internal harmony, which can be achieved by correct orientation to objects in the physical realm and to God. By not respecting the hierarchies of value and beauty in the world, and thus becoming a source of discord in the ordered scheme of the universe, a creature falls into an internal state of discord, as well. Augustine thinks that

> all physical beauty depends on a harmony between the parts of the body, combined with an attractive complexion. When there is not this harmony and proportion the appearance is displeasing, either because of distortion, or because of some excess or deficiency (*City of God* 1061).

The same applies to the shape of the creature's soul. As Plato points out, "the reason ought to rule, having the ability and foresight to act for the whole, and the spirit ought to obey and support it" (*Republic* 194). The reason is in command when the creature willingly subjects him- or herself to God and respects the ordered beauty of the universe: "it is better for every creature to be under the control of divine wisdom. That wisdom and control should, if possible, come from within" (368). Thus, we can see how important order, harmony and discipline are in Augustine's and Plato's thinking. A creature who abandons such order ends up in a state of internal chaos. The creature becomes disproportionate and truly deformed, losing all sense of order.

For Milton, right reason is the soul's being, and, as Thomas Stroup points out, "[s]in for Milton is the subjection of the reason to the lower powers," it is "self-subordination of reason [… by] deliberate actions" (Stroup 62). The Chorus' description of Samson is an illustration of such a state of subjection:

> See how he lies at random, carelessly diffused,
> With languished head unpropped,
> As one past hope, abandoned,
> And by himself given over (*SA* 118–21).

Here Samson's bodily state and posture reflect his spiritual state, caused by his carnal vision and idolatry. Samson's way of lying randomly and carelessly reflects his spiritual disorder. I will argue that Samson's physical state of captivity has been caused by an internal loss of order, and that Samson is misaligned with God, himself and other creatures. He is unable to judge correctly, to see the true aspects of objects, creatures and ideas. Indeed, he has lost his ability to see his own actions in the light of the spirit.

Samson's state of mind and his reactions are witness to the inner chaos of his being. In his captivity, Samson is vengeful, he rages, hates, and lets his ill-proportioned passions control him. Samson's mind is constantly troubled and fermenting. In this, he resembles Satan in *Paradise Regained.* Satan is "with envy fraught and rage" (1.38). He needs to "vent his rage / And [is] mad beside" (4.445–46), an "[a]mbitious spirit" (495) often "in a careless mood" (450), "swoll'n with rage" (499), "inly stung with anger and disdain" (1.466). Like Satan, Samson "lies at random, carelessly diffused" (*SA* 118). This torpor, inner disorder, leaves room for unchecked passions to take control of Samson's mind. His careless diffusion creates and feeds the aggressions that rage inside him. He is full of aggression, as his words to Harapha show: "My heels are fettered, but my fist is free" (1235). He also threatens Dalila, who wants to touch his hand, with violence, his standard solution to every problem: "Not for thy life, lest fierce remembrance wake / My sudden rage to tear thee joint by joint" (952–53). Satan's "rash revolt" (*PR* 1.359) can also be compared to Samson's impulsive actions of destruction and slaughter, committed in torrents of rage. He has "[s]purned [… his enemies] to death by troops" (*SA* 138). Samson's mind seems to be in total chaos.

In contrast, Jesus has an "untroubled mind" in *Paradise Regained* (4.401). He is the "patient Son of God" (420) who always remains "in calm and sinless peace" (425) "as a rock / Of adamant" (533–34). He is "our Saviour meek" (636), who can "sternly" (1.406) reply to Satan with "unaltered brow" (493), with well-balanced mind and emotions. Jesus is like Job who with "his patience won" (426), whereas Samson and Satan are rash, violent and impatient. Jesus' being is in harmony with the universe, whereas Samson finds himself fallen away from this unity. This fall has been caused by his carnal understanding of beauty and value. The higher realms of beauty which require spiritual vision are beyond the reach of his fallen senses.

The Chorus talk about the power of beauty:

> Yet beauty, though injurious, hath strange power,
> After offence returning, to regain
> Love once possessed, nor can be easily
> Repulsed, without much inward passion felt
> And secret sting of amorous remorse (*SA* 1003–07).

This kind of a reaction to bodily beauty is a result of lust. It evinces an excessive appreciation of a low order of beauty. Before going physically blind, Samson has been susceptible to mere show and outward appearance, taking it for the essential quality of things. He has only seen the various representations, not the unchanging Form – the reality behind those representations. Samson's physical loss of sight can therefore be seen as a natural consequence of his idolatrous concentration on the carnal senses and his lack of spiritual vision. His carnal vision has caused him to be "awry enslaved / With dotage" (1041–42). He has fallen prey to Dalila's "enchanting voice [...] / The bait of honeyed words" (1065–66), her charms and beautiful looks – mere surfaces.

Carnality has also always been evinced in Samson's perception of strength. He thinks that physical strength is real strength – even if he understands that it needs wisdom to guide it. Augustine points out: "when our support rests on our own strength, it is infirmity" (*Confessions* 71), and Samson's carnal vision has indeed led to his current weakness and captivity. He still prioritizes physical, violent action and has a mental image of himself as a beautiful champion of God, even when he inflicts pain and suffering on people, and his actions cause horror and could certainly be rather called ugly. Pulling down the temple, for example, before being legitimized by the Chorus and Manoa, is intuitively described as an aesthetically repellent action by the characters of Milton's drama. Manoa asks:

> O what noise?
> Mercy of heaven what hideous noise was that?
> Horribly loud unlike the former shout (*SA* 1508–10).

The noise is horribly loud and hideous. It is not harmonious with the beautiful music of the spheres that represents the harmony of the universe. There is nothing well and fair in the noise. The Chorus is also horrified: "Blood, death, and deathful deeds are in that noise / Ruin, destruction at the utmost point" (1513–14). The Hebrew messenger's value judgement is quite clear, as well. He calls Samson pulling down the temple a "horrid spectacle" (1542), "the sad event" (1551) and the location "the place of horror" (1550).

The aesthetic perspective is always also a moral perspective in Milton's works. Therefore, the intuitive reactions of the characters should make the reader question the following appropriation of Samson's action into the cultural narrative of national heroism and the justification of his deeds by the rhetoric of national liberation. It is exactly these kinds of narratives that have captured Samson's mind in the first place, formed his identity and enslaved him under the desire of becoming a beautiful national hero.

Dalila is not free either. She too has a warped understanding of beauty. David Robertson argues that "Dalila [...] is an example of a self that is constructed from her own desires" (Robertson 314). She idolises her outward beauty and thus subjects herself to it. Her judgment has been corrupted and she sees her charming appearance as an inherent, defining feature of herself. She does not understand that her beautiful appearance is only a reflection of the beauty of God, in Augustinian terms the "supremely good Father, beauty of all things beautiful" (*Confessions* 41). For Milton beauty is always related to goodness, wisdom and justice – real beauty is inseparably linked to ethics and morality, that is. Beauty should always direct the creature towards the Good, affirm the relationship between the creature and God. Used rightly, beauty can teach virtue. Dalila's outward beauty is a gift, a talent like Samson's strength, and it should be used well and responsibly, not abused or wasted. However, Dalila uses her beauty as a weapon. She turns it into a commodity, just like Comus urges the Lady to do:

> Beauty is Nature's coin, must not be hoarded,
> But must be current [...]
> Beauty is Nature's brag, and must be shown
> In courts and feasts (*A Masque* 738–39, 744–45).

By commodifying and politicising the beauty of her body, Dalila debases her beautiful appearance and loses the beauty of her spirit, thus becoming enslaved by the mere appearance she idolises. By incorrectly valuing physical beauty and the benefits that can be achieved by abusing it, Dalila falls into idol worship. This happens because she abandons the true hierarchy of beauties in the universe.

David Harper thinks that "Dalila arrives not to comfort Samson or even to ask sincerely for forgiveness, but to tempt Samson once again in a ploy to get him back under her control" (Harper 147). Indeed, she arrives:

> [...] so bedecked, ornate, and gay
> Comes this way sailing
> Like a stately ship [...]
> With all her bravery on, and tackle trim (*SA* 712–14, 717).

Dalila is described as being "stately" (714), which can be read as her having a public function rather than a private one. She arrives dressed to kill, and she is perfectly composed, which suggests that her professed feelings are affected and false. She expects her body to be transported into the realm of myth by people's gazes. She lets these gazes construct an identity for herself from the outside. We are told that

> with head declined
> Like a fair flower surcharged with dew, she weeps
> [...]
> Wetting the borders of her silken veil (727–28, 730).

This is a controlled, well-thought-out performance meant to draw attention to her false charm and enacted beauty. Samson is able to recognise this now, whereas before, when he could still see, he was blind to Dalila's deceits and the hollowness of character in her.

Dalila is wearing perfume to tempt Samson now that he is blind (720–21), and she says: "though sight be lost, [...] / other senses want not their delights" (914, 916). At this point, having lost his sight and living physically enslaved, Samson finally understands how he has let himself be enslaved before:

> The base degree to which I now am fall'n,
> These rags, this grinding, is not yet so base
> As was my former servitude, ignoble,
> Unmanly, ignominious, infamous,
> True slavery, and that blindness worse than this,
> That saw not how degenerately I served (414–19).

He explains his weakness to Dalila: I was "overpowered / By thy request, who could deny thee nothing" (880–81). This is exactly the attitude that has got him into trouble in the first place. His relationship to Dalila has been idolatrous. He has fallen to the base degree he finds himself in because of his base understanding of beauty. As Harper argues, Samson "was enthralled in the sinful practise of worshipping a false idol – Dalila" (Harper 144). Harper is mistaken, however, in stating that Samson's "sin was one of overvaluation, of loving [Dalila] too well" (149). It is rather undervaluation – treating Dalila as an object of desire – that has caused his fall. Edmund Burke makes a distinction between love and lust:

> I likewise distinguish love, by which I mean that satisfaction which arises to the mind upon contemplating any thing beautiful, of whatsoever nature it may be, from desire or lust; which is an energy of the mind, that hurries us on to the possession of certain objects, that do not affect us as they are beautiful, but by means altogether different (Burke 83).

Samson feels desire to possess Dalila, lust, not true love or respect. This wrongly directed, disproportionate passion of his originates in his concentration on the carnal senses. It enslaves him and blinds him spiritually. As Augustine points out: "[t]o be far from your [God's] face is to be in the darkness of passion" (*Confessions* 20).

Samson is now outwardly subjected to "servile toil" (*SA* 5), he is "a prisoner chained" (7). However, this is a natural consequence of him subjecting himself to the beauty of things of a lower order. In other words, his physical state can be derived from his mental captivity. Samson complains that his

> glorious strength
> [has been] Put to the labour of a beast, debased
> Lower than bond-slave (36–38),

but it is he who has himself put his glorious strength to such usage in the first place. He is able to recognise this to a degree: "servile mind / Rewarded well with servile punishment!" (412–13).

> [...] Manoa thinks that
> if he [Samson] through frailty err,
> He [God] should not so o'erwhelm, and as a thrall
> Subject him [Samson] to so foul indignities (369–71).

What Manoa cannot see is that Samson's thraldom and the indignities are not extra punishments from God but simply a natural consequence of his idolatry and spiritual blindness. Augustine holds that "Your [God's] punishment is that which human beings do to their own injury because, even when they are sinning against you, their wicked actions are against their own souls" (*Confessions* 47). Samson has subjected his mind, spirit and reason to his passions and carnal senses. Therefore, his being is in a state of disorder. There is a marked contrast to Jesus in *Paradise Regained.* Whereas he fasts in the desert for forty days, finding plenty of food for his spirit,

Samson, by indulging his carnal desires, becomes "to [him]self a region of destitution" (St. Augustine, *Confessions* 34).

All in all, Jesus' words about a person who lets his passions rule him or her can be used to describe Samson:

> he who reigns within himself, and rules
> Passions, desires, and fears, is more a king;
> Which every wise and virtuous man attains:
> And who attains not, ill aspires to rule
> Cities of men, or headstrong multitudes,
> Subject himself to anarchy within,
> Or lawless passions in him which he serves (*PR* 2.466–72).

Samson's mind is in a state of anarchy, liable to be ruled by random thoughts and passions. There is no order, balance, or harmony in his mind – it is indeed lawless. However, the physically blind Samson is finally able to see Dalila. He says: "These false pretexts and varnished colours failing, / Bare in thy guilt how foul must thou appear!" (901–02). He can now see the spiritual and moral debasement of character underneath the outward show of beauty in Dalila. Samson has gained some degree of insight now that he is not distracted by visual stimuli. Dalila's actions and words show the ugliness of her motivations, and, in this sense, Samson's blindness is a strength.

However, Samson is still unable to see the hideous nature of his own exploits as a deliverer of his people. Neither does he understand the mental hold that the cultural model of heroism has over him. He is concentrated on the carnal aspects of his situation and is eventually unable to develop his understanding. Samson thinks that he is much easier to take advantage of now that he is physically blind:

> How wouldst thou use me now, blind, and thereby
> Deceivable, in most things as a child,
> Helpless (941–43).

However, the worse blindness that he suffers from is in fact spiritual, and it is more dangerous because he does not have an adequate conception of it like he does of his physical blindness. He has indeed been like a helpless child already before going physically blind. Not only has he been vulnerable to be manipulated by Dalila, but also by the violent cultural images of heroism that construct his mind. The elevated position of a worshipped idol that he has enjoyed has also contributed to his corruption. As Joseph Wittreich points out, "Samson's blindness emblematizes his past failings and failures of vision" (Wittreich 280). He has been blind among enemies before losing his eyesight, now it is only manifest in a new way:

> the vilest here excel me,
> They creep, yet see, I dark in light exposed
> To daily fraud, contempt, abuse and wrong,
> Within doors, or without, still as a fool,
> In power of others, never in my own;
> Scarce half I seem to live, dead more than half.
> O dark, dark, dark, amid the blaze of noon,
> Irrecoverably dark, total eclipse
> Without all hope of day! (*SA* 74–82)

This is indeed an adequate description of Samson's mental state already before his physical blindness.

True virtue, living by the standard of the spirit, provides one with inner light, wisdom, and vision:

> He that has light within his own clear breast
> May sit I' the centre, and enjoy bright day.
> But he that hides a dark soul, and foul thoughts
> Benighted walks under the midday sun;
> Himself is his own dungeon (*A Masque* 380–84).

This light is what Samson has been lacking. Samson's mind has not been properly aligned with the reality of Milton's cosmos, and he has therefore been making blind choices, deprived of spiritual vision. In this sense, he has been a dungeon to himself and has walked benighted amid the blaze of noon already before going physically blind.

It should now be evident how Samson has been imprisoned by his carnal mind and bodily senses due to his incorrect orientation to the different orders of beauty in the world. He lacks the light of the Spirit – inner beauty that illuminates the world and gives one wisdom to perceive the truth. This inward light in the soul is received from God by the creature that achieves and maintains the right relation to him.

In this sense, Samson is and has indeed been "exiled from light" (*SA* 98) from the start. What he misses most, even in his final blindness, are the delights provided by the sense of sight, not true vision:

> Light the prime work of God to me is extinct,
> And all her various objects of delight
> Annulled, which might in part my grief have eased (70–72).

He has no interest in concentrating on the higher orders of beauty – he just misses looking at delightful objects. The loss of bodily sight is an opportunity for Samson to gain spiritual sight, but he is too much a slave to the habitually carnal processes of his mind to be liberated from the darkness that clouds his understanding. Eventually, Samson's lack of spiritual vision leads to his ruin, which he brings upon himself:

> So fond are mortal men
> Fallen into wrath divine,
> As their own ruin on themselves to invite,
> Insensate left, or to sense reprobate,
> And with blindness internal struck (1682–86).

The Semichorus is here talking about the Philistines, but there is good reason to apply their words to Samson, as well. Due to his carnal idolatry, he is truly insensate, not just physically blind, but spiritually devoid of light, truly reprobate to sense.

In Milton's works, the way a creature sees beauty always reflects on his or her freedom. Dalila idolises her beauty and debases it by abusing it. Samson concentrates too much on the carnal aspects of beauty as well, and he is blind to true beauty of the spirit. He idolises the beauty of things of a lower order of reality, thus subjecting his mind to those things. In fact, both Samson and Dalila enslave themselves to the carnally oriented structures of their own minds. It can be argued that Samson's mental enslavement finally reaches its natural outcome in his physical enslavement, just like his lack of spiritual vision finally leads to his loss of physical sight. In other words, Samson lets his mind be captivated by beautiful appearances and thus loses his freedom – both physical and intellectual. As a consequence, his mind becomes deformed – lacking order, harmony and beauty – and his judgement cannot be trusted.

Works Cited

St. Augustine. *Concerning the city of God against the Pagans.* Trans. Henry Bettenson. London: Penguin Books, 1972.

–. *Confessions.* Trans. & ed. Henry Chadwick. Oxford: Oxford UP, 1992.

Burke, Edmund. *A Philosophical Enquiry into the Origin of Our Ideas of the Sublime and Beautiful.* Ed. Adam Phillips. Oxford: Oxford UP, 1990.

Harper, David A. "'Perhaps More Than Enough': The Dangers of Mate-Idolatry in Milton's *Samson Agonistes.*" *Milton Quarterly* 37 (2003): 139–51.

Milton, John. *John Milton: Complete Shorter Poems.* Ed. John Carey. 2nd ed. London and New York: Longman, 1997.

Plato. *The Republic.* Trans. H. D. P. Lee. Harmondsworth: Penguin Books, 1955.

–. *Symposium and the death of Socrates.* Trans. Tom Griffith. Ware: Worthsworth Editions Limited, 1997. 1–58.

Robertson, David. *"My self / Before me": Self-Love in the Works of John Milton.* Tampere: Tampere UP, 1992.

Stroup, Thomas B. "Psychology and Milton." *A Milton Encyclopedia.* Ed. William B. Hunter et al. Vol. 7. Lewisburg: Bucknell UP, 1979. 59–64.

Wittreich, Joseph. *Interpreting Samson Agonistes.* Princeton: Princeton UP, 1986.

Sherry Lutz ZIVLEY and Chase HAMBLIN

The Prosody of *Samson Agonistes*

Two problems relating to *Samson Agonistes* have continued to perplex Milton scholars. One involves the prosody of the poem. The other involves the date of composition. Both problems merit further study.

Eleven percent of the lines of the poem have fewer than ten syllables. I will call such lines "hypometrical."[1] Likewise, I will use the traditional term "hypermetrical" for lines with more than ten syllables.[2] Over 1200 of the 1758 lines (68.2 percent) of the poem are in decasyllabic blank verse – a blank verse rich in prosodic devices. There are hypermetrical lines of eleven syllables, created either by the use of a feminine ending or, rarely, lines of twelve syllables. In contrast, the hypometrical lines may have anywhere from four to nine syllables. And there are relatively few substitutions for the iambic feet that dominate the poem.

Although various critics have tried to explain the poem's prosody, none have analyzed the prosody of the entire poem. Instead, they have focused their attention on those examples that support their own theories (usually relating prosody to theme, to the dramatic intensity of various scenes, or to the poetic excellence of the poem).[3] Many of the critics who have argued that *SA* was composed in the 1640s or at a date decades later have relied on evidence external to the poem.[4] Ants Oras, however, analyzed internal pro-

1 Although "hypometrical" is generally used to describe a *whole* poem wit lines shorter than the norm for a poem of that genre and form, I am using it here to describe lines within a single poem that are shorter than the normal length for that poem. In *Samson Agonistes* the overwhelming majority of the lines are decasyllabic.

2 Of the possible terms for a shortened line ("catalectic," "acephalous," and "hypometrical"), "hypometrical" is the most accurate for the phenomenon being discussed here.

3 Robert Beum, "The Rhyme in *Samson Agonistes,*" *Texas Studies in Literature and Language* 4 (1962) and Keith N. Hull, "Rhyme and Disorder in *Samson Agonistes,*" *Milton Studies* 30 (1993).

4 The most thorough and objective recapitulation of the various scholarly articles on the date of composition of *Samson Agonistes* is the appendix to Mary Ann Radzinowicz's *Toward Samson Agonistes: The Growth of Milton's Mind* (Princeton: Princeton University Press, 1978).

sodic evidence. Using Oras's evidence, Shawcross drew conclusions that differ from those of Oras. Given that the poem contains two very different kinds of poetry, it is not surprising that critics have held divergent opinions about its date of composition.

Part of the poem employs a blank verse similar to that of *Paradise Lost* and *Paradise Regained.* The other part, the lyrical, seems a logical progression

---

Some of the primary arguments for a composition date in the 1640s are William Riley Parker, "The Date of *Samson Agonistes,*" *Philological Quarterly* 28 (1949), 145–66; "The Date of *Samson Agonistes* Again," *Calm of Mind: Tercentenary Essays on* Paradise Regained *and* Samson Agonistes, (Cleveland: Press of Case Western Reserve University, 1971), 163–74; "The Date of *Samson Agonistes*: A Postscript," *Notes and Queries* 203 (May 1958), 201–2. Ernest Sirluck presents a point-by-point rebuttal to those who argue for a composition date in the 1640s in the appendix, entitled "Some Recent Suggested Changes in the Chronology of Milton's Poems," to "Milton's Idle Right Hand," *Journal of English and German Philology* 60 (1961), 749–85.

Some of the primary arguments for a composition date at the end of Milton's career are the following: Robert Beum, "The Rhyme in *Samson Agonistes,*" *Texas Studies in Literature and Language*, 4.2 (Summer 1962) 177–82; Edward LeConpt, "New Objections to a Pre-Restoration Date for *Samson Agonistes,*" *Poets' Riddles: Essays in Seventeenth-Century Explication* (Port Washington, NY, 1975), 129–53; Ants Oras, "Milton's Blank Verse and the Chronology of His Major Poems," *SAMLA Studies in Milton,* ed. J. Max Patrick (Gainesville, FL: 1953), 128–97; J. Max Patrick, "Milton's Revolution against Rime, and Some of Its Implications," *Milton and the Art of Sacred Song,* ed. J. Max Patrick and Roger H. Sundell (Madison: University of Wisconsin Press), 99–117; and John Shawcross, "The Chronology of Milton's Major Poems," *PMLA* 76 (1961), 345–58.

In "Is *Samson Agonistes* Unfinished?" *Philological Quarterly* 28 (1949), 101, Allan H. Gilbert argues that *Samson,* like Milton's other works, underwent various revisions, but that "Milton repeated so often in this tragedy because he did not undertake the labor of blotting out and varying redundant lines" (105). I would also argue that the redundancies in this work are the result of the interfoliated nature of the work: the later sections Milton dictated sometimes overlapped the sections which were written earlier.

Gilbert also states that "[t]he text suggests lack of care" (105), but I would argue that the lack of care is only manifest in the longer-lined speeches, which I believe to have been dictated at the end of Milton's career.

In Paradise Regained*: Worthy T'Have Not Remain'd So Long Unsung* (Pittsburgh: Duquesne, 1988) John Shawcross suggests – in comments that are merely tangential to his discussion of the date of composition of *Paradise Regained,* and he does not develop – that Milton may have worked on *Samson Agonistes* at two or more periods of his life. He believes it was "completed as we know [it] before mid-1670," [16] and that had "quite a lot of 'free' time, especially between 1642 and 1649" [26], time between March 1645 and December 1648 "for the incomplete development of *Samson Agonistes*" [28].

in the prosodic innovations Milton used in *On Time* and continued through *Upon the Circumcision*, and *At a Solemn Musick* and *Lycidas*. The lyrical passages are never free verse, but are made up of ode-like (alleostrophic) parts with varied line length and intermittent rhyme. This second form of prosody I shall term "early" because it is similar to Milton's prosodic practices which climax in *Lycidas*. My thesis is that Milton worked on an early version of *Samson* using the "early" prosody, probably in the 1640s, and that he put it aside unfinished. He may, as Shawcross suggests, have revised it between 1640 and 1658. Then later, probably after writing *PL* and *PR,* he returned to the work, amplified it considerably, and completed it using blank verse.[5] Separating and analyzing each of these parts can suggest what the earlier effort comprised and lead to further understanding of the poem.

The Date of Composition

Persuasive arguments for early composition have been advanced. In 1944 William Riley Parker (*PQ* 162) argued that *SA* was composed between 1647 and 1653. Likewise, Allen H. Gilbert in the same issue of *PQ* (98–106) argued that it could have been composed in the early 1640's. In 1957 Merritt Y. Hughes and others judged that it followed soon after Milton made a "draft of plans for five Samson plays as we have them in the Trinity Manuscript" (531). And although one may not agree with Gilbert that *SA* demonstrates sufficient, as Hughes puts it, "crudity to confirm that it was an unfinished work" (532), most readers would agree that the episodes with Manoa, Dalila, and Harapha fail to measure up to the seriousness, dignity, and emotional power of Samson's earlier dialogues with the chorus. In *Milton: A Biography*, Parker argues at length against a late date of composition "because it is quite unsupported by objective evidence" (904). He then presents a summary of his arguments, which include the following:

5 Milton had created two other assembled poems, *Mask* and *Paradise Regained*, as William B. Hunter points out in "A Bibliographical Excursus into the Trinity Manuscript" and "The Double Set of Temptations in *Paradise Regained*," *The Descent of Urania* (Lewisburg: Bucknell University Press, 1989).

- that since Edward Phillips does not know when *SA* was composed "it was evidently written at some time when he was not an intimate observer of his uncle's activities" (906),
- that "documentary evidence and riming … cast … doubt on the traditional date" (904),
- that there are no definitive political or personal allusions (905),
- that "from about 1641, he [Milton] intended to write drama" (905),
- that Milton's "later minor poetry, through *Lycidas*, exhibits experimentation with irregularity of line length, stanzaic form, and rime pattern" (907),
- that, unlike Milton's later works, *SA* "is almost devoid of theology" (907),
- that one can not assume the tragedy is a veiled biography (908), and
- that "the language of the poem" frequently replicates – nearly or exactly – language Milton used in other works known to have been written in the 1640s, an assertion for which Parker gives more than ninety examples.

Similarly, Evert Mordecai Clark, in his report on Milton's utilization of the Samson story, asserts that in the Trinity manuscript there is "a kind of *Samson Agonistes* in embryo," which Clark believes to be "the fifth act of the tragedy of Samson's successive failures" (154).

Equally persuasive arguments have been offered for late composition. Because *SA* was published with *PR* in 1671, the date traditionally assigned for its composition has been between 1666 and 1670. Since Parker's essays and biography, many of the arguments for late publication have been focused on refuting his arguments. Chief among Parker's critics is Ernest Sirluck, who makes the following points, as summarized by Thomas Kranadas in *A Milton Encyclopedia*. He points out that Sirluck

- believes that Parker "underestimated the evidence for late composition and points out that the authoritative Richardson (in the 1734 Life) declares without any uncertainty that *SA* was written after *PL* and *PR*"
- asks "If Phillips thought *Samson Agonistes* was written before Paradise Lost, why did he not say so?" and
- claims that "Parker has underestimated the rhymes in *PL*."

Kranadas summarizes other arguments for late composition. He explains

- that "The game of autobiographical inference can be played toward different conclusions,"
- that the metrics of the poem have not been thoroughly analyzed,
- that "the plans for drama in *TM* and *RCG* are no argument for assuming that Milton worked on a drama during 1645–1648" (143).

Mary Ann Radzinowicz and others argue for late composition on the basis of Milton's "stylistic practices and intentions," his "thematic and intellectual concerns," and the "autobiographical and historical references" she finds in the play. She seems to speak for all who support late composition when she concludes,

> Objective evidence is not lacking for the late date; artistic practices and theories do not militate against it; thematic links between *Paradise Regained* and *Samson Agonistes* confirm it; and the existence of allusions from autobiography and current affairs points so strongly to the late date that early daters have to expend heroic effort to discredit it (407).

It is hardly surprising then that some critics believe that Milton may have worked on *SA* at different times in his life, perhaps both before and after he wrote *PL*. Parker argues that Milton began the poem in 1646–47 and then returned to it in 1652–53 (Carey and Fowler 331). Shawcross concludes "[t]he period from March 1645 to December 1948 (almost four years) allows time for the *incomplete* development of *Samson Agonistes* and of *Paradise Regain'd*" (*PR* 28). It is clear that there are strong arguments for *both* early and late composition. However, these divergent arguments can function together if part of the poem was indeed composed early and the rest much later.

Many of the daters – early and late – either (1) argue to disprove daters with whom they disagree, or (2) use inflated rhetoric because their evidence is *not* definitive. That they resort to such argumentative approaches suggests that their proofs of early or late composition are not airtight. The analysis of *SA* becomes much simpler if one separates the sections by prosody.

Evolution of Milton's Prosody

In his early poetry Milton explored innovative verse forms. Only a few of his English sonnets follow the Italian sonnet form exactly. Seven begin with two quatrains with the traditional ABBA rhyme scheme and conclude with a sextet that rhymes CDCDCD. Each of the other four has a different rhyme scheme in the sextet (#7, "[How Soon Hath Time]" ends with CDEDCE; #11, "[I Did But Prompt the Age]" with CBBCBC; #15, "[Fairfax]" with CDDCDC; and #16, "[Cromwell]" with CDDCEE.)

L'Allegro and *Il Penseroso* each have a ten line introduction in which hexasyllabic and decasyllabic lines alternate, except for one seven-syllable line. The body of the poems, as Robert Bridges points out, is iambic tetrameter, with a few "seven-syllable line[s] with falling stress" and "a few inverted first feet" (52). Milton will continue these practices in *SA*. Bridges shows that Milton utilized various rhythmic innovations in *L'Allegro* and *Il Penseroso*.[6] *Arcades* and *Comus* contain a variety of forms because they are dramas which include songs and were intended for performance. Because of these genre-determined variations in form, they are not relevant to this study.

Milton's sixteen- to twenty-eight-lined poems contain further prosodic variations. The sixteen-line *On Shakespeare*, is comprised of a series of iambic pentameter rhymed couplets, and the twenty-two-line *On Time* interrupts decasyllabic with hexasyllabic lines in patterns which anticipate those of *Lycidas* and *SA*. In *On Time*, line 20 is octasyllabic and line 22 is dodecasyllabic. The poem has two quatrains (ABAB and CDDC), followed by five rhymed couplets (EE FF GG HH II) and a concluding quatrain (JKKJ) that functions, in meaning, like a coda.

6 Bridges identified the following rhythmic variants:
- There are nine lines that begin with trochees in which the word "the" is the second syllable.
- Nine lines have initial two-syllable words that are normally accented on their first syllable.
- Five lines have a trochee in the middle of a line.
- There are five lines whose sense demands an initial trochee "more, woful Shepherds" (165), and "Flames in the forehead" (171).
- There are two lines with feminine endings (one seven-syllable and one eleven-syllable line).

Two double sonnets, *On the Circumcision* and *At a Solemn Music* contain still more variations in form. The twenty-eight-line *On the Circumcision* has eighteen deca-, two hepta- six hexa-, and two tetrasyllabic lines. It has a complicated rhyme scheme of ABCBA CCDDC EFFE GHIHG, JJKKJ LMML. The twenty-four-line *At a Solemn Music* has four deca-, one dode-ca-, and three hexasyllabic lines, and a rhyme scheme of ABAB DDCC EFFGGHHE II JJ KK LL. In neither of these poems nor in the sonnets are there any unrhymed lines. Also, the twenty-line *On the Forcers of Conscience* is an Italian sonnet with a tail of six lines (CDEDEC), a hexasyllabic line (C), a couplet (FF), a hexasyllabic line (F), and a concluding couplet (GG).

John S. Diekhoff shows that in *Comus* (excluding the songs) Milton maintained decasyllabic regularity by using the following tactics: (1) eliding open vowels and (2) eliding vowels separated by the liquids *l*, *n*, and *r*, (3) using the elided "second person singular verbs" such as "told'st" (157), and (4) using feminine endings (164). He also shows that Milton utilized what he calls "theoretical stress" (165). After analyzing the pentameter verse of *Comus*, *Lycidas*, and other short poems from the Trinity Manuscript, Diekhoff concludes that in pentameter verse "Milton is for the most part scrupulously careful to provide ten syllables and only ten syllables" and never allows "truncation." He explains that should an extrametrical syllable be allowed, it "occurs without exception at the caesura" (173). Except for the addition of the extra caesura syllable, these practices are continued in *PL*.

Lycidas is even more prosodically innovative.[7] Only two of the verse paragraphs are the same length, and none have the same rhyme schemes.

7 In order to present a fair analysis, if a line of poetry can be read as either regular or irregular I have consistently read it as regular. The number of lines per stanza, rhyme schemes, and number of syllables in a line if other than ten are as follows:

¶#	Lines per paragraph¶	Rhyme schemes and syllables per paragraph line
1	1–14	x a b b a. a c: d a c d. a x a.
2	15–24	x a a. b b c c x. e e.
3	25–36	a b a b c c d. e e: d f f.
4	37–49	a a! x b b. c c d. e d f e f.
5	50–63	a x? a b b c c: d? e d f e f e
6	64–84	a b a? c b a? d e d; e d f d f; g g h h x i i
7	85–102	a b a b: c c x x d e e d f; g f h h g.
8	103–131	a b b a. b? a c d d c d c e? c f f e. f g! H; g i h i h i h j j
9	132–164	a b a b. b c c d e e. d f g g f h i: h i d. j d j k j l k l m xm n n
10	165–185	a b a b b a c: c d e d e f. f g. H; h i i.
11	186–193	a b; a b; a b; c c.

Milton utilizes far more variation of rhyme length and includes a few (seven or 3.6 per cent) unrhymed lines. As John S. Diekhoff points out, "Milton accepts and uses freely … heptasyllables" (173), as he will also do in the lyrical sections of *SA*.

Robert Bridges uses *PL* as the prosodic standard to which he compares *SA* and *PR*. In *PL* he finds that no line has "less than ten syllables" (4), that some lines have "supernumery [extrametrical] syllables," (5), that some lines may contain a "[v]ariety in number of stresses" (37), including "[l]ines with … four accents" (38) or with "three full stresses" (39), and that "inversion of feet" (40) can occur in *PL* in any foot of the line (41), but very rarely in the fifth. Bridges finds similar variations *SA*; in *SA* "the lines are of various lengths" (53). He explains that Milton takes such liberties "on account of their rhythmical resources, in order to introduce true trisyllabic rhythms into his verse" (53–54). Bridges specifies four ways that the prosody of *SA* varies from a traditional iambic pentameter pattern. First, there are "[l]ines of falling rhythm [trochaic, or lines lacking an initial syllable] … [that] are all … in the choric or lyric verse" (55). Second, there are ten lines in which "the first two feet of the line are inverted." (Of the examples he cites, all but two are from what I shall term the "early" version of the poem, and can be read as regular iambic pentameter lines.)[8] Third, there are "twelve-syllable lines [with] six stresses" (59), with caesuras in various positions or no breaks. Fourth, Milton employs "examples of free rhythms" by inverting various iambic feet, substituting a trochee for an iamb, and including extra metrical syllables.[9]

Bridges concludes that Milton utilized such variations in order "to make a good use of natural English stress rhythms, without falling into their sing-song, or setting all his verse to dance" (66). In discussing the prosody of *SA*, he presents 16 examples of elision in *PR* and *SA*, which he says Milton would not have admitted in *PL* (47). Of these 16 examples, 15 are from *PR*.

This analysis agrees with that of Diekhoff (178–79), much of whose analysis is from George Saintsbury, *A History of English Prosody*, II, 220–21 (London: Macmillan, 1906-1910).

8 Bridges reads "Or by evasions thy crime uncoverst more" (842) as beginning with a trochee (/ u u) followed by a trochee (l u), but it can as easily be read as beginning with two iambs. And he reads "For his people of old; what hinders now?" (1553) as beginning with two trochees, but it can be read as beginning with an iamb followed by a trochaic or pyrrhic foot.

9 Only two of Bridges's examples are from the lyrical parts of the play.

This suggests that although Milton relaxed his rules of elision in *PR*, he allowed very few such variations in *SA*. Although the title to Part II of Bridges' study is "On the Prosody of *Paradise Regained* and *Samson Agonistes*," he devotes three of 21 pages to *L'Allegro* and *Il Penseroso*, and, except for the examples of relaxed elision, 57 of his 70 examples (or 81 percent) are from what I regard as the "early" section of *SA*. It would be a natural step for Milton to utilize these and further innovations – especially more and varied types of what Diekhoff calls "truncated" lines – in his early version of *SA*, whose lyrical sections have the most varied prosody of all of Milton's works.

Dividing the Poem

To consider the possibility that part of the poem was written prior to *PL* and part of it afterward, it is necessary to find a rationale on which to date the sections. Two objective criteria can be used: one can start by separating out the sections which repeat the Samson story told in the book of Judges, or one can separate out the passages which contain hypometrical lines.[10] Except for the four-line introduction to Manoa and the fifteen-line introduction to Dalila (both of whom are present in Judges), these two ways of dividing the poem present congruent results. The introductions to Manoa and Dalila would suggest, however, that when Milton wrote his original draft of the poem he intended to come back to it and add the dialogues with Manoa and Dalila. There are 446 lines of speeches containing hypometrical lines and 1312 lines of speeches containing only decasyllabic lines or decasyllabic and hypermetrical (more than ten-syllable) lines. I have left all paragraphs and speeches intact. The early speeches may include some revisions, but to try to isolate such lines is beyond the scope of this paper.[11]

10 Most readers will come very close to agreement when they count syllables, whereas they may differ widely about matters of accent, elision, caesura, and other prosodic details that depend on performance.

11 If one were to identify such lines and count them among the later lines, the changes in numbers would be minimal and would only enhance the results of the data shown in this paper.

The lines that can be determined to be included in the earlier and later sections are as follows:

Earlier section	*Later section*	*Characters present*	*Total of*	*Number lines*
			Earlier section	*Later section*
	1–79	Samson		79
80–186		Samson, Chorus	107	
	187–276	Samson, Chorus		90
277–325		Chorus	49	
326–329		Intro to Manoa	4	
	330–605	Chorus, Samson, and Manoa		276
606–709		Samson and Chorus	104	
710–724		Intro to Dalila	15	
	725–1009	Samson, Chorus, and Dalila		285
1010–1060		Chorus	51	
	1061–1075	Intro to Harapha		15
	1076–1267	Samson and Harapha		192
1268–1300		Chorus	33	
	1301–1307	Intro to Public Officer	7	
	1308–1426	Samson, Chorus, and Harapha		119
1427–1440		Chorus	14	
	1441–1659	Manoa, Chorus, and Messenger		219
1660–1707		Chorus and Semichorus	48	
	1708–1744	Manoa		37
1745–1758		Chorus	14	
			446	1312
			Total	1758

Other reasons support such a division. The lyrical passages of *SA* contain Milton's most innovative prosody and would be likely, therefore, to have been written after *Lycidas* but before he attacked rhyme in the introduction to *PL*.

Many critics of the poem's prosody have apparently found it difficult to do a prosodic analysis of the entire poem and have, therefore, resorted to either evaluating the effectiveness of various passages or interpreting the meaning of various passages. The critics who have written about the use of rhyme in *SA* have tended either (1) to focus on a few, selected passages, which they interpret and/or evaluate (usually the latter); or (2) to assert that a certain percentage of lines of the poem manifest certain prosodic traits. One problem with the former selective approach is that one can choose to discuss only those passages that support one's thesis. Evaluation is always subjective – dependent on the performance and personal taste of the evaluator. Therefore, such passages can be interpreted in ways that may or may not apply to the work as a whole.

Other critics have tried to account for the apparent prosodic disjunction among various parts of the poem by arguing that what they call the "lyrical" parts are moments of ode-like high emotion and that what they call the "nonlyrical" parts present more pedestrian ideas or moments of flatter affect. A problem with such an explanation is that it seems inappropriate that so many of the moments of "high" emotion should be spoken by the Chorus, when it is Samson who is suffering the most. Even Manoa, Dalila, and Harapha are more emotionally engaged in the events than the Chorus.

Two critics, S. Ernest Sprott and Ants Oras, have considered dividing the poem into sections nearly like the above divisions. In 1953 Sprott explained that *SA* consists of blocks of iambic verse pentameters interspersed in the classical fashion with groups of so-called lyrical verses spoken for the most part by the Chorus. An exact delimitation of the extent of these groups is difficult to make, because Milton obviously has not intended it (129).

Sprott divides the poem into the following parts. What he calls "lyrical verses" include lines 80–186, 277–339, 606–731, 997–1075, 1268–1307, 1427–1444, 1660–1707, and 1745–1758 (129). Ants Oras, in his 1953 study, explains, "Since this study is confined to Milton's blank verse, the figures do not include the songs or tetrameters in *Comus* or the lyrical passages in *SA*. The short lines of the tragedy have also been left out of account" (133). In his revised, 1966 study he specifies that he will analyze only the following "nonlyrical" parts of *SA*. He then divides the "nonlyrical" part into the following three sections:

- the pentameters in the first two act-like divisions, lines 1–276, and 331–605,
- the next two subdivisions, lines 721–1009 and 1061–1267,

and

- the final section, lines 1307–1744 (11).

Since Oras considers only the nonlyrical portions of the poem, his conclusions (and those of Shawcross, who utilizes Oras's numbers) about the dating of the poem can only apply to those sections I am stipulating as "late."

Following a different technical approach, Janel Mueller has analyzed various lines of *SA*. But since her analysis rests on her performance of the lines, it is idiosyncratic.[12] Furthermore her claim that rhythm and meter can have symbolic meaning is unsupportable.

There are various reasons for concluding that lyrical parts of the poem were written much earlier than the nonlyrical sections. The early (or lyrical) portion of the play follows the model of Thespis's very simple dramas. These lyrical sections contain only one character, Samson, who engages in a dialogue with the chorus. When Parker claims, "*SA* could not have been written until a re-study of Greek tragedy overcame his [Milton's] strong preference for the Italianate form" (II, 207), he is referring to the complete play, not the lyrical sections, which do conform to the Italianate form.

As Gretchen Ludke Finney points out, this early section of *SA* also has a structure like that of the oratorio, a form which "appealed to the ear, not the eye. It had all the suggestion of action but was not acted. It was not meant for the stage" (660). As Finney also points out, "The Samson story was a favorite one for writers of oratorio from its beginnings up to the time of Handel's *Samson*" (659). In his definition of *oratorio*, Owen Jander explains that the oratorio "was performed without scenery, costume or action" and instead emphasized "contemplation" (570). Like such oratorios, the early section of *SA* is focused on contemplation rather than action.

It is probable, therefore, that Milton's initial work on *SA* resulted in a simple structure like that of Thespis's plays and that of the oratorio. Such a composition would never have been intended to be a complete tragedy. In fact, what dramatic conflicts there are in the play all occur in the "later" sections: the arguments with Dalila, with Harapha, and with the Public Officer. The additions of these confrontations then complete a play about

12 Most reasonable readers would agree with Mueller that the prosody and syntax of good poetry is compatible with the meaning of the poem, but they would be unlikely to agree with her when she states that the "verse design encodes" meaning (47) or when she uses phrases like "metrical typology" (66), "metrical symbolics" (79), and "symbolics of rhythm" (67). When she suggests that specific meanings are encoded in certain prosodic patterns, she is making insupportable claims. She even claims that the sound effects of the Chorus proves (her word is "hence," by which she means "therefore") "their [the Chorous's unreliability as observers and commentators" (75). Finally, her – almost undecipherable, analytical bracketing of words and phrases in individual lines considers only a few lines, not the entire poem.

which analysts like Radzinowitz note a "structure … [that] is shaped with both Greek and contemporary practice in mind," a structure Radzinowicz divides into the traditional five acts with scene divisions (13). That Milton studied Greek tragedies before he added the first 79 lines of the poem would account for the parallels that Louis L. Martz sees in "the opening of Sophocles' redemptive tragedy, *Oedipus at Colonus*, where the blind Oedipus is led on stage by … Antigone" (117).

Prosody in Lyrical and Nonlyrical Sections of *SA*

There are several significant differences in the lyrical and nonlyrical sections of the poem.

Hypometrical Lines: The most obvious difference is that there are hypometrical lines only in the lyrical sections.

End Rhymes: As Mary Anne Radzinowitz points out, "[r]hyme is virtually limited to the lyrical parts of the play" (394), all of which are included in what I am stipulating as the early section. In *Lycidas*, Milton used 183 total end rhymes in the poem's 193 lines (94.8 percent). He uses far fewer rhymes in *SA*, where most are in the lyrical section of the poem. In the lyrical section of *SA*, he uses 173 end rhymes (33.8 percent). This percentage is over five times as great a percentage of rhyming lines as in the nonlyrical section, in which he used only 81 rhyming lines (6.2 percent). Furthermore, in the earlier section of *SA*, Milton used rhyme patterns that retain vestiges of the rhyme patterns he had used in *Lycidas*.

Twelve-Syllable-Lines: in the early, rhymed sections of *SA*, there are more twelve-syllable lines (Alexandrines) than in the later sections. In the earlier sections 37 of the 446 lines have twelve syllables (37%). In the later sections 205 of the 1312 lines have twelve syllables (5%), which means that there are 6.5 times as great a percentage of twelve-syllable lines in the earlier speeches as there are in the later ones. The twelve-syllable lines make up 4.2 percent of the earlier speeches but only 0.6 percent of the later speeches.

Alexandrine lines tend to subdivide themselves – especially if they contain strong caesuras – into lines which, when performed, would be indistinguishable from a pair of three-stress lines (for example, lines 118, 131, 138, 144, 146, 148, and 157) or a pair of lines in which one has four stresses and the other two (for example, lines 124 and 149). These Alexandrines are very compatible with the stress patterns in the 2-, 3-, 4-, and 5-stress lines in the earlier sections. Because these Alexandrine lines nearly always have six stresses, they can produce rhythmical patterns that differ from and even undermine the five-stress pattern of blank verse. This would explain why Milton used fewer of them in the later sections of the poem.

Eleven-Syllable (Feminine) Lines: Shawcross explains that Milton used significantly more feminine endings in *Comus* and *SA* than in his other long poems[13] because those two works are composed predominantly of dialogue (Chron 348). However there are far fewer in the early section (5.4 percent) than there are in the late section (16.5 percent), although dialogue dominates both parts. Perhaps when Milton moved to the predominantly decasyllabic lines of the late section, he cared less about avoiding these non-accented endings because they do little to disturb the overall rhythm of the lines.

Total Extrametrical Lines: because there is a larger number of twelve-syllable lines in the early section of the poem and a larger number of eleven-syllable lines in the nonlyrical section of the poem, there is not much difference in the total number of extrametrical lines in the two sections. Sixty-one of the 446 lines (13.7%) of the early section and 210 of the 1312 lines (16.0%) of the later section are extrametrical.

Hypometrical Lines: Milton only uses hypometrical lines (lines with fewer than ten syllables in primarily decasyllabic poems) in *On Time*, *Upon the Circumcision*, *At a Solemn Music*, *Lycidas*, and *SA*. There are 31.8 percent in *On Time*, 28.6 percent in *Upon the Circumcision*,10.7 percent in *At a Solemn Music*, 7.3 percent in *Lycidas*, and 43.3 percent in the early parts of *SA*. Of these examples, by far the highest percentage appears in *SA*.

Variety of Line Lengths: the lyrical sections of *SA* contain the greatest variety of line lengths. The 446 lines in the lyrical sections can be broken down as follows:

Four-syllable lines	7	1.6%
Five-syllable lines	3	0.7%
Six-syllable lines	73	16.4%
Seven-syllable lines	14	3.1%
Eight-syllable lines	80	17.9%

13 10.2% in *Comus* and 18.0 per cent in *SA*, as compared with 4.4 per cent in *PR* and 1.3 per cent in *PL*.

Nine-syllable lines	16	3.6%
Ten-syllable lines	177	39.7%
Eleven-syllable lines	24	5.4%
Twelve-syllable lines	37	8.3%

If the lyrical sections of the poem represent Milton's "First" *SA,* a poem with such enormous variation is far more likely to have been written close to the time of *Lycidas* rather than after *PL* and *PR.*

Run-on Lines: Shawcross has argued that "the use of run-on lines … is increasingly employed as the poet matures and achieves command of his talent" (*PR* 10) and says "we should be struck at the increase in run-on lines as we move from *Comus* … to *PL*" (*PR* 11). Utilizing Oras's criterion that "those lines that have no punctuation at the end of lines are considered run-on" (*PR,* 10, n.), Shawcross produced the following chart:

Sonnets 8–11	32.1%
Comus	39.9%
Odes	41.0%
Samson Agonistes	42.1%
Sonnets 12–15	42.9%
Paradise Regained	45.2%
Sonnets 16–23	48.2%
Psalms 1–8	*58.4%*
Paradise Lost	58.8%

These percentages lead Shawcross to conclude that *SA* and *PR* "are earlier in composition than *PL*" (*PR* 12).

However, a separate examination of the percentage of run-on lines in the short-lined section and in the long-lined section of *SA* and of *Lycidas* produces the following chart:

Sonnets 8–11	32.1%
Lycidas	35.8%
Comus	39.9%
Samson Agonistes – lyrical (early)	40.0%
Odes	41.0%
Samson Agonistes	42.1%
Sonnets 12–15	42.9%
Paradise Regained	45.2%
Samson Agonistes – non-lyrical (late)	45.8%
Sonnets 16–23	48.2%

Psalms 1–8	58.4%
Paradise Lost	58.8%

It is clear that almost from his earliest poems, Milton had shown an interest in prosodic and formal innovation. In a relatively small number of sonnets, he utilizes more variations than many other writers did in scores of them.

One might reasonably expect his next long poem to manifest even more variations. And certain *portions* of *SA* do just that – utilizing even more innovations in rhyme patterns and line lengths than he used in *Lycidas.* But the prosody of other portions of *SA* are entirely different – almost at the opposite end of the prosodic spectrum from *Lycidas*, but more like the prosody of *Paradise Lost* and very much like the prosody of *Paradise Regained.*

Biographical Arguments

Milton seems to have made extreme shifts in prosody between *Lycidas* and *PL.* But these are the kinds of changes that would have to be made by a man going blind. A fully-sighted person could utilize a variety of line lengths and consider the visual impact of these various line lengths on a reader. An example is the visual impact of the short lines of John Donne's "Go and Catch a Falling Star." *Seeing* the lines "And swear / Nowhere" makes for a more powerful emphasis on "swear" and "where" than if written as one line "And swear nowhere" or as part of a longer line. Such effects might not be impossible for a blind poet, but Milton would have found them extremely hard to sustain over hundreds of lines of poetry when he could no longer see the page.

There are reasons that suggest at least part of *SA* was written as Milton was going or had just gone blind. In Parker's estimation, "The *Agonistes* is Milton's darkest piece of writing," to which Parker adds, "In Milton's life story, as in Samson's at the end of the Manoa episode, this is the depth from which he has to rise" (II, 937). Furthermore, probably the most emotionally powerful lines in all of Milton's poetry are those of the short-lined section of Samson's first soliloquy, ll. 80–109.

O dark, dark, dark, amid the blaze of noon,
Irrecoverably dark, total Eclipse
Without all hope of day!
O first created Beam, and thou great Word,
Let there be light, and light was over all;
Why am I thus, bereav'd thy prime decree?
The Sun to me is dark
And silent as the Moon
When she deserts the night
Hid in her vacant interlunar cave.
Since light so necessary is to life,
And almost life itself, if it be true
That light is in the Soul,
She all in every part; why was the sight
To such a tender ball as th' eye confin'd?
So obvious and so easie to be quench't,
And not as feeling through all parts diffus'd,
That she might look at will through every pore?
Then had I not been thus exil'd from light;
As in the land of darkness yet in light,
To live a life half dead, a living death,
And buried; but O yet more miserable!
My self, my Sepulcher, a moving Grave,
Buried, yet not exempt
By priviledge of death and burial
From worst of other evils, pains and wrongs,
But made hereby obnoxious more
To all the miseries of life,
Life in captivity
Among inhuman foes.

As Parker argues, these lines "have about them the eloquence and conviction of newly met reality" (I, 431). They also express powerful self-pity and anger at God, which would be one's first reaction to such a loss. The only other line which approaches this degree of power is the last line of Sonnet 23 (which is generally believed to have been dictated between 1656 and 1658), "I wak'd, she fled, and day brought back my night."

The other passage, the following long-lined section on blindness, is also a part of Samson's first soliloquy. It too complains of blindness, but has the calmer, more resigned tone of a man who has come to terms with his affliction (ll. 60–79), suggesting it was written later.

But peace, I must not quarrel with the will
Of highest dispensation, which herein
Happ'ly had ends above my reach to know:
Suffices that to me strength is my bane,
And proves the sourse of all my miseries;
So many, and so huge, that each apart
Would ask a life to wail, but chief of all,
O loss of sight, of thee I most complain!
Blind among enemies, O worse then chains,
Dungeon, or beggery, or decrepit age!
Light the prime work of God to me is extinct,
And all her various objects of delight
Annull'd, which might in part my grief have eas'd,
Inferiour to the vilest now become
Of man or worm; the vilest here excel me,
They creep, yet see, I dark in light expos'd
To daily fraud, contempt, abuse and wrong,
Within doors, or without, still as a fool,
In power of others, never in my own;
Scarce half I seem to live, dead more then half.

This passage no longer rails against blindness. Samson no longer lashes out at God, but presents a rational description of his situation as he evaluates his condition and frets at being thought a fool.

These kinds of variants – especially in line length – require that a poet be able to *see* the layout of the poem on the page. After Milton lost his vision, he would almost inevitably be more comfortably utilizing prosody that sounds most natural to the English ear – blank verse (decasyllabic line with a preponderance of iambic pentameter feet). It makes more sense that he would explore such innovative patterns immediately after writing *Lycidas* than that he would suddenly return to them *after* writing *PL* and *PR* and after writing his attack on rhyme. Being unable to continue his innovative treatment of rhyme and being unable to expand the plot, Milton would have ample reason to abandon *SA* after writing only the short-lined sections.

Many of the problems that have been associated with the play disappear if the play is considered to have been written in two parts – first as a simple dialogue between Samson and the chorus, in the manner of the drama of Thespis and of the oratorio, a play with great variety of rhyme lengths, irregular rhyme, and powerful emotion. In this section Samson laments his condition and the foolish decisions that led to that condition. Milton then later amplified it with blank verse into a five-act Greek drama, which includes confrontations with his father, Dalila, Harapha, and the officer, as well as Samson's offstage destruction of the temple and death.

Conclusion

Good – and great – English poetry can be performed in three ways: syntactically (by reading in accordance to the syntax of the poem), prosodically (by reading in accordance to the rhythms of the metrical feet of the verse), or auditorily (by focusing on the natural stresses, which sometimes emphasized by alliteration, that naturally occur in the language, that linger as vestiges of strong-stress poetry, and that some poets, such as Wordsworth and Hopkins, employ in their poetry). The greatest poets in the language manage to attend to all three. And none do so better than Milton.

One can imagine several scenarios that led to the printed version of *Samson Agonistes.*

- He could have begun *SA* with some plan to follow the general structures of Greek Latin odes, then expanded his poem beyond the restrictions of those forms.
- He could have begun *SA* with plans to use the hypometric variable-length lines for the lyric parts of the poem and to use blank verse for the less lyrical parts – following the kind of shifts he makes in *Arcades* and *Comus* between dialogue and song.
- He could have planned a whole poem of various, nonrepeatable structures like those in *Lycidas.* Although he announces his intentions to use such a form, "[a]llaeostopha," in the choruses, he uses allaeostropha in some of Samson's speeches, but fails to use it in some of the chorus's speeches.
- With any of these approaches, he would have been aware that the visual layout would influence the way a reader read the poem. Visual format would not, of course, have eradicated the impact of the auditory format, but would have complimented it.

Any of these scenarios would result in a long poem with complicated prosody.

Any of these plans would, however, have been heavily dependent on his being able to see the page – to see the poem as his readers would see it. But the onset of his blindness would have changed all of that. First, it would have given him reason to abandon the poem entirely, either because he felt too handicapped to continue writing or because he felt too much despair. Second, in the nature of the English language there remains – to paraphrase Hopkins – the dearest power and deep-down accents and alliterations. Such accents and alliterations are the stuff of which Old English oral poetry was constructed, and they are there in the language for Milton to mine after he was blind. Third, blank verse itself (or blank verse with the kind of variants that Bridges and Diekhoff and others have found in Milton's blank verse) is remarkably close to the language of everyday speech.

Although we may never know exactly what Milton's original intentions were for the prosody of *SA* – because of his blindness, because he ran out of material when he had covered the events recounted in Judges, or even because his attentions were drawn away from the poem to political activity and to political and theological writing – there is reason to believe that he began the poem, abandoned it, and returned to it later in his life. Certainly there are many similarities between his early work in some of the sonnets and slightly longer poems, *Arcades* and *Lycidas*, with what I have isolated as the early section of the poem. There are equally strong similarities between the form of *PL* and *PR* with what I've stipulated as the later part of the poem. I am convinced that Milton began utilizing one prosodic form, abandoned the form – and probably the poem itself for a substantial period of time – and completed it using another prosodic principle.

Whether the latter part of the poem was written before or after *Paradise Regained* or before or after *Paradise Lost* remains a question for further exploration.

Works Cited

Beum, Robert. "The Rhyme in *Samson Agonistes*." *Texas Studies in Literature and Language* 4 (1962): 177–82.

Bridges, Robert. *Milton's Prosody with a Chapter on Accentual Verse*. Oxford: Oxford UP, 1921.

Gilbert, Allan H. "Is *Samson Agonistes* Unfinished?" *Philological Quarterly* 28 (1949): 98–106.

Hull, Keith N. "Rhyme and Disorder in *Samson Agonistes.*" *Milton Studies* 30 (1933): 163–81.

Hunter, William B. *The Descent of Urania.* Lewisburg: Bucknell UP, 1989.

Le Comte, Edward. "New Objections to a Pre-Restoration Date for *Samson Agonistes.*" *Poets' Riddles: Essays in Seventeenth-Century Explication.* Port Washington, NY: Kennikat Press, 1975.

Oras, Ants. "Milton's Blank Verse and the Chronology of His Major Poems." *SAMLA Studies in Milton*, ed. J. Max Patrick. Gainsville, FL: University of Florida Press, 1953. 128–195.

Parker, William Riley. "The Date of *Samson Agonistes.*" *Philological Quarterly* 28 (1949): 145–66.

–. "The Date of *Samson Agonistes*: A Postscript." *Notes and Queries* 203 (May 1958): 201–2.

–. "The Date of *Samson Agonistes* Again." *Calm of Mind: Tercentenary Essays on* Paradise Lost *and* Samson Agonistes. Cleveland: Press of Case Western Reserve University, 1971. 163–174.

Patrick, J. Max. "Milton's Revolution Against Rime, and Some of Its Implications." *Milton and the Art of Sacred Song*, ed. J. Max Patrick and Roger H. Sundell. Madison: University of Wisconsin Press, 1979. 99–115.

Radzinowicz, Mary Ann. *Toward "Samson Agonistes": The Growth of Milton's Mind.* Princeton: Princeton UP, 1978.

Shawcross, John. "The Chronology of Milton's Major Poems." *PMLA*: 70 (1961): 345–58.

–. *John Milton: The Self and the World.* Lexington: University Press of Kentucky, 1993.

–. Paradise Regained*: Worth T'Have Not Remain'd So Long Unsung.* Pittsburgh: Duquesne UP, 1988.

Sirluck, Ernest. "Milton's Idle Right Hand." *Journal of English and German Philology* 60 (1961): 749–85.

Part IV

French Perspectives

Nicole BERRY

John Milton, ou l'aigle blessé

Dans le contexte du Symposium «Milton, Droits et Libertés», il convient de considérer la liberté intérieure. Quelque chose d'inconnu, par lui-même ignoré, peut venir entraver la liberté de penser et la capacité créative du poète. Tel est mon thème.

Au temps de «d'heureux matin», *happy morn*, dans la rigueur de l'hiver, un enfant est né, *born*: ces deux mots apparaissent dans le poème *On the Morning Christ's Nativity*[1]: Milton est l'enfant de la Nature.

On Time[2] introduit ensuite l'indice d'une frayeur devant une si longue éternité:

> And last of all, thy greedy self consum'd (v. 10).

Dans la soif de vivre, le soi risque d'être dévoré. Et Milton éprouve un vif désir de vivre; il ne sera pas *A Philosopher on his way to Death!*[3]Il compose *On May Morning*: ruisseaux bruissants et bois si verts, il est

> Unheard, unsought for, or unseen.[4]

On ne peut l'entendre et non plus le chercher, il est invisible.

Cette liberté résonne comme un plaisir.

La tentative d'écrire sur le sujet de la Passion du Christ a été un échec: Milton est incapable de penser la souffrance ou la mort. Cela ne l'empêche pas d'être témoin de la décapitation du roi Charles sans frissonner d'horreur et d'écrire sa réplique au Français Saumaise qui l'accuse d'approuver le régi-

1 John Milton, *Complete Poetical Works*, edited by Douglas Bush, New Haven, CT, Harvard University Press, 1965. 65–72.

2 Id., pp. 105–106.

3 Par allusion à son poème *Philosophus ad regem [...] haec subito misit* ("A Philosopher on his way to execution").

4 Robert Burton, *The Anatomy of Melancholy* (Londres, 1621); poème préfacé à la sixième édition de 1652: "The Authors Abstract of Melancholy," v. 20.

cide, *Pro Defensio pro Populo Anglicano*[5] (1651); dans ce texte, il se montre provocant, brutal et même insolent; il utilise le grotesque: c'est une appréciation de Markus Klinge.[6] Milton, personnellement impliqué dans le *Defensio*, dit: «vous, l'esclave», «vous, mouche du coche» et cela semble être une identification projective: «vous êtes, mais je ne suis pas… et j'ai bien peur de l'être! Milton n'est-il pas hanté par le fantôme d'un père symbolique? «Un roi qui se dresse comme un fantôme.»

Alors il se met au travail pour le Bien des hommes: *On Reformation, The Discipline of Divorce, Of Education, Areopagitica.* Milton n'a aucune conscience qu'une pensée mauvaise puisse l'habiter et il n'a pas l'idée du mal en général. Il n'a pas conscience d'être personnellement impliqué lorsqu'il écrit ses *Prose Works*: il est un bon écrivain au service du bien pour l'humanité.

Il avait confié à son ami Charles Diodati qu'il écrirait une œuvre qui lui offrirait l'immortalité[7], mais il différa le projet du grand poème de 1626 à 1658! Etait-ce un sacrifice nécessaire à l'accomplissement de son désir[8] ou bien avait-il le sentiment d'avoir un précieux trésor à garder en lui, avec une singulière confiance dans sa capacité à créer?

Il nous faut attendre les mots de Satan dans le *Paradis Perdu* pour connaître le vrai soi de Milton. Comme bien des critiques, j'entendrai la voix de Satan comme étant celle de Milton lui-même.

> […] si ce qui est mal
> Est réel, pourquoi ne serait-il pas connu et ainsi plus facilement évité?
> Dieu ne peut donc vous frapper et être juste;
> S'il n'est pas juste, il n'est pas Dieu, il n'est donc pas digne d'être craint ni obéi.
> (*Paradis Perdu* 9.698–701)

5 John Milton, *Complete Prose Works*, 8 vols., general editor Don M. Wolfe. New Haven: Yale University Press, 1953–81. IV, pp. 308–330.

6 Markus Klinge, *The Grotesque in Defensio.* Intervention au Congrès International de Pittsburgh, Mars 2004. Communication personnelle.

7 *Complete Poetical Works,* I, pp. 211–459. *Elegia Prima.* To Charles Diodati, 1626.
"But now I wish you have your curiosity satisfied. You ask me many questions, even at to what I am thinking of. Listen, Theodotus, but let it be in your ear, less I blush […] so may the good God help me, of immortality! And in fact, what am I doing? Growing my wings and meditating flight […]." «A présent je sais que vous voudriez voir votre curiosité satisfaite. Vous m'interrogez sur ce que je pense. Ecoutez, Theodotus, mais que votre oreille seule reçoive la confidence, autrement je rougirais: si Dieu veut me prêter secours, d'immortalité! Et qu'est-ce que je suis en train de faire? Laisser pousser mes ailes, méditant de prendre mon vol.»

8 Nicole Berry, Intervention au Congrès International de Pittsburgh, Mars 2004.

Milton, par la voix du Tentateur, dénonce l'injonction paradoxale par laquelle le Dieu Père tient l'homme en son pouvoir, le mettant devant un choix impossible. L'injonction paradoxale ou *double bind* rend compte d'une entrave dans la pensée et d'une interdiction de disposer librement de son destin. Avoir à obéir comme un petit enfant constitue une grave blessure narcissique; à l'opposé, si l'homme veut connaître le Bien et le Mal, il est un rebelle. Obéissance ou rébellion, le choix est impossible.

> Le bien inconnu, certes, on ne l'a point, ou si on l'a
> Et qu'il reste encore inconnu, c'est comme si on ne l'avait pas.
> (*Paradis Perdu* 9.756–57)

Le bien inconnu n'est pas véritablement bon. Dieu nous défendant ce qui est bon n'est pas bon. Et la liberté n'est pas libre. Pour être bon, il faut donc se rebeller. L'injonction paradoxale, ou *double bind*, c'est-à-dire un ordre doublé de son contraire, est un défi à la pensée logique, inacceptable pour l'auteur de *The Art of Logic.*

Le terme d'»injonction paradoxale» a été introduit par l'école de Palo Alto, en Californie; Bateson et Jackson l'ont décrit comme trouble de la communication entre deux êtres.[9] Didier Anzieu, en France, a repris la situation ainsi créée en terme de relation: l'injonction paradoxale induit une inhibition de la vie affective, avec un sentiment de persécution qui confronte l'homme à une terreur d'annihilation: elle est décrite par Satan à l'instant de sa chute dans le monde infernal. Obéissance ou rébellion, les deux modes de réactions sont inconciliables. L'obéissance met le sujet sous le pouvoir d'un autre, la rébellion lui donne le sentiment d'être mauvais.

L'injonction paradoxale suscite soit un désir de perfection, soit un renoncement à penser, c'est-à-dire une mort psychique, un sentiment de perte du sentiment d'existence, *loss of being.* Au contraire, la révolte est une réaction normale pour ne pas perdre son être: il faut donc être désobéissant et dire: «que le mal soit mon bien»![10] *"Evil be thou my good"!*

Selon la théorie freudienne des pulsions, la tentative d'exercer un pouvoir sur une autre personne soumise à sa toute-puissance est liée à la pul-

9 Ecole psychanalytique de Palo Alto, en Californie. Paul Watzlawick, *Une logique de la communication*, Paris, Le Seuil, 1973.

10 Didier Anzieu, «Le transfert paradoxal», *Revue française de Psychanalyse,* Paris, Gallimard, 1975. Il conclut sa réflexion par les termes du Satan du *Paradis Perdu* qu'il n'avait pas lu!

sion de mort. Dans la lutte, en chacun de nous, entre la pulsion de mort et la pulsion de vie, les dérivés de la pulsion de mort doivent être dirigés vers l'extérieur afin de ne pas détruire le soi: telle est l'origine de l'agressivité.

La tyrannie du Ciel, Milton la refuse et avec Satan, il a le courage de «ne jamais se soumettre ou céder» (*Paradis Perdu* 1.108). Le choix de Milton est d'être un rebelle, il refuse tout pouvoir exercé sur lui et affirme la grandeur de l'esprit:

> Pour autant que des dieux ou des substances célestes
> Peuvent périr, car la pensée et l'esprit demeurent
> Invincibles [...]
> (*Paradis Perdu* 1.138–41)

Au contraire de la soumission, il projette de s'envoler «d'un vol non tempéré», *"to soar with no middle flight"* comme l'aigle prend son essor dans l'*Iliade*, volant haut, à la droite du «divin Hector» avant le combat contre Achille. «Le divin Hector» est comme Satan, «semblable à la flamme».[11] Et avec hauteur, un trait de caractère que nous lui connaissons, Milton dé-fie:

> L'esprit est à soi-même sa propre demeure et peut faire en soi
> Un Ciel de l'Enfer et un Enfer du Ciel.
> (*Paradis Perdu* 1.254–55)

Satan désire compenser la blessure narcissique par un «narcissisme destructeur.» Et «cruel est son œil» bien que le souci demeure sur sa joue fanée, *"care sat on his faded cheek"* (1.601–602). Pourtant son cœur se dilate d'orgueil! *"His heart distends with pride."*

Milton avait été le fils choisi mais il n'aurait pas dû disposer librement de son destin; puis il avait été méprisé, perdant sa position politique; il traduisit alors les psaumes de Job comme sa propre plainte.

> O Dieu abaisse ton regard vers moi
> O entends moi qui te prie
> Car je suis pauvre et dépéri
> Réponds moi quand je te supplie.[12]

11 Homère, *L'Iliade*. Paris: les Belles Lettres, 1937. I. XIII, 688.
12 Psaume 88. *Complete Poetical Works,* I, p. 184.

De quelle hauteur est-il tombé, lui, si estimé et défendant le bien des hommes! De la fierté hautaine à l'humiliation, Milton en choisissant les Psaumes de Job, se fait soumis:

C'est toi, Yahvé ma lampe
Mon Dieu éclaire ma ténèbre.[13]

Dans l'humiliation, il trouve une exaltation: Albert Labriola en a donné une extraordinaire illustration. Le Fils humilié, mais d'une nature angélique, est exalté.[14]

Et en tant que défense contre le sentiment d'humiliation, nous voyons souvent dans le *Paradis Perdu* le «renversement dans le contraire» décrit par Freud comme un trait caractéristique de la personnalité de Milton. Le vol superbe, d'un pôle à l'autre, de «l'Ange indompté» est l'inverse de la chute décrite comme une perte de l'être; on l'a souvent comparé aux vols baroques.[15] De la chute à la grandeur, *"uplift,"* 2.929, affreusement inquiet, Satan s'écrie:

[...] de quel état
Je suis tombé, combien je resplendissais jadis au-dessus de ta sphère.
(*Paradis Perdu* 4.38–39)

Mais il se relève:

Eveillez-vous, levez-vous ou soyez à jamais tombés
(*Paradis Perdu* 1.330).
Awake, arise or be for ever fall'n

Le vers, shakespearien, a été remarqué par Châteaubriand.

Triomphe et découragement. Humiliation et exaltation, arbre de vie et arbre de mort côte à côte, 7.324, l'humeur et les pensées du poète sont aussi «troublées» que celles de Satan.

Renversement dans le contraire, inexactitudes, illogismes: la pensée du poète était perturbée par un conflit intérieur. Le comble du renversement est exprimé par Belzebuth, au Livre II, 369–370: que le créateur lui-même

13 Psaume 18.

14 Albert Labriola, "Thy Humiliation shall exalt. The Christology of *Paradise Lost,*" In *Milton Studies*, XV, Pittsburgh University Press, 1981.

15 Eugenio d'Ors, *Du Baroque.* Paris: Gallimard, «Idées», 1935 et Robert Ellrodt, *Figures du Baroque dans le Paradis Perdu,* Paris, Ed. Benoît, 1983.

«d'une main repentante abolisse son propre ouvrage»! Ce sera lui, le Mauvais!

Milton, en effet, avait été lui-même l'objet d'une injonction paradoxale de la part de ses parents: ils avaient voué à Dieu le fils qu'ils avaient longtemps attendu et celui-ci devrait se faire pasteur si Dieu le leur accordait. Aussi le jeune étudiant pouvait-il bien chanter et jouer de l'orgue, sa destinée serait de devenir un homme d'église, destinée d'un «soi-objet»[16], sacrifié à… la sainte union de ses parents, il n'avait qu'à obéir. Ne pas être maître de son destin, cela constitue une grave blessure narcissique.

> Mais devrai-je vivre une mort vivante […]
> (*Paradis Perdu* 10.788)
> But shall I die a living Death […]

dira Adam.

Le père de Milton s'était rebellé contre son propre père qui était catholique, lisant seul et sans maître la bible. Il fut rejeté et déshérité. Milton se faisant rebelle, n'est-il pas le digne fils de son père?!

Obéissance ou rébellion?

Milton choisit d'être rebelle et va jusqu'à dénier la filiation paternelle:

L'invocation à l'Esprit, à l'ouverture du poème, est précise:

> Instruis-moi, car tu sais: toi au premier instant
> Tu étais présent; avec tes puissantes ailes éployées
> Pareil à une colombe tu couvas l'immense abîme
> Et le rendis fécond […]
> (*Paradis Perdu* 1.19–22).

Il n'y aurait pas de Père Créateur mais, au commencement du monde, l'Esprit.

Milton, les ailes puissantes comme un aigle, prendrait son essor et volerait d'un pôle à l'autre avec une évidente exaltation. Un aigle: comme l'aigle de Dante dans le *Paradis*[17], le symbole de l'assemblée des âmes, le contraire du noir cormoran, corbeau de mer avide.[18]

16 Heinz Kohut, *Le soi,* traduit par Monique André Lussier. Paris: PUF, «le Fil rouge», 1974. *The Analysis of the Self.* New York, International Universities Press, 1971.

17 Dante, *La Divine Comédie.* Le Paradis, XIX, 1–3. In *Œuvres Complètes*, Paris: Gallimard, «La Pléiade», pp. 1539–1540. Note d'André Pézard. Flammarion, Paris, 1985, Trad. J. Risset.

18 Harry Redman, Communication personnelle.

Mais l'aigle est l'emblème inscrit sur la maison paternelle! Comme il est divisé!

Milton, «des pensées troublées», a puisé sa force auprès des hommes qu'il admirait. Refusant toute paternité, il se veut fils de l'Esprit. Il serait comme l'un de ces hommes qui ont eu un destin exceptionnel, décrits par Machiavel:

> La totalité ou la plupart de ceux qui ont accompli de grandes choses en ce monde et ont excellé parmi les hommes de leur temps ont eu une naissance ou des débuts humbles et obscures [...].[19]

Moïse, Œdipe, Romulus et Remus, Castruccio Castracani del Antelminelli.[20]

Milton avait sans doute une connaissance de Machiavel.

La construction d'un savoir considérable relevait du désir d'être un homme exceptionnel: Milton luttait ainsi contre un «préjudice». Le désir de savoir et l'insubordination viennent compenser une grave blessure de l'amour de soi. Pour Freud, les «Etres d'exception» cherchent une compensation à un préjudice et elle porte à la haine: le Richard III de Shakespeare s'écrie, tout comme le Satan de Milton, *the Fiend,* le scélérat, «je suis déterminé à être un scélérat».[21] Le savoir tente aussi de conjurer une angoisse de vide. Milton n'est pas un mélancolique frère d'Hamlet; cependant, son esprit est peuplé de visions, occupé de pensées: la confrontation de la pensée avec la mort porte l'homme à méditer et, alternant avec la joie et le plaisir de vivre, elle est féconde: *Allegro, Il Penseroso,*[22] les deux beaux poèmes mis en musique par Händel, décrivent les deux versants d'une personnalité. L'agressivité contre soi-même se mue en créativité, l'œuvre en train de se

19 «[...] ou bien ils ont été exposés aux bêtes sauvages ou bien ils ont eu un père si vil que par vergogne, ils se sont déclarés fils de Jupiter ou de quelque autre dieu.» Machiavel, *Œuvres Complètes.* Paris, Gallimard, «La Pléiade», 1952.

20 Machiavel, La *vie de Castruccio Castracani.* Paris, Gallimard, La Pléiade, p. 545 et pp. 913–940. La vie de Castruccio del Antelminelli da Lucca. Toulouse, PBO 1992. Castruccio est le héros du «roman italien» de Mary Shelley, *Valperga.* Trad. Nicole Berry, Lausanne, L'Age d'Homme, 1997.

21 Sigmund Freud, «Quelques types de caractères. Les êtres d'exception», in *Essais de psychanalyse appliquée.* Traduction Marie Bonaparte. Paris: Gallimard, 1933.

22 John Milton, *Allegro, Il Penseroso, Samson Agonistes*, Paris, Aubier, traduction de Floris Delattre, 1963, Cf. *Complete Poetical Works,* I, pp. 88–96.

faire est un autre mode d'existence, un soi qui se crée lui-même![23] Le défi de Satan est:

> Cette horreur deviendra douceur, cette obscurité lumière.
> (*Paradis Perdu* 2.220)

L'affirmation de Milton dans son désarroi est:

> My weakness will be my strength.

Sa faiblesse fera sa force. Aveugle, il verra dans l'inconnu.

Le pari, inconscient lorsqu'il commence, est faire du mal du beau, de faire de sa rage une création. Et il assume ainsi, par son invention poétique, sa propre paternité:

> Nous ne connaissons point de temps où nous n'étions comme maintenant;
> Nous ne connaissons personne avant nous, engendrés de nous-mêmes, sortis de nous-mêmes
> Par notre propre force vive [...]
> (*Paradis Perdu* 5.52–53)

Aussi Milton, par retournement contre lui-même de l'hostilité dirigée contre un père, ne peut-il être père de ses propres enfants et peut-être a-t-il inconsciemment négligé le petit John, mort à neuf mois après sa mère, Mary. Il ne peut non plus être père de ses œuvres et nous ne voyons apparaître sa signature qu'avec la parution du *Paradis Perdu*![24]

Il existait un clivage dans le moi, à cause d'une haine ignorée jusqu'au temps où l'œuvre donna naissance à l'homme. Car devoir sa vie à un père est un poids intolérable, une dette humiliante. Par Satan Milton dit sa rébellion: il voulait être lui-même un poème, comme son modèle, Spenser, *"myself a true poem"*, il écrit *"a poem, a true self"*. Et ainsi il est libre:

> [...] je m'affranchirais
> De la dette immense d'une gratitude éternelle

23 Ma pensée diffère de celle de Mélanie Klein pour qui la mélancolie est un vide intérieur. M. Klein. «Les situations d'angoisse de l'enfant et leur reflet dans l'œuvre d'art et dans l'élan créateur», 1929. In *Essais de Psychanalyse*, Paris, Payot, 1967; traduction de Marguerite Derrida, pp. 254–263. Tavistok Publications. Les états mélancoliques admettent des représentations.

24 J. Martin Evans, "The Birth of the Author: Milton's poetic self construction." *Milton Studies*, XXXVIII, Pittsburgh, PA, Pittsburgh University Press, 2000.

> Si lourde, payant toujours et toujours à payer.
> (*Paradis Perdu* 4.52–53).

En ce qui concerne sa mère, Milton était aussi devant une injonction paradoxale: on la disait dévouée aux œuvres charitables, elle était donc bonne. Mais nous savons qu'elle avait perdu six enfants avant lui.[25] Pouvait-elle voir le petit garçon vivant devant elle? Les portraits de Milton enfant le montrent regardant au loin, tristement. Mauvaise ou bonne, sa mère n'était-elle pas une «mère morte»[26], une mère glacée, «un continent gelé», *"a frozen continent"* (*Paradis Perdu* 2.386)? La figure maternelle héritée du Moyen-Age, moitié femme, moitié serpent, est la mère de Satan dans les Enfers! Milton tout enfant avait sans doute fantasmé cette figure d'une mauvaise mère, et ceci avait un lien avec l'envie: la fécondité d'une mère suscite l'envie; John Leonard l'a aussi noté.[27] A cause de l'envie, les mauvais Anges désirent les trésors cachés de la terre Mère et se livrent au pillage avec une énergie extraordinaire.

> Ils saccagèrent le centre de la terre, et avec des mains impies
> Pillèrent les entrailles de leur terre Mère.
> (*Paradis Perdu* 1.686–87)

Pour ses plaisirs et aussi pour les pensées impies, Milton prend souvent Ovide comme complice[28]: dans les *Métamorphoses*, les hommes arrachent du sein de la Terre ce qui était caché là. Les similitudes avec les fantasmes d'envie et les pulsions qui cherchent à détruire l'intérieur du sein maternel décrites par Mélanie Klein à propos des très petits enfants sont frappantes.[29] Envie, pulsions destructrices à l'égard du sein maternel, le malaise

25 Louise Simmons, "Philadelphia. A possible Milton Family Portrait: Sara Jeffrey Milton." Présentation au Milton Congress, Pittsburgh, 2004. Communication personnelle.

26 André Green, «La mère morte», in *Narcissisme de vie, Narcissisme de mort.* Paris, Editions de Minuit, 1983, pp. 222–253.
Nicole Berry, «Le sentiment d'existence», in *Le sentiment d'identité,* 1987, Paris, L'Harmattan 1990; pp. 145–167.

27 John Leonard, "'Thus they relate erring.'" *Milton Studies*, XXXVIII, Pittsburgh, Pittsburgh University Press, 2000.

28 Ovide. *Les Métamorphoses*, Paris, Les Belles Lettres, 1928; traduction Georges Lafaye, Vol I. Chant I, 137–144.

29 Mélanie Klein, «Comme fantasmes des petits enfants à l'égard de leur mère.» M. Klein. *Envie et gratitude et autres essais.* Paris, Gallimard, 1968. Traduction de Victor Smirnoff et Marguerite Derrida. *Envy and Gratitude,* Mélanie Klein Trust, 1957.

était dans le «puits infernal» de soi, inconscient. Ce peut être pour le figurer que Milton invente un Fils qui, dans la Bible, n'existe pas dans l'Ancien Testament: sa détestation est justifiée par l'existence du rival que le Père lui préfère. Ainsi peut-il expliquer une souffrance archaïque impensable.

Milton écrivit *Ad patrem*, un poème de gratitude adressé à son père pour «le don des six langues»: cent vingt vers pour le remercier, seulement trois fois sept vers quelque temps plus tard pour dire son amour à Leonora Baroni. L'insistance est suspecte. La haine avait toujours été dirigée vers des figures représentant l'autorité, par transfert de son ambivalence.

Au sujet de sa mère, Milton n'a jamais écrit, la bonne mère est toujours la Terre Mère, dans *Lycidas*, déjà.

Pour clarifier son monde intérieur, Milton avait à entreprendre son aventure périlleuse et affronter l'angoisse de la perte du sentiment d'existence. L'angoisse archaïque d'une chute vertigineuse fut l'expérience initiale, initiatrice, une chute, très différente de la descente aux Enfers de Dante que Virgile accompagne et rassure, comme un «bon père» ou parfois «une mère» dans le monde infernal. Milton écrit:

> Je m'expose seul, d'un pas solitaire je vais
> (*Paradis Perdu* 2.828).
> My self expose with lonely steps to tread

Le sentiment d'une chute vertigineuse dans un monde sans haut ni bas a été décrit par Frances Tustin au sujet des enfants autistes.[30] Trois siècles plus tôt, Milton a trouvé les mots pour exprimer son angoisse, par la voix de Satan.

> Me miserable! Which way I flie
> Infinite wrauth and infinite despaire?
> Which way I flie is hell: myself am hell.
> (*Paradise Lost* 4.73–75)

N'est-ce pas pathétique?

Au livre IV, il a une claire conscience de composer un poème qui le concerne intimement.

Il faut se référer au conflit intrapsychique pour comprendre son cheminement.

30 Frances Tustin, *Le Trou noir de la psyché*, Paris, Le Seuil, 1989. *Autistics Barriers in Neurotic Patients*, London, Karnak Books, 1986.

Les pulsions destructrices menacent de submerger le moi et réclament que des limites soient posées aux désirs. Le père de Milton ne lui avait jamais rien refusé et sa bonté pouvait apparaître comme une faiblesse. Milton devait être son propre censeur et cela était inquiétant. Ni les désirs, ni les pulsions destructrices n'avaient rencontré d'obstacle ou d'interdit; Satan-Milton est habité d'une puissante rage qui le submerge:

> Qu'il soit donc maudit cet amour, puisque l'amour ou la haine
> Sont pour moi semblables et que l'amour m'apporte éternel malheur.
> (*Paradis Perdu* 4.69–70)

Un Tortureur fait face à un Tentateur en chacun de nous. Freud a décrit le fantasme masochiste comme une demande d'être traité comme un enfant en détresse et surtout comme un mauvais enfant souhaitant d'être battu afin de satisfaire à son désir d'être humilié. La délectation sadique est forte dans le *Paradis Perdu* et non moins la satisfaction masochiste.[31]

Mais la blessure narcissique a eu aussi un effet positif (c'est mon hypothèse): renonçant à la revendication virile, Milton se montre libre du savoir et capable de cultiver une réceptivité à la venue de la Muse, une *nightly visitation.* La complicité avec la Muse est une sublimation du désir amoureux. Elle le visiterait la nuit et chuchoterait à son oreille, comme le serpent dans Eden chuchote à l'oreille d'Eve. Les mêmes mots, les mêmes images.

> Que tout près de mon oreille quelqu'un d'une voix douce
> M'invitait à me promener
> (*Paradis Perdu* 5. 36–37).
> Nightly I visit [...]
> (*Paradise Lost* 3.32)

Visit, la répétition du mot ressemble à la plainte d'une femme que l'amant ne visiterait pas souvent.

La *nightly visitation* peut être aussi l'attente de la venue de l'Esprit. Et, dans le *Paradis Perdu,* la recherche de la terreur, comme quelque chose qui viendrait de la Nature, spécialement terrifiante,[32] un éclair, un tonnerre, peut être l'expression de l'espoir d'une révélation divine, une terreur sacrée,

31 Sigmund Freud, *Le problème économique du masochisme.* 1924. iIn *Névrose, Psychose et Perversion*, Paris, P.U.F., 1973. Traduction de Jean Laplanche. Standard Edition, XIX, 162.

32 C'est une suggestion de Townley Chisholm, Phillips Exeter Academy, U.S.A.

awe, avec une aspiration à la spiritualité. Par la terreur, Milton est un précusrseur du Gothique anglais.

Pour Milton, l'Esprit a toujours été là, *"from the first"* (I, 19–22). Mais le mal?

Nous savons dans le Livre I, par la trinité des anges mauvais que Satan désire faire le mal. L'origine du mal, pour Milton, apparaît être une blessure narcissique, la rage d'avoir été considéré comme un objet et aussi l'envie à l'égard du pouvoir fécondant de la mère, déjà décrite par Ovide après Hésiode. Il y a d'autres explications plus générales de l'origine du Mal.

Milton ne savait pas au commencement pourquoi il était tellement concerné par la question du Mal. Il commence à comprendre. Mais comment fut-il capable de créer un aussi grand poème à partir du mal?

> L'opinion chez les hommes de valeur n'est que la connaissance qui s'élabore.[33]
> Opinion in good men is but knowledge in the making.

«*In the making*»: la création n'est possible que si l'esprit, *mind,* est relativement libre. L'esprit de Milton s'est trouvé libéré après l'épreuve de la chute avec Satan, une expérience qu'il vécut lui-même avec un grand courage. Au temps où il était déjà totalement aveugle, il devint clairvoyant devant son monde intérieur.

Il y a aussi une exaltation à être libéré de la pensée et de la vision des choses réelles.

L'origine de la pensée, pour Milton, ne fut-elle pas la musique? Il pouvait entendre son père chanter et jouer de l'orgue lorsqu'il était un tout petit enfant. Il ne voyait pas son visage, mais il intériorisa une force et aussi une douceur et, sans doute, aveugle au monde, il voyait dans le ciel sombre des étoiles dessinant les notes d'une musique inouïe. Il se trouvait réconforté, exalté comme autrefois: le monde n'était pas vide mais plein:

> […] je suis celui qui emplit
> L'infini.
> (*Paradis Perdu* 7.168–169)

Se délivrer de la préoccupation de savoir permet de rêver et d'entendre l'inspiration, la «*visitation*». Mais cela ne suffit pas pour être créatif.

33 John Milton, *Areopagitica*, Paris, Aubier, bilingue, 1956, traduction d'Olivier Lutaud, p. 203.

On est frappé de voir les images du Livre sacré que Milton lit chaque jour alterner avec des images profanes venues d'Homère, d'Ovide, du monde Ancien, comme d'une égale valeur. Le sacré et le profane sont confondus. Est-ce là le «péché»?

La condition, pour créer, est la transgression. Milton écrivant sa propre bible transgresse la foi admise. Il avait toujours admiré les transgresseurs: Samson, Prométhée, Galilée, Jésus, Cromwell. (Il expierait en écrivant le *Paradis Regagné.*)

La transgression est une solution créative à l'injonction paradoxale.

Le pari de Satan était de créer un nouveau monde avec sa rage, le pari de Milton fut de créer un magnifique poème avec sa désobéissance.[34]

Après la lecture du *Paradis Perdu*, nous ne sommes plus semblables à nous-mêmes: la *wilderness* n'est plus si *wild,* si rude et si sauvage, elle est sacrée et parle d'immensité.[35]

«Là vient la nuit et la nuit mérite qu'on l'écoute», dit Homère.[36]

Du *whirlwind* au *whispering,* le ciel étoilé est tremblant de lumière pour que les hommes posent leurs questions. *Unseen, unheard, unborn, uncreated...* La négativité répétée signifie une question et poser des questions est être en vie.[37]

34 Nicole Berry, *John Milton, Le Paradis Perdu, des Ténèbres à la lumière*, Lausanne, L'Age d'Homme, 2005.

35 Risa S. Bear, "'Eden Rais'd in the Waste Wilderness': *Milton and the obedient moment.*" University of Oregon, 1992. Web: http://www.uoregon.edu/~rbear/milton.html

36 Homère. *L'Iliade*, Paris, Les belles-Lettres, 1937, VV, 182.

37 Voir l'essai sur Milton dans: Nicole Berry, *Trois textes: le récit, le paysage, les sonorités. Essais sur P. B. Shelley, Henry James, Joseph Conrad, John Milton*, à paraître prochainement chez Peter Lang.

Miriam Andrade MANSUR

Milton and Derrida: Deconstructing Milton's *Paradise Lost* Through a "Darkness Visible" Perspective

The purpose of this research upon the visual metaphors of *Paradise Lost* is to demonstrate that Milton's phrase "darkness visible" (1. 63), and other lines of *Paradise Lost*, adumbrated the post-structuralists's stance upon vision, that is, the need to mistrust in the immediacy of the physical sight and search for a more deeply reflection upon the superficiality of images. Milton's "darkness visible" perspective is compatible, in the view of this project, with that of the post-structualists', particularly with the one of Jacques Derrida in his book *Memoirs of the Blind* (1993) and in his theories. This research, as a product of an informed reading, displays a careful observation on the visual metaphors of *Paradise Lost* and it may prove that Milton would have proposed in his epic poem of the seventeenth century that the dialectics of the traditional philosophy on the issue of vision/blindness should be placed under erasure. Such attempt follows with a cancellation of the literal eye and the insertion of the figural I in the scope of interpretation. The methodology of this text will provide a critical guide for the visual metaphors of *Paradise Lost* which will be negotiated with the Derridean questions on the contemporary philosophical problematic over sight.

The ambivalences of the visual words in *Paradise Lost* demonstrate an oscillation between the use of the figural and the literal vision. This oscillation suggests that a type of threshold is established and its reference leaves the scope of stabilized concepts for a more debatable perspective. *Paradise Lost* is itself a written debate. Its debate can be ensured if an analysis of the textual structures of this epic is made. This analysis may uncover questions over the metaphysical conceptions that constitute the Western philosophy and attack the symbolic order of the *logos*. The line of thought of the traditional philosophy is characterized by the orderly distinctions of the binary oppositions. Questions on the concept of stabilized antinomies, on fixed points of reference mark the main locus of discussion of logocentrism.

Logocentrism is a term coined by the French philosopher Jacques Derrida that refers to traditional philosophy as based on the "metaphysics of presence". Logocentrism demonstrates how the structures of the binary oppositions work as determinate forms that serve as the basis of the Western philosophical thought. In such basis, the logocentric assumptions claim that defined truths reside beyond the presence of a signified in a way as to assure the signifiers with the limited meanings they convey. Derrida puts the limited operation of the signifiers and signifieds in the logocentric ideas under erasure, particularly for the fact that such operation attempts to frame the principles with concepts of absolute truths.

In *Writing and Difference* (1978), Derrida exposes his arguments against the matrix of the metaphysics of presence.

> This matrix "is the determination of being as *presence* in all the senses of this word. It could be shown that all the names related to fundamentals, to principles, or to the center have always designated an invariable presence-*eidos, arché, telos, energeia, ousia* (essence, existence, substance, subject) *alétheia*, transcendentality, consciousness, God, man, and so forth" (280).

Derrida argues for the dangers of the stabilized system of signs as structures that bear the essence of presence and operate with a transcendent meaning of the I/eye.

The tendency in logocentrism of the conceptualization of a center, which marks the I/ eye and denotes the privilege of this sign over the marginal, breaks the possibilities of the negotiation of meanings in their various (con)texts. Derrida explains that such privilege fails. He sets forth his view denying the limitation or separation of both signifier and signified and the prevalence of a center. In his claim, Derrida contends that a signifier may be either interior or exterior to other signifiers, according to their relation to the signified. The combination of these two possibilities of signification, the decentralization of the signified, the intermingling of the signifier and signified in a play of signification, and the consequent movement to the margin open the possibility of abstaining from the absolute truths and negotiating meanings with the matters of *differánce*. In the approach towards *differánce* the signs do not have a unique signification, instead, their meanings oscillate between assertions and subversions, marking the problematic state of a fixed present concept or signified. The word *differánce* summarizes the "undecidability of signs" and it implies the impossibility of a single, unified, monocular view of interpretation. The sign should be incorporated and brought into question up to a moment of un-veiling its hidden meanings, and in this procedure, reading would be taken to the realm of darkness.

The interpretation of the sign, according to Derrida, should perform an act that "must proceed in the night" and escape "the field of vision" (1993: 45). For the accounts related to the experience of darkness to reach visibility, Derrida's book *Memoirs of the Blind* demonstrates the articulations of two types of blindnesses, the transcendental and the sacrificial. These two blindnesses intervene and repeat each other. Derrida's transcendental and sacrificial blindnesses are indeed two scopes of interpretation and rhetoric that proliferate meaning in the powerless aspect of the literal, and consequently, decentralize the essence of the physical eye leading interpretation to a "darkness visible" realm.

The phrase "darkness visible" appears in the first Book of Milton's *Paradise Lost.* The "darkness visible" perspective is a type of experience that takes one to a blind state. There is the undecidability of these two elements, darkness and visible. Milton, like the post-structuralit's view of Derrida, plays and (de)stabilizes a concrete division between these two signs. In this phrase, these two opposing concepts are conflated and there is no evidence of the privilege of one over the other; on the contrary, their meanings cannot be approached independently. "Darkness visible" orients the direction of the ambiguities of the visual metaphors of *Paradise Lost*, for it implies the experience of the loss of an external and physically visible paradise and the accomplishment of seeing through darkness the unveiling of a "paradise within" (12. 311). According to the dictionary definition, a paradise is an enclosed park, an intermediate place or state and, in this matter, it reflects the outside, the external. "Paradise within" is another oxymoron and in its combination of (in)congruous[1] elements, the external is brought to the internal, in other words, the visibility out of darkness is through the mere experience of blindness *(OED).*

As mentioned previously, the orientation of this paper may proceed with a "darkness visible" perspective that opens the epic for the visual metaphors. The visual metaphors of Book 1 demonstrate that there is an

1 Although the word *incongruous* may commonly be understood for its negative significations as lacking congruity, as being not harmonious or incompatible, I have opted for its in-congruous form. The prefix *in* is not serving to produce a derivative word with a negative form, instead, it is employed based on its adjective function, which means: directed or bound inward *(OED).*

oscillation between two points of signification. The sentence "darkness visible" contributes to mark these two extremes. Darkness is outside and inside the words of this Book. It is outside in the whole description of Hell as the setting of the fall. It is also inside because the reader can have access to the mixture of doubt, hopelessness, and fear that confuses the choices of the fallen angels. Even Satan, although motivated for the regaining of his seat among the angels in Heaven, feels remorse and passion.

The oscillation of the visual metaphors between darkness and visibility comes to terms with Derrida's blindnesses. Darkness corresponds to the sacrificial blindness, especially because its meaning involves a loss that is represented by a sacrifice. The fall for the fallen angels stands for the loss of the presence of God and, at the same time, serves as a symbol of their deprivation of the light of Heaven. In this manner, it seems that in their state they face the dark realm of blindness. Visibility, on the other hand, represents the awakening after the fall and is similar to the transcendental blindness. Out of darkness, the angels' inward attempt may symbolize the possibility of reaching light again. The fallen angels' traces recall the inner capacity of their minds that open their (in)sight and motivate their fight for the conquest of their paradise. In their recovery attempt their outward frailties can be overcome by their inward resistance for submission. The position of these two extremes does not conduct this study to the frame of two distinct possibilities of signification, on the contrary, it is exactly on the oscillation of these two possibilities that the experience of blindness takes place.

The blind state in the beginning of Book 1 when Satan sees himself in Chaos and tries to wake up after the fall is repeated when he falls in the profound abyss of Chaos in the end of Book 2. The inner strength that helps the recovery after the fall comes up again in the dark abyss of Chaos when "the sacred influence of light appears" (2. 1034–1035). All the darkness of Satan's experiences is replaced by the visibility of a "pendent World, in bigness as a star" (1. 1052). In the seeing of light out of dark surroundings, darkness becomes visible, and blindness brings the restoration of sight.

Darkness leaves Hell with Satan's attempt to violate boundaries and perform his conquest and the visibility of light apparently takes control of the narrative in the beginning of Book 3. For the persona, who in the first lines of Book 3 seems to represent the blind poet himself, light is the purest expression from within and, through it, one may erase the literal eye, "that roll in vain" (3. 23) and insert the figural I with its "shine inward" that sees and tells "things invisible to mortal sight" (3. 52–55). Yet for Satan, the light from within is symbolized by all the negative features that sprang from his mind to motivate the revenge against God's new creation and aspire to possess God's power. These two opposing views will not go hand in hand for the rest of the epic, with a clear separation of their two poles; it is, on the contrary, in the intermingling of both and the consequent crossing of the limits of their signification, that this reading may proceed with its scope through the metaphorical "darkness visible" perspective.

Satan's attempt, immersed in his own passion and in his ungoverned desire to conquest and to power, is the best proof of the recoil of one's own self before the outward appearance and temptation that meet his/her physical eyes. The lack of vision is blindness itself, within its physical and transcendental aspect, and it demonstrates Satan's lack of containment with the withdrawal of his view, and in this manner, Satan's trespasses the limits of his own self as well as the boundaries of his external and internal sight. Once again, the crossing of the limits of Hell and his arrival on the Earth do not prevent Satan from the very same losses that assailed him when he leaves Hell. Blindness from without and blindness from within, demonstrate Satan's losses that depart with himself for his attempt, "with hoped success" (3. 740), against man.

Satan's losses continue tempting him in the beginning of Book 4. The traces of his memories "of what he was, what is, and what must be" (4. 25) or become of him keep on affecting his view in his enterprise. In his despair, "horror and doubt distract /His troubled thoughts, and from the bottom stir /The Hell within him, for within Hell" (4. 18–20) continue assailing his mind wherever he goes. Even the changing of places from Hell to Earth does not alter his inward and outward distress. When he sees the beauty and order of the Earth, his "bitter memory" (4. 24) is recalled fiercely, and his former state comes to his mind to reinforce the differences on his shape and condition. With the views of the new world, he contrasts his deformed shape and realizes his fallen and weak being. Satan's thoughts turn inwardly and outwardly up to the moment that he comes to the conclusion that he is to blame God for his fall. Satan's inconsistency in blaming God reflects his doubtful experience of losing God's light as well as the reference of God in his being. In this sense, Satan's losses represent his detachment from his only referent, or better saying, from order itself, which symbolizes God, and, because of it, he experiences disorder and confusion.

The order experienced by Satan in Heaven is all gone and he suffers from the disorder of his state. His disordered mind cannot cope with the seeing of God's order represented by the new world. Satan's "disorder bursts out in blindness" and through it the blind Satan "does not know what to make of the order brought forth with the heavy change" (Sá 1996: 165) before his sight.

The failure of Satan's sight corresponds to a lack of insight. Under the aspect of seeing "undelighted all delight, all kind /Of living creatures, new to sight and strange" (4. 286–287), Satan suffers from the absence of a referent once he is freed from the presence of God, but imprisoned in his own view. In the new world, with the perfection of order shown by the characters of Adam and Eve and the other creatures, Satan's limitless view does not find a copartner. He is alone, in the middle of perfection. In his limitless view, Satan can only see God around him with all the representations of goodness. His invisibility is thus marked by the idea that the world before Satan is filled with creatures that are literally unable to see his real nature.

At the end of Book 4, despite the chances Satan has to see the other side of his fallen condition and from those views analyze the distress of his losses and search for his own light, he resists light and flees from paradise "murmuring, and with him" flees "the shades of Night" (4. 1015). Thus, Milton's "darkness visible" perspective, which would demand from one a moment of reflection of the images presented to his/her eyes before an interpretation of them are made, is not applied to Satan's character. In Satan's case, his inner motivation for revenge blinds his eyes and he can only see through the lenses of the aspiration of God's world. Satan leaves paradise and with him goes the "shades of Night" which demonstrate the darkness from within in the purest expression of his inability to see and from without with the shades of Night surrounding him. With Satan's and the shades of Night's departure of paradise, light is established in Eden, and from this moment on, an attempt to open the eyes of Adam and Eve for the dangers of the temptation before their sight takes place.

From Book 5 to Book 8, the retelling of the stories of creation is all invaded with the light of God. The first temptation of Eve in Book 5 brings forth the need to open the eyes of the two human creatures for the risks of the external beauty and seducement. The light of God is represented by the presence of Raphael in Eden and his efforts to convey the goodness of God are attempts to make God visible for Adam and Eve. Raphael is the archangel that works as a messenger between Heaven and Earth, and as Derrida suggests when he analyses the drawings on Tobit's healing of blindness, Raphael represents the "visible signs of the invisible" (Derrida 1993: 29). In this sense, Raphael stands for the visible aspect of the invisibility of God's acts.

The presence of Raphael with his view and report of the world before Adam's eyes, may suggest Adam's need to find his personal fulfillment in the other. When Adam is together with Raphael, he disregards Eve's presence and she becomes sightless to them. Adam incorporates, in this case, his humanly necessity for companion and care. The presence of the other reinforces Adam's own presence. Adam, as the being that is the image and resemblance of God in his inward and outward world, is also the possessor of a fissure from within. The fissure in God's world is represented by his two creations according to *Paradise Lost*'s lines, the Son and Satan. The crack is from within provided that the interpretation of these two creations is regarded as the fruits of God's womb, symbolized by His world. The inner lacuna humans possess would demand to be filled. The other would, for Adam, represent his wholeness. Nevertheless, it seems that in this matter, Milton's writings, especially *Paradise Lost* in its calls for reason, may imply that the gap in the inner self of man should be filled through knowledge that stands for reason and wisdom. Knowledge would be the filling need one must approach to find his fulfillment from within and become aware from a passive condition that all humans bear.

Adam's passivity before Eve's power foreshadows the events to come, already implying the dangers of the external unwise seducement in denigration of an inward expression. The words of Raphael bring his retelling act to the end and in its end he reinforces the caution Adam has to hold to avoid the outward guidance of passion. Raphael denounces Eve's figure as "an outside; fair, no doubt, and worthy well /Thy cherishing, thy honouring, and thy love – Not thy subjetion" (8. 568–570). In this matter, Raphael admonishes Adam anew to "stand fast; to stand or fall /Free in thine own arbitrament it lies /Perfect within, no outward aid require" (8. 640–642). Thus, Raphael lesson is completed and with it, Adam learns about the capacity of his own inner sight to perform a positive praise of the other, but not a negative subjection before the other's view. Milton's warning lesson is finally expressed with Raphael's words. In this matter,

Milton seems to condemn the endangered attitude one may carry out if he/she prefers to trust in his/her physical eyes and subjects his/her self to an outward conformity and seduction without a pondering reflection upon his/her choices. Furthermore, the implication of an unware reliance on the eyes of the other might cause the disregard of one's mind and reason and in this sense, blindness from within and blindness from without may conduct the passive path towards submission. Milton's sentence "darkness visible" would conclude these books displaying the dangers of visibility if an inward reflection does not take place before the images presented to one's eyes. Moreover, the need for wholeness found in the other may express the risks for the external to complete the internal self, and as for Milton, the process of wholeness might go the other way round.

The problematic instance posed by the previous books is summed up in Book 9 in which the losses and the envious state of Satan are fulfilled in the shallowness of Adam and Eve, and, in this matter, their falls will be intermixed in their different types of blindnesses. The visual metaphors support the two conditions of the characters' behavior. Satan's eyes cannot cope with what they see: all brightness of his former state presently lost at the view of the new magnificent creation of man. Besides that, the distress of his losses is strengthened by the fact that man's creation substituted Satan's own. Satan is the example of the two sides of blindnesses, the external and internal ones as previously discussed. On the other hand, there stand Adam with his need to see the other to complete his self-formation, and Eve still invisible to her own eyes. Adam and Eve also experience blindness, however their blindness is demonstrated by their inner lack that controls their outer dependence.

In Books 10, 11, and 12, Milton's lesson is settled and the visual metaphors used in these final lines of the epic support his words. It is in these three last books that the oscillation in the usage of the visual metaphors helps prove their importance in Milton's approach towards vision. The evocation of the literal eye in the first lines of Book 10 seems to set the two opposing views to show how Milton's lesson concentrates on the variation that slides from the need to erase the literal eye and validate a deeper concern with the exercise of the figural eye as placed in the end of Books 11 and 12.

The narrator continues tracing that the two opposing sides may conduct the direction towards the final view(s) of the epic. As soon as the visibility of God's Son is depicted leaving paradise, the narrator shifts his words to "the gates of Hell" where "Sin and Death, in counterview" (10. 230–231) appear. The contrast of the scenes seems to request the reader to abstain from the literal expression of Adam's and Eve's views to counterview with Sin's and Death's. In this matter, in the last three Books, there is a play with the visual words that moves to and fro the two poles of signification and the reader's eyes follow the oscillation between them. On the one hand, there is an end of the references of Hell and its creatures. It seems that with the punishment inflicted on the fallen angels there is the presentation of the final view of the devils, however, another change of vision occurs and the reading goes back to Paradise. In Paradise the view of "the hellish pair" (10. 585), Sin and Death, leaves the scope open and suggests that although the devilish machine of Satan and his peers is brought to an apparent end with their punishment, Satan's traces will go on affecting God's and his creation's views.

The traces and the sliding movement from the literal to the figural sight, from darkness to visibility, from blindness to evidence, help reinforce the major concentration of Milton's lesson, that is, a search for an inner light, reason, that may guide one through the best path to choice. However, Milton's leaving the hellish pair available in the humans' realm also implies that the search and the accomplishment of reason may undergo through darkness, but it may also culminate in a deep expression of eternal darkness presented by the last scene of the devil's part. Michael's final words to Adam and Eve displaying a "paradise within" (12. 587) demonstrate the possibility of reaching reason in another view, through reflection and an inward exercise of the sight.

In *Paradise Lost* the presence of visual metaphors (de)stabilize the wordplay between the literal and the figural sight and in these two poles, a sliding movement takes place. Such movement tends to establish, according to Derrida, a communication between two opposing values, the literal and the figural. Instead of a limit or a slash between these two opposing concepts, the lines of *Paradise Lost* invite the readers to experience vision and blindness, to leave the literal and reach the figural and at the same time to see with the figural sight the risks of the physical one. The two possibilities of the process of self-formation based on the elimination of the eye and the trust in the I are more emphasized in the last three Books, as if this strategy would display the coming of an end. The highest and the lowest extremes in the presence of the visual metaphors conclude the tension between the literal and figural sight, however, the end of the epic resists a closure. It seems that the lesson is ended, yet the enormous scope before Adam's and Eve's eyes demonstrates that a closure is impossible with the gates of the world wide open before them and before the reader.

Like Derrida, Milton's rhetoric in *Paradise Lost* "violates the relationship between word (signifier) and meaning (signified)" (Rapaport 1983: 12). The language of *Paradise Lost* is abstract and stylish, and to a certain extent, it contrasts with the ordinary ideal of the spoken language. In this opposition, *Paradise Lost* reassures that Milton was not the poet that emphasized presence or the idealization of the present represented by speech, on the contrary, he invented various types of comparisons in his metaphors that lead to an endless path of interpretations, distancing his writing from the mere act of the spoken word. For this reason, the ideal present applied to the signifier and signified in the logocentric conception is banished in *Paradise Lost.*

The experience of the Derridean blindnesses, the movement from the outward vision towards the (in)sight, in a "downward path to wisdom" (Shattuck 1996) is mastered into an inward process of self-formation and inner reflection. In *Paradise Lost* the same blinding attempt takes place in the experience of the eye/I as a lost paradise that is invaginated through a "darkness visible" perspective into an inwardly act up to its recovery as a "paradise within". In the movement from the external to the internal sight, a careful observation and the chance of pondering the risks of the immediacy of the physical vision and a concomitant "submission to external interpretative authority" (Rumrich 1990: 257), provide the ground for the institution of a more aware individual. The individual in this manner experiences a type of reasoning process and due to it, he/she can exercise his/her choices in the public sphere in a more rational way and not simply place himself or herself in a condition of outward acceptance and conformity of pre-existing principles.

The articulation of the visual metaphors in *Paradise Lost* does take the reading to a dimension in which perception must be exercised. The elevation of the reading to the realm of external and internal senses gives life to the lines of the poem. Sight, for the sake of reading or interpretation, should be exposed to blindness in an attempt to erase the act from the outside and invite the exercise of the inner one. The "darkness visible" metaphor and Derrida's blindnesses are articulated in the lines of *Paradise Lost,* and in such articulation, sight is absorbed into a blinding state and the (in)sight is activated, hence, out of darkness, visibility is achieved. The visual metaphors of *Paradise Lost* are the focus of this study and their references in the epic reach the number of 869 times. As their number is high, the length of this study is also of great size, which makes this paper only a prolegomenon to the whole research that is currently under process.

Finally, according to the words of the head curator of the exhibition in the preface of *Memoirs of the Blind,* from which the Derridean hypotheses of blindnesses come up:

> Jacques Derrida's reflection goes to the heart of the phenomena of vision, from blindness to evidence... It thus will have seen it to interrupt the legacy of a monocular vision in order to lead us by the hand toward this other legacy that is passed down in darkness. Opening eyes, then, yes – but in order to cancel them.

In this matter, blindness may be interpreted as a seeing experience in another dimension, in the scope of reflection, in the articulation with the outer and the inner worlds. Through blindness, Derrida and Milton take us by the hand to see how the eyes can be opened to the fallacies of the world.

Works Cited

Derrida, Jacques. *Aporias.* Stanford: Stanford University Press, 1993.

–. *Dissemination*, trans. Barbara Johnson. Chicago: The University of Chicago Press, 1981.

–. *Memoirs of the Blind: The Self Portrait and Other Ruins*, trans. Pascale-Anne Brault and Michael Naas. Chicago: The University of Chicago Press, 1993.

–. *Of Grammatology,* trans. Gayatri Spivak. Baltimore: John Hopkins University Press, 1976.

–. *Positions*, trans. Alan Bass. Chicago: The University of Chicago Press, 1981.

–. *The Ear of the Other: Otobiography, Transference, Translation*, trans. Avital Ronell. Lincoln and London: University of Nebraska Press, 1988.

–. *Writing and Difference*, trans. Alan Bass. Chicago: The University of Chicago Press, 1978.

Frye, Norhrop. *Five Essays on Milton Epics.* London: Routledge & Kegan Paul, 1966.

Guss, Donald L. "Enlightenment as Process: Milton and Habermas," *PMLA*, v. 106, n. 5, pp. 1156–1169, October 1991.

Herman, Peter. "'Warring Chains of Signifiers': Metaphoric Ambivalence and the Politics of *Paradise Lost*". *Texas Studies in Literature and Language*, v. 40, n. 3, pp. 268–292, Fall 1998.

–. "*Paradise Lost*, the Miltonic 'Or', and the Poetics of Incertitude". *SEL*, v. 43, n. 1, 181–211, Winter 2003.

Jay, Martin. *Downcast Eyes: The Denigration of Vision in Twentieth-Century French Thought.* California: University of California Press, 1993.

Milton, John. *Paradise Lost.* London: Penguin Popular Classics, 1996.

OED, 7th ed 2005.

Rapaport, H. *Milton and the Postmodern.* Lincoln: University of Nebraska Press, 1983.

Rumrich, John. "Uninventing Milton". *Modern Philology*, v. 87, n. 3, 249–265, February 1990.

Sá, Luiz Fernando F. *The Myth of Orpheus in Milton's 'L'Allegro', 'Il Penseroso', and 'Lycidas'*. Belo Horizonte: UFMG, 1996.

Schwartz, Regina. "From Shadowy Types to Shadowy Types: The Unendings of *Paradise Lost*". In: Simmonds, J. D. (Ed.). *Milton Studies* 24. Pittsburgh: University of Pittsburgh Press, 1988. 123–139.

Shattuck, Roger. *Forbidden Knowledge: From Prometheus to Pornography.* New York: St. Martin's Press, 1996.

Marie-Dominique GARNIER

From Dagon to Deleuze and Derrida: *Samson Agonistes* and Particle Poetics

Literary itineraries

"Grand style", as Christopher Ricks was among the first to show, is a matter of small things. The minor mechanics of diminutive differentials and discreet displacements is what forms the subtle scaffolds on which the "grand" poetics of *Paradise Lost* finds one of its strongest supports. While Christopher Ricks' epoch-making study of the minor beneath the major devotes its critical attention to the specific scale-length of the word, what this essay aims to do is to displace the reader's gaze towards the smaller scale of a particle-oriented, "molecular" reading. Beneath, between, or just beside "words" and signifiers, what could be called Milton's particle poetics awaits reappraisal.

While many Miltonists, among whom Joseph Wittreich, agree on the many places in which Milton's *Paradise Lost* reveals its disorienting effects as a "field of opposing stresses and signals," few accept to return to the discontinuities of Milton's writing as a pregnant component of his "style." Recently Peter C. Herman has shown the importance of the Miltonic "or," in an article on Milton's poetics of "uncertainty," in which the critic bravely refuses to base his reading on a semblance of consistency – although what Peter Herman newly conceptualizes as "incertitude" manifests an implicit need to "make sense", to reconstruct or historicize (181).

In the wake of such readings, the following study looks at Milton's stylistic craftsmanship as a matter of "small things", significant smithereens and sub-signifying parts, on the assumption that, "yet once more," the question of style needs to be re-opened. Like the floating, hesitant particle "or," the syllable "on" can be shown to affect much of Milton's later poetic corpus, quite notably in *Samson Agonistes*. Unlike "or", however, "on" cannot be monolithically given any significant, semantic weight, no more that it can be attributed any stable syntactic status. A preposition used to indicate contact with or position on a surface, "on" also serves as an adverb, as a verbal particle. But rather than being safely contained as a dictionary item, the particle "on" gestures towards a number of uncouth and unruly interpretive directions. Its affects the surface of Milton's text, understood as one vast, continuous, single poetic expanse, from Milton's first epic punning on Satan's name ("Satan sat on…") to Dalila's first entrance into the text of *Samson Agonistes*, in the subtle, stubborn undertones of "yet on she moves." "On" recurs freely as a partial, less than significant subatomic marker originating from the poet's own name, whose signature tune ranges across a number of resonant syllabic effects in *Samson Agonistes*, the stage of an "agon" between Samson and Dagon. Re-envisaged from this novel, non-semantic angle, *Samson Agonistes* reads as a vast territory of articles, particles, adverbs and suffixes, additions and disarticulations, strewn with diminutive yet minutely important pre-or postpositional odds and ends – without which no language, no process of articulation, can take place. After several critical decades, Christopher Ricks' approach in *Milton's Grand Style* – itself a "grand" and ideally slim book – belongs to the transitional period that both preceded and prepared deconstruction, a period best described as that of "verbal" criticism. Since then, structures, post-structures and signifiers have emerged. The late sixties in France saw the publication of a Lacanian review, aptly called *Ornicar?*, which devotes a fair amount of its analytic energies to the study of the signifier. As appears in its prepositional title, which fuses three French operators of coordination ("or"/ "ni"/ "car") the importance of the finer particles language cannot be neglected – "Ornicar" becoming another name for hermeneutics, based on the mnemonic rigmarole with which schoolchildren are enticed to remember coordinates *(mais où est-donc Ornicar?)*. An important study by Charles Méla in *Ornicar 25* (*"La lettre tue: Crytographie du Graal,"* 142) refers to the effects of what he calls "cryptography," to how letters, in the wake of such an important book as Isidore of Seville's *Etymologies*, can – and have – signified, if one devotes enough attention to them. His reading develops a number of tactics based on one of Isidore's creative etymologies: "Letters *(littera)* are so called as if the term were *legitera*, because they provide a road *(iter)* for those who are reading *(legere)*, or because they are repeated *(iterare)* in reading" (I, 3, 3). On which Isidore adds that Hebrew is the "mother of all languages and letters", and begins with Moses' law *(lege)* (I, 3, 4). A similarly cryptographic deciphering of the literal in *Samson Agonistes* should bring out novel ways of "reading" Milton, whose texts are suspended in the equivocating directions of what the "letter" means: between the law of proper reading and the free path of iteration.

One of the ways of addressing this issue is to look at what goes on in the finer grain of Milton's poetic utterances, on the double assumption that his "texts" are what matters, and that we still need to keep wondering what a "text" is, what and how a text means, and where to place or displace its theoretical and practical boundaries. Beneath the textural metaphor imported in the term "text", what goes on in a poem may not agree with the binary rules of warp and weft, paradigm and syntagm, signifier and signified. One of my aims in insisting on the efficacy of a "nano-reading" of Milton is to resist the rule of orthogonality in the process: "on", as a particle/adverb/syllable, can no longer be pigeon-holed into any semantic category. It becomes, on the other hand, the locus of an "agon", which matters, and matters "on". "On", as the following "subatomic" reading of *Samson Agonistes* hopes to show, behaves as a sonorous, free linguistic constituent, a detachable, re-combinable poetic electron. On a larger scale, "On" also seems to operate smoothly yet surely throughout the Miltonic corpus, where its audible presence emerges in key-moments of *Paradise Lost*, to recur, with unique force, in Milton's last dramatic poem. On the "nano-scale" of particle poetics (as in particle physics), "on" informs *Samson Agonistes* and provides a form of micro-tutorial to close-reading, as well as close-scanning. Put differently, *Samson Agonistes* is, quite literally, a "cellular" poem, a text about incarceration, captive thoughts, blind confinement, deprivation, yet about the need to resist and read "on", into the cellular possibilities of a new language. Between Samson's initial isolation "in the common prison" (l.6) and his live burial beneath the final debris, the force of a mere adverb, "on", opens up a resonating, iterative zone of sense, in which can be found the beginning of an answer to the haunting questions recently revived in *Milton Studies 44* – why, and how, Milton matters, in the detail of the sub-signifiers, local scanning issues, and the resistance to textuality of his major "texts".

Literary iteration: On "on"

A curiously generative or proliferative principle seems to operate from the first, foreign, and slightly uncouth letters of *Samson Agonistes*' "Jewgreek" title, which welds words from two linguistic worlds around a shared, echoic syllable. A principle of continued growth and exponential increase affects the dissemination of its two programmatic letters, S/A, involved, as it were, in a pattern of repetition and dissemination. First introduced as a closely-knit wedded pair in the name "Samson," they recur in a divided pattern, as two severed, disseminating capitalized initials. An increased sense of echoic tangling is achieved prosodically by the twice repeated, nasal syllable "on," which Milton makes audible and readable again as a full-fledged signifier in Samson's initial utterance: "a little onward," a phrase suggestive of an "on"-going direction which both liberates and contains the power of insistence, or of resilience, attached to the particle. A sense of agonistic trial and confinement, in other words, is nicely counterbalanced, in such an inter-play, by the suggestion that something can, and will, go "on," in the force of a linguistic exodus attached to Samson's Hebraic name.

"On" borrows its force from its ill-defined, syllabic/adverbial status in the text, where it operates as a viral principle that connects and tangles opposing semantic and syntactic threads or scales in the dramatic poem. The force of "on" rests in its infectious power, a force which cuts across existing patterns of opposition between God and Dagon, Dagon and Milton/Samson, *agon* and Dagon, signifier and signified. The syllable begins, quite literally, Milton's dramatic piece, which also leads to it, although, as I shall show later, with a slight twist. "On" ties together a number of loose threads. It operates, one could show, as one of the text's living stigmata, first found in that key adverb, "onward", which initiates the poem, then at the turn in the poem when Dalila stalks on stage ("yet on she moves"), then, finally, in one of the poem's most resonant terms, "passion." Between a Samson and a Dagon, the possibility of viral contagion is rendered palpable, audible, with the discreet force of the syllable "on."

The speeches attributed to Dalila in particular make her operate less as a full-fledged, psychologically coherent voice, than as a flexible, mobile network of free adverbial particles, among which "on" predominates. To Samson's refusal to have anything more to do with her, the chorus replies: "yet <u>on</u> she moves", attaching a minor, yet insistent adverbial undercurrent to the feminine figure. Dalila's lines re-introduce a bonding, rhyming pattern into the text, with rhymes based on just that syllable:

> With doubtful feet and wav'ring resolution
> I came, still dreading thy displeasure, Samson,
> Which to have merited, without excuse
> I cannot but acknowledge; yet if fears
> May expiate (though the fact more evil drew
> In the perverse event that I foresaw)
> My penance has not slackened, though my pardon
> No way assured. But conjugal affection
> Prevailing over fear and timorous doubt
> Hath led me on [...] (731–741).

The last lines uttered by Dalila before her final disappearance hammer in a similar end-rhyme that belongs to the same phonetic family, with the chiming association of "shown" and "own" (994–996). Such cases of repetition cannot be merely explained as semantic choices suggestive of Milton's intention to signify Dalila's connections with bondage or with ornate vulgarity. Dalila's minor language "moves on" to disseminate the syllable in a series of half-rhymes, internal rhymes and other iterative figures which disrupt the constraining patterns of rhyme, and resist rhyme altogether. At once a combination of "resident" nominal suffix and a mobile adverb, "on" encompasses the play's semantic specter.

"On" operates, in other words, as a syntactic field which entangles two threads into one: as a preposition, "on" is about superimposing, constraint and bondage, about the Satanic politics and poetics of Dagon, the god of idolatry, ornament and rhyming – a palindrome of God's own name, to which is appended a fish tail, "upward man and downward fish" (*PL* I.462–63), the likely Hebrew source for the name being *dag*, fish. Yet "on" as an adverb introduces an active subtext implying iterated, continuous growth, forward motion, and the power of gaining-anew or regaining, as in *Paradise Regained* – a force which in the words of the Chorus is explicitly associated to Dalila:

> Yet beauty, though injurious, has strange power
> After offence returning, to regain
> Love once possessed, nor can be easily
> Repulsed, without much inward passion felt (*SA* 1003–1006).

"Passion" reads as a two-syllable term here, unlike the dramatic poem's final use of the same term, in "calm of mind all passion spent," where "passion" (l. 1758), as we shall see, can only be scanned with a dieresis, if one seeks to retain the "proper" pentametric feel of the line. Samson's own regained passion (a word which semantically looks both ways, towards God and Dalila) is a matter of growth, a function of growing "on", on the strength of a short energetic syllable that re-emerges in another strategic dieresis in the poem, when the freedom-fighter begins to feel "some rousing moti<u>on</u>s" (l. 1383).

"On" operates less a signifier than as a "scale" of writing, a dovetailing, micro-chip of sense affecting the poem, and converting the orthogonality of a "textural" poem into a scaly, slippery, undecidable surface of interrogation. As a one-dimensional, less-than-signifying part, "on" undermines the stability attached to the binary concept of text (conceived, in the present case, as an agonistic space of conflict between two sides, which *Samson Agonistes* in many ways resists becoming). A detached, movable part, the particle "on" (whether adverbial, prepositional, phonetic, or merely parasitic), operates as a loose bolt, that finds one of its origins in an on-going pun that runs across *Paradise Lost* on Satan's name: "Satan/sat on" (*PL* I.639). "On" sits between semantics and syntax, between adverbial force and prepositional hesitancy. It comes dangerously close to parading, associatively, as God's "other" name, inscribed in the lines spoken by the Chorus, who introduces "the Holy One /of Israel", a phrase given particular prosodic promotion and visibility in the meta-stable arrangement of an enjambment, on the falling edge of line 1426.

"On" is phonetically invasive, syntactically bi-fold, and semantically tied to what could be termed a non-textual, paradoxical logic. Milton's poem exposes a Greek "*agon*" in the vicinity of a Semitic "Dagon," itself invited to re-emerge, after a process of mutation and reverse-engineering, in its metamorphic, Saxon twin form as a "dragon," to which Samson is likened (l.1692). As made clear in Michael Lieb's study of the notion of dread in relation to the God of *Samson Agonistes*, beyond the derivation of the name Dagon from *dag* (fish), "one might note the etymological association between *dag* as "fish" and *daag* (a form of *dag*) as both "fish" and "dread" [...] Whether Milton was aware of it remains to be seen" (Lieb, 1997, 24 note 25).

Whether Milton was aware of these dovetailing, contradictory etymologies or not matters in fact very little. The poem, the language at work in the poem, is more, or less, than aware of it, in Milton's own stead: the poem actually does circulate the possibility of such an overlap, and therefore contributes to a shattering sense that the "temple" of language is affected at its roots.

A type of Samson manacled at a real yet emblematic mill in the poem's opening lines, Milton "grinds" poetry to infra-semantic pieces, submitting inherited patterns of textual oppositions to a process of literal milling or matting – pressing the fibers of a textual fabric into a "locked," resistant material. The growth and progress of Milton's "text" is a factor of the length, volume, split ends and extensions of Samson's matted locks and curls. What locks the "agon" and the "dagon" together is the reversible, scaly logic that operates at the primitive roots of language, which Milton, as this poem testifies, was well familiar with long before Freud.

As recently shown by John Rogers, Milton's exploitation of the narrative detail of the growth or, in French, the "regain" of Samson's hair goes against the grain of all Calvinistic expectations. Instead, Milton exploits "the embarrassing folkloric remnant left untouched by the biblical writers" (Rogers, 117). What the critic elbows aside as a "folkloric remnant" may in fact be in touch with a primeval capacity for resistance and resilience at the "root" of language.

Scales: Justice and a Kettle of Fish

A "fishy" strain runs across *Samson Agonistes*, a work steeped in Milton's rereading of the *Book of Judges* – a book one could emblematize with the allegory of the "scales" of Justice, used in the process of distinguishing between two parties, two moral issues. While *Samson Agonistes* pays lip service to the semantics of the law, the poem's prosodic and aural imagination, on the other hand, runs counter to it: its homophonic strain, as well as its audible passion for strange phonetic attractors, revise the scales of justice into alternative homophonic "scales": the horny, overlapping outgrowths that cover the skins of reptiles and fish. Following this associative, burning trail, one stumbles on a serendipitous case of *nomen omen*, as Milton's own name appears to contain a discreet yet insistent "fishy" strain inscribed at its core: it yields, in its productive first syllable, *milt,* or fish-roe. It is hardly a surprise, one might venture to add in a creative onomastic (though perhaps unwelcome) vein, that one of Milton's most inventive critics happens to bear the name of S. Fish, a promising, scaly cognomen, a fertile outgrowth imped on Milton's own scale-backed poetics.

Yet another example of such grafting can be found in Milton's alliterative linking of Samson's "locks" to "laws", in the last paragraphs of *The Reason of Church Government.* There, Milton compares the state and person of a king to that "mighty Nazarite Samson, who [...] grows up to a noble strength and perfection with those his illustrious and sunny locks, the laws, waving and curling about his godlike shoulders" (Milton 688–689). In Milton's extended metaphor, the clippers of regal power – the prelates – are called the "shavers of the laws," before the text resorts to two more tropes: paronomasia and a palindrome, where "locks" and "laws" are metamorphosed into "looks" and "walls":

> And if they be such clippers of regal power and shavers of the law, how they stand affected to the law-giving parliament, yourselves, worthy peers and commons, can best testify, the current of whose glorious and immortal actions hath been only opposed by the obscure and pernicious designs of the prelates, until their insolence broke out to such a bold affront as hath justly immured their haughty looks within strong walls (688).

The prelates' "haughty looks" curiously echo the mighty locks and laws of Samson. A mere palindrome separates "laws" from "walls," while the subtleties of paronomasia differentiate "locks" from "looks," God from Dagon. The logic of the overlap threatens to render meaning less and less probable. Although God and Dagon are clearly made to belong to opposed paradigms – insightful blindness versus excessive showmanship and visibility – an *"agon"* is being staged, which a mere letter separates from (D)agon.

In the Name of the law

The language of minimal differences and minor disparities at work in the *Reason of Church Government* reaches a much more perceptible form in *Samson Agonistes*, where the "name" of the law is made to recur in a series of non-concordant acceptations. Its last occurrence imports the Greek sense of fate or dire necessity, in the lines spoken by the Chorus to clear Samson of the guilt of suicide – as he now "li'st victorious [...] tangled in the fold of dire necessity / whose law in death conjoined" (1660–1667). Samson literally lies victorious, where "lie" entangles the semantic polarities of victorious rest and of possible dissimulation, gain and loss, in a pattern of semantic *agonistes.* The above lines contain a meta-phrase or (double) translation of the term "law," based on two diverging roots or linguistic contexts – etymological split-ends: the old Aryan *"lag,"* to lie, to place, and the Latin *"legere"*, to read. The Greek term for the law, *nomos,* from an Indo-European root, "Nem," which indicates distribution (Laroche 116–124) is itself nomadic, and roams towards antithetical paths. The law belongs with the uncouth space of the *nomos,* originally a space of scattering, an expanse of "pastures new" or common grazing land (before it came to designate an enclosed space, a share, a possession, a name). The space of the "law" is, in other words, etymologically reversible as commonwealth, an expense of commonly exploited land. *Nomos*, originally a shared piece of grazing land, operates as a primitive linguistic pastureland where loose particles float across lexicographic boundaries, where etymologies roam free from their roots, like adventitious shoots: if one disregards the Hebraic *shimshon*, and its solar associations, another possible root, "to sam" (to gather, to collect) patiently waits beneath the surface of Samson's name. Several readings of "what's in a name" can rub elbows in a common signifier. Heard, rather than read, from a similar open angle, a "dag" (Samson's body-double) is a piece of fleece or unshorn cloth.

Samson in three "D's"

At a further stage in the process of reading into the 'nano' constituents of Miltonic poetry, the reader comes across the single, recurring letter "d", abundantly pressed into service in the opening lines of *Paradise Lost.* Like other fine constituents of Milton's "unshorn" poetic cloth, "d" can be traced gathering, folding and pressing together the opposite ends and fibres of *Samson Agonistes.* The letter is generative of a series of Philistine names – Dalila, Dagon – but also harps on the leitmotiv of deliverance at the hands of divine power. D is the letter of Dread, as in Samson's own name, or "great dread" (Lieb 14). The letter is disseminated in Samson's narrative of his successive marriages, in lines which render palpable the dental accidents linked to his successive wedlocks, telling "how [he] sought to wed, the daughter of an Infidel," because "[he] motion'd was of God", and "urged the marriage on," that he might begin "Israel's Deliverance" (221–26). More d's can be heard than meet the eye, as the phoneme emerges phonetically as well as graphically. Some of Milton's d's, as in /marriage/, operate blindly, invisibly, as if the ingrained, pre-programmed letter of divorce haunted the text of a union meant to receive divine sanctification.

An initial d-ridden texture is made visible or audible from the opening lines of the play-poem, from the four-fold beat of "a little onward lend thy guiding hand", to recurrent words and phrases which hammer in the same resounding, battering sound-track: dark steps, day, idol, forbid, not to mention the final "d" of *Paradise Regained*, to which *Samson Agonistes*, if one quotes the 1671 title, has been, Milton says, *"added."* Reading *Samson Agonistes* can become, in other words, an early-Derridean exercise in "d-reading", or perhaps a nomadic process of rhizoming reading, after Deleuze.

Why Milton Matters, or Milton at the Mill

To return to the question posed by the community of American critics in the wake of 9/11, "why Milton matters", the term "matter" calls for re-readings in "material" terms, as well as a reappraisal of the silent metaphors at work beneath critical tools. Beyond, and regardless of the textual, Milton "matters" in the sense that new cut-off points in the "matted" material of Milton's text can be brought to light. The "text" of *Samson Agonistes* invalidates a number of assumptions and expectations attached to the textual or textural, words based on a metaphor that takes its origin in the binary, orthogonal procedures of the economics of weaving and textile-making. The "mill" on which *Samson Agonistes* opens – whether a grinding-mill, an oil-mill, or a water-extracting device – cannot be sidetracked as a mere stage prop or as an element of external or mental scenery. The initializing moment presenting Samson at the mill reads as a critical nucleus, a significant, uncouth, salient feature. The initial "milling" moment in the opening lines of Milton's "text" establishes the sense of a new, yet untapped, blind or tactile form of criticality. Beyond decorum and metaphor, the initial, productive "mill" reads as an allegory of the reading process, which involves interpretive and prosodic milling, as well as page-churning.

What "matters," then, is how Milton's power of inventiveness has produced a "matted" text, that perhaps challenges Western textual culture to the advantage of Eastern traditions in cloth-making and story-telling. Milton's "fable", to borrow the author's own category, seems to belong, ultimately, to the slippery field of spoken, rather than written, tales. As a fable, it bars and promotes the desire to interpret, and has generated a wealth of "agonistic" interpretations. Two dominant critical currents rule the field: the re-generational, and the iconoclastic, – opposing, to take quick examples, Mary Ann Radzinowicz's sense of a "progressive revelation" in *Samson Agonistes*, to David Loewenstein and Michael Lieb's analyses of the inscrutable meaning of Milton's notion of deity, a "God whose name is Dread" (Lieb, 1997, 5). The two approaches, however, can coexist like dovetailing scales rather than as opposing threads in a two-dimensional grid. Milton, it seems, has entangled the "scaly" threads of his fine poem as densely as the "hyacinthine locks" that adorn the heads of nearly all of his characters, from Comus to Eve, including his own luscious head of hair. As early as *Manso* and *Comus*, which means, etymologically, endowed with much hair, a "locked" form of approach seems in order.

Samson Agonistes' thick-set, resilient lines curl and proliferate in synchronicity with Samson's locks of hair, "regained" in the process – a term which implies new growth and recovery, not necessarily the return of a repressed, but simply a re-pressing, discontinuous fit of re-emergence. *Samson Agonistes*'s style is a matter of hairstyle.

The growth of Milton's lines, rather than the growth of Milton's mind, is, in other words, what matters. The "measure of verse", which the poem's prefatory epistle identifies as "of all sorts," generates an adverbial field which seems obsessively connected with growth, of hair in particular: "at length" significantly occurs twice in the poem's opening Argument, first in the presentation of Samson who happens "at length to be visited," and is later "at length persuaded inwardly" (*SA* 9) that the invitation to fight is from God. The poem's title generates a letter-locked frame, caught in the enclosed space of two s's – an initial one, and a final, Greek "s", suggestive of the tail-biting circularity of the mill. No relief from the "task of servile toil" is granted to whoever enters the play-poem, bond in a contract of "servile toil", until the dismissal of readers or "servants" in the concluding lines.

On a micro-scale *Samson Agonistes* lends itself to a series of "locked" readings, deadlocks of interpretation, twists and turns and conundrums. The snarled, restive, refractory fibers of Milton's poetics have entailed interpretive deadlocks opposing humanist to subversive approaches. They have also made it possible to entangle, against all interpretive and historical odds, poetic inventiveness and recent near-Eastern history. Nothing is more poetic and polemic perhaps than the uncouth connections between a name partly sprung from Milton's onomastic imagination, Harapha – a term grounded on an Arabic root for gigantism, or possibly on *rafa,* meaning a hill – and a more recent, wild offshoot, in the echoes of an Arafat, which it reverberates and uncouthly resembles "to a t." Such metamorphic "becomings" have been perhaps best described as cases of an "after-language" by Gilles Deleuze and Felix Guattari, an after-language being a proliferating series of micro-resonances and loci of resistance to the rule of signifier and signified. In such a logic, key terms can become reversible and open up contrary meanings, as in the open-ended series of ambivalent primitive terms described by Freud, quoting "a pamphlet by K. Abel, *The Antithetical Meaning of Primal Words*" (Freud 318). The term "lock", to return to one of *Samson Agonistes'* key terms, figures foremost in Abel's (and Freud's) list of reversible roots. It designates a passageway as well (as in "loch") as a shutting point. In connection with the logic of dreaming in the context of which Freud mentions this type of research, the function of such words, which Freud finds helpful to resort to in the context of his early work on dreams, make it possible to prevent interpretation, and yet, in an uncouth way, to generate it, in a hair-splitting fashion.

From Matting to Metering

At the split-end of *Samson Agonistes* looms a metric conundrum. Edward Weismiller's comprehensive essay on the subject of Miltonic verse begins by questioning "the nature of meter itself", and by stating that although the "English ten-syllable line was secure," it was "not wholly understood" (256). Some hundred pages later, the question of what Milton understands by "apt numbers" in his declaration of prosodic intentions in the note on the "verse" prefixed to *Paradise Lost*, remains open: "in this respect also there is more to do" (363).

The tail-end of *Samson Agonistes* – the place where, strategically, meaning, or what sentence-based linguistics has called "end-weight", is expected to reside – a curious, apparently cathartic phrase concludes the tragedy: "calm of mind." It reads, however, as a split-end, to follow the capillary strain, linguistically suspended or caught between two opposed meanings in English and Greek. The entire line, "calm of mind all passion spent" concludes a final stanza of fourteen lines that appears both to mimic and mock the rules of sonnet-writing. Rhythmically, the last line must either be scanned as short of one foot or stress, given the dominant pentametric context of the preceding lines, or, on the other hand, it must be scanned with a dieresis on the word passi/<u>on</u>, rendered as a sonorous, harsh, uncouth two syllable word – a "dreadful" sound effect, if one remembers how close "dread" itself stands to being an actual name of God (Lieb, 1997, 5).

The semantics of "calm" corroborate the metrics of the last line: calm, like "agonistes", is Greek and must be read with Greek in mind. The cathartic purgation or spending of all passion is contradicted rather than supported by the inconclusive, Greek-based "calm of mind", which implies heat and fire, the opposite of a calm conclusion. "Calm" has generated an extensive etymological OED entry which explores its Greek sources:

> "Calma" in Old Spanish and Portuguese means also "heat of the day" [...] Possibly derived from the Greek cauma, burning heat, fever heat, heat of the sun, heat of the day, which has given the possible development "rest during the heat of the day."

In addition to the etymological factor, the hammered plosives and the chiastic formation of "passi/on spent" provide a supplement of resistance that goes against the semantic grain of purgative "spending" – a term which, in the immediate vicinity of "acquist", takes on the monetary hue that Samson earlier associates with meretricious Dalila. A further development on the two pregnant initial letters of "SPending", which Milton's poetics aptly press, full and entangle in a literal, milling procedure, would be of Derridean inspiration – S and P being two letters on which Derrida's deconstructive *Postcard* rests (Derrida 47).

If one sticks to Milton's advice not to be "driven from the letter", "on" is the poem's penultimate syllable, which many insist should be "dead", like Mallarmé's *"pénultième."* Whether it is stressed or unstressed, the syllable is placed in an attention-grabbing position, suggestive of either surfeit or lack. If reduced to a common-or-garden two-syllable word, ("pass/ion"), the resulting reading will retain the sense of a missing beat (thus semantically relaying the spending of passion). Whether one hears it as a three-syllable or as a two-syllable term, a jarring effect on passion is achieved, bringing either excess or lack, the frustrating sense of an "un-ending".

If one ties together the two ends of *Samson Agonistes*, what emerges is an economic network of lending ("A little onward lend thy guiding hand" (l.1)) and spending ("passi/on spent" (1758). Money matters, in other words, are never severed from what "matters," although neither hoarding wealth nor capitalizing are promoted in either gesture. In the dual economy of lending and spending, what transpires is the suggestion that reading and writing, too, lend and spend. If one agrees to lend an ear to the "ore" contained in a mere syllable, a tight network links Samson to Dagon in the initial twelve lines of the play-poem, through such phonetic relays as "wont" (5), "common prison" (6), "enjoin'd" (6), "imprison'd" (7), "unwholesome" (8), "born" (11), until Dagon appears in the appropriately numbered line 13.

To return, yet once more, to "why Milton matters," this paper has brought a micro-textual confirmation of what Joseph Wittreich, in *Milton Studies* XLIV, has called "a whole series of meldings," in particular "Milton / Samson / Cromwell / Satan blurring into one another as *Samson Agonistes* proceeds" (27). In the face of such meldings, Joseph Wittreich hastens to add that "the dramatic form in which this poem is cast militates against such identifications" (27–28). What is a dramatic form not meant for acting, but a poem?

A hair's breadth separates the figures of Samson/Milton at the mill. In his early literary tribute to Manso, Milton fascinatingly envisages his own future access to posterity, by stating he would "rest in perfect peace," if a Manso-like friend agreed to "weave [his] locks with Paphian myrtle" (CP 130). A disinterred body was examined on August 17, 1790, and identified as Milton's, on the faith of a lock of hair: "On a paper, enclosing a bit of the hair, the surgeon had written, Milton's hair" (Lieb 7). Of a scaly nature, like poetry perhaps, hair (or style) lives "on".

Works Cited

Barney, Lewis, Beach, Berghof, *The Etymologies of Isidore of Seville*, Cambridge: Cambridge UP, 2006.

Deleuze Gilles and Guattari Félix, *A Thousand Plateaus*, Minneapolis: University of Minnesota Press, 1987.

Derrida, Jacques, *The Postcard*, transl. Alan Bass, Chicago and London: The University of Chicago Press, 1987.

Fish, Stanley, "Why Milton Matters; or, Against Historicism", *Milton Studies* 44, Pittsburgh: The University of Pittsburgh Press, 2005.

Freud, Sigmund, *The Interpretation of Dreams*, vol. IV, London: The Hogarth Press, 1953.

Hermann, Peter C., "Paradise Lost, the Miltonic 'or,' and the Poetics of Incertitude", *SEL, Studies in English Literature 1500–1900*, volume 53 Number 1 (Winter 2003): 181–211.

Laroche, Emmanuel, *Histoire de la racine "nem" en grec ancien*, Paris: Klincksieck, 1949.

Lieb, Michael, *Milton and the Culture of Violence*, Ithaca, NY: Cornell UP, 1994.

–. "'Our Living Dread': The God of *Samson Agonistes,*" *Milton Studies* 33 (1997): 3–26.

Milton, John, *Samson Agonistes*, ed. Michael Davis, Houndmills Basingstoke: Macmillan Education, 1977.

–. *Complete Poems and Major Prose*, ed. Merritt Hughes, New York: Macmillan Publishing Company, 1957

Mueller, Janel, "Just Measures? Versification in *Samson Agonistes*", *Milton Studies* 33 (1997): 47–82.

Ornicar? La Revue du champ freudien, ed. Jacques-Alain Miller, Paris: Navarin, numéro 25, 1982.

Roger, John, "The Secret of *Samson Agonistes*", *Milton Studies* 33 (1997): 111–132.

Weismiller, Edward R., *A Variorum Commentary on the Poems of John Milton*, Volume Four, *Paradise Regained*, London: Routledge and Kegan Paul, 1975.

Part V

Milton's Influence in Non-Anglophone Cultures

Luis Fernando Ferreira SÁ

Enjoined By Fate: Private and Public Miltons in a Nineteenth-Century Portuguese Play[1]

Je n'aime guère le mot influence, qui ne désigne
qu'une ignorance ou une hypothèse.
Paul Valéry

In literary studies in general and Milton studies in particular, the term "influence" suggests at least three related meanings. In the first sense, it implies a political position: at one time Milton's works were so well known and so widely read that they formed part of what was commonly called the national consciousness of the British Isles. In this sense, literary influence, or Milton's influence to be more specific, relates to the power or capacity from a major writer and his *œuvre* to cause an effect in indirect or intangible ways. In its temporal and historical sense, "influence" describes the social and cultural conditions related to publication, readership, and the so-called biographical tradition. Complete editions of Milton's works have succeeded each other since the last decades of the seventeenth century. Milton's readership, which was established in his own lifetime, has been on a constant increase in terms of the proportion and diversity of the readers in any given age that he has reached, let alone the degree to which biographers have succeeded in creating an enduring image of the writer: sometimes as an emanation of spiritual and moral force and at other times as an emanation of some occult power said to derive from stars or celestial muses. As a critical category, "influence" both encapsulates and exceeds its political and temporal connotations: literary influence purports to analyze not only the logic of acquired authority and prestige but also the capacity of the term itself to articulate viable critical takes on an author's or work's "weight," "credit," and persuasion.[2] Although there are many long-standing critiques

1 I use the verb "enjoin" both as to direct or impose by authoritative order or with admonition and also, as in a Derridean play, to enjoy a yoke or burden or fate from which there is no escape.

2 In relation to the notion of influence and its various connotations in literary and Milton studies, Havens (1922) provides a list of critical claims for correspondences be-

of literary influence, scholars are still struggling to adapt this word to their own critical vocabulary. How can alternative views on influence enhance our critical apparatus? What barriers do we – informed readers and critics – confront when we attempt to employ it as an analytic concept? If we turn our attention to the epigraph, why have we been forced to love it less and less each day?

In this paper, I want to use Francisco da Costa Braga's *Milton: A Comedy in One Act*[3] to think more about the value and limitations of the term "influence" for Milton scholarship. This one-act comedy takes place at "Honton," Buckingham County, and had as its main characters: the old and blind poet Milton; his daughter Emma; William Davenant's son, Lord Arthur Davenant; the Quaker judge Godwen; and Godwen's niece, Miss Carlota. The dramatic narrative centers on Emma and Carlota's machinations to have Arthur enter Milton's service without his knowing that Arthur was a young man. What Milton and the other characters did not know, however, was that Arthur was the son of William Davenant, the Parliamentary member and poet, and a favorite of Charles II. Arthur engaged himself as Milton's amanuensis and reader in order to "save" the old poet from political persecution. Alongside this dramatic "political" narrative, there is also a comic "romantic" narrative running through the play: Carlota thought Arthur is in love with her, but Arthur loves Emma instead, who renounces her love for Carlota's sake. In the end, love conquers Emma and Arthur with Milton's consent. This paper will then discuss how the private and the public Miltons enjoined the play, in terms of a contemporary assessment of literary influence, so as to produce a provocative critical reception of this

---

tween one poem and the other; Sanderlin (1938) reads influence and genre in terms of (inter)textual relationship; Bate (1970) addresses influence in terms of a burden; Bloom (1973) proposes a series of revisionary ratios inscribed in an Oedipal struggle; McArthur (1988) assesses influence in terms of stolen writings or re-writings; Hogan (1995) advocates a grammar of influence inserted in an economy of innovation; and DuRocher (2001) conjoins influence and pedagogy. Recent studies show scholars either debating with Bloom, such as Reid's (2003: 667) – "Eighteenth-century poets imitated the classics with an inventiveness that is remarkably free from anxiety of influence" – or assessing influence in terms of depth/surface borrowings, of close intertextual reinterpretation, and of a "literary debt owed Milton" (Urbanczyk 2003: 281).

3 I warmly thank Angelica Duran for having shared with me this nineteenth-century Portuguese play.

major English Renaissance writer in the Portuguese world of the nineteenth century.

With this in mind, it would be relatively easy to argue that Braga's *Milton* demonstrates the critical need for a more contemporary theory of influence. Read in this way, the play's romantic and comic effects suggest that there is more to influence than the mere acts of alluding to, imitating, rewriting, or (violently) rejecting a precursor, be it an author or a work. Like Milton, who, as a character in need of a reader (Arthur), ends Braga's play by an act of consent and recommendation, it would be tempting to read this play trying to rethink Milton as an analogy for literary influence. But, Braga's Milton's words first: "Well, well, I consent. Emma, the dearest daughter of my soul, is yours, milord. Tranquil about my fate and my daughter's, I will consecrate whatever is left of my past hectic life to the muses, looking forward to recommending my name to the memory of Men."[4] Furthermore, we could feasibly interpret the play's temporal horizon as a weapon of writers and scholars concerned with influence. Along these lines, Braga's *Milton* may be read as suggesting that influence is the act or power of producing an effect without an apparent exertion of force – recommendation – or without direct exercise of command – consent. Influence, Milton and Braga seem to propose, supersedes consenting to someone or something and means recommending a name to memory and its writing, tradition. We could argue plausibly that Braga's play is a replay of Miltonic themes and, as a consequence, renews (a Miltonic) tradition. The play simultaneously refutes the idea of influence as corrupt interference with authority for personal gain while exploring the possibility of influence as an emerging site of influx and inflow of power: the power of a name and of memory. In short, I propose "influence" here be taken as an influx of power in the sense of "a coming in of a name to memory" and as an inflow[5] of power in the sense of "a flowing in of memory to tradition."

4 All translations from the Portuguese are mine. Braga's words run as follows: "*Milton.* Pois bem, consinto. Emma, a filha querida da minha alma é sua, milord. Tranqüilo a respeito da minha sorte e da de minha filha, irei consagrando ás muzas, o resto de uma vida agitadíssima, procurando recommendar o meu nome á memória dos homens" (1867: 25).

5 An inflow should be viewed as deriving from "Influere," that is, to flow in. An inflow and an influx have the same etymological origin, diverging, though, in usage. Influx means "a coming in" as in "an influx of tourists" and an inflow means "a flowing in" as in "the inflow of air" and "an inflow of funds." In short, whereas an influx has a to-

But any attempt to read the play as an argument for the usefulness of "influence" as a critical term must be complicated by the text's deployment of historically specific social and political relationships in England during the Restoration. We need to evaluate, in other words, whether or not a theory of influence based on influx and inflow may be extracted from Braga's play and Milton. In the case of an influx of influence, one of Braga's subplots in *Milton* concentrates on Godwen returning from court after having appealed to the King's magistrates in Milton's favor. However, the appeal had no effect and he returns only to report that Milton's name is on the fatal list, a list that would contain the name of those who would be put to death or imprisoned. Court emissaries are already on the look-out for those on the list, but Milton's place of self-exile is unknown. Godwen then reassures Carlota and Emma that there is nothing to worry about, since there is a last hope. Since Milton had saved Lord Davenant from death penalty at the time the Protectorate (under Oliver Cromwell) were executing the so-called enemies of the Republic, Lord Davenant can now repay Milton by saving him from the wrath of Charles II, the restored King. But to no avail: to Godwen's ears there comes no reply from Lord Davenant and they all conclude help is not coming so that an escape to Scotland is all the hope there is. Milton confides this piece of information to Arthur, who, Milton thinks, being old, cannot bear the burden: "How would your feeble arm draw the enemy back, supplant danger?"[6] Arthur convinces Milton that he, though past his youth, would serve the (un)glorious poet best by his side. There is a turn of events: Arthur, the reader and amanuensis Carlota introduced to Milton's service, was visited by a servant who happened to call him milord. A second time, the servant from the House of the Davenants brings Arthur news and Godwen then realizes that he must be a traitor to Milton's cause. There is another turn of events: Arthur produces a letter from the Minister of State declaring to Lord Davenant, Arthur's father, that Milton is saved by the intercession of such a good friend both to the King and Milton. The subplot in question exemplifies a coming in of several names to memory: Arthur's, Davenant's, Milton's. Furthermore, Milton's name is brought to memory (recalled) on different levels: as an old friend to both nobility and protectorate, as an old poet exiled at

tality in view (building, country, national site), an inflow does not necessarily hold a totality in view.

6 "Como é que o seu debil braço arredaria os inimigos, supplantaria o perigo?" (Braga 1867: 18).

home, as an old man beguiled by his reader (Arthur), as the poet who once suffered his readers to know that Satan deceived Uriel: "For neither man nor angel can discern / Hypocrisy, the only evil that walks / Invisible" (*PL* 3.682–84).[7]

The play demonstrates how theories of influence must be read through very specific situations and material circumstances. Arthur's hypocrisy, whether his act of playing a part on the stage or his feigning to be what he is not, definitively reminds readers of Milton's previous depiction of Satan as a false dissembler. The case in question, its material circumstance, is not only Milton as historical figure, nor is it only Milton the bio-graphed subject, but Milton's *Paradise Lost.* "Milton's achievement commanded admiration, encouraged emulation, and offered opportunities" (Griffin 1989: 247) on various levels of influence and as an influx of power: names that are converted to memory. Furthermore, this memory appears to play around ignorance (not knowing and not discerning), on the one hand, and on hypotheses (or hypocrisies), on the other. The material name that had been causing "hate" – influence –, to return once more to the epigraph, seems now to be circumstantiating an influx.

In the case of Braga's *Milton,* I argue that the play reads the way it does – as a site of emergence for influx and inflow of influence – because the play's trajectory is not fully compatible with the historical circumstances it wishes to dramatize. History, at least the officially written (graphed) one, may tell us another story. But what counts here is the appropriation and assimilation of Milton's language and conception of human history. Braga's *Milton* stages, as another subplot, a love story of romantic misdemeanors (Adam and Eve in *Paradise Lost,* or Arthur and Emma in *Milton*) very much based on artifice, salvation, and sacred debt: "*Arthur.* Pardon an innocent artifice which demanded your own salvation, for the necessity of surely paying this sacred debt off."[8] One might even say that what is the "economic basis" here, to use a dear term to Marxists of all persuasions, may be Milton's creative pressure, Milton's stature, or even Milton exerting a powerful, multiform influence. And on the other hand, the superstructure that underwrites the play is Milton, the name followed by its memories: not as a

7 I might add Milton as a hypocritical old Oedipus. "*Milton.* Isn't it true, Arthur, that I take after Oedipus?" My translation of: "*Milton.* Não é verdade, Arthur, que me pareço muito com Oedipo?" (Braga 1867: 14).

8 "*Arthur.* Perdoe um innocente arteficio que demandava a sua propria salvação, pela precisão de mais seguramente saldar essa divida sagrada" (Braga 1867: 24).

pre-emptor or a blocking figure, but an inspiration and a resource. Milton/name/memory may even represent a walk on memory lane: an imaginary path through the nostalgically remembered past when both writer and reader were free from any anxiety of Miltonic influence.[9] What one owes to Milton is not knowledge but power. In other words, one owes him the "exercise and expansion to (one's) own latent capacity of sympathy with the infinite," as written by Thomas De Quincey, one of the last Romantics, cited by Joseph Wittreich (1970: 492), a Milton scholar keen on influence. In yet other words, one owes him nothing because influence should not be gauged in terms of debit and credit, which are accounting notions. It is rather an inflow of memory to and towards tradition. The latter may as well be a "line of vision" (Wittreich 1975: 141): a Miltonic tradition of prophecy in which the poets regarded themselves, and also committed themselves to memory, as the spiritual men who would usher in a new order and a new age. Whether this new order and age have ever been ushered in does not lie within the scope of this paper, but what is of cardinal importance in relation to the constitution of any such tradition is the possibility of a true name to be distrusted, a name whose material circumstance is to be found in the play in question: "*Arthur.* If Charles II's favorite had presented himself in this house with his true name, it would only intensify your distrust".[10]

This distrust of history and of a true name becomes very clear, for example, when we examine (Milton's) influence as an inflow of power. In the logic of Ezra Pound (1979) and T. S. Eliot (1997), Milton was either a sort of poison or a ghost that had not been laid to rest. To put it more provocatively, literary influence and Milton's influence in particular would grow on

9 On a similar note, Renza (1995: 201) views Bloom's anxiety of influence as such: "From the poststructuralist perspective, Bloom's theory of influence and its machines of fluxing ratios thus only eventuates in a Freudian 'science fiction': a repressed knowledge of its own fictionality, all the more repressed for giving itself room to entertain this self-fictionality. Yet even for Derrida, 'writing' always already transpires through the desire for self-presence – or in Bloomian terms through the writer's (and reader's) quest for radical textual independence. And if 'writing' disseminates this willful desire, such desire also tends to reclaim or identify with this very act of dissemination, which act in turn becomes reducible as yet another 'latecomer's defense, since it seeks to make of [writing] a perpetual earliness,' or to repress 'the shadows of anteriority' [Bloom]".

10 "*Arthur.* Se o favorito de Carlos II se tivesse apresentado nesta caza com o seu verdadeiro nome, só excitaria a sua desconfiança e a de seus amigos" (Braga 1867: 24).

the fertile soil of being simultaneously a poison and a ghost. Both terms are inserted in the play of memory[11] in the sense that memory as a mark will tell one what drug is to kill (poison) and what to cure. Furthermore, memory as a mark will be in charge of alerting one when and where a spectral apparition is to be recalled as such and in opposition, for instance, to delusion, hallucination, fantasy, desire. In the long run, sedimentary memory (mark) will turn into a tradition, whether the tradition of asserting Milton's Latinisms and his aggravating the dissociation of sensibility in the late seventeenth century, the tradition of a line of prophetic vision, or the tradition of "Miltonizing."[12] In this sense, Milton becomes a name, a memory, a tradition, a mark whose lineaments have to do more with an absence than with a presence. In other words, Milton is a presence that is simultaneously an absence and a presence/mark of this absence.

John Shawcross (1991), for example, looked at what he called "presence," focusing less on direct quotations or sources from one author to another, as the word "influence" might usually connote, and not being concerned with anxiety that might arise for one author toward the other who is being emulated. According to Shawcross,

> 'Presence' suggests the way in which intertextuality may exist as one author or work may be discerned as having a relationship with another, not necessarily as source and not necessarily as direct influence. This kind of intertextuality allows us to understand one work in terms of its related text, regardless of chronological sequence. Such 'presence' evokes a sense in a later or in an earlier writer that may supply an allusion, a comparison, a contrast, simply an understanding that might otherwise be missed by the reader but that leads us to reading of one of those authors or both that might be otherwise overlooked (1998: 41).

When properly done, a study of influence does not merely recount a causal sequence that led to the production or reception of a novel, poem, or play. Rather, it places the novel or poem or play in a literary context that (geo/bio)graphically enhances it in terms of an absent presence and in view of (im)possible rewritings/re-readings. As the homely Milton states in

11 I read memory as stemming from the Greek *mermera* – care, as an activity closely associated with re-membering. Memory is the wife of Zeus and mother of the Muses. It is thus power as an ordering principle, as that which links past-present-future.

12 I use the term as a free play on the notion of influence as translating the impossible debt to Milton, his name, and of influence as meaning borrowings from a Miltonic memory.

Braga's play: "*Milton.* The perfume I breathe in as I enter this room makes me acknowledge that there is in here a flower which is not vulgar."[13] This perfume/flower that is breathed in, that flows in, is not the generally used, applied, or accepted term influence. The flower to which *Milton* refers suggests to me an enjoined fate that reaches the ear as enjoyed. Milton's private and public names – the memories associated with these names, and the tradition that results from such associations – have been directed, but not imposed, by a will to order (name/memory/tradition). This ordering principle, though urgent and admonitory, is influence in progress. Vulgar (referred to texts written in a vernacular) and in/vulgar (referred to those unwilling to simply display knowledge), both writer and reader (Braga, Milton, Arthur, myself) have been entangled by the influx and the inflow of power, which is influence at work. Under the influence of power, we should always already enjoy both haunting the text and hunting for texts.

Works Cited

Bate, W. J. *The Burden of the Past and the English Poet.* Cambridge: Cambridge UP, 1970.

Bloom, Harold. *The Anxiety of Influence.* Oxford: Oxford UP, 1973.

Braga, Francisco da Costa. *Milton: a comedia em um acto.* Lisboa: Ferreira & Franco, 1867.

DuRocher, Richard J. *Milton Among the Romans: The Pedagogy and Influence of Milton's Latin Curriculum.* Pittsburgh: Duquesne UP, 2001.

Eliot, T. S. *The Sacred Wood: Essays on Poetry and Criticism.* London: Faber and Faber, 1997.

Griffin, Dustin. "Milton's Literary Influence." In: Danielson, Dennis (Ed.). *The Cambridge Companion to Milton.* Cambridge: Cambridge UP, 1989. 243–260.

Havens, R. D. *The Influence of Milton on English Poetry.* Harvard: Harvard UP, 1922.

Hogan, Patrick Colm. *Joyce, Milton, and the Theory of Influence.* Gainesville: University Press of Florida, 1995.

McArthur, Murray. *Stolen Writings: Blakes's Milton, Joyce's Ulysses, and the Nature of Influence.* Ann Arbor, Mich.: UMI Research Press, 1988.

Milton, John. *John Milton: Complete Poems and Major Prose.* Hughes, Merritt Y. (Ed.). New York: Odyssey Press, 1957.

Pound, Ezra. *Literary Essays.* Westport, Conn.: Greenwood Press: 1979.

Reid, David. "Thomson's Poetry of Reverie and Milton." *Studies in English Literature 1500–1900*, 43 (2003): 667–82.

13 "*Milton.* Pelo perfume que respiro ao entrar n'este gabinete conheço que há aqui uma flor que não é vulgar" (Braga 1867: 12).

Renza, Louis A. "Influence," In: Lentricchia, Frank and McLaughlin, Thomas (Eds). *Critical Terms for Literary Study*. Chicago: The University of Chicago Press, 1995. 186–202.

Sanderlin, George William. "The Influence of Milton and Wordsworth on the Early Victorian Sonnet." ELH, *A Journal of English Literary History*, 5 (1938): 225–51.

Shawcross, John T. *John Milton and Influence: Presence in Literature, History and Culture*. Pittsburgh: Duquesne UP, 1991.

–. "John Milton and His Spanish and Portuguese Presence," *Milton Quarterly*, 32 (1998): 41–52.

Urbanczyk, Aaron. "Melville's Debt to Milton: Inverted Satanic Morphology and Rhetoric in *The Confidence-Man*." *Papers on Language and Literature*, 39 (2003): 281–306.

Chia-Yin HUANG

The Miltonic Personality: Milton as a Model of Liberty in China*

In 1923, the article "Milton and China" written by Tian Han appeared in the July issue of *Young China* magazine. The article began by quoting in Chinese translation the first eight lines of Wordsworth's sonnet "London" (1802), in which the speaker invoked Milton's spirit to rise again and rekindle virtue and liberty in England. Comparing the socio-cultural crisis of China at the turn of the century to the political turmoil in Wordsworth's England nearly a century earlier, Tian Han hoped that his introduction of Milton to China could help alleviate China's present maladies. Using Wordsworth's invocation "Milton! thou should'st be living at this hour: / England hath need of thee …" as the lead-in for his biographical account of Milton, Tian Han's treatment of Milton illustrates the interesting phenomenon of the reception of Milton in China. Like the eighteenth and nineteenth century English writers who appropriated Milton as a symbol of freedom and moral integrity for nineteenth century England, the Chinese writers in the 1920s and 30s appropriated Milton as a model of liberty for modern China.

China in the late nineteenth and early twentieth century was undergoing drastic transformation resulting from a series of political, diplomatic, economic, and social crises. As the traditional norms were considered stagnant and insufficient to cope with the changes of the modern world, new cultural norms had to be developed. Consequently a new class of young, foreign-educated intellectuals in the early twentieth century looked to the Western culture for new ideas to propose new norms for modern China. Among the diverse fields of knowledge that were influenced by these West-

* I would like to thank Professor Hideyuki Shitaka, professor at Hiroshima Prefectural Women's University, who kindly provided me with the original Japanese text of Zhang Changgong's translation of Iichiro Tokutomi's *Toho to miruton*. I am also very grateful for Ms. Lynn Sauvé, editing consultant of Bookman Books, Ltd., who gave me many useful suggestions on the structure and English style of this paper.

ern ideas, literature played an important role. Many of the new intellectuals devoted themselves to introduce and translate foreign authors and works into China. They believed that the reform of Chinese literature was fundamental to the modernization of Chinese culture. Western literature reflected new ideas, norms, and models formerly unavailable in China like naturalism and symbolism. The new intellectuals dug into this rich reserve of new resources, looking for new perspectives, genres, and styles, which could be incorporated into modern Chinese literature. They found role models – that is, foreign writers, politicians, and intellectuals who exemplified the ideals or actions they sought. Liang Qichao extolled Oliver Cromwell as a political hero who opened the space of liberty for the English people (2). Lu Xun lauded Byron as an advocate of freedom, national independence, and resistance to oppression (66). Shelley was praised for his undaunted statements against Christian doctrines and dominant ideologies (Lu Xun 83–87).

Among these personal models adopted from the West, Milton occupied a unique position. He was the only pre-modern poet lauded not simply for literary achievements but for political contributions. As the new elites generally paid more attention to Western literature of the nineteenth and twentieth century, only a limited number of pre-modern authors and works were introduced to China.[1] The works before the Romantic period were often considered remote or irrelevant to the goal of modernizing China. Some elites believed that the Western classics such as *Divine Comedy*, *Faust*, and *Paradise Lost* should not be translated for the time being because they did not answer the pressing need of reform in China.[2] Nevertheless, Milton stood out as a distinct foreign pre-modern hero. He was highly praised by the new elites not because his poetic works answered their immediate concerns, but because his character, thoughts, and political contribution were perfect materials for fashioning an intellectual hero who served the cause of liberty with unrelenting devotion. As the character Chen in Liang Qichao's novella *The Future of New China* (1902–3) asserted, "Milton helped Cromwell accomplish the great enterprise of the English Revolution; Byron … gave up his life for the independence of Greece. Such personalities deserve our worship. They are reputed not merely for literature" (51). Therefore, it was

1 For the foreign literary influences in early twentieth-century China, see Leo Ou-Fan Lee, "Literary Trends I: The Quest for Modernity, 1895–1927." In *The Cambridge History of China* 464–504.

2 There was a series of debates in literary journals on what works should be translated in the 1920s. See Shen, Zou, and Zheng's remarks on the issue.

the "Miltonic noble personality" – in Liang Zhinan's word – that touched the new intellectual hearts across time and cultural difference (154: 2).

This article examines the Chinese portrayals of Milton in literary writings during the 1920s and 30s. It discusses the ways in which Milton was fashioned as an ideal poet-statesman who committed his pen to the pursuit of liberty and the political revolution in his country. It examines the terms "liberty," "liberalism," "democracy," and "republic" frequently associated with Milton in Chinese writings and compares these terms to the idea of liberty presented in Milton's own political tracts. Revealing the Chinese appropriation of Milton, this paper shows how a different culture may transform foreign models to meet its specific historical context and cultural needs.

To the new intellectuals, Milton was an unusual foreign hero who maintained his integrity in the face of many challenges and devoted himself whole-heartedly to poetry and at the same time to politics. He was admired as a foreign model that inspired them to push for political and cultural reforms in China. Liang Zhinan, for instance, extolled Milton as a "shining star of world poetry, an unprecedented poet in England," whose works epitomized his splendid heroic actions and sacred thoughts. To him, Milton was not only a poet but also "a diligent scholar, a devoted patriot, and an enthusiastic admirer of liberty" (153: 2). He encouraged the Chinese poets to follow Milton's example and produce works that could elevate the declining spirit of China (153: 2).

Moreover, Milton was often elevated to the position of great statesman equal to Cromwell or as literary counterpart of Cromwell in the English political scene. Jin Donglei said, "When Cromwell directed the government, Milton was the Chief Secretary. With these two great men, one in literature and the other with military exploits, who led the Puritans and the people to implement the republican rule, the English political scene was sure to be secure" (152).

Understood as a major intellectual leader in English Revolution, Milton was often portrayed as the spokesperson for liberty and the English Commonwealth against monarchy. In Chinese writings of the period, three points in Milton's life were frequently presented as manifestations of his commitment to liberty: (a) Milton's decision to cut short his tour in Europe due to the revolution; (b) Milton's declaration that his left hand was his weapon to fight for liberty; and (c) Milton's willingness to sacrifice his sight for liberty. In most Chinese portrayals of Milton, *ziyiou*, the Chinese term for "liberty", became the poet's signature trait. He was often described as a poet who used his pen and ink, rather than swords, to fight for liberty. Tian Han characterized Milton as a polemicist who advocated liberty in both the public and the private sectors:

> He condemned censorship and promoted three liberties: religious liberty, domestic liberty, and individual liberty. Domestic liberty included the freedom of marriage, of education, and of expression. He believed that the three liberties were the foundation for one's happiness as a member of society. Apart from a few sonnets, Milton devoted his pen almost entirely to the struggles for liberty and justice in politics and religion in the subsequent decades. For the time being, he gave up the ambition to write a great national narrative poem. His aspiration for literary creativity yielded to concern for the troubled times! (3)

In addition to *ziyiou*, the Chinese writers often qualified Milton's liberty with political terms such as *ziyiou zhuyi* (liberalism), *minzhu* (democracy), and *gonghe* (republic). They seemed to use these terms as synonymous expressions that denote a set of interrelated political concepts.

Milton's liberty was sometimes labeled as *ziyiou zhuyi*, the Chinese translation for "liberalism" – especially in the writings derived or translated from Japanese sources.[3] In Zhang Changgong's "Milton and Du Fu," a partial translation of Iichiro Tokutomi's *Toho to miruton*, the poet's political stance was described as such: "Milton's basic principle was liberalism. His goal was to make this liberalism applicable to religion, politics, education, and thoughts." (19) Sun Lianggong, who consulted the Japanese reference work *Sekai nihyaku bungō* for his biographical sketches of world authors, said that Milton wrote to defend Puritanism and liberalism (6).

The frequent association of *minzhu* (democracy) with *ziyiou* in these writings makes it almost an alternative term for liberty in the portrayals of Milton. For instance, Jin Donglei praised Milton's devotion to defend the Commonwealth as a commitment to democracy and described his continental rival Salmasius, the author of *Eikon Basilike*, as an enemy to democracy:

> in response to *Eikon Basilike*, the work written by an anti-democratic scholar, [Milton] wrote numerous tracts to defend the new government and criticize Charles I for vio-

3 Many of the new intellectuals studied in Japan. Some of the writers learned Western literature through Japanese sources. For the history of the new intellectuals' foreign education in Japan, see Paula Harrell, *Sowing the Seeds of Change: Chinese Students, Japanese Teachers, 1895–1905* (Stanford: Stanford UP, 1992).

> lating the constitution and for inadequate handling of the parliament. While completing these tracts, he gradually lost his eyesight. When he was writing the tracts, his friends and relatives advised him not to work so hard, he answered steadfastly, "I am willing to sacrifice my eyes for liberty." What a commitment to democracy! (155–56)

Recurrently allied with "democracy" was the term *gonghe* (republic). The Chinese writers often used it to characterize the English Commonwealth Milton defended vehemently. Tian Han described the Commonwealth during the interregnum as a "democratic republic" that deposed the king, promoted religious freedom, and implemented parliamentary representation (4).

With these Chinese terms for "liberty," "liberalism," "democracy," and "republic," the Chinese writers established Milton's image as the poet-statesman who promoted liberty and defended the democratic republic throughout his life. However, these terms do not necessarily correspond to the idea of liberty presented in Milton's works.

Studies on Chinese political terms in the late nineteenth and early twentieth century show that these terms were drawn from ancient Chinese texts and adapted for translations of modern Western political concepts.[4] According to Xiong Yuezhi, the term *ziyiou* was first used in the Western sense in a newspaper article "On the Principles of Liberty and Mutual Love in the West" in 1887 (72). It also appeared in a translation of Herbert Spencer's treatise "On Liberty" serialized in *A Review of the Times* between May 1900 and January 1902. In the preface to his translation of John Stuart Mill's *On Liberty* in 1903, Yan Fu explained his use of *ziyiou* as the translation of "liberty" despite *ziyiou*'s traditional connotation of "without restraint" or "unbridled." (1) *Minzhu* was first used to denote a democratic political system in W. A. P. Martin's Chinese translation of Wheaton's *Elements of International Law* published in 1864 (Xiong 74). According to Jin Guantao and Liu Qingfong's analysis, *minzhu* (literally "lord of the people") usually designated a leader elected by the people, as opposed to the monarch (*junzhu*, "a monarchical lord") in nineteenth-century discussions of Western political systems (31–32). *Gonghe* in the classical texts means the joint rule of two or more aristocrats (Feng 7). In the late nineteenth century, it often appeared

4 Some studies suggested that the Chinese terms used to translate Western political concepts were often influenced by Japanese translations. See Xie and Feng. Also Xiong, Yueji, *Zhongguo jindai minzhu xixiangshi (The Democratic Ideas in Modern China: A History)* (Shanghai: Shanghai People's Publisher, 1986), 10–13.

in the phrase *gonghe guo*, a term used interchangeably with *minzhu guo* to designate a commonwealth or a republic (Fang 54). It was later adopted by Dr. Sun Yat-Sien and his fellow revolutionaries in their revolutionary discourse against imperial rule (Feng 11). As these were new terms developed through translation, they were unfamiliar concepts to the Chinese intellectuals. The translations have not been stabilized and these three terms were often used interchangeably to denote a constitutional democracy with parliamentary representation.

These terms emerged in late nineteenth-century Chinese political discourse as China was transforming from a traditional empire to a modern nation. Young Chinese intellectuals observed Western political systems in action and translated major political writings from the West in the hope of finding feasible political alternatives and building China into a strong modern nation. Yan Fu, for instance, translated Huxley's *Evolution and Ethics*, John Stuart Mill's *On Liberty*, and other nineteenth-century political writings in his efforts to find a path to wealth and power for China in the modern world (Schwartz 63). To Yan, the Western theories of social evolution, liberty, and democracy provided both a conceptual framework and a practical option for reforming the Chinese political system. The intellectuals' understanding of these concepts was generally shaped by the ultimate concern for reorganizing China with the most rational and effective political system available in the modern era – that is, a democratic government of the people, whose rights and freedoms were protected by law.[5]

In the early twentieth century – especially after the May-Fourth Movement[6], "democracy" became a watchword that epitomized the political and cultural ideals shared by the new intellectuals. Chen Duxiu proposed Mr. Democracy and Mr. Science as the symbolic models that could solve the problems of China: "Now we are confident that only these two gentlemen [Mr. Democracy and Mr. Science] can save China from political, moral,

5 See studies on the Chinese elites' understanding of "democracy" in Gu, Xiong, Xie, Fang, and Zhu.

6 [NB] The May Fourth Movement was an anti-imperialist, cultural, and political movement in early modern China. It began on May 4, 1919 and marked the upsurge of Chinese nationalism, and a re-evaluation of Chinese cultural institutions, such as Confucianism. The movement grew out of dissatisfaction with the Treaty of Versailles settlement, termed the Shandong Problem. Coming out of the New Culture Movement, the end result was a drastic change in society that fuelled the birth of the Communist Party of China (1921).

intellectual, and mental darkness" (98). Li Dazhao said: "All aspects of modern life are influenced by Democracy and run according to Democracy. You can find it in the political, economic, social, ethical, educational and religious realms, even in literature and art. Everything in modern life is dominated by it" (Translation cited from Gu 604) (138). At the personal level, *minzhu* or "democracy" was grounded on independence, freedom, and equality of individuals (Wu 18–9). At the public level, it referred to an ideal political and moral order of a democratic republic founded on the principles of freedom, equality, and independence (Wu 19). To the new intellectuals, only when the principles of freedom, equality, and independence were fully integrated into the political system and social life could China really established itself as a modern democracy. Thus, the new intellectuals conflated the modern political ideas such as liberty, equality, personal and political independence, and republican government into the one big word "democracy." In their writings, *ziyiou*, *minzhu*, and *gonghe* usually came together as interrelated concepts that defined the ideal political principles for modern China.

Not surprisingly, the new intellectuals had a very different understanding of liberty from Milton's pre-modern conception. Although Milton favored a commonwealth ruled by a permanent group of elected representatives, he was not necessarily thinking about universal suffrage and franchise. Dzelzainis observed, "Milton managed to remain equivocal on the subject of monarchy as such [...], he displayed a high degree of indifference with regard to constitutional forms" (19). In his regicide tract *The Tenure of Kings and Magistrates* (1649), Milton redefined Kings and Magistrates as deputies to whom the people entrusted authority, not masters who ruled by arbitrary power. Milton stressed the people's right to replace the King or the Magistrates when they failed to perform their duties according to the Laws. However, his argument centered on the covenantal relationship between the king (or the magistrates) and the people. The people entrusted authority and power to the king (or the magistrates) by common consent, so the actual power was still in the hands of the entrusted deputies:

> Not to be thir Lords and Maisters [...] but, to be thir Deputies and Commissioners, to execute, by vertue of thir intrusted power, that justice which else every man by the bond of nature and of Cov'nant must have executed for himself, and for one another (*CPW* 3: 199).

Although Milton proposed the elected Grand Council as the ideal form of political representation in *The Ready and Easy Way to Establish a Free Commonwealth* (1660), by no means did he conceive it in the sense of modern democratic elections. The term of the Council members was permanent; no succession was necessary except by death or just accusation. The members would not be elected by universal suffrage. Only those who met certain socioeconomic requirements were qualified for the election:

> if the people [...] will seriously and calmly now consider thir own good, thir own libertie and the only means therof, as shall be heer laid before them, and will elect thir Knights and Burgesses able men, and according to the just and necessarie qualifications decreed in Parlament, men not addicted to a single person or house of lords, the work is don (*CPW* 7: 367–8).

The numerous local commonwealths, which came together to form the greater Commonwealth, were still controlled by the nobility and gentry rather than the general public:

> if every county in the land were made a little commonwealth, and thir chief town a city, if it be not so call'd already; where the nobilities and chief gentry may build, houses or palaces, befitting their qualitie, may bear part in the government, make their own judicial lawes, and execute them by their own elected judicatures, without appeal, in all things of civil government between man and man (*CPW* 7: 383).

Moreover, Milton's idea of liberty had a strong connection with Christian ideology and the Bible – a phenomenon entirely ignored by the Chinese writers. His civil liberty was deeply rooted in Christian theology of creation and free will. For Milton, God's creation presupposes universal free will and equality. No single person or group of persons can assume absolute authority before the rest of the human beings, because God is the only Supreme Power that everyone answers. It was Adam's transgression and men's corruption that caused men to fall from the originally free state and required human delegation (*CPW* 3: 198–9). The kings and magistrates were human institutions designed to remedy the postlapsarian loss of harmony. People submit to such a "human ordinance" only for the maintenance of justice and order. Yet they should not submit "to any civil power unaccountable, unquestionable, and not to be resisted" as it violates God's supreme ordinance of free will (Id., 209)

The Chinese writers of Milton showed no knowledge of Milton's arguments on civil liberty, regicide, the Commonwealth, and the divine ordinance of freedom. I can find no evidence of any mention or discussion of Milton's actual statements on liberty and the institution of government. They saw no difference between Milton's definition of liberty and their own. Not taking into account the context of Milton's discourse, they saw his prose works as an abstract body of work manifesting his commitment to liberty and democracy.

The discrepancy between Milton's liberty and the liberty attributed to Milton by the Chinese writers was produced through two levels of mediation. Firstly, the Chinese writers learned about Milton mainly from secondary sources. Milton's political writings were not available in Chinese translation till the 1950s. There were only translations of Milton's poetical works – *Paradise Lost* and a few shorter poems – in the 1920s and 30s. According to the references presented in the texts, the writers mainly consulted nineteenth-century European criticism on Milton and often cited complimentary statements on Milton by the critics. Tian Han and Jin Donglei, for instance, both quote a long passage by Hippolyte Taine on Milton's later life (Tian 6; Jin 159). Jin Donglei also cited Wordsworth, Tennyson, and George Saintsbury to characterize Milton's achievements (158). According to Liang Zhinan's bibliography, he consulted David Masson's edition of *Milton's Poetical Works* and several critical accounts of Milton by George Saintsbury, Henry S. Pancost, R. B. Halleck and others (154: 3). It was very likely that the nineteenth-century European criticism helped shape some of the Chinese portrayals of Milton. Tian Han's and other writers' reference to Wordsworth's remarks on Milton suggests a strong connection between the Chinese interpretations of Milton and the images of Milton in nineteenth-century European literary criticism – although this is yet to be proven.[7]

Secondly, the Chinese writers read secondary accounts of Milton analogously, not in an attempt to understand him in his original cultural context, but to discover his cultural significance for modern China. Liang Zhinan, for instance, illustrated Milton's life with Chinese analogies (e.g. citing Chinese poems and idioms) and urged modern Chinese poets to follow Milton's example in producing "true" poetry for China (153: 2). As shown

7 The writers might have consulted Japanese translations of nineteenth-century European criticism, considering that some had studied in Japan or used Japanese writings on Milton as their sources. Unfortunately the writers rarely specified their sources or provided bibliographies for the works they have consulted. It will require detailed biographical research on the writers in order to determine the extent of Japanese influences in their portrayals of Milton.

earlier, Tian Han drew analogy between Wordsworth's invocation and his recruiting of Milton; he attempted to establish Milton as a foreign intellectual remedy that could save China from political and social crises. Gao Changnan and Yi Zhen pointed out the similarity between Milton's Satan and the Monkey King in the Chinese novel *A Journey to West* as symbols of free spirit, independence, and resistance against oppressive authority – symbols that they believed Milton secretly endorsed for the promotion of liberty (230; 58).

In these Chinese portrayals, Milton was twice removed from the seventeenth-century context and re-encoded into Chinese political discourse. When reading their nineteenth-century sources, they selected elements compatible to their modern discourse of democracy and wove them into an ideal intellectual hero who inspired their efforts to reform and modernize China. Through such refashioning, Milton embodied the modern political and cultural ideals the Chinese intellectuals attempted to import from the West. The idealized image of Milton was the junction where Western ideas and the Chinese intellect joined to spark off reform efforts in China. Thus, the appropriation of Milton may be considered an epitome of cross-cultural transformation in early twentieth-century China. It shows how a canonical writer in one culture can be reincarnated in another with a new image and significance customized for that receptor culture. It presents how a culture negotiates between the foreign and the familiar and how the foreign may be integrated into the domestic discourse to motivate cultural change.

Works Cited

Chen, Douxiu. "Xinqingnian zueian zhi dabianshu (Rejoinder to Accusations Against *New Youth*)." *Xin Qingnian (New Youth)* 6.1 (Jan. 1919): 97–98.

Dzelzainis, Martin. "Milton's Classical Republicanism." *Milton and Republicansim.* Ed. David Armitage, Armand Himy, and Quentin Skinner. Cambridge: Cambridge UP, 1995. 3–24.

Fang, Weiguei. "'yihuei,' 'minzhu,' yu 'gonghe' gainian zai xifang yu zhongguo de tanbian (The Transformation of 'yihuei,' 'minzhu,' and 'gonghe' in China and in the West)." *Ershiyi shiji shuangyuekan (Twentieth Century Bimonthly)* 58 (April 2000): 49–61.

Feng, Tianyu. "'Geming,' 'gonghe': qingmin zhiji zhengzhi zhongjian gainian de xingcheng ('Revolution,' 'Republic': The Consolidation of Political Ideas between Qing Dyansty and the Republic)." *Wuhan daxue xuebao (Journal of Wuhan University [Humanities]* 55.1 (Jan. 2002): 5–14.

Gao, Changnan. "Shijen mierdun (The Poet Milton)." *Dushu guwun jikan (Reading Consultant Quarterly)* 4 (1935): 224–31.

Gu, Edward X. "Who was Mr. Democracy? The May Fourth Discourse of Populist Democracy and the Radicalization of Chinese Intellectuals (1915–1922)," *Modern Asian Studies* 35.3 (2001): 589–621.

Jin, Donglei. "Diqizhang qingjiaotu shidai: dierjieh geming de dashiren (Chapter 7, the Puritan Era: Sec. 2. The Great Poet of Revolution)." *Yingguo wenxue shigang (A Historical Outline of English Literature).* Minguo Series 3, no. 57. Shanghai: Commercial Press, 1937. 155–59.

Jin, Guantao, and Qingfeng Liu. "Xinqingnian minzhu guannian de yanbian (The Development of the Concept of Democracy in *Xinqingnian*)." *Ershiyi shiji shuangyuekan (Twentieth Century Bimonthly)* 56 (Dec. 1999): 29–41.

Lee Dazhao (Shou Chang). "Laodong jiaoyu Wunti (The Question of Labor Education)." *Chenbao (Morning Daily)* Feb. 14 & 15, 1919. In *Li Dazhao xuanji (The Collected Works of Li Da zhao).* Beijing: People's Publisher, 1959. 138–39.

Lee, Leo Ou-Fan. "Literary Trends I: The Quest for Modernity, 1895–1927." *The Cambridge History of China: Republican China, 1912–1949.* Pt. 1. Vol. 12. Ed. Twitchett, Denis, and John K. Fairbank. New York: Cambridge University Press, 1978–1986.

Liang Qichao. "Xin yingguo juren Kelinweier zhuan (A New Biography of the English Hero Cromwell)." *Xinming (New Citizen)* 25–26 (11 Feb. 1913), 54–56 (9 Oct. 1914). In *Yinbingshi heji (Writings in the Ice-Tasting Room).* Vol. 6. Beijing: Zhonghua Booksstore, 1989. 1–20.

–. "Xinzhongguo weilai ji (The Future of New China)." *Xin Xiaoshuo (New Short Stories)* 1–3 (Nov.–Jan., 1902–1903). In *Yinbingshi heji (Writings in the Ice-Tasting Room).* Vol. 6. Beijing: Zhonghua Booksstore, 1989. 1–57.

Liang, Zhinan. "Mierdun erbaiwushinian jinian (The 250th Anniversary of John Milton)." *Wenxue (xunkan) (Literature [Trimonthly])* 153 & 154 (Dec. 22 & 29, 1924): 1–3; 1–3.

Lu, Xun (Ling Fei). "Muoluo shili shuo (On the Power of Mara Poetry)." *Henan* 2–3 (Feb.–March 1908). In *Lu Xun chuanji (Complete Works of Lu Xun).* Vol. 1. Beijing: People's Publisher, 1981. 63–115.

Milton, John. *Complete Prose Works of John Milton.* Ed. Don M. Wolfe. New Haven, Conn.: Yale University Press, 1953–1982.

Schwartz, Benjamin. *In Search of Wealth and Power: Yen Fu and the West.* Cambridge, Mass.: Beknap Press of Harvard University Press, 1964.

Shen, Yanbing (Bing). "Jieshao waiguowenxue zuopin de mudi (The Purpose of Introducing Foreign Literature)." *Wenxue xunkan (Literature Trimonthly)* 45 (1 Aug. 1922): 2–3.

Sun, Lianggong. "Mierdun (Milton)." *Shijie wenxuejia liezhuan (Biographies of World Literary Figures).* Shanghai: China Books, 1926. 5–7.

Tian Han. "Mierdun yu zhongguo (Milton and China)." *Shaonian zhongguo (Young China)* 4.5 (July 1923): 1–7. Also reprinted in *Tien Han quanji (Complete Works of Tian Han).* Vol. 14. Shijiazhuang: Huashan Literature and Art Press, 2000. 358–346.

Wu, Naihua. "Lun wusi shiqi zhushifenzi de minzhu sixiang (On the Idea of Democracy of the May-Fourth Intellectuals)." *Zhongyan shehuizhuyi xuebao (Central Journal of Socialism).* 1995.6: 18–22.

Xie, Fang. "Wushu qianhou guoren dei 'minquan,' 'minzhu' de renzhi (The Understanding of 'minquan' and 'minzhu' before and after the Wushu Reform)." *Ershiyi shiji shuangyuekan (Twentieth Century Bimonthly)* 65 (June 2001): 42–51.

Xiong, Yuezhi. "'Liberty', 'Democracy', 'President': The Translation and Usage of Some Political Terms in Late Qing China." *New Terms for New Ideas: Western Knowledge and Lexical Change in Late Imperial China.* Ed. Michael Lackner, Iow Amelung, and Joachim Kurtz. Leiden: Brill, 2001. 69–93.

Yan, Fu. Translator's Preface. *Qunji quanjielun (On the Boundaries of the Rights of Society and the Rights of the Individual).* Taipei: Commercial Press, 1966. 1–5.

Yi Zhen. "Shileyuan han xiyiouji (*Paradise Lost* and *A Journey to West*)." *Funu yuekan (Women Monthly)* 7.2 (1948): 57–58.

Zeng, Xubai. "Yingguo wenxue: wu yuehan mierdun (English Literature, 5: John Milton)." *Xiyang wenxue jiangzuo (Lectures on Western Literatures).* Minguo Series 2, no. 63. Facsimile. World Bookstore, 1935. 24–27.

Zhang, Changgong. "Mierdun yu Du Fu (Milton and Du Fu)." *Chengxing yuehkan (Morning Star Monthly)* 2 (1930): 13–36. Summarized from Tokutomi Sohō cho, Toho to miru ton. Tōkyō: Min'yūsha, 1917.

Zheng, Zhenduo (Xi Di). "Zatan (24): Mangmu de fanyijia (Miscellaneous (24): The Blind Translators)." *Wenxue xunkan (Literature Trimonthly)* 6 (June 1921).

Zhou, Zuoren. "Fanyi wenxueshu de taolun (Discussions on Translating Literature)." *Xiaoshuo yuebao (Short Stories Monthly)* 12.2 (Feb. 1921). In *Zhouzuoren jiweiwen (The Uncollected Writings by Zhou Zuoren).* Vol. 1. 334–35.

Zhu, Zhimin. "Wusi yundong qianho Democracy yiyu yanbian zhi kaocha (The Development of Translated Terms for Democracy before and after the May Fourth Movement)." *Wusi yundong yu ershishiji zhongguo (The May Fourth Movmeent and Twentieth Century China).* Vol. 1. Ed. Bin Hou and Zhesheng Ouyang. Beijing: Social Science Documents Press, 2001. 173–82.

List of Abstracts

Anderson, Kemmer: "Those Tenured Tyrants: How Milton's *Tenure of Magistrates and Kings* Influenced Jefferson's *Declaration of Independence*

How much does Jefferson's "Declaration of Independence" owe to Milton's "Tenure of Kings and Magistrates?" With a focus on tyranny, the paper argues that Milton provided a vocabulary and structure for part of the Declaration. Through speeches and characters, *Paradise Lo*st emphasizes how the word "tyrant" became a part of Jefferson's education and writing. Milton's epic poem offers a narrative definition of a tyrant. Milton and Jefferson both walked a Socratic divided line in framing their preamble for the case against a tyrant king. Milton and his tract provide vision for the American document of liberation from kings and tyrants.

Borgogni, Daniele: "'Real Or Allegorical I Discern Not'": *Paradise Regained* and the Problem of Representation in Early Modern England

Before the Civil War, the problem of how words and people could represent transparently what they expressed played a primary role in seventeenth-century England not only from a religious, but also from an ideological point of view. Two decades later, the same problems reappear with a deeper hermeneutic relevance in *Paradise Regained.* The various temptations culminate with Satan's claim that "relation stands" between his heavenly and hellish identity, while Christ's reign is deemed ambiguous and thus non-representative. Satan aims at denying Christ's representativity and thus the existing political hierarchies in Heaven and Earth, but even if Christ overcomes the temptations, the solution to the hermeneutic problems raised by the text is left to the reader.

Clutterbuck, Charlotte: "The Sinner's View of God in the Invocations and Book III of *Paradise Lost*"

Unlike any other major English poet, Milton makes God the Father a character in *Paradise Lost.* Many readers, finding his Father repellent, have considered the poem flawed as a result. This paper suggests a new reading of the Father's relationship with the persona. The invocations dramatize an increasing distance between the persona and God as the persona secures his poem at the cost of endangering his relationship with God. This anxiety about his personal salvation permeates Book III, in the Father's negative language, the debate between the Father and Son, and the Persona's timid appropriation of the angelic prayer.

Dawes, Martin: "Adam's Co-creation of Eve: Taking Liberties with Milton's Ironic God"

In *Paradise Lost* 8, Adam takes the liberty of recounting his own co-creation of Eve not simply to detain Raphael but mainly because he has learned an important lesson from wrestling with God. In negotiating for "Collateral love" (8.426), Adam learns that God invites his creatures to healthy trial by means of irony, rewarding not unquestioning obedience but "embold'nd" response (cf. 8.434–40). Indeed, reading the Father as characteristically wielding "irony's edge" (L. Hutcheon 1995) reveals him as a Lord Protector challenging his subjects to become citizens or co-creators. In taking the liberty of commissioning his maker as matchmaker, Adam comes to epitomize the dialogical humanism of Milton's political prose.

Dean, Margaret J.: "Martyrdom Reconsidered: Adam's Profit from Abdiel's Example"

What purpose does the Abdiel narrative, prominent within Raphael's account of the War in Heaven, serve in Milton's epic? Milton models Abdiel upon his definition of martyrdom in *De Doctrina Christiana* in order to present him as an example for Adam. Abdiel is marked as a martyr in Milton's estimation, not as one who suffers death, as an angel Abdiel is immortal, but as one who suffers for truth. In Book Nine Adam misconstrues Abdiel's example, presenting himself as Eve's defender by offering to die with her. In the context of the seventeenth-century martyrological controversy in which Milton participated, Adam fails to discern Augustine's touchstone for martyrdom, "Not the punishment, but the cause makes the martyr." Adam substitutes idolatrous disobedience for Abdiel's truth.

Dolloff, Matthew K.: "Urania, Antidote to Tyranny"

If we read the Book VII invocation of *Paradise Lost* as both poetical and political, then Milton's Muse, Urania, should pertain to both. Having surveyed many literary precedents that mention her in one guise or another, I have noticed that she, of or beyond the Muses nine, seems most qualified to oppose tyranny. Most significantly, she stands in contrast to the licentiousness of kings and courtiers even as she remains a vehicle for relating heavenly truths and divinely inspired poetry.

Frison, Danièle: "Droits & Libertés dans *Le Mandat des Rois & des Magistrats*"

Dans *The Tenure of Kings and Magistrates*, écrit peu après l'exécution de Charles Ier dans le but de justifier le régicide, Milton affirme le droit des sujets à déposer leur souverain lorsque celui-ci s'avère un tyran. Il pose les bases du concept de contrat social, à l'opposé du droit divin des rois défendu par Filmer mais aussi du contrat social défini par Hobbes.

Milton fixe les limites des pouvoirs des gouvernants et les droits des gouvernés sur le fondement d'arguments religieux, historiques et juridiques. Il définit le contrat social entre le peuple et le souverain en termes d'un *trust*, par lequel les pouvoirs du peuple sont dévolus au souverain pour qu'il en use dans l'intérêt du peuple, faute de quoi le peuple est fondé à le déposer.

Garnier, Marie-Dominique: "From Dagon to Deleuze and Derrida: *Samson Agonistes* and Particle Poetics"

"Grand style," as Christopher Ricks has been among the first to show, is a matter of small things. This essay proposes a "subatomic" reading of *Samson Agonistes* based on a few of the poem's linguistic, movable parts, such as the proliferating syllable "on". From the poem's very first line to its final key-word "passion," "-on-" informs the nano-textuality of *Samson Agonistes* (as well as its onomastics) and invites the reader to switch into different speeds of reading, to revisit by-passed loci of poetic interest (such as the adverb cum prefix and phoneme "on"). A "cellular" text about incarceration blind confinement and deprivation, the poem also generates the "cells" or seeds of a resilient, cellular, proliferating language bound to break free from rhetorical and linguistic bondage. The essay submits the poem to close-readings as well as to concepts borrowed from Deleuze and Guattari (the "rhizome") and from Derrida (his questioning the differential logic of language) in order to lead, ultimately, to an unorthodox, perhaps uncouth form of a new "on-tology."

Huang, Chia-Yin: "The Miltonic Personality: Milton as a Model of Liberty in China"

This article examines the Chinese portrayals of Milton in literary writings during the 1920s and 30s. It discusses the ways in which Milton was fashioned as an ideal poet-statesman who committed his pen to the pursuit of liberty and political revolution. It examines the terms "liberty," "liberalism," "democracy," and "republic" frequently associated with Milton in Chinese writings and compares these terms to the idea of liberty presented in Milton's own political tracts. Revealing the Chinese appropriation of Milton, this article shows how a different culture may transform foreign models to meet its specific historical context and cultural needs.

Jockims, Trevor Laurence: "Pastoral Lost and Regained in 'Lycidas'"

Death's interruption of pastoral's harmonious, cyclic view of time in "Lycidas" offers one example of the sort of inflection which the pastoral grounding of pastoral elegy is liable to cause. With the event of death, Milton's shepherd-elegist has lost not only friend and fellow shepherd, but singing partner as well; death, that is, has incised pastoral's fundamentally dialogic construction and made of it a monody. The generic speaker of "Lycidas" is a belabored representative of an ontologically unstable pastoral landscape. The purpose of my paper is to trace out the ways in which death does violence to the pastoral landscape and leaves the shepherd-elegist, that mode's representative, to repair the rift done to his pastoral place.

Jordan, Matthew: "The Bourgeois Utopianism of Milton's Anti-Prelatical Tracts"

"Revisionist" historiography has downplayed the significance of questions of liberty and class as causes of the English Revolution. While the concerns of Milton's notional allies, the Smectymnuuans, tend to confirm this view, Milton's own texts evince an enthusiasm for a conception of liberation informed by a class-based perspective on social issues. Where the Smectymnuuans look forward to a form of church-government which will enhance the status and power of their clerical caste, Milton embraces what he senses is the emergence of a new, more popular, less generally repressive social order, a commitment encapsulated in his coinage of the term "self-esteem."

Leasure, Ross T.: "Spenser's Diabolical Orator and Milton's 'Man of Hell'"

More than akin to Milton's Belial is Spenser's allegorical figure of Despayre who constitutes a "belialist" in his own right. As quintessential adoxographers, both are more than mere sophists. The connaturality of these characters rests in certain specific rhetorical strategies each employs while plying their adoxographical trade in the manner of a litigator or advocate. Particularly striking is the pervasiveness of anthypophora and anacoenosis within the virtuosic oratory of Belial and Despayre. By means of such strategies, these demonic rhetors effectively attempt to supplant the volition of their auditors with their own will-to-inaction, thereby de-moralizing the gullible through pointed argumentation.

Mäkelä, Suvi: "'[E]xiled from light'": Beauty, the Senses and Freedom in *Samson Agonistes*"

Milton's interest in the idea of the beautiful can be seen informing a great many of his writings. For instance, beauty plays a decisive role in the loss of freedom of Milton's Samson. This paper focuses on studying the effects of Samson's understanding of beauty. Some philosophical aspects of St. Augustine's and Plato's works are the most important theories used in the paper. They are used to shed light on Milton's conception of the ordered harmony of the universe, and the importance of the right appreciation of beauty.

Mansur, Miriam: "Milton and Derrida: Deconstructing Paradise"

This essay tries to examine blindness as a visible perspective, as a form to erase the risks of the literal sight and approach, through an inner reflection, to the exercise of the (in)sight. This reading analyses the visual metaphors of John Milton's *Paradise Lost* and attempts to place Milton's epic together with Jacques Derrida's *Memoirs of the Blind* on the post-structuralist's stance towards vision.

Noro, Yuko (Kanakubo): "On Milton's Proposal for a *'Communitas Libera'* Reconsidered"

The 1658 edition of *Defensio Prima* plays an important role in relation with *PL*, and simultaneously, with the second edition of *The Readie and Easie Way*. My aim in this paper is to reassess the 1658 edition of *Defensio Prima* in terms of the second edition of *The Readie and Easie Way* and *PL*. The three main additions in the revised version of *The Readie and Easie Way* will be the focus of the paper; one on the law of nature, another on the society of ants, and the last on the perpetual senate based on a three-layered governmental system.

Ortega-Tillier, Virginie: "Qualités plastiques de l'évocation poétique & caractéristiques des illustrations du *Paradis perdu* de Milton"

Une édition parisienne de 1863 du *Paradis perdu* est ornée d'une vingtaine de planches de belle facture, de même que ses publications londoniennes de 1795 et 1827; toutes mettent en lumière la grande qualité plastique de l'évocation de l'Eden de Milton et son caractère novateur au regard d'une tradition iconographique abondante. Milton demeure généralement fidèle au texte de la Genèse et à la tradition exégétique dans les descriptions du Paradis terrestre et dans la formulation de certaines séquences narratives; il s'en écarte cependant par plusieurs aspects. A la source de la Genèse, Milton joint le souvenir du *locus amœnus* antique et les débats érudits sur la localisation et la pérennité du Jardin d'Eden. Certains vers définissent de plus la topographie du Paradis terrestre, et différents passages du poème rappellent la vision ptoléméenne de l'Univers. L'Eden de Milton compose aussi le premier jardin anglais, dans lequel Adam et Eve doivent ordonner la nature sauvage et luxuriante. L'abondance descriptive d'une foisonnante réalité matérielle compose une autre caractéristique plastique des vers miltoniens, qui appartient aussi à l'éloge de la variété de l'Œuvre de Dieu. Les relations du premier couple sont décrites avec tendresse et sensualité, dans une union du sensible et du spirituel que les graveurs ont su transposer, de même que la scène de la Tentation et celle du désespoir d'Adam après la faute. Dans le poème de Milton, la Chute du genre humain paraît à la fois comme acte de transgression qui marque le refus de soumission de la créature à son créateur et comme acte tragique qui n'est toutefois pas irréparable. La mort ouvrira l'accès à un paradis céleste qui est conçu à l'image du Paradis terrestre, au climat tempéré, d'une «agréable vicissitude». La reconquête est annoncée et sera effective dans le *Paradis reconquis* (Livre I, 1–7).

Piazza, Antonella: "Milton and Galileo: An Endless War or an Early Modern Compromise?"

The idea of Nature as a book written by God is the most meaningful Galilean allusion in Milton's sacred poem. Galileo's most revolutionary and long lasting 'contribution' to modernity was his differentiation of the Bible from Nature: he argued that they were both books written by God and aiming at one and the same truth, but with different languages and for different readers. Galileo's differentiation was to prove the beginning of a dangerous dichotomy between the sciences of man and those of nature. By making a distinction between Adam and Eve's and the Poet's ways of access to Galileo's new astronomy (between what I call their astronomical diets), Milton attempts a cultural, poetic reparation, in trying to keep together ethics and science, the heaven of God and the sky of astronomy. Which was Milton's extreme defence of his poetic monistic materialism.

Pironon, Jean: "The Five Senses as Origin of Milton's Poetic Idiom in the University Exercises and the Minor Poems (1626–1645)"

To understand how young Milton constructed his poetic idiom during his education years, one needs to confront his response to the stimulation of the world outside the schoolroom and his ethical approach to corporeity through his reading of the Classics and the Fathers. An examination of the early works (from the Latin Elegies to A Mask), illustrates the "modes" – conceptual, perceptual, or both – through which the experience of the senses found its way into the poetry. The efficiency of the poetic form is the result of a tension between words as replacement for sense-impressions and a Christian poet's ethical control over them.

Rovira, James: "Milton's Ontology of Books and *Areopagitica*"

"Milton's Ontology of Books and the *Areopagitica*" supports a historically grounded reading of Milton's treatise on free speech contra Stanley Fish's "Driving from the Letter: Truth and Indeterminacy in the *Areopagitica*" and Lana Cable's *Carnal Rhetoric*, maintaining the *Areopagitica's* status as a foundational document on freedom of the press while acknowledging and accommodating the contradictions and complexities of Milton's argument. Intellectual history in the form of Milton's conception of the vegetable, sensitive, and rational souls common in his day and before is emphasized as central to understanding Milton's ontology of books and to resolving some of the apparent contradictions within Milton's text.

Sá, Luis Fernando Ferreira: "Notes on a Postcolonial Fall in Milton's Paradise"

In John Milton's *Paradise Lost* epic and empire are dissociated. Contrary to many misreadings, this all-important writing of the English Renaissance intersects post-colonial thinking in a number of ways. By using Edward Said's, Gayatri Spivak's, and Homi Bhabha's circuit of post-colonial theory and practice, this paper enacts a counterpointal (mis)reading of Milton's text: Paradise Lost may at last free its (post-)colonial (dis)content. Since every reading is a mis-reading, my (mis)reading of Milton's paradise is a mo(ve)ment of resistance against and intervention in a so-called grand narrative of power (Milton's epic) with a view to proposing both a post-colonial conversation with this seventeenth-century English work and post-colonial counterscene for this text.

–. "Enjoined By Fate: Private and Public Miltons in a 19th-Century Portuguese Play"

Francisco da Costa Braga's *Milton: A Comedy in One Act* was staged on April 29, 1866 at the Theatro das Variedades Dramaticas in Lisbon with much "applause." The play received an *imprimatur* seal by C. C. Menezes on March 17, 1867 and enjoyed a rather long career. This one-act comedy took place at "Honton," Buckingham County, and had as its main characters: the old and blind poet Milton; his daughter Emma; William Davenant's son, Lord Arthur Davenant; the Quaker judge Godwen; and Godwen's niece, Miss Carlota. The dramatic narrative centered on Emma and Carlota's machinations to have Arthur enter Milton's service without his knowing that Arthur was a young man. What Milton and the other characters did not know, however, was that Arthur was the son of William Davenant, the Parliamentary member and poet, and a favorite of Charles II. Arthur engaged himself as Milton's amanuensis in order to "save" the old poet from political persecution. Alongside this dramatic "political" narrative, there was also a comic "romantic" narrative running through the play: Carlota thought Arthur was in love with her, but Arthur loved Emma instead, who renounced her love for Carlota's sake. In the end, love conquered Emma and Arthur with Milton's consent. This paper discusses how the private and the public Miltons enjoined the play so as to produce a provocative critical reception of this major English Renaissance writer in the Portuguese world of the nineteenth century.

Tahvanainen, Antti: "The Role of Rhetoric in the Political Thought of John Milton"

Rhetoric, while an essential part in the education of t he virtuous citizens of classical republicanism, has often been condemned as leading to demagogy and flattery. This paper argues that Milton was well aware of such abuses, but he consistently argued that they could be countered with the kind of rhetoric that would follow the ideals of moral, learning and eloquence. Accordingly, these ideals were also the essentials in Milton's views on republican educational reform. Milton aimed at a preventive policy: how to create soothing orators instead of inflammatory demagogues, wise counsellors instead of vicious courtiers.

Urban, David V.: "Talents and Laborers: Parabolic Tension in Milton's Sonnet 19"

This essay explores, in Milton's Sonnet 19, the tension evident between the parable of the talents (Matt. 25.14–30) and the parable of the laborers in the vineyard (Matt. 20.1–16). Milton's tendency to identify himself with the unprofitable servant of the parable of the talents is seen clearly in the anguish-filled octave of the sonnet in question. But this unsettling tendency is mitigated in the sonnet by the autobiographical speaker's comparable sense of self-identification with the last-chosen laborers of the parable of the laborers, a mitigation offers the speaker the hope of God's favor amidst his failures.

Vasilev, Georgi: "Philosophie et figures dualistes dans les pamphlets de John Milton"

A lot of studies have been dedicated to Milton's rather specific religious views. Here we can quote Arthur Lovejoy's idea of *felix culpa* (The Fortunate Fall? 1937), reiterated by Hugh White (1994) and the studies of Maurice Kelley and Barbara Lewalski. In more recent times we have the volume Milton and Heresy (1998), published by Stephen Dobranski and John

Rumrich or the book of A. D. Nuttall, *Alternative Trinity: Gnostic Heresy in Marlowe, Milton, and Blake*, which appeared in the same year. They posed the question, they did some intuitive findings, but failed to provide sufficient clarification of Milton's theology. This was actually done by Milton himself when he declared his appreciation for the Waldensian or Cathari church or when he set as his example "the divine and admirable spirit of Wiclef" in *Areopagitica*, as well as in other works. The poet complemented his views of a reformed Presbyterian Church by questioning the icons or even the cross, the liturgies, the Old Testament church scenery or Donatio Constantini, among other things. These were fundamental arguments for Bogomilism, albeit in their Cathar and Lollard variants. Milton repeatedly used terms like good men and inward man, which were inherent to dualistic vocabulary. In addition, he propounded the fundamental Dualistic idea quite directly: "Good and evil we know in the field of this world grow up together almost inseparably; and the knowledge of good is so involved and interwoven with the knowledge of evil, and so many cunning resemblances hardly to be discerned, that the knowledge of good and evil, as two twins cleaving together, leaped forth into the world."

The study reveals some of the ways by which Cathar manuscripts came to England in Milton's time.

Wilson, Hugh: "Milton and Wordsworth: Reflections on *L'Allegro*, *Il Penseroso*, and *Tintern Abbey*"

Although previous scholars have noted that Wordsworth's "Tintern Abbey" recalls a number of Milton's works, the relevance of Milton's companion poems, "L'Allegro," and "Il Penseroso" has been neglected. In addition to echoing *Paradise Lost* and *Samson Agonistes*, Wordsworth parallels the antinomies and evokes the imagery of Milton's companion poems. Both men dramatize the genesis of their moral orientations. Both poets, the militant defender of the English revolution and the ardent partisan of the initial phases of the French revolution, confronted disappointment, depression, and threats of government repression with heightened aspirations and lyrical intuitions that issue in impassioned resolves and allusive poetry.

Zivley, Sherry and Hamblin, Chase: "The Prosody of *Samson Agonistes*"

There is evidence that Milton wrote an early version of *Samson Agonistes*, put it aside unfinished for a variety of reasons, and completed it much later. The earlier version can be identified by both its prosody, which seems to evolve from his earlier prosodic innovations, and the fact that it includes only information that is included in Judges. The later version utilizes decasyllabic lines, like those of *Paradise Lost* and *Paradise Regained,* introduces dialogues with Manoa and Dalila, introduces Harapha, and shows Samson to be more resigned to his blindness.

List of Contributors

Kemmer ANDERSON teaches world literature at the McCallie School in Chattanooga, Tennessee. A poet, he has published poems in the *Sewanee Review*, *Christian Century*, *Christ College Magazine*, *Chard School Magazine*, Davidson *Miscellany*, *Poetic Page*, *CER*BER*US*, *Poets Against War*, and *Counterpunch*. He has published the following chapbooks: *Poem Sightings at Hunting Island* (1993), *A Compass Reading for Ithaca* (1994), *Acropolis Fire* (1998), *Just Light: A Poetics of Human Rights* (2001), *Stratford upon Avon at 49* (2002), *Voyage to Ithaca* (2003), and *Sparrows and Soldiers* (2005).

Nicole BERRY is an honorary member of the French Psychoanalytical Association and of the International Psychoanalytical Association. She has written a biography of Mary Shelley, *Mary Shelley, du monstre au sublime*, 1997, and a monograph on Milton, *John Milton, Le Paradis perdu, des ténèbres à la lumière* (2005), both published in Lausanne at l'Age d'Homme. Her previous psychoanalytic and literary works include studies of the writings of Thomas Mann (*Le sentiment d'identité.* Paris: Ed. universitaires, 1987), of Hawthorne's *The House of the Seven Gables* (*Le présent de l'analyse.* Paris: L'Harmattan, 1998), and of James's *The Turn of the Screw* and Dickens's *The Haunted Man* (*Anges et fantômes.* Toulouse, Ombres, 1993). She has participated in many international psychoanalytic and literary conferences in France, England and the USA. She is a member of the Milton Society of America.

Daniele BORGOGNI took his doctorate in English Literature in 1996. He is currently a high school teacher in Turin but regularly teaches Translation and English Language at the University of Turin. He published a monograph on John Milton's *Paradise Regained* (1998) and articles on John Bunyan, George Wither, and translation and emblematics. He edited a collection of essays on religious and literary discourse in Early Modern France and England (2004), and is currently working on emblematics and Translation Studies.

Charlotte CLUTTERBUCK completed her PhD in English Literature at Sydney University in 2001. She has taught Literature and Communication courses at Macquarie University, the Australian Catholic University, and the University of Western Sydney. She now teaches English at Abbotsleigh School for Girls, Sydney. She has published *Encounters with God in Medieval and Early Modern English Poetry* (Ashgate 2005) and a volume of poetry, *Soundings* (Five Islands Press 1997).

Martin DAWES is a doctoral candidate at McGill University. He holds an M.A. from the University of Manitoba. Publications include "An Orphic Lament for Orphic Lament: 'Lycidas' and the Persistence of Orphic Desire," in *Milton Quarterly* 38.3 (2004); and "Cinema's Imprinting of *The English Patient*: Self, Community, and the Gravitational Pull of *Casablanca*," in *Essays on Canadian Writing* 84 (2005).

Margaret Justice DEAN is Professor of English at Eastern Kentucky University in Richmond, Kentucky, where she teaches Milton and early modern literature. In 1998 she completed her dissertation under the direction of John Shawcross and David Lee Miller at the University of Kentucky and recently served as President of the Kentucky Philological Association. Her research interests include discourses of martyrdom in English and early American literature. Publications include "Choosing Death: Adam's Temptation to Martyrdom in *Paradise Lost*" in *Milton Studies* 46 (2007): 30–56.

Matt DOLLOFF was born in 1966 in Maryland, USA and grew up in Tennessee. He received his BA from San Francisco State University (1998), and Masters (2001) and Ph.D. (2006) in English from the University of Texas at Austin, with John Rumrich supervisor. He presented a paper on Milton and Audience at the Milton Society session at the MLA (2006). He is currently a Lecturer at the University of Tennessee, Knoxville. For IMS 9, London 2008, he has prepared "Gabriel's Trumpet: Milton and the Seventeenth Century Conceptualization of Infinity."

Danièle FRISON is Full Professor at the University of Paris X – Nanterre, where she teaches English Constitutional Law, English Religious History and Public Liberties. She is Director of a postgraduate program of legal studies in French Law and English Law, and of a Master's Degree program in Legal Translation. She created at Paris X a Centre of Jewish Studies. Her main publications are: *Le Juif dans la tradition anglaise*, Paris, Publidix-Editions de l'Espace Européen, 1992; *Histoire constitutionnelle de la Grande-Bretagne*, Paris, Ellipses, 1997, new edition 2005; *Le schisme d'Henri VIII*, Paris, Ellipses, 2004; *Introduction au Droit anglais et aux institutions britanniques*, Paris, Ellipses, 3rd ed. 2005.

Marie-Dominique GARNIER is Professor of English literature at the University of Paris VIII, where she teaches courses and seminars on seventeenth-century poetry and drama, on modernism, and on literature and philosophy (Cixous, Derrida, and Deleuze). She has published essays and book chapters (mostly on Shakespeare, Donne, Milton, De Quincey, Dickens, Joyce, T. S. Eliot, V. Woolf), and a book on George Herbert. She has worked in the field of literature and photography, and edited *Jardins d'Hiver* with the *Presses de l'Ecole Normale Supérieure*. She is also a translator (Samuel Pepys, Thomas Browne, Madeline Gins).

Chase HAMBLIN was a senior English major at the University of Houston. He worked with Sherry Zivley in the University Scholar Program, which provided talented seniors who planned to go to graduate school with the opportunity participate in a research project under the direction of a faculty mentor.

Chia-Yin HUANG is Language & Literature Assistant Professor in the Department of English at Chinese Culture University, Taiwan. Her areas of interest include John Milton, English Renaissance and seventeenth-century Literature, Translation Studies, and Chinese-English Literary Relations.

Trevor Laurence JOCKIMS is a PhD student in the Department of Comparative Literature at The Graduate Center of The City University of New York. He works primarily on Modernism – especially questions concerning Modern poetry and its relationship to philosophy, and the history and theory of lyric poetry – and on Early Modern literature and culture. His Early Modern work centers around the Renaissance literatures of the English, French, Croatian, and Italian traditions, with a special emphasis on issues of East and West interchange within the Early Modern Mediterranean. Recent publications include articles on Modern ekphrastic poetry, figures of evil in Marlowe's plays, and the reception of Shakespeare within Bosnia and the former Yugoslavia. He teaches World Humanities and World Literature at The City College of The City University of New York.

Matthew JORDAN is Senior Lecturer in Literature and Cultural History at Liverpool John Moores University. He is the author of *Milton and Modernity: Politics, Masculinity and 'Paradise Lost"* (Palgrave Macmillan, 2001) and *Twenty-First Century Literary Theory* (Palgrave Macmillan, 2007). He is working on *A Reader's Guide to 'Paradise Lost"* (Palgrave Macmillan). He is currently conducting research toward a book-length project on the discursive contexts of Milton's early prose, specifically his probable coinage of the term "self-esteem."

Ross T. LEASURE is an assistant professor at Salisbury University in Maryland (USA), specializing in medieval and early modern English literature. His recent dissertation examines the demonic figure of Belial (Cornell 2004), and he has authored two related articles in *Milton Quarterly*. Ross has also contributed entries to the forthcoming *Milton Encyclopedia* (Yale 2008). His current research projects involve Icelandic and French translations of *Paradise Lost.*

Suvi MÄKELÄ, M.A., is a post-graduate student of English Philology at the University of Tampere, Finland. Currently, she is working on a Ph.D. thesis on the concepts of beauty in Milton's works.

Miriam MANSUR is a graduate student at the Univerdade Federal of Minas Gerais in Brazil. Her line of research is English Literature and other Semiotic Systems. She is completing her Master's with a project on "Deconstructing Milton's *Paradise Lost* through a Derridean 'darkness visible' perspective" and plans to write a thesis on Milton's writings in Brazil.

Yuko (Kanakubo) NORO is Professor of English, Department of English, College of Humanities and Sciences, Nihon University, Japan. She wrote several essays on Milton, including "A Comparative Study of 'The Ultimate Love' between *Paradise Lost* and *Shitsurakuen*," Bulletin of Tokyo Seitoku University 9 (2002): 43–51, a comparative study of *PL* and the movie "Paradise Lost" (1997) adapted from a work by the renowned Japanese writer Junichi Watanabe. The paper is translated into German and published in a German magazine, IKONEN (2003). She translated into Japanese Milton's *Pro Populo Anglicano Defensio* and *Defensio Secunda*, Seigakuin University Press (2002). She also translated into Japanese Neil Forsyth's *The Old Enemy: Satan and the Combat Myth*, Hosei University Press (2001).

Virginie ORTEGA-TILLIER is an Art Historian, writer, teacher and an Art Gallery owner. She got her PhD in Art History from the University of Bourgogne. She did her doctoral research on the representation of the Garden of Eden and her work was subsequently published as *Le jardin d'Eden: iconographie et topographie dans la gravure, XVe-XVIIIe* siècles. Dijon: Editions universitaires de Dijon, 2006. Today her interests have led her to pursue her studies along three axes: iconography, especially that of Biblical gardens; book art and the relationships between visual arts and literature; and engraving.

Antonella PIAZZA teaches English Literature at the University of Salerno. Her research area concentrates mainly on the cultural and literary transformations of the early modern age. Her most recent publication is on the Elizabethan domestic tragedy and the origin of the nuclear family: *'IV: Onora il Padre'. Tragedie domestiche sulla scena elisabettiana'.* (2000). She has also edited a book on D. H. Lawrence (*Lawrence. Arte e Mito*, 2000) and another on Shakespeare (*Shakespeare in Europa,* 2004).

Jean PIRONON, Professor Emeritus of English Literature at MSH, Blaise Pascal University, Clermont-Ferrand, France. Etat thesis on *The Criticism of Milton's Poetry from 1945 to 1978,* University of Montpellier, France (Vanth-Adosa, 1979). Other works, in totality or partly on Milton: *Le temps figé et l'inexprimable distance,* Clermont-Ferrand, ADOSA, 1984, and *Au Cœur brilliant des nuits* (CERHAC, 2001). Has also produced articles on several other poets of the period, and on Shakespeare *(Etudes anglaises).* Major interest: the imagination in the English Renaissance and the Seventeenth Century.

James ROVIRA (ABD) is a Lecturer in English at Rollins College in Winter Park, Florida and a Ph.D. candidate in English at Drew University in Madison, New Jersey, living with his wife and children in Central Florida. He is currently writing 'Blake, Kierkegaard, and Creation Anxiety,' a study applying Kierkegaard's Concept of Anxiety to the trope of creation in William Blake's mythological works of the 1790s. His most recent publications include "V for Vindictive" and "The Curse of the Were-Rabbit" for *Metaphilm*; "Justice: A Semi-Autobiographical Fiction" for *The New Pantagruel*; "Subverting the Mechanisms of Control: Baudrillard, *The Matrix Trilogy*, and the Future of Religion" for the *International Journal of Baudrillard Studies*; and "Gathering the Scattered Body of Milton's *Areopagitica*" for *Renascence.*

Luiz Fernando Ferreira SÁ has his PhD on Comparative Literature and his MA on English Literature. He is Associate Professor at the Faculty of Letters of the Federal University of Minas Gerais – Brazil. He has published widely both in Brazil and abroad and his most recent book is titled *The Orpheus Myth in John Milton's "L'Allegro," "Il Penseroso," and "Lycidas".*

Antti TAHVANAINEN is a graduate student at the Department of History, University of Helsinki. He is currently completing his doctoral dissertation on the relationship between rhetoric and republicanism in late seventeenth-century England.

Christophe TOURNU is Associate professor of English at the School of Law of Grenoble, France. Secretary to IMS 8 and to the Société d'Etudes Miltoniennes, he holds a D.Phil from Blaise Pascal University, Clermont-Ferrand, France, on the relationships between theology and politics in Milton's prose works (published 2000: Villeneuve d'Ascq, Septentrion). He has also translated *The Doctrine and Discipline of Divorce* (Paris: Belin, 2005) and edited Milton's texts that were translated and adapted during the French Revolution (*Milton, Mirabeau: rencontre révolutionnaire.* Paris: Edimaf, 2002). He is co-editor, with Olivier Abel, of *Milton et le droit au divorce* (Geneva: Labor et Fides, 2005), with Jean-Luc Chabot, of *L'héritage religieux et spirituel de l'identité européenne* 2004) and with Jean-Luc Chabot and Stéphane Gal, of *Figures de la médiation et lien social* (2006), both at L'Harmattan. His *John Milton, penseur républicain à l'époque de la première revolution anglaise* (written mostly in English) is forthcoming at CNED/ Armand Colin. At the ESSE Conference in London in 2006 he co-convened a workshop on "Milton, Rights and Liberties" and read a paper on "Milton, from family to politics", which has been extended into a book, *John Milton, pamphlétaire: de la famille à la République*, to be published in 2008. The Academic Steering Committee of IMS9 to be held in London next year has just accepted his proposal for a panel on 'Milton's Politics of Divorce' (Neil Forsyth, Chair; Christophe Tournu, 'John Milton, from Family to Politics'; Olivier Abel, '*The Doctrine and Discipline of Divorce* and the Puritan Rupture'; Sandra Laugier, '*The Doctrine and Discipline of Divorce* and the Public Stakes of Private Life').

David V. URBAN is Assistant Professor of English at Calvin College. His articles and reviews have appeared in *ANQ*, *Christianity and Literature*, *Cithara*, *Leviathan*, *Milton Quarterly*, *Milton Studies*, *Religion and Literature*, *Seventeenth-Century News*, and as chapters in several books. He is completing and editing the late Calvin Huckabay's *John Milton: An Annotated Bibliography, 1989–1999* and is working on a monograph on Milton's use of and self-identification with figures from biblical parables. Along with Peter Medine and John T. Shawcross, he is co-editing a collection of essays on vision and violence in Milton's writings, a festschrift for Michael Lieb.

Georgi VASILEV, PhD, D.Litt., is Professor of European & Medieval Studies at The State University of Library Studies and Information Technologies, Sofia, Bulgaria. His book *Bogomil and Apocryphal Ideas in Medieval English Culture: The Bulgarian Image of Christ Plowman as Piers Plowman in William Langland's 'The Vision Of Piers Plowman'* was published in Bulgaria in 2001, sponsored by the Bulgarian Ministry of Culture. His latest work is: *Heresy and the English Reformation: Bogomil-Cathar Influence on Wycliffe, Langland, Tyndale and Milton* (McFarlands Publishers, USA, 2007). He is member of the Bulgarian Society for British Studies and of the Société d'Etudes Miltoniennes, France. He is the author of a website: http://www.cl.bas.bg/ Balkan-Studies/bogomilism/index.html.

Hugh WILSON earned his B.A. at Johns Hopkins University, his M.A. and Ph.D. at the University of Chicago. He has taught at Kenyon College, Texas Tech University, and SUNY-Plattsburgh. Wilson has received the Allen Breck Award from the Rocky Mountain Medieval Renaissance Association for his essay on Anne Southwell, the Drescher Fellowship from SUNY, a Ford Foundation Fellowship, and a Woodrow Wilson Fellowship. He currently chairs the English department at Grambling State University. He has presented conference papers on Shakespeare, Milton, Donne, Cowley, Southwell, and Montrose; he has published essays on Shakespeare, Milton, Ben Jonson, Anne Southwell, and David Masson.

Sherry Lutz ZIVLEY is an associate professor at the University of Houston, where she teaches contemporary fiction, literature by women, the poetry of Milton, the poetry of Plath and Hughes, and analysis of poetry. Her most recent writings have been on the phenomenology of space in contemporary fiction and film.